# Microsoft® Windows® Scripting Self-Paced Learning Guide

*Ed Wilson*

PUBLISHED BY
Microsoft Press
A Division of Microsoft Corporation
One Microsoft Way
Redmond, Washington 98052-6399

Library of Congress Cataloging-in-Publication Data
Wilson, Ed.
    Microsoft Windows Scripting Self-paced Learning Guide / Ed Wilson.
        p. cm.
    Includes index.
    ISBN 0-7356-1981-6
    1. Microsoft Windows (Computer file) 2. Operating systems (Computers) I. Title.

    QA76.76.O63W5596  2004
    005.4'46--dc22                                              2004040306


Printed and bound in the United States of America.

5  6  7  8  9      QWT      9  8  7  6

Distributed in Canada by H.B. Fenn and Company Ltd.

A CIP catalogue record for this book is available from the British Library.

Microsoft Press books are available through booksellers and distributors worldwide. For further information about international editions, contact your local Microsoft Corporation office or contact Microsoft Press International directly at fax (425) 936-7329. Visit our Web site at www.microsoft.com/learning/. Send comments to *mspinput@microsoft.com*.

**Acquisitions Editor:** Martin DelRe
**Project Editor:** Valerie Woolley
**Technical Editor:** Alex K. Angelopoulos
**Indexer:** Julie Bess


Body Part No. X10-46139

*This book is dedicated to Bobby R. Wilson—*
*teacher, friend, and dad.*

# Contents

## 4    The Power of Many                  65

## 7    Fun with Folders                                                                              129

## 8    Why Windows Management Instrumentation?                                                        143

## Part 3  Advanced Windows Administration

### 11  Introduction to Active Directory Service Interfaces    187

### 12  Reading and Writing for ADSI    201

## 17    Working with the Registry    277

## 18    Working with Printers    293

## Part 4   Scripting Other Applications

### 19   Managing IIS 6.0      309

### 20   Working with Exchange 2003      323

# Acknowledgments

A book simply does not appear out of thin air, and no book is the work of a single individual. This book would not have happened without the tireless efforts of my agent Mike Meehan of the Moore Literary Agency, who ensured the proper publisher for this book. Martin DelRe at Microsoft Press immediately saw the value of a Visual Basic Script tutorial and helped everything get going. Valerie Woolley and Sally Stickney, also at Microsoft Press, guided the project to completion and provided much encouragement. Alex K. Angelopoulos, MVP, provided awesome and enthusiastic technical review. Victoria P. Thulman contributed immensely by forcing me to make my writing more specific. David Schwinn, MCSE, and Bill Mell, MCSE, reviewed much of the book and provided valuable suggestions. Lastly, my wife Teresa read the entire book and offered many insightful comments.

# About This Book

Network administrators and consultants are confronted with numerous mundane and time-consuming activities on a daily basis. Whether it is going through thousands of users in Active Directory Users and Computers to grant dial-in permissions to a select group, or changing profile storage locations to point to a newly added network server, these everyday tasks must be completed. In the enterprise space, the ability to quickly write and deploy a Microsoft Visual Basic Script (VBScript) will make the difference between a task that takes a few hours and one that takes a few weeks.

As an Enterprise Consultant for Microsoft, I am in constant contact with some of the world's largest companies that run its software. The one recurring theme I hear is, "How can we effectively manage thousands of servers and tens of thousands of users?" In some instances, the solution lies in the employment of specialized software packages—but in the vast majority of the cases, the solution is a simple VBScript.

In Microsoft Windows Server 2003, enterprise manageability was one of the design goals, and VBScript is one path to unlocking the rich storehouse of newly added features. Using the techniques outlined in *Microsoft Windows Scripting Self-Paced Learning Guide*, anyone can begin crafting custom scripts within minutes of opening these pages. I'm not talking about the traditional Hello World script—I'm talking about truly useful scripts that save time and help to ensure accurate and predictable results.

Whereas in the past scripting was somewhat hard to do, required special installations of various implementations, and was rather limited in its effect, with the release of Microsoft Windows XP and Windows Server 2003, scripting is coming into its own.

This is really as it should be. However, most Administrators and IT professionals do not have an understanding of scripting, because in the past scripting was not a powerful alternative for platform management.

However, in a large enterprise, it is a vital reality that one simply cannot perform management from the GUI applications because it is too time-constraining, too error prone, and after a while too irritating. Clearly there needs to be a better way, and there is. Scripting is the answer.

## A Practical Approach to Scripting

*Microsoft Windows Scripting Self-Paced Learning Guide* will equip you with the tools to automate setup, deployment, and management of Microsoft Windows 2003 networks via the various scripting interfaces contained with the product. In addition, it will provide you with an understanding of a select number of VBScripts adaptable to

xx   About This Book

your own unique environments. This will lead you into an awareness of the basics of programming through modeling of fundamental techniques.

The approach I take to teaching you how to use VBScript to automate your Windows 2003 servers is similar to the approach used in some of the executive foreign language schools. You'll learn by using the language. In addition, concepts are presented not in a dry academic fashion but in a dynamic real-life manner. When a concept is needed to accomplish something, it is presented. If a topic is not useful for automating network management, I don't bring it forward.

This is a practical application-oriented book, so the coverage of VBScript, Windows Scripting Host, Active Directory Service Interfaces (ADSI), and Windows Management Instrumentation (WMI) is not exceedingly deep. This is not a reference book; it is a tutorial, a guide, a springboard for ideas perhaps, but not an encyclopedia.

## Is This Book for Me?

*Microsoft Windows Scripting Self-Paced Learning Guide* is aimed at several audiences, including:

- **Windows networking consultants**   Anyone desiring to standardize and automate the installation and configuration of .NET networking components.

- **Windows network administrators**   Anyone desiring to automate the day-to-day management of Windows .NET networks.

- **Windows Help Desk staff**   Anyone desiring to verify configuration of remotely connected desktops.

- **Microsoft Certified Systems Engineers (MCSEs) and Microsoft Certified Trainers (MCTs)**   Although not a strategic core competency within the MCP program, a few questions about scripting do crop up from time to time on various exams.

- **General technical staff**   Anyone desiring to collect information, configure settings on Windows XP machines, or implement management via WMI, WSH, or WBEM.

- **Power users**   Anyone wishing to obtain maximum power and configurability of their Windows XP machines either at home or in an unmanaged desktop workplace environment.

## Outline of This Book

This book is divided into four parts, each covering a major facet of scripting. The following sections describe these parts.

# Part 1: Covering the Basics

OK, so you've decided you need to learn scripting. Where do you begin? Start here in Part 1! In Chapter 1, "Starting From Scratch," you learn the basics: what a script is, how to read it, and how to write it. Once you move beyond using a script to figure out what your IP address is and print it to a file, you need to introduce some logic into the script, which you do in Chapters 2–5. You'll learn how to introduce conditions and add some intelligence to allow the script to check some stuff, and then based upon what it finds, do some other stuff. This section concludes by looking at troubleshooting scripts. I've made some mistakes that you don't need to repeat! Here are the chapters in Part 1:

- Chapter 1, "Starting from Scratch"
- Chapter 2, "Getting in the Loop"
- Chapter 3, "Adding Intelligence"
- Chapter 4, "The Power of Many"
- Chapter 5, "The Power of Many More"

# Part 2: Basic Windows Administration

In Part 2, you dig deep under the covers of VBScript and WMI and really begin to see the power you can bring to your automation tasks. In working with the file system, you see how to use the file system object to create files, delete files, and verify the existence of files. All these basic tasks provide loads of flexibility for your scripts. Next, you move on to working with folders, learning how to use VBScript to completely automate the creation of folders and files on your servers and users' workstations. In the last half of Part 2, you get an in-depth look at the power of WMI when it is combined with the simplicity and flexibility of VBScript. Here are the chapters in Part 2:

- Chapter 6, "Working with the File System"
- Chapter 7, "Fun with Folders"
- Chapter 8, "Why Windows Management Instrumentation?"
- Chapter 9, "WMI Continued"
- Chapter 10, "Using WMI Queries"

# Part 3: Advanced Windows Administration

This section will shave at least four points off your handicap (because you will get to play an extra 18 holes a week due to the time you save)! At least three things are really lame when it comes to administering Windows servers: all those click, click, and save motions; all the time spent waiting for the screen to refresh; and loosing your place in a long list of users. Guess what? In this section, some of that pain is relieved. When

Human Resources hires 100 people, you tell them to send you a spreadsheet with the new users, and you use your script to create those users. It takes 2 minutes instead of 2 hours. (Dude—that's the front nine!) In addition to saving time, scripting your administrative tasks is more accurate. If you have to set a particular set of access control lists on dozens of folders, a script is the only way to ensure all the flags are set correctly. Here are the chapters in Part 3:

- Chapter 11, "Introduction to Active Directory Service Interfaces"
- Chapter 12, "Reading and Writing for ADSI"
- Chapter 13, "Searching Active Directory"
- Chapter 14, "Configuring Networking Components"
- Chapter 15, "Subs and Other Round Things"
- Chapter 16, "Logon Scripts"
- Chapter 17, "Working with the Registry"
- Chapter 18, "Working with Printers"

## Part 4: Scripting Other Applications

Once you learn how to use WMI and VBScript to automate Windows Server 2003, the logical question is, "What else can I do?" Well, with the latest version of Microsoft Exchange and Internet Information Services (IIS), the answer is quite a lot. So in this part of the book, you look at using WMI and VBScript to automate other applications.

In IIS 6.0, nearly everything that can be configured via GUI tools can also be scripted. This enables the Web administrator to simplify management and to also ensure repeatable configuration of the websites from a security perspective.

In Exchange administration, many routine tasks can be simplified by using VBScript. In Part 4, you look at how to leverage the power of VBScript to simplify user management, to configure and administer Exchange, and to troubleshoot some of the common issues confronting the enterprise Exchange administrator. The chapters in Part 4 are as follows:

- Chapter 19, "Managing IIS 6.0"
- Chapter 20, "Working with Exchange 2003"

## Part 5: Appendices

The Appendices in this book are not the normal "never read" stuff—indeed you will find yourself referring again and again to these four crucial documents. In Appendix A you will find lots of ideas for further work in developing your mastery of VBScript. Appendix B will save you many hours of searching for the "special names" that unlock the power of ADSI scripting. Appendix C helps you find the special WMI namespaces that enable you to perform many cool "tricks" in your scripting—and last but certainly not least is Appendix D, which contains my documentation "cheat sheet"—actually you will want to read it rather early in your scripting career.

- Appendix A, "VBScript Documentation"

- Appendix B, "ADSI Documentation"

- Appendix C, "WMI Documentation"

- Appendix D, "Documentation Standards"

## About the Companion CD

The CD accompanying this book contains additional information and software components, including the following files:

- **Lab files**   The lab files contain starter scripts, same-text files, and completed lab solutions for each of the 40 labs contained in this book. In addition, each of the scripts that is discussed in the book is contained in the folder corresponding to the chapter number. So for instance, in Chapter 1 we talk about enumerating disk drives on a computer system. The script that makes up the bulk of our discussion around that topic is contained in the \Labs\Ch01 folder.

- **eBook**   You can view an electronic version of this book on screen using Adobe Acrobat Reader. For more information, see the Readme.txt file included in the root folder of the Companion CD.

- **Scripts**   Sample scripts and starter scripts for all labs.

- **Tools**   Scriptomatic 1.0, Tweakomatic, EZADScriptomatic,  WMI Admin Tools, selected Windows Resouce Kit tools, and an evaluation of PrimalScript 3.1.

## System Requirements

- Minimum 233 MHz in the Intel Pentium/Celeron family or the AMD k6/Atholon/ Duron family

- 64 MB memory

- 1.5 GB available hard disk space

- Display monitor capable of 800 x 600 resolution or higher

- CD-ROM drive or DVD drive

- Microsoft Mouse or compatible pointing device

- Windows Server 2003 or Windows XP

# Technical Support

Every effort has been made to ensure the accuracy of this book and the contents of the companion CD-ROM. Microsoft Press provides corrections for books through the World Wide Web at *http://www.microsoft.com/learning/support*.

To connect directly with the Microsoft Press Knowledge Base and enter a query regarding a question or an issue that you might have, go to *http://www.microsoft.com /learning/support/search.asp*.

If you have comments, questions, or ideas regarding this book or the companion CD-ROM, please send them to Microsoft Press using either of the following methods:

| | |
|---|---|
| **E-Mail** | mspinput@microsoft.com |
| **Postal Mail** | Microsoft Press<br>Attn: Editor, *Microsoft Windows Scripting Self-Paced Learning Guide*<br>One Microsoft Way<br>Redmond, WA 98052 |

Please note that product support is not offered through the preceding addresses.

# Part 1
# Covering the Basics

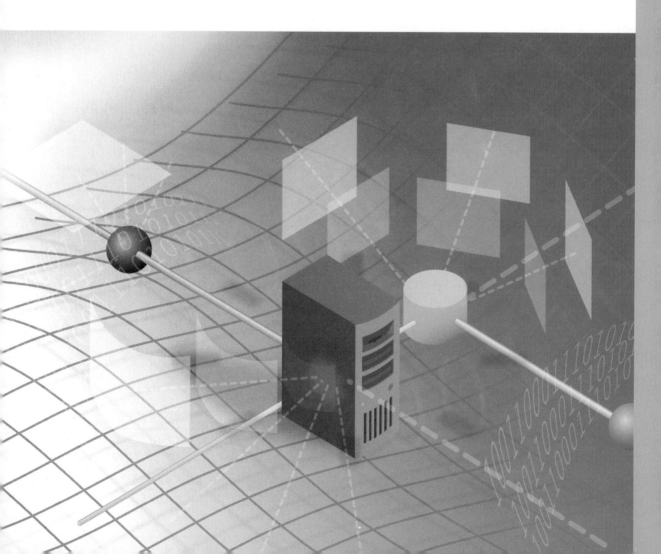

# 1 Starting from Scratch

In this chapter, you begin your journey down the winding road that leads to the automation of Microsoft Windows Server 2003. Our first step will be to examine several scripts written in Microsoft Visual Basic Scripting Edition (VBScript). Then you'll dissect a few scripts so that you can see what elements make up a script. Finally—and this is the best part—you'll write several scripts from scratch. Many of the concepts covered in this chapter will come up throughout this book, as well as in your day-to-day life as a network administrator, so be sure you understand the material here before moving on.

## Before You Begin

**To work through this chapter, you should be familiar with the following concept:**

- Basic Windows Server administration

**After completing this chapter you will be familiar with the following:**

- Basic error handling
- Connect to the file system object
- Four parts of a script
- Declaring variables
- Producing output
- Reading the registry
- Running scripts
- Using *Option Explicit*

## Running Your First Script

It is late at night and the cold air conditioning is drying your eyes out, making it impossible to keep them open. You have drunk nearly a dozen cups of coffee, and you try to steady your hands. The last item on your migration check-off list stares out at you from the page eerily: "Ensure all servers have the administrator tools installed." Slowly your predicament begins to sink in, through the caffeine cloud surrounding your eyes. "I should have been doing this hours ago." The hum of the equipment room seems to grow louder, and the rows of servers stretch for miles and miles. Supper is a distant memory and sleep a fleeting dream. "How in the world am I supposed to check 1000 servers for administrator tools?"

The darkness of foreboding doom begins to envelop you but then suddenly vanishes with a single fulgurant idea: I bet we can script this! Within five minutes, the following script is tested on a single server and works like a charm:

*Maybe case sensitive if in quotes*

*Can also pass a path c:\<dir>\<dir>*

```
Set objShell = CreateObject("Shell.Application")
Set colTools = objShell.Namespace(47).Items
For Each objTool in colTools
    WScript.Echo objTool
Next
```

---

### Just the Steps

▶ **To run an existing script**

1. Open a command prompt. (From the Start menu, select Run\CMD).
2. Change the directory to **\BookScripts\ch1**.
3. Type **CScript CheckAdminTools.vbs**, and press Enter.

---

A good way to learn how to write scripts is to read scripts. So what is a script? For our purposes, a script is nothing more than a collection of commands that we include in a text file. In this regard, scripts are like batch files that many network administrators have used since DOS days. Just like batch files, scripts can be written using nothing more sophisticated than Microsoft Notepad. An important difference between a batch file and a script is that a script has greater flexibility and its language is more powerful. In this section, you'll look at several scripts and learn to identify their common elements. I know some of you probably want to start typing your first script, but be patient. In the long run, you'll benefit from taking the time now to understand the elements found in all scripts.

---

### Just the Steps

▶ **To open an existing script**

1. Open Notepad.
2. From the File menu, choose Open. In the Files Of Type box, choose All Files from the drop-down list.
3. Navigate to the location of the VBScript you want to read.
4. Select the file, and choose Open from the Action menu.

---

Take a look at the following script, which you'll be referring to in the next few sections:

```
Option Explicit
On Error Resume Next
Dim objShell
Dim regActiveComputerName, regComputerName, regHostname
Dim ActiveComputerName, ComputerName, Hostname

regActiveComputerName = "HKLM\SYSTEM\CurrentControlSet\Control\" & _
    "ComputerName\ActiveComputerName\ComputerName"
```

```
regComputerName = "HKLM\SYSTEM\CurrentControlSet\Control\" & _
    "ComputerName\ComputerName\ComputerName"
regHostname = _
    "HKLM\SYSTEM\CurrentControlSet\Services\Tcpip\Parameters\Hostname"

Set objShell = CreateObject("WScript.Shell")
ActiveComputerName = objShell.RegRead(regActiveComputerName)
ComputerName = objShell.RegRead(regComputerName)
Hostname = objShell.RegRead(regHostname)

WScript.Echo ActiveComputerName & " is active computer name"
WScript.Echo ComputerName & " is computer name"
WScript.Echo Hostname & " is host name"
```

As you can see, this script contains a lot of information. Let's break it down piece by piece so that it's not too overwhelming. For the purposes of our discussion, you can think of the script as being made up of four main parts:

- Header information
- Reference information
- Worker information
- Output information

## Header Information

You can think of the header information as administrative overhead for your script. For most scripts, you can leave out the Header information section and lose none of the functionality. In fact, the preceding script would run just fine if the Header information section were deleted. (And it just so happens that you'll get a chance to prove this assertion during the labs at the end of this chapter.) If this information is so unrelated to the script's functionality, why should you include it? The header information should be a standard part of your script for two reasons: it makes the script easier to read and maintain, and it controls the way the script runs (as opposed to the way it might run by default). You'll learn more about how it controls the script later in the chapter when we look at the *Option Explicit* command and the *On Error Resume Next* command.

In the earlier script example, the header information consists of the following lines of code:

```
Option Explicit
On Error Resume Next
Dim objShell
Dim regActiveComputerName, regComputerName, regHostname
Dim ActiveComputerName, ComputerName, Hostname
```

Although this code might look complicated, in reality, only three different commands are being used: *Option Explicit*, *On Error Resume Next*, and *Dim*. Each of these commands is covered in detail in the following sections, but before we dive into the nuts and bolts, let's do a quick reality check.

**Quick Check**

**Q.** **What is one way to run a VBScript?**

**A.** Type **CScript** before the name of the .vbs file at the command prompt.

**Q.** **What is one tool you can use to read the text of a .vbs file?**

**A.** Notepad.

**Q.** **What are three commands found in the Header information section of a VBScript?**

**A.** *Option Explicit, On Error Resume Next,* and *Dim.*

### Option Explicit

The *Option Explicit* statement tells the script that each variable used in the script is going to be listed specifically before it is actually used.

**Note**   Not sure what a variable is? The official definition of a *variable* is a named storage location capable of containing data that can be modified during program execution. For now, however, it's sufficient to think of a variable as a kind of "nickname" for a piece of information stored in a script.

If you want to use a variable and you specify *Option Explicit* in the Header information section of the VBScript, you have to tell the script you're going to use this variable *before you actually use it.* If you omit *Option Explicit,* VBScript assumes by default that any statement it doesn't recognize is a variable. To declare a variable, you must use the command *Dim,* as illustrated in the preceding code. *Dim* stands for *dimension.* "Dimming" is how variables are treated. (This dimensioning of variables is actually setting aside a portion of memory used to contain the data.)

### On Error Resume Next

What does *On Error Resume Next* sound like it's trying to do? Let's break it down. *On Error* means that you want the computer to do something if it finds an error. *Resume Next* is what you want it to do. But *Next* what? A very good question. The *Next* you want it to resume is the next line of code in the script. So *On Error Resume Next* tells the computer that when something is messed up (causing an error), you want the computer to just skip that line and try the next line in the script. This process is called *error handling,* and it's a very basic task when writing scripts. You should probably consider using *On Error Resume Next* when you're using VBScript for logon scripts so that you don't get lots of phone calls right at 9:00 A.M. when your script has a problem. Of course, you'll test the script prior to deploying it, but we all know that tests don't always catch every eventuality. You'll learn about error handling in more detail later, including some pretty cool tricks, so stay tuned.

> **Note**   Even though we show it here for a complete script, your best practice is to *not* use *On Error Resume Next* while developing scripts; it will prevent you from seeing any errors produced during normal script execution. If you are using it and a script fails to work the way you expect, your first troubleshooting step should be to remove the *On Error Resume Next* statement.

### *Dim*

This code has a whole bunch of *Dim* stuff. As mentioned earlier, you use the word *Dim* to declare a variable. For instance, in the code at the end of this section, *objShell* and all the other words (except for *Dim*) are variable names I made up. I could have just as easily used *a*, *b*, *c*, *d*, and so on as the variables names (kind of like the variables you used in high school algebra) and saved myself a lot of typing. However, a good variable name makes the code easier to read and to understand. For example, in the following code, you can assume that the variable named *ComputerName* actually holds a computer name. (I think you'd agree that *ComputerName* is much more descriptive than *a*.) And notice how similar *regActiveComputerName*, *regComputerName*, and *regHostName* are (except for the *reg* part) to the following variables: *ActiveComputerName*, *Computer-Name*, and *HostName*. The variables are arranged according to how they will be used, that is, variables used to hold registry keys are on one line, and variables containing the corresponding output values of those registry keys appear on the next line.

```
Dim objShell
Dim regActiveComputerName, regComputerName, regHostName
Dim ActiveComputerName, ComputerName, Hostname
```

> **Quick Check**
>
> **Q.** For what purpose is *Option Explicit* used?
>
> **A.** To inform VBScript that all variables will be declared prior to use.
>
> **Q.** What functionality does *On Error Resume Next* provide?
>
> **A.** Basic error handling.
>
> **Q.** What is the command *Dim* used for?
>
> **A.** To declare variables.

## Reference Information

The Reference information section of the script gives you the ability to assign values to the variables you named in the Header information section of the script. Another reason for using a variable is to create a shortened alias for some value. Aliases make the script easier to work with. In the following code, values are assigned to some of the variables created in the Header information section of the script.

```
regActiveComputerName = "HKLM\SYSTEM\CurrentControlSet\Control\" &_
    "ComputerName\ActiveComputerName\ComputerName"
regComputerName = "HKLM\SYSTEM\CurrentControlSet\Control" &_
    "\ComputerName\ComputerName\ComputerName"
regHostname = "HKLM\SYSTEM\CurrentControlSet\Services" &_
    "\Tcpip\Parameters\Hostname"
```

*(handwritten annotations: "not (no space)", "ampersand space underscore")*

Notice that everything on the right-hand side of the equal sign looks like a registry key. If you caught that, you can probably figure out what the *reg* part of the variable name stands for. You got it—registry! Did you also notice that the three variable names (on the left-hand sides of the equal signs) are the same ones we talked about in the preceding section? What you're doing in this code is tying each of those variables to a registry key. For example, the first line of code shows that *regActiveComputerName* is equal to the very long string *HKLM\SYSTEM\CurrentControlSet\Control\Computer-Name\ActiveComputerName\ComputerName*. (By the way, *HKLM* is shorthand for HKEY_LOCAL_MACHINE. Since VBScript understands this abbreviation, using *HKLM* will save you some typing.)

## Getting the Proper Registry Key

One easy way to make sure you get the proper registry key for your scripts is to use the Copy Key Name feature of the Registry Editor (Regedit.exe). As shown in Figure 1-1, you select the registry key containing the information you want VBScript to extract, open the Edit menu, and select Copy Key Name from the list. The entire key name is pasted on the clipboard, and from there you paste it into your script.

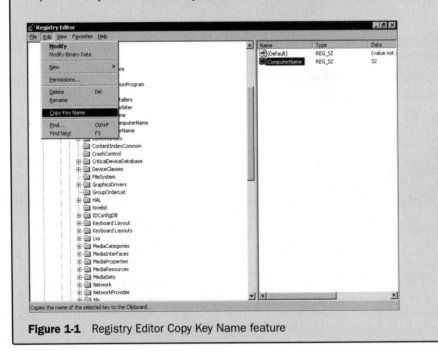

**Figure 1-1**   Registry Editor Copy Key Name feature

The Reference information section has the following purposes:

- Minimizes typing, and therefore ensures accuracy. You have to type long strings only once.

- Makes the script easier to read. If a variable is used several times in the script, the variable is "referenced" to the actual item only once.

- Makes it easier to change the script later. For example, the sample script you've been examining pulls out computer names. By changing the registry key and nothing else, you can make the script pull out any other information in the registry.

## Worker Information

The Worker information section of the script gets its name because it actually does something. The variables are declared in the Header section and referenced in the Reference section; in the Worker information section, the variables get busy.

> **Note**  I haven't yet explained WScript, which can also be used to create objects, or how to create file system objects. These subjects are covered in later chapters. At this point, you should focus on understanding the flow and the functionality of the script.

Let's look at some code.

```
Set objShell = CreateObject("WScript.Shell")
Set objFileSystem = CreateObject("Scripting.FileSystemObject")
ActiveComputerName = objShell.RegRead(regActiveComputerName)
ComputerName = objShell.RegRead(regComputerName)
Hostname = objShell.RegRead(regHostname)
```

Because you've read through the header information and looked at all the *Dim* statements, you know which names in the preceding code are variables. For instance, *objShell* and *objFileSystem* are both variables; that is, they are shorthand for something. The question is, shorthand for what? Let's walk through the first line of code:

```
Set objShell = CreateObject("WScript.Shell")
```

Notice that the sentence begins with *Set*. *Set* is a command in VBScript that is used to assign an object reference to a variable. For VBScript to be able to read from the registry, it must have a connection to it. This requirement is similar to that for reading from a database—you must first establish a connection to the database. To create an object reference, you use the *Set* keyword to assign the reference to a variable.

VBScript uses *automation objects* as a way to use the capabilities of other programs to provide more power to the system administrator who needs to create powerful scripts to manage today's complex networking environments. For example, instead of dumping output to a black and white, text-only command prompt, you can use an automation object to leverage the display and formatting capabilities of the products in the Microsoft Office System and create multicolor, three-dimensional graphs and charts.

You are setting the variable name *objShell* to the reference you created by using *CreateObject*. Notice the equal sign following *objShell*. It indicates that *objShell* should be equal to something else—in this case, to everything to the right of the equal sign, or *CreateObject("WScript.Shell")*. For now, pay attention to the *CreateObject* part of the expression. The use of the verb *Create* is a tip-off that some action is about to take place. As you'll see in a moment, this line assigns to *objShell* a connection that will allow the script to read the registry.

> **Note**   You might also see *WScript.CreateObject* used to assign an object reference to a variable instead of VBScript's plain *CreateObject*. For our purposes, both ways to assign an object reference will work.

You can now use the variables *ActiveComputerName* and *regActiveComputerName* to read the registry by using the newfound power of the variable *objShell*. Remember that earlier you defined *regActiveComputerName* as equal to the registry key that contains the active computer name. You now define *ActiveComputerName* to be equal to the name that comes out of the registry key when you read the registry. You do the same thing for the other two registry keys.

Let's take a moment to recap what you've done so far. You've stored three computer names into memory by using the variables named *ActiveComputerName*, *ComputerName*, and *Hostname*. To get the computer names into those variables, you read the values that are stored in three different registry keys on the computer. To do this, you created three variables named *regActiveComputerName*, *regComputerName*, and *regHostname*. You used the prefix *reg* to denote that the variables contain strings for the actual registry keys. You then used the *RegRead* capability of the *objShell* variable that you assigned to the object reference by using the *CreateObject* command. Now that you have this information stored into three variables, you need to do something with it. In the script you are examining, you will use the output capability of VBScript, described in the next section.

## Output Information

Being able to read from the registry, though cool, doesn't do you much good when you can't use the information. That's why it's important for a script to have an Output section. Of course, you can write a script that uses the information to perform tasks other than creating output, such as monitoring the status of a service and re-starting it when it failed, but even then most network administrators would want at least a log entry stating that the service was restarted. In our script, output is provided through a series of *Echo* commands. The use of the *WScript.Echo* command is illustrated in the following code:

```
WScript.Echo activecomputername & " is active computer name"
WScript.Echo ComputerName & " is computer name"
WScript.Echo Hostname & " is host name"
```

The *WScript.Echo* command is used to type text inside a command prompt or to produce a pop-up message box, depending on how the VBScript is actually run. When the VBScript is run by using CScript, as detailed in the earlier procedure titled "Just the Steps: To run an existing script," the script writes inside the command shell.

Each variable name that you just set is equal to the registry key information in the last section of our script. So what does *Echo* do? You guessed it—it repeats something. Since the variables are now linked to the strings contained within the registry keys (via the Reference information section), we can use *WScript.Echo* to write the information currently held by the variables. In the code, the ampersand (&), which simply means "and," is followed by a phrase within quotation marks. The current value of the variable on the left side of the ampersand gets put together with the string value contained inside the quotation marks on the right side of the ampersand. This "putting together" of two things with the ampersand is called *concatenation*. You are echoing what is stored in memory for each of our three variables, and you're also adding some text to explain what each variable is. When you run this script, you're rewarded with the results in Figure 1-2.

**Figure 1-2**  Screen output of DisplayComputerNames.vbs

Dealing with only three dialog boxes is a bit tedious, so imagine the frustration that dealing with a thousand or even just a hundred dialog boxes could cause. Some scripts can easily return a listing of over a thousand items (for example, a script that queried all the users in a medium-sized domain). Clearly you need a more efficient way to write data. In fact, you have several ways to do this, such as using VBScript's MsgBox to display a pop-up box containing text, but I am going to save that for Chapter 2, "Getting in the Loop."

## Enhancing Your Script

You've worked your way through your first script, and now let's see how we can modify it to enhance its capabilities. Here is the new functionality you will add to your script:

- Creating documentation that will keep track of what you learned in the previous section

- Obtaining information in addition to the three computer names

## Docs That Make House Calls

Let's first add some documentation to the script so that when you look at it six months from now, you'll know what you're looking at.

To add documentation, you simply type information into the script. To prevent the script from choking, you need to indicate that you are adding the text. You can do this in several ways. Perhaps the most efficient way is to preface each note with a single quotation mark (') followed by explanatory text (often called a *comment*). Here's what the script looks like with the added documentation:

```
' This script displays various Computer Names by reading the registry

Option Explicit      'Forces the scripter to declare variables
On Error Resume Next 'Tells VBScript to go to the next line
                     'instead of exiting when an error occurs
' Dim is used to declare variable names that are used in the script
Dim objShell
Dim regActiveComputerName, regComputerName, regHostname
Dim ActiveComputerName, ComputerName, Hostname

' When you use a variable name and then an equal sign (=)
'you're saying the variable contains the information on the right.
'The registry keys are quite long, so make them easier to read on
'a single screen by splitting the line in two.

regActiveComputerName = "HKLM\SYSTEM\CurrentControlSet" & _
    "\Control\ComputerName\ActiveComputerName\ComputerName"
regComputerName = "HKLM\SYSTEM\CurrentControlSet\Control" & _
    "\ComputerName\ComputerName\ComputerName"
regHostname = "HKLM\SYSTEM\CurrentControlSet\Services" & _
    "\Tcpip\Parameters\Hostname"


Set objShell = CreateObject("WScript.Shell")
ActiveComputerName = objShell.RegRead(regActiveComputerName)
ComputerName = objShell.RegRead(regComputerName)
Hostname = objShell.RegRead(regHostname)

' To make dialog boxes you can use WScript.Echo
' and then tell it what you want it to say.

WScript.Echo activecomputername & " is active computer name"
WScript.Echo ComputerName & " is computer name"
WScript.Echo Hostname & " is host name"
```

---

**Just the Steps**

▶ **To add documentation to a script**

1. Open the script in Notepad.

2. Preface the line with a single quotation mark (').

3. On the first line of script, after the single quotation mark, type a short description of the script's purpose.

4. Save the script.

---

# Modifying an Existing Script

Now that your script is fully documented, you can modify it to pull in additional information. Thus far, you can retrieve the active computer name, the host name, and the computer name. (Actually, these names could be different in certain situations, so this script really is useful.) What kind of information could you be interested in retrieving at this juncture? Look at Table 1-1 for some ideas. (Notice in Table 1-1 that the registry keys are spelled out completely—HKEY_LOCAL_MACHINE, for instance—and the script you worked on earlier was abbreviated *HKLM*. VBScript allows you to reference the registry using several forms. These forms are covered in depth in the section on the registry.)

**Table 1-1   Useful registry keys for script writers**

| Information | Location |
|---|---|
| Service information | HKEY_LOCAL_MACHINE\SYSTEM\CurrentControlSet\Services |
| User name used to log on to the domain | HKEY_CURRENT_USER\Software\Microsoft\Windows\CurrentVersion\Explorer\Logon User Name |
| Microsoft Exchange 2000 domain information | HKEY_CURRENT_USER\Software\Microsoft\Exchange\LogonDomain |
| Exchange 2000 domain user information | HKEY_CURRENT_USER\Software\Microsoft\Exchange\UserName |
| Group policy server | HKEY_CURRENT_USER\Software\Microsoft\Windows\CurrentVersion\Group Policy\History\DCName |
| User's home directory | HKEY_CURRENT_USER\Volatile Environment\HomeShare |
| The server that authenticated the currently logged-on user | HKEY_CURRENT_USER\Volatile Environment\LOGONSERVER |
| The DNS domain name of the currently logged-on user | HKEY_CURRENT_USER\Volatile Environment\USERDNSDOMAIN |

> **Note**   Much of the information that you can gather via the registry can be obtained by other approaches, such as using Active Directory Service Interface (ADSI) or Windows Management Instrumentation (WMI) (which you'll learn about in later chapters). These are two other ways you can use the power of VBScript to gather information you need to manage our network. You should be aware of this because the registry is a dynamic environment, and keys get moved around from time to time. Thus, the registry is not always consistent among all machines on the network. For instance, there are obviously differences between Microsoft Windows 95 and Microsoft Windows XP, but there are also differences between Microsoft Windows 2000 and Windows XP, and even between Windows XP and a version of Windows XP that has been upgraded from Microsoft Windows Me, for example. Mining information from sources other than the registry can assure a more consistent result. If at all possible, try to read the registry for items that cannot be obtained via other methods.

To modify your script to gather some of the information listed in Table 1-1, you need to make a few changes in each of its four sections. Much of your script will be exactly the same, and a few sections will be similar (meaning that you'll need to change a few names to ensure clarity in your documentation). Now you'll look at each section of your script to see what needs to be changed.

## Modifying the Header Information

The first three lines of your script can remain exactly the same. You still want to make sure you specify which variables you plan to use in the script, so leave *Option Explicit*. You also don't want the script to blow up when a value is absent or some other problem arises, so leave *On Error Resume Next* in place. In addition, since you're connecting to the registry to read items, you'll need the *objShell* variable in place. There is really no point in renaming these variables or changing them in any other way. By keeping the same name for *objShell*, for example, you'll always know its purpose. In this respect, you are developing your own *naming convention* for your scripts.

```
Option Explicit
On Error Resume Next
Dim objShell
```

The first three lines are in place and working fine, so now you need to create variables that you will use for the new registry values you want to read. For this example, we use some (but not all) of the values identified in Table 1-1. These variables are here:

```
Dim regLogonUserName, regExchangeDomain, regGPServer
Dim regLogonServer, regDNSdomain
Dim LogonUserName, ExchangeDomain, GPServer
Dim LogonServer, DNSdomain
```

Notice that we use our previous naming convention: we preface with *reg* all names of variables that will hold registry keys, and we leave *reg* off the names of all variables that will hold the information contained in the registry keys. (The variable item names are the same except for *reg*.)

---

**Just the Steps**

▶ **To modify the header information**

1. Open Notepad.
2. Ensure *Option Explicit* is listed.
3. Ensure *On Error Resume Next* is listed.
4. Delete variables that are not required.
5. Add variables for new information.
6. Save the script with a new name.

---

## Modifying the Reference Information

Because you are changing the registry keys you will pull information from, you'll need to completely replace the Reference information section. The good news is that the format for the section is exactly the same. The pattern looks like this:

Variable name             =       Registry key in quotation marks

*regLogonUserName*      =       "HKEY_CURRENT_USER\Software\

Microsoft\" & _"Windows\CurrentVersion\Explorer\Logon User Name"

There are three parts of the script involved in reading a registry key, and all the information we want to obtain can be easily modified by changing the assignment of values to the variable names listed in the preceding syntax example. In addition, because you listed all the variable names we want to use to hold the registry keys in the Header information section of the script, you can simply cut and paste the variables into the reference information section. In the next listing, you remove the *Dim* portion and the commas and place each variable name on a separate line. The resulting code will look like Figure 1-3.

```
Dim regLogonUserName, regExchangeDomain, regGPServer
Dim regLogonServer, regDNSdomain
```

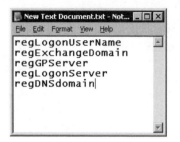

**Figure 1-3**   Using Notepad to speed script modification

After the variable names and the equal signs are inserted, add each registry key and enclose it in quotation marks. Remember to use the copy key feature of Regedit. Once all the registry keys are pasted into the script, the modified Reference information section looks like the following listing. Remember that the ampersand and underscore are used to indicate line continuation and are included here for readability. I also include them in production scripts to avoid having to scroll to the right while revising code.

```
regLogonUserName = "HKEY_CURRENT_USER\Software\Microsoft\" & _
    "Windows\CurrentVersion\Explorer\Logon User Name"
regExchangeDomain = "HKEY_CURRENT_USER\Software\Microsoft\" & _
    "Exchange\LogonDomain"
regGPServer = "HKEY_CURRENT_USER\Software\Microsoft\Windows\" & _
    "CurrentVersion\Group Policy\History\DCName"
regLogonServer = "HKEY_CURRENT_USER\Volatile Environment\" & _
    "LOGONSERVER"
regDNSdomain = "HKEY_CURRENT_USER\Volatile Environment\" & _
    "USERDNSDOMAIN"
```

---

**Just the Steps**

▶ **To modify the reference information**

1. Open Notepad.

2. Copy the *Dim* section of the header information.

3. Paste the *Dim* section from step 2 into a new Notepad file.

4. From the Edit menu, select Replace to display the Replace dialog box. In the Find What box, type **Dim**. Do not type anything in the Replace With box. This will erase all occurrences of the word *Dim*.

5. Place each variable on a separate line and remove the commas.

6. Open Regedit and locate the desired registry keys.

7. Using the Copy Key Name feature, paste the key after each variable name.

8. Ensure the variable name is separated from the registry key name with an equal sign.

9. Ensure the registry key name is enclosed in quotation marks.

10. Save the script.

---

## Modifying the Worker Information

You are halfway through creating the new script. The first line in the Worker information section of the script is fine and does not need to be changed.

```
Set objShell = CreateObject("WScript.Shell")
```

Notice that same two variables listed in the third line of the Header information section are used here. The challenge now is to modify each line so that it assigns the variables you created *without* the *reg* prefixes to the variables you created with the *reg* prefixes. This command has four parts associated with it:

| Variable name | = | Worker | Registry variable in () |
|---|---|---|---|
| *LogonUserName* | = | *objShell.RegRead* | *(regLogonUserName)* |

Here's the entire Worker information section of the new script:

```
LogonUserName = objShell.RegRead(regLogonUserName)
ExchangeDomain= objShell.RegRead(regExchangeDomain)
GPServer = objShell.RegRead(regGPServer)
LogonServer = objShell.RegRead(regLogonServer)
DNSdomain = objShell.RegRead(regDNSdomain)
```

The variables were all listed in the Header information section and were copied and pasted on separate lines in this section of the script without the *Dim* statements—just as we copied and pasted information for the Reference information section of our script. In the next part of the script, insert the equal sign and the same worker component (you always do this), which in this case is the *objShell.RegRead*. The last part of the script contains the registry variable created in the Reference section enclosed in parentheses. This again can be a really quick cut and paste job from the Reference information section.

---

**Just the Steps**

▶ **To modify the worker information**

1. Open Notepad.

2. Copy the *Dim* section of the Header information.

3. Paste the *Dim* section from step 2 into a new Notepad file.

4. From the Edit menu, select Replace to display the Replace dialog box. In the Find What box, type **Dim**. Do not type anything in the Find What box. This will erase all occurrences of the word Dim.

5. Place each variable on a separate line and remove the commas.

6. Paste an equal sign and the worker component *objShell.RegRead* onto each line.

7. Paste the appropriate variable from the Reference information section and enclose it in parentheses.

8. Save the script.

> **Note** I tend to use the cut-and-paste feature when working with scripts because some of the variable names I create are a little long. Although the names are typically not case-sensitive, for the most part *spelling counts*, to rephrase something I learned in first grade. The best way I've found to avoid messing up the script is to copy and paste the variable names between my Header information section and my Worker information section.

After you finish modifying the Worker information section of our script, double-check that all declared variables are in place and that everything else is accounted for. Save your script under a different name if you were editing the DisplayComputerNames script. You could try to run it, but it won't do too well because you need to change the last section—the Output information section.

## Modifying the Output information

The Output information section of the script takes what you've learned from the registry and displays it in an easy-to-understand format. This section is what really makes the script usable. It's amazing that we spend a lot of time figuring out how to find information but not too much time formatting the data we get. You'll beef up your knowledge of displaying and writing data quite a bit in later chapters. For now, you'll use *WScript.Echo* to bounce data back.

You can't really salvage much from the old script—the process would be too confusing because you'd have to change every variable that holds information from the registry, as well as all the comments added after the keys. So all you will keep are the *WScript.Echo* lines. Delete everything after *WScript.Echo* and start cutting and pasting. Make sure you include every variable name identified in the Worker information section of the script. The syntax for this section is made up of four parts and looks something like this:

| Command | Variable | & | Comment |
|---|---|---|---|
| *WScript.Echo* | *LogonUserName &* | | *" is currently Logged on"* |

Notice that there's a space after the first quotation mark in the comment section. You include the space because the ampersand is used to glue two phrases together, and VBScript does not add spaces when concatenating lines. Our new code section looks like this:

```
WScript.Echo LogonUserName & " is currently Logged on"
WScript.Echo ExchangeDomain & " is the current logon domain"
WScript.Echo GPServer & " is the current Group Policy Server"
WScript.Echo LogonServer & " is the current logon server"
WScript.Echo DNSdomain & " is the current DNS domain"
```

To put this section together, you just cut and paste each variable assigned to a registry key in the Worker information section of the script, add an ampersand, and put quotation marks around whatever text will be echoed out. Later on, you'll use *WScript.Echo* to troubleshoot problems because it's an excellent way to follow progress in a script.

---

**Just the Steps**

▶ **To modify the output information**

1. Open Notepad.

2. Copy each variable added to the Worker information section.

3. Paste the variables from step 2 into the Output information section.

4. Add an ampersand after each variable.

5. Place quotation marks around any text to be echoed out to the screen.

6. Paste an equal sign and the worker component *objShell.RegRead* onto each line.

7. Preface each line with *WScript.Echo*.

8. Save the script.

---

## How to Run Scripts

You can run scripts in several ways on Windows Server 2003, each of which has advantages and disadvantages. Let's look at some of these approaches now.

### Double-Clicking a File with a .vbs Extension

By default, when you double-click a file with a .vbs extension, the file runs within an instance of WScript.exe. Therefore, using *WScript.Echo* in the Output information section of the script results in the cute little pop-up boxes. This might not be a big deal when we're talking about two or three variables, but it can be a real pain when we're listing all the user names in our domain—which has 11,000 users! Perhaps a better alternative is the CScript approach.

### CScript

CScript can be thought of as the command-line version of the Windows Scripting Host (Figure 1-4). CScript is nice because you don't have to click any dialog boxes to make the script continue. (Yes—that's right—with the default Windows Scripting Host, the entire script pauses until you click OK in the dialog box, and then the script waits for you to do the same in each dialog box after that.) In addition, you can pretty easily capture output from CScript because you can enable Quick Edit mode from the command window. To do this, click C:\ in the upper left part of the window, and select Properties from the Action menu. Then click on the Options tab, and select the Quick Edit Mode box. Next, choose Save Properties For Future Windows Of The Same Title, and you're finished. This feature enables you to highlight text and copy it to the clipboard from the CMD window. Once the data is on the clipboard, you can do everything from pasting the data into Notepad to using the text driver for Microsoft Excel and sorting the data into various cells that you can use to produce graphs. You'll learn more about this feature later in the book.

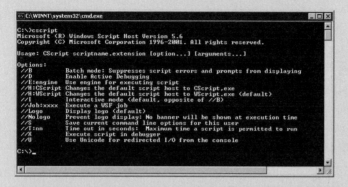

**Figure 1-4**   CScript offers many options, which can be set from the command line

### Embedding Scripts in Web Pages

You can embed scripts inside Web pages. This has some potential use in the enterprise environment in which users who have access to a particular Web site on the intranet can click a button to launch a particular script. This might be a useful and valid use of VBScript for, say, information gathering or troubleshooting. There are some security concerns, however, which you'll learn about later in the book.

### Dragging and Dropping a .vbs File to an Open Command Prompt

You can drag and drop a .vbs file to an open command prompt, which launches the script with the default scripting host. The nice thing about this is that you do not have to type the path to the file because Windows Explorer automatically puts it onto the command prompt line.

### Dragging and Dropping a .vbs File to Notepad

You can drag and drop the .vbs file to an open Notepad file with a blank page to automatically open the file and display the text.

### Adding Notepad to the SendTo Menu

You can easily edit the script by opening it in Notepad. Just add Notepad to the SendTo menu by going into C:\Documents and Settings\%USERNAME%\SendTo and adding a shortcut to Notepad.exe.

## Summary

In this chapter, you looked at your first script. Recall that the script is broken into four parts: the Header information, the Reference information, the Worker information, and the Output information sections. You also looked at variables and how to make the script engine aware of their presence. We learned how to read from the registry and how to get information out to the user. Finally, you looked at modifying scripts and learned to determine which parts of the script can be re-used and which parts need to be re-created.

## Quiz Yourself

**Q.** What is the reason for including *Option Explicit* as the first line of a VBScript?

**A.** *Option Explicit* forces you to list each variable you are going to use in your script. It is useful in that it guards against misspelled words and helps you to know which parts of the script are real commands and which parts are made-up variable names. When you do not use *Option Explicit*, a misspelled variable automatically becomes a new variable.

**Q.** You are trying to read from the registry; however, every time the script gets to a particular key, the script fails. What can be done to prevent this?

**A.** You can use two approaches to prevent the script from failing when an error is present. The first is to include *On Error Resume Next* in your script. The second is to simply place a single quotation mark (') in front of the line that is failing. If you run the script again and it doesn't fail, you've found the problem.

**Q.** What does it mean to *Dim* a variable?

**A.** To *Dim* a variable is to declare it to the script. The operating system then allocates memory for the variables. In addition, *Dim* is a good place to add documentation that explains the purpose of each variable.

**Q.** To produce a pop-up dialog box, which command do you use?

**A.** The command *WScript.Echo* will produce a pop-up dialog box in WScript or send output to the console window when run under CScript.

**Q.** Name the four parts of a VBScript.

**A.** The four parts of a VBScript are the Header information section, Reference information section, Worker information section, and Output information section.

## On Your Own

## Lab 1 Exploring a VBScript

In this section, you will explore the parts of a VBScript.

## Lab Instructions

1. Open the Lab1 folder located on the companion CD-ROM. From there, open the DisplayComputerNames.vbs script in Notepad.

2. Add comments that identify each section of the script. (Make sure to include all four parts of the script: Header information, Reference information, Worker information, and Output information.)

3. Save the script with a different filename, such as **lab1.vbs**.

4. Delete the entire Header information section.

5. Save the script, and then try to run it. Does it run?

6. Add the *Option Explicit* command again, and save the file. Now does it run?

7. Put a comment mark (') in front of *Option Explicit*, and save the file. Does it run?

# Lab 2 Customizing an Existing Script

In this lab, you learn to customize an existing script.

## Scenario

You are a new network administrator at a Fortune 500 company. You recently had a server crash, and it did not generate a dump file. Because you have several servers on your network, you don't want to have to "mouse around" very much; rather, you'd like to simply run a script to confirm the crash recovery configuration. Since your company is fortunate to have a college intern working for the summer, and you haven't yet learned how to remotely run the script, you've decided to do the following:

1. Create a script that reads crash recovery information from the registry. Your research has revealed the following keys to be of interest:

   ```
   "HKLM\SYSTEM\CurrentControlSet\Control\CrashControl\AutoReboot"
   "HKLM\SYSTEM\CurrentControlSet\Control\CrashControl\MinidumpDir"
   "HKLM\SYSTEM\CurrentControlSet\Services\Tcpip\Parameters\Hostname"
   "HKLM\SYSTEM\CurrentControlSet\Control\CrashControl\LogEvent"
   "HKLM\SYSTEM\CurrentControlSet\Control\CrashControl\DumpFile"
   ```

2. Copy the script to a share on a local server.

3. Run the script under CScript.

4. Have the intern copy the output from the command prompt and paste it into a Notepad file that has the same name as the server.

## Lab Instructions

1. Still using the CD-ROM, open the Lab2 folder, which contains the Display-ComputerName.vbs file.

2. Open the DisplayComputerName.vbs file, and save it as **ReadCrashRecoveryInformation.vbs**.

3. Edit the Header information section of the script, and include variables for each of the items you are going to read from the registry. (Remember, you'll need two variables for each registry item: one for the registry key itself, and one for the data contained in the registry key.)

4. Edit the Reference information section of the script. (Use the *reg* variable names you created in step 3 of this procedure and assign them to the appropriate registry keys.)

5. Edit the Worker information section of the script. (Assign the non-registry variable names you created in step 3 to the *regRead* Worker part of the script.)

6. Edit the Output information section of the script. (Use the *same* variables you assigned to the *regRead* parts in step 5.)

7. Add any documentation to the script you need. (Make sure you *over*-comment your script. Concepts that are perfectly clear today will be a dull memory within a few days.)

8. Save your script.

9. Open a command prompt.

10. Type **CScript ReadCrashRecoveryInformation.vbs** and press Enter. (If you get a File Not Found comment, change to the directory where you saved your script and repeat the command.)

# 2  Getting in the Loop

If you thought the last chapter went fast, wait until you get a load of our objectives for this chapter.

## Before You Begin

**In order to work through the material presented in this chapter, you need to be familiar with the following concepts from earlier chapters:**

- How to run a script
- How to declare a variable by using the *Dim* command
- How to perform basic error suppression by using *On Error Resume Next*
- How to connect to the file system object
- How to read from the registry

**After completing this chapter you will be familiar with the following:**

- Using *For Each Next*
- Defining constants
- Implementing collections
- Using *For…Next*
- Controlling script execution by using the *Sleep* command
- Implementing line concatenation
- Using *Do While…Loop*
- Using *Do Until*

## Adding Power to Scripts

Reading the registry and echoing the results on the screen are useful tasks. At times, however, you need to perform repetitive operations. Even the most casual observer knows that network administration involves many tasks performed over and over again. As Yogi Berra once said, "It's déjà vu all over again."

How can you harness the power of VBScript to relieve some of the banality of day-to-day network administration on Microsoft Windows Server 2003? At least four constructs are ideal for the task:

- *For Each…Next*

- *For…Next*

- *Do While*

- *Do Until*

This chapter begins by examining a real script to see how you can use these powerful tools in your daily duties as network administrators.

# For Each…Next

The *For Each…Next* tool is really the "For something—do it again" tool. *For Each…Next* lets you walk through a collection of objects and perform a particular action on the object, and then perform that action again on the next object.

In the following script, you use *For Each…Next* to examine characteristics of fixed drives on a server:

```
Option Explicit
On Error Resume Next
Const DriveType = 3
Dim colDrives
Dim drive

set colDrives = _
GetObject("winmgmts:").ExecQuery _
    ("select DeviceID from Win32_LogicalDisk where DriveType =" & DriveType)

For Each drive in colDrives
    WScript.Echo drive.DeviceID
Next
```

Let's peruse this script and see what it's doing. In your initial reading, you see some common elements you learned about in Chapter 1, "Starting From Scratch": the Header information section of the script (*Option Explicit*, *On Error Resume Next*, and *Dim*); and the Reference information section (the part with *set colDrives*). Those are the only elements that should look familiar. This script introduces a number of new concepts, such as constants, Windows Management Instrumentation (WMI), and collections, in addition to the *For Each…Next* construct. Dive in! The scripting waters are fine.

---

**Just the Steps**

▶ **To use *For Each…Next***

1. On a new line in a script, type **For Each** and then a variable name.

2. On the next line, enter a command you want repeated.

3. On the line following the command you want repeated, type **Next**.

# Header Information

The Header information section of your script contains commands that are rapidly becoming old hat:

```
Option Explicit
On Error Resume Next
Const DriveType = 3
Dim colDrives
Dim drive
```

This script begins by using *Option Explicit*, which says that each variable must be specifically listed (declared) by using the *Dim* command. *On Error Resume Next* is a rudimentary error handling technique that says "when an error occurs, skip the line that caused the problem and go on to the next line in the script." You also see a new item in the third line—*Const*. Let's talk about it now.

### Defining Constants

The *Const DriveType = 3* line is a new concept. In this line, you define a constant. This line says that the word *DriveType* is equal to the number 3. Why do you do this? You want to use the number 3 later in the script when you build the WMI query. Rather than hard-coding the number 3 into your query (hard-coding a value into a script is called *creating a literal*), you replace it with the constant *DriveType*. Just like a variable, the constant can be called anything you want. But since WMI uses the number 3 to refer to the type of drive, you called the constant *DriveType*.

### Constants vs. Variables

Why did you use a constant instead of a variable? This is a good question, and the answer is that you could have used a variable in this instance. It would look something like this:

```
Dim colDrives 'Holder for what comes back from the WMI query
Dim drive 'Holder for name of each logical drive in colDrives
Dim DriveType
DriveType = 3
```

In this particular case, using a variable instead of a constant wouldn't have made any difference. However, variables have a dark secret that will come back to haunt you one day (guaranteed). Their value can change during script execution, whereas the value of a constant is set before execution. This is illustrated in the following rather silly script. First is the normal Header information section: *Option Explicit, On Error Resume Next*, and a few *Dim* statements to declare the variables. Next, in the Reference section, you assign values to each variable and echo out the total. So far so good. However, you then reassign the *FirstValue* to be equal to the total, and echo out the total. Because the variable *total* is assigned to *FirstValue + SecondValue* before the *FirstValue* is reassigned to the *total*, the script produces illogical results. If you added *total = FirstValue + SecondValue* right before the second echo, the script would work as expected.

```
Option Explicit
On Error Resume Next

Dim total
Dim FirstValue
Dim SecondValue

FirstValue = 1
SecondValue = 3
Total = FirstValue + SecondValue

WScript.Echo " the total of " & FirstValue & " and " & _
    SecondValue &  " Is " & (total)
FirstValue = Total
WScript.Echo " the total of " & FirstValue & " and " & _
    SecondValue &  " Is " & (Total)
```

## Shared Benefits of Constants and Variables

You gain several advantages by using either a constant or a variable:

- The script is easier to read. When you read the WMI query, notice that you're filtering by *DriveType*. This makes more sense than filtering out number 3 drive types.

- The script is easier to revise. To change the script to filter out CD-ROMs, simply change the constant to the number 5.

- Reusing the value in the script later on is easier. This script does not reuse the constant *DriveType*. However, in longer scripts, you'll do this, and using constants is a good habit to get into.

- The script is easier to document. You can easily add a comment or a series of comments such as the following:

```
Const DriveType = 3 'used by WMI for fixed disks
'other drive types are 2 for removable, 4 for Network, 5 for CD
```

After the constant is defined, you list a couple of variables used by the script. In this case, you declared two. The first one is *colDrives*. Now, why did you call this colDrives? Because the WMI query returns a collection of drives. Let's look at collections and see what they do for you.

---

**Quick Check**

**Q.** **Name one advantage of using *For Each...Next*.**

**A.** Using this construct provides the ability to iterate through a collection without knowing the number of members in advance.

**Q.** **What is the difference between a variable and a constant?**

**A.** A variable can change value, whereas a constant retains a constant value.

**Q.** **List three reasons for using constants.**

**A.** Using constants makes the script easier to read and revise. Reuse later in the script is also easy.

---

## Collections

When you have the possibility of seeing a group of related items, thinking of them as a *collection* is useful. A collection is a familiar concept. For instance, my wife has a collection of key chains. Although each of the key chains is different (some have city names, some have college names, and others have product names), they are also similar enough to be in her collection called key chains. That is, they all have a ring on which keys are hung—without that common purpose, they would not be key chains. In a similar fashion, when you run your script, the script will return all the permanently fixed hard disk drives on the server. These drives might be IDE or SCSI, but they will all be hard disk drives.

What's so groovy about having a collection of hard disks (aside from the fact they're pretty)? Consider the alternative. If you couldn't return a collection of hard drives from a server, you'd need to know which drives are actually installed on the machine. You'd have to connect to the server and list the necessary information for each drive—for example, you'd need to connect to drives A, C, D, E, F, and so on. In addition, to keep the script from failing when a drive did not exist, you'd need error handling (such as *On Error Resume Next*), or you'd have to test for the presence of each drive prior to querying information about it. Although that approach would work, it would be kludgy, to say the least.

There is only one bad thing about collections: you cannot simply perform a *WScript.Echo* (or a *WriteLine* for that matter) of the information returned from a query. Instead, you have to do something like a *For Each...Next* loop and go through the loop as many times as there are items in the collection. If you had five drives in your collection, guess what? We, in our current script, make five passes through the loop and echo each of the drives out. Walking through the loop multiple times, once for each member of the collection, is called *iteration* and is a task routinely performed in administrative scripting.

If you have only one drive, guess what? It's still returned as a collection, and you have to iterate through the collection using *For Each...Next* to get out your single drive. Major bummer! Fortunately, by the end of this chapter, you'll have so much experience doing this, it will seem like a piece of cake (or a piece of celery, if you're on a diet like I am).

## Reference Information

In the Reference information section of the script is a new concept mentioned earlier— WMI. We're using it here to look at our drives, but you'll learn more about WMI later in this chapter. To connect to WMI, you have to use a string that looks like *GetObject("winmgmts:")*. Then you simply run a query that selects the desired drives. Remember that in the Reference information section of our script, you say that *colDrives* is equal to all the information on the right side of the equal sign. You are creating an alias for the long *winmgmts* connection string that we call *colDrives*. You can see this in the following code:

```
Set colDrives =_
GetObject("winmgmts:").ExecQuery _
    ("select DeviceID from Win32_LogicalDisk where DriveType =" & _
    DriveType)
```

## Worker Information

The Worker information section is really small in this script. In addition, the Output information section is sandwiched inside the *For Each...Next* loop. Let's look at it:

```
For Each drive In colDrives
    WScript.Echo drive.DeviceID
Next
```

Because you sent a fine-tuned query to WMI in the Reference information section of the script, and the purpose of the script was simply to list drives, the Worker information section has little work to do. All it really needs to do is to walk through the collection of drives returned from WMI. You use *For Each* and then the variable drive that you created to hold each of the drives returned from *colDrives*. Once you have the drive in your hands, you look for the *DeviceID* of the drive. But, interestingly enough, you use this in the Output information section of the script, which is the *WScript.Echo* part. After you echo the *DeviceID*, you do it again for the next drive in the collection using the *Next* command.

## *For...Next*

I know what you're thinking: "We just got finished looking at *For...Next!*" Well, sort of, but not really. An important difference between *For Each...Next* and *For...Next* is that with *For Each...Next*, you don't have to know how many times you want to do something. With the *For...Next* construct, you must know exactly how many times you want to do something. Using *For...Next* is not necessarily a bad thing, however, because it gives you a lot of extra control. For example, the next script checks a number of performance indicators on the server (that is, process thread counts, page faults, working set sizes, and the like). The values for these items can change quite often, so you want to check them on a regular basis. However, frequent checking can cause a performance hit on either the server or the network (depending on how the script was utilized), so you want to check the status only at certain times. The solution here is to take measurements of all the running processes, then wait an hour and do it again. You do this for an 8-hour cycle and then quit. You could use this type of script to monitor performance on a server that was heavily utilized during working hours.

---

**Just the Steps**

▶ **To implement *For…Next***

1. On a new line in the script, type **For** followed by a variable and a count (such as **For i = 1 to 10**).

2. On the next line, type the command to be performed.

3. On the next line, type **Next**.

---

## Header Information

Our Header information section begins with the *Option Explicit* command that tells VBScript that all our variables will have to be formally announced by using the *Dim* command. One issue to keep in mind about *Option Explicit* is that it must be the first non-commented line in the script. For instance, in the electronic version of the next script, notice that several lines have been commented out by using the single quotation mark character ('). These lines are used to tell basic information about the purpose of the script, provide documentation on the use of various variables, and explain some of the syntax peculiarities. Once all that work is done, the first line without a single quotation mark (') must be *Option Explicit* if you want *Option Explicit* to work. The reason for this is that when the line without the single quotation mark is not the first line in the script, some variables can sneak in without being declared. *On Error Resume Next* uses the second line in our script. As you no doubt have noticed, *On Error Resume Next* and *Option Explicit* seem to appear in all scripts. If you were going to create a template for script creation, *Option Explicit* and *On Error Resume Next* would be a couple of good lines to include, because more than likely you'll want them in all your scripts. However, you might want to comment out the *On Error Resume Next* line by placing a single quotation mark in front of it. In this way, while you are writing and testing your script, you will be able to catch all the errors, because *On Error Resume Next* is turned off. Once testing is completed, you simply remove the single quotation mark from in front of *On Error Resume Next*, turning it back on.

Next, you define a constant named *ONE_HOUR* and set it equal to 3600000. You're going to use this constant in conjunction with the *Sleep* command, which counts in milliseconds. To calculate, you'd multiply 60 minutes by 60 seconds, and then multiply the result by 1000, which yields 3600000. By defining the *ONE_HOUR* constant, you make the script easier to read. In the complete script (on the companion CD), this constant is commented to explain that it will be used with the *Sleep* command, which requires a millisecond value. In addition, you might want to add several other constants in the script, such as *HALF_HOUR*, *QUARTER_HOUR*, and *FIVE_MINUTES*, and then you could easily change the sleep timeout value later in the script. Defining constants but not utilizing them in the script doesn't adversely affect the running of the script, because you comment them to that effect. This script has only three variables: *objWMIService*, which is used to hold the connection to WMI, allowing you to query for performance information about the running processes; *objProcess*, which is used to hold the name of each process that comes back from *objWMIService*; and lastly *i*, which is one of the weird little variables used to increment the *For...Next* loop. Since *i* is, however, a variable, and you turned on *Option Explicit*, you need to declare it by using the *Dim* command.

```
Option Explicit
On Error Resume Next
Const ONE_HOUR = 3600000
Dim objWMIService
Dim objProcess
Dim i

Set objWMIService = GetObject("winmgmts:") _
    & .ExecQuery _
    ("SELECT * FROM Win32_Process")

For i = 1 To 8
    For Each objProcess In objWMIService
        WScript.Echo Now
        WScript.Echo ""
        WScript.Echo "Process: " & objProcess.Name
        WScript.Echo "Process ID: " & objProcess.ProcessID
        WScript.Echo "Thread Count: " & objProcess.ThreadCount
        WScript.Echo "Page File Size: " & objProcess.PageFileUsage
        WScript.Echo "Page Faults: " & objProcess.PageFaults
        WScript.Echo "Working Set Size: " & objProcess.WorkingSetSize
    Next
    WScript.Echo "******PASS COMPLETE**********"
    WScript.Sleep ONE_HOUR
Next
```

## Reference Information

The Reference information section of the script consists of a rather nasty WMI query string and its attendant assignment to the *objWMIService* variable. One line of code is all that the Reference information section takes up in this script. The nasty code is shown here:

```
Set objWMIService = GetObject("winmgmts:") _
    & .ExecQuery _
    ("SELECT * FROM Win32_Process")
```

This line of code connects to WMI and then executes a query that lists all Win32 processes running on the machine. As mentioned earlier, you'll learn about WMI in later chapters, but it is important to notice now that the query looks exactly like a regular SQL Server query. The code says to select (which means to choose something) from the Win32 process. The "something" that is being chosen is *. As you no doubt recognize, * is the wildcard character and means "everything." So this query chooses everything from the Win32 process.

> **Note**   Notice in the preceding code the underscore (_) that appears at the end of the first and second lines in the Reference information section. These are used to break up the code into more than one line to make the code easier to read. The important aspect to pay attention to is the placement of the open and close parentheses and the quotation marks (" ") as you break up the lines. Notice also that in the beginning of the second line, the ampersand was used, which as you'll recall from Chapter 1 is the concatenation character. This ampersand was used because you're inside of the parentheses, and you need to stick the two lines together. At times, you'll need to embed spaces to ensure commands are not messed up when you break the lines. The line continuation following *ExecQuery* does not include the ampersand because it falls outside of the parentheses.

## Worker and Output Information

As in the first script in this chapter, the Worker and the Output information sections kind of merge together. This section begins with the *For i = 1 To 8* command, which means that you're going to count to 8 and on each pass increment the value of the variable *i*. With each pass, the variable *i* changes its value. In the second line of the Worker information section is a *For Each...Next* command. This tells you that the information returned from the *objWMIService* variable is a collection. Since it is a collection, you need to use *For Each...Next* to walk (*iterate*) through the collection. As the code walks, it echoes out the value of the information you want (such as the process, process ID, and thread count). At the end of the grouping of *WScript.Echo* commands is a *Next* command. The problem with nested *Next* commands is trying to keep track of which *Next* belongs to which *For* or *For Each*. Indenting them a little bit will help you see which *For* command lines up with which *Next* command. This technique makes the script easier to read.

The *Now* command is used to echo out the date and time, providing an easy way to timestamp logs and other output obtained from scripts. In addition, since *Now* is inside the *For Each...Next* loop, it will timestamp each process as it is reported. This allows you to see how long it takes the script to complete its processing—the *Now* command reports down to the second.

The *WScript.Sleep* command is used to pause the execution of the script for a specified amount of time. As mentioned earlier in this chapter, the *Sleep* command takes its input in the form of milliseconds. To pause the script for one second, you would write the code like this:

```
WScript.Sleep 1000
```

I've been calling this the *Sleep* command, but in programming speak it would be called the *Sleep* method of the *WScript* object. However, if I called it that, this book would sound like a programmer's reference and therefore would be boring. So I'll just call it the *Sleep* command and be done with it.

This ability to pause the script can have a number of uses. For instance, it allows you to have a very flexible running schedule. If you attempted to pause the script using the scheduler service on Windows Server 2003, you would need eight different schedules, because there is no notion of "pause for an hour, and only do it for 8 hours." One other very useful aspect of the *Sleep* command is that it allows for "spin-up time." By using the *Sleep* command, you can cause a script to wait for a slower component to come on line prior to execution. The *Sleep* command is not an atomic clock. Although it's fine for generic pausing of a script, don't think you can use it for scientific timing—it was never designed for that purpose. In general, it's not accurate for periods of time less than a second.

The only other issue that needs to be pointed out in this Worker/Output information section is the use of *WScript.Echo*. I know you're all familiar with this command by now; however, notice what is done in the fourth line:

```
WScript.Echo ""
```

By doing an echo with "", you're essentially echoing a blank line. This helps to format the output. You have the date and time, then a blank line at the start of each listing for each process in the collection of Win32 processes. In addition to the blank line, *WScript.Echo* is used to indicate that the script has finished its pass through the processes. Remember that anything inside the quotation marks will be echoed to the screen. By padding the script with a bunch of *****, you can more easily find your information.

```
For i = 1 To 8
    For Each objProcess In objWMIService
        WScript.Echo  Now
        WScript.Echo ""
        WScript.Echo "Process: " & objProcess.Name
        WScript.Echo "Process ID: " & objProcess.ProcessID
        WScript.Echo "Thread Count: " & objProcess.ThreadCount
        WScript.Echo "Page File Size: " & objProcess.PageFileUsage
        WScript.Echo "Page Faults: " & objProcess.PageFaults
        WScript.Echo "Working Set Size: " & objProcess.WorkingSetSize
    Next
    WScript.Echo "******PASS COMPLETE**********"
    WScript.Sleep ONE_HOUR
Next
```

---

**Quick Check**

**Q.** *WScript.Sleep* **is expressed in what unit?**

**A.** *WScript.Sleep* is expressed in milliseconds.

**Q.** **What is an important difference between** *For Each...Next* **and** *For...Next*?

**A.** With *For Each...Next*, you don't need to know the number of elements in advance.

---

# Do While...Loop

The *Do While...Loop* allows you to run a script as long as a certain condition is in effect. If you were in Kauai, the *Do While...Loop* might look like this:

```
Do While sun_is_shining
    Surf
Loop
```

*Do While...Loop* means that as long as the specified condition remains true, the listed action continues to perform—it just loops around and around. In our silly preceding example, as long as the sun is shining, we surf. (Not a bad way to spend an afternoon.)

---

**Just the Steps**

▶ **To use the** *Do While...Loop*

**1.** On a new line in the script, type **Do While** followed by a condition to be tested.

**2.** On the next line, type the command to be performed.

**3.** On the next line type, **Loop.**

---

In the following script, you monitor the disk space on a server to let you know when it falls below 100000000 bytes. If the free space falls below 100000000, a message is echoed to the screen every 5 seconds. Read through this script and see which parts you can identify. After you finish reading it, we'll discuss it.

```
Option Explicit
On Error Resume Next
Const FIVE_SEC = 5000
Const LOCAL_HARD_DISK = 3
Dim colMonitoredDisks
Dim objWMIService
Dim objDiskChange
Dim i

Set objWMIService = GetObject("winmgmts:" _
    & "{impersonationLevel=impersonate}").ExecQuery _
    ("SELECT * FROM Win32_Process")
```

```
Set colMonitoredDisks = objWMIService.ExecNotificationQuery _
    ("Select * from __instancemodificationevent within 30 where " _
    & "TargetInstance isa 'Win32_LogicalDisk'")
i = 0
Do While i = 0
    Set objDiskChange = colMonitoredDisks.NextEvent
    If objDiskChange.TargetInstance.DriveType = _
        LOCAL_HARD_DISK Then
        If objDiskChange.TargetInstance.Size < 100000000 Then
            WScript.Echo _
                "Hard disk space is below 100000000 bytes."
            WScript.Sleep(FIVE_SEC)
        End If
    End If
Loop
```

## Header Information

The Header information section, as shown in the next segment of code, begins with the *Option Explicit* command. You can think of *Option Explicit* as a cheap spelling checker. Since it forces you to list all your variables, if you later misspell a variable, VBScript gives you an error, such as the one shown in Figure 2-1.

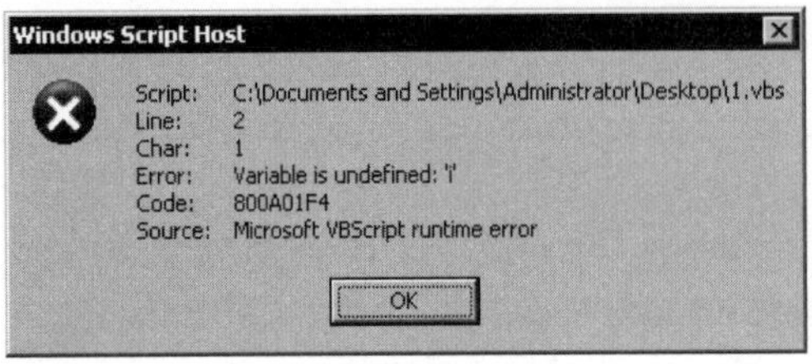

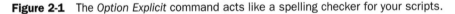

**Figure 2-1**   The *Option Explicit* command acts like a spelling checker for your scripts.

After the *Option Explicit* command, you see *On Error Resume Next*. This is one command you want to comment out during testing of the script. The reason for this is that while you're in testing and development mode, the *On Error Resume Next* command suppresses error messages, and you won't know what's going on with the script. One of the easiest errors to see is failure to declare a variable while using *Option Explicit*. The rest of the Header information section of our script is shown here:

```
Option Explicit
On Error Resume Next
Const FIVE_SEC = 5000
Dim colMonitoredDisks
Dim objWMIService
Dim objDiskChange
Dim i
```

In the Header information section, we declare the constant *FIVE_SEC*, which is set to 5000. This will be used by the *WScript.Sleep* command, which requires the time to be specified in milliseconds (5000 milliseconds is 5 seconds). By changing the value of this constant, you can vary the length of time the script will pause before echoing messages. You should be aware that creating a loop statement that does not exit, with a *Sleep* command that is very short, can cause VBScript to eat up all your CPU time and make your server unstable. The variables are listed here:

- ***colMonitoredDisks***  Used to hold the collection of disks that is returned by the WMI query.

- ***objWMIService***  Used to hold the connection string and query to WMI.

- ***objDiskChange***  Used to hold the notification event that comes from WMI, which lets you know you have a change in disk status.

- *i*  This is a trick variable in this script. Since you want the script to run continuously, you set *i* to zero, and then tell the *Do* loop to *Loop While i* is equal to zero. In this script, the value of *i* will never change, and thus the script will never end.

## Reference Information

In the Reference information section, shown next, you make your connection to WMI and then execute a query:

```
Set objWMIService = GetObject("winmgmts:" _
    & "{impersonationLevel=impersonate}").ExecQuery _
    ("SELECT * FROM Win32_Process")

Set colMonitoredDisks = objWMIService.ExecNotificationQuery _
    ("Select * from __instancemodificationevent within 30 where " _
        & "TargetInstance isa 'Win32_LogicalDisk'")
```

## Worker and Output Information

The Worker and Output information section of the script is where you do some pretty cool stuff. Let's take a look at what is going on in this section of the script:

```
i = 0
Do While i = 0
    Set objDiskChange = colMonitoredDisks.NextEvent
    If objDiskChange.TargetInstance.DriveType = _
    LOCAL_HARD_DISK Then
        If objDiskChange.TargetInstance.Size < 100000000 Then
            WScript.Echo _
                "Hard disk space is below 100000000 bytes."
            WScript.Sleep(FIVE_SEC)
        End If
    End If
Loop
```

First let's look at the *Do While...Loop* construction. Notice that the second line of this section is *Do While i = 0*. This tells VBScript that you want to invoke a *Do While...Loop*. Everything between *Do While* and *Loop* will continue to run as long as the *Do While* statement is true. So as long as *i* is equal to zero, our code in the middle will run.

After you set up the *Do While...Loop*, you assign the *objDiskChange* variable to be equal to the next event that comes out of *colMonitoredDisks*. Once that assignment is done, you go into a couple of nested *If...Then* statements. (We'll look at *If...Then* in Chapter 3, "Adding Intelligence," so let's skip over this section of the script. Also, we'll cover WMI events in later chapters, so we'll skip over that as well.) If the disk space falls below 100000000 bytes, however, you'll get an echo message every 5 seconds.

---

**Quick Check**

**Q.** **What is the primary function of a *Do While...Loop*?**

**A.** It allows you to run a script as long as a certain condition is in effect.

**Q.** **What is one reason for turning off *On Error Resume Next* during development and testing?**

**A.** During development and testing, you want to be presented with error messages to facilitate testing and debug operations.

---

**Note**   This script is one you would want to run in CScript. To do so, open up a CMD prompt, and type **cscript** and the filename. The complete command line would look something like this: *cscript c:\scripts\doWhile.vbs*. CScript is nice because when you want to break out of the program, all you do is press Ctrl+C. If the script is run under WScript (which is the default), to end the program, you have to open up Task Manager and kill the wscript.exe process.

---

# Do Until...Loop

As you know by now, *Do Loop* allows the script to continue to perform certain actions until a specific condition occurs. *Do While...Loop* allows your script to continue to perform these actions as long as the specified condition remains true. Once the specified condition is no longer true, *Do While...Loop* exits. In contrast, the *Do Until...Loop* has the opposite effect—the script continues to perform the action *until* a certain condition is met.

"So what?" you might ask. In and of itself, *Do Until* is not all that exciting, but you can use it to perform certain tasks. Here are common uses of *Do Until*:

■ Read text from a file

■ Read through records in a record set

■ Create a looping condition for monitoring purposes

Each of these implementations will be used in coming chapters. For now, let's look at a typical use of *Do Until*, which is illustrated in the following script:

```
Option Explicit
On Error Resume Next
Dim error1String
Dim objFSO
Dim objFile
Dim strLine
Dim SearchResult

error1String = "error"
Set objFSO = CreateObject("Scripting.FileSystemObject")
Set objFile = objFSO.OpenTextFile("C:\windows\setuplog.txt", 1)
strLine = objFile.ReadLine

Do Until objFile.AtEndofStream
    strLine = objFile.ReadLine
    SearchResult = InStr(strLine, error1String)
    If SearchResult <> 0 Then
        WScript.Echo(strLine)
    End if
Loop
WScript.Echo("all done")
objFile.Close
```

In this script, you begin with the Header information section, which is where you declare your variables and turn on error handling. Here is the Reference information section:

```
Option Explicit
On Error Resume Next
Dim error1String
Dim objFSO
Dim objFile
Dim strLine
Dim SearchResult
```

As in other scripts, *Option Explicit* tells VBScript that you're going to tell VBScript about each variable before you use it. If an unnamed item comes up and it's not a command, an error is generated. This helps to save us from misspelled variable names and typos. *On Error Resume Next* tells VBScript to ignore all the errors it can and to go to the next line. You don't want this turned on when you're writing scripts, because scripts will fail and not let you know what's going on.

After the two standard lines of the script, it's time to declare some variables. Since you can give variables any name you want (except the names for built-in commands or names already used for constants), it makes sense to use names that are self-explanatory. In addition, as you have already noticed, in VBScript you seem to always be using the same types of connections and commands. For instance, by the end of the book, you will certainly know how to create the file system object, and I tend to use the variable name *objFSO* for this. The *obj* part tells me that the item is associated with an object, and the *FSO* portion is simply shorthand for *file system object*. This object could just as well be named *objFile-SystemObject*, but I use it a lot and that name requires way too much typing.

Anyway, since this section is not about the file system object but rather about using *Do Until*, let's plunge ahead. The next part of the script is the Reference information section. It's here that you tell VBScript that you're going to define things to make it easier to work with them. In the following code, you create several reference assignments:

```
error1String = "error"
Set objFSO = CreateObject("Scripting.FileSystemObject")
Set objFile = objFSO.OpenTextFile("C:\windows\setuplog.txt", 1)
strLine = objFile.ReadLine
```

The *error1String* is set equal to the word *error*. This is what you want to search for in the log file you're going to open. The word assigned to *error1String* can easily be changed to search the log file for other words such as "failure," "failed," "unable," or even "can not," all of which show up in log files from time to time. By using a variable for the text you are searching for, you are facilitating the ability to change the script to search for other words.

Once *error1String* is assigned to the word you're searching for, you use two *Set* commands to talk to the file system and open a text file. We'll be covering these commands in detail in Chapter 3. For now, it's sufficient to note that the text file you're opening to read is "C:\windows\setuplog.txt", which is the file that Windows Server 2003 creates during installation. The file is huge and loaded with needed troubleshooting information if setup were to ever fail. But the installation doesn't have to be a complete bust for the file to be useful. For instance, if you're having problems with Windows Product Activation (WPA), just change *error1String* and look for WPA. Error codes found in this section of the setuplog.txt are standard HTTP 1.1 messages (for example, 403 is access denied, 404 is file or directory not found, and 407 is initial proxy authentication required by the Web server). Armed with this information and the script, you can search setuplog.txt, parse the return information, and match it with standard HTTP 1.1 messages.

The last line in the Reference information section is *strLine = objFile.ReadLine*, which tells VBScript to read one line from the text file referenced by *objFile*. You use the variable *strLine* in the Worker information section of the script, which we talk about next. *StrLine* holds the line of text that comes out of the file via the *ReadLine* command. If you printed *strLine* by using the *WScript.Echo* command, the line of text would be echoed to the screen. You can also use the *strLine* variable to hold the line of text so that you can search it for our keyword "error." In fact, you do both of these actions in our script, as seen in the next section.

## Worker and Output Information

In the same way that the other scripts in this chapter combined the Worker and Output information sections, our current script also combines these sections. Let's look at *Do Until...Loop*. In the next script part, notice that *Do Until* is in effect until *objFile.AtEnd-ofStream*. Think of the *ReadLine* command as a pump—you're going to pump text into *Do Until...Loop Until* until you reach the end of the text stream. This means that you read a line of text, one line at a time, until you reach the end of the file. You can see this process in the first two lines.

```
Do Until objFile.AtEndofStream
    strLine = objFile.ReadLine
    SearchResult = InStr(strLine, error1String)
    If SearchResult <>0 Then
        WScript.Echo(strLine)
    End if
Loop
WScript.Echo("all done")
objFile.Close
```

Once the text pump is set up and you have a nice steady stream of letters coming across, you use the next command in the Worker and Output information section of the script. You now use the *SearchResult* variable that you declared earlier. You assign *SearchResult* to the result of using the *InStr* command (think of it as "in string"), which looks through a string of text and tries to find a match. The command is put together like this:

| Command | String 1 | String 2 |
|---------|----------|----------|
| *InStr* | String to be searched | String being searched for |

In this script, you look through each line of text that comes from the Setuplog.txt file to find the word "error," which you assigned to the variable named *error1String*. This part of the script looks like the following:

```
SearchResult = InStr(strLine, error1String)
```

Now the situation gets a little complicated, because the *InStr* command is rather peculiar in the way it hands back information, as detailed in Table 2-1:

**Table 2-1   Use of the *InStr* function**

| Condition | Result Returned |
|-----------|-----------------|
| String 1 is zero in length | *0* |
| String 1 is null | *Null* |
| String 2 is zero in length | *Start* |
| String 2 is null | *Null* |
| String 2 is not found | *0* |
| String 2 is found in string 1 | Position at which the match is found |

In Table 2-2, the only value we're interested in is the one that is not equal to zero. (Although a null value contains no valid data, it is not the same as zero or as the empty string "", often referred to as a *null string*. You'll learn more about that when we talk about data types.) To evaluate the results of the *InStr* function, use *If...Then* to make sure that what came back from *InStr* is not equal to zero—which tells us that *InStr* is indicating where in the line the word "error" was found. We really don't care where in the line the word occurs, only that the word is present. You use *WScript.Echo* to echo out the value of *strLine*. Note that you print out *strLine*, which is the variable that contains the line of text that you read from the log file. You don't echo out *SearchResult* because it contains only a number, as explained in Table 2-1.

After you print out the line containing the error message from the Setuplog.txt file, you end your *If* statement by using the *End If* command, and you *Loop* (which sends us right back to the *Do Until* command). You continue to *Loop Until* until you reach the end of the file, at which time, you echo out "all done" and close your file. The "all done" statement just lets you know (while you watch stuff scroll on the screen) that you've completed running the script (otherwise, there is no indication that the script completed).

---

**Quick Check**

**Q.** **What is the difference between *Do Until* and *Do While*?**

**A.** *Do Until* does not run once a condition becomes true, whereas *Do While* runs as long as a condition is true.

**Q.** **What is the *InStr* command used for?**

**A.** *InStr* is used to look through a string of text to find a specific sequence of characters.

---

# Summary

In this chapter, you saw the power that you can bring to scripts by using looping types of constructs. Tools such as *For...Next*, which perform specified operations a certain number of times, allow you to easily perform repetitive actions. As you saw in several script examples, *For...Next* and *For Each...Next* are often used in tandem to walk through collections of information and to perform actions together and in tandem. You are not, however, limited to just manual counting through collections. You can also devise looping conditions that will monitor until a condition either becomes true or ceases to be true by using either *Do While* or *Do Until*. These two commands are often used to read through a record set or a text file. Along the way, we also talked about collections, constants, the *Sleep* command, and *InStr*. Stay tuned—the next chapter is even more exciting.

# Quiz Yourself

**Q.** **What is one reason for using *For Each...Next*?**

**A.** One reason for using the *For Each...Next* construction is to walk through a collection of items such as that often returned by WMI.

**Q.** **What is the advantage of defining either a constant or a variable?**

**A.** Constants allow you to define numbers that could be confusing if they were embedded within a script. In addition to making scripts easier to read and maintain, constants allow you to easily change values that could be utilized throughout a long script.

**Q.** **How do constants differ from variables?**

**A.** Constants do not change their values during script execution as variables can.

**Q.** **How can *For...Next* and *For Each...Next* be used together?**

**A.** You can put *For...Next* commands outside of a *For Each...Next* construction to allow you to perform the *For Each...Next* operation many times.

**Q.** **You want to create a looping condition that occurs only as long as a particular condition is true. What command will you use?**

**A.** A looping condition that occurs only when a condition is true is a *Do While* statement.

**Q.** **You want to create a looping condition that does not run when a certain condition is true. What command will you use?**

**A.** A looping condition that does not run when a certain condition is true is a *Do Until* statement.

**Q.** **How do you pause a script for a specified period of time?**

**A.** To pause a script for a certain period of time, you can use the *WScript.Sleep* command.

**Q.** **What unit does the *WScript.Sleep* command count in?**

**A.** The *WScript.Sleep* command counts in thousandths of a second.

# On Your Own

# Lab 3 Using the *For Each...Next* Command

In this lab, you'll explore using the *For Each...Next* command and the *For...Next* command.

## Lab Instructions

1. Open up the ping.vbs script in Microsoft Notepad.

2. Change the values *strMachines = "s1;s2"* to one or more computers reachable on your network.

3. Save the script with a different name, such as **lab3.vbs**.

4. Open a CMD prompt and switch to the directory where you saved the script.

5. Type **cscript lab3.vbs** and see whether the script runs. If it does not, do a regular ping to your networked machine and ensure it is reachable. If so, make sure you have the quotation marks and the semicolon, as shown in step 2.

6. Set *Option Explicit*.

7. *Dim* each variable that is used in the script.

8. Set *On Error Resume Next*.

9. Add comments to identify each section of the script.

10. Change the values *strMachines* = *"s1;s2"* to one or more computers reachable on your network.

11. Examine the construct of the *For Each...Next* statement.

12. In the Worker and Output sections of the script, put in a *For...Next* statement that makes the script send three pings.

13. Save the script and test.

14. If it runs properly, add the *On Error Resume Next* statement.

15. Save the script and see whether it runs. If it does, you're finished.

16. Extra: Play around with the script and see what optimizations you can add.

17. Extra, Extra: Add additional comments to the script that explain why certain items are required.

# Lab 4 Modifying the Ping Script

In this lab, you will modify the ping script so that it can be used to monitor your servers.

## Lab Instructions

1. Open lab3.vbs and save it as **lab4.vbs**. (You can also use pingsolution.vbs if you change *strMachines* = *"s1;s2"* to your local servers.)

2. Comment out *On Error Resume Next* so that you can test the script.

3. Define a constant called *ONE_HOUR* and set it equal to 100 for testing purposes. In the real world, 3600000 is equal to 1 hour for the *WScript.Sleep* command.

4. Declare a variable to be used to count to 8, such as *ihours*.

5. Add a *For ihours = 1 To 8* command to the beginning of the Worker section. It will go under *aMachines = Split(strMachines, ";")*.

6. Add the *WScript.Sleep(ONE_HOUR)* command to the bottom of the script (after all those *Next* commands). When you define a constant as you did in step 2, testing your script is a lot nicer.

7. Save the script. Try to run the script. (You should get an error.)

8. Add another *Next* command after the *WScript.Sleep* command.

9. Save the script and run it. (It should work now.)

10. Add a *WScript.Echo* command to the bottom of the script with a message letting you know when the script is finished.

# 3 Adding Intelligence

Much of the daily work of the intrepid network administrator involves making decisions. It's true that upgrades to network operating systems can't be automated, but many tasks, such as reading the event log and responding to critical events, can be scripted. In this chapter, you build on the skills you learned in Chapter 1, "Starting from Scratch," and Chapter 2, "Getting in the Loop," and combine them with three powerful tools: *If...Then*, *If...Then...ElseIf*, and *Select Case*.

## Before You Begin

**To successfully complete this chapter, you need to be familiar with the following concepts, which were presented in Chapters 1 and 2:**

- Declaring variables
- Basic error handling
- Connecting to the file system object
- Using *For Each...Next*
- Using *Do While*

**After completing this chapter you will be familiar with the following:**

- *If...Then*
- *If...Then...ElseIf*
- *If...Then...Else*
- *Select Case*
- Intrinsic constants

## *If...Then*

*If...Then* is one of those programming staples (like fried chicken and mashed potatoes are staples in the southern United States). What's nice about *If...Then* is that it makes sense. We use this kind of logic all the time.

The basic operation is diagrammed here:

| **If** | **condition** | **Then** | **action** |
|--------|---------------|----------|------------|
| If | store is open | Then | buy chicken |

The real power of *If...Then* comes into play when combined with tools such as those we looked at in Chapter 2. *If...Then* is rarely used by itself. Although you could have a script such as this one, you wouldn't find it extremely valuable:

```
Const a = 2
Const b = 3
Const c = 5
If a + b = c Then
    WScript.Echo(c)
End If
```

In this script are defined three constants: a, b, and c. We then sum the numbers and evaluate the result by using the *If...Then* statement. There are three important elements to pay attention to in implementing the *If...Then* construct:

- The *If* and the *Then must* be on the *same* line.

- The action to be taken must be on the *next* line.

- You must end your *If...Then* statement by using *End If*.

If any of these elements are missing or misplaced, your *If...Then* statement generates an error. If you do not see an error and one of these elements is missing, make sure you have commented out *On Error Resume Next*.

Now that you have the basic syntax down pat, let's look at the following more respectable and useful script, named GetComments.vbs, which is on the companion CD. *If* you put lots of descriptive comments in your VBScripts, *Then* GetComments.vbs pulls them out and writes them into a separate file. This file is used to create a book of documentation about the most essential scripts you utilize in your network. In addition, *If* you standardize your documentation procedures, *Then* the created book will require very little touch-up work when you are finished. (OK, I'll quit playing *If...Then* with you. Let's look at that code, which is described in the next few sections.)

```
Option Explicit
On Error Resume Next
Const ForReading = 1
Const ForWriting = 2
Dim scriptFile
Dim commentFile
Dim objScriptFile
Dim objFSO
Dim objCommentFile
Dim strCurrentLine
Dim intIsComment
scriptFile = "C:\scripts\displayComputerNames.vbs"
commentFile = "C:\scripts\comments.txt"
Set objFSO = CreateObject("Scripting.FileSystemObject")
```

```
Set objScriptFile = objFSO.OpenTextFile _
    (scriptFile, ForReading)
Set objCommentFile = objFSO.OpenTextFile(commentFile, _
    ForWriting, True)
Do While objScriptFile.AtEndOfStream <> True
    strCurrentLine = objScriptFile.ReadLine
    intIsComment = InAtr(1,strCurrentLine,"'")
    If intIsComment > 0 Then
        objCommentFile.Write strCurrentLine & vbCrLf
    End If
Loop
WScript.Echo("script complete")
objScriptFile.Close
objCommentFile.Close
```

---

**Just the Steps**

▶ **To implement** *If…Then*

1. On a new line in the script, type **If** *some condition* **Then**.

2. On the next line, enter the command you want to invoke.

3. On the next line, type **End If**.

---

## Header Information

The first few lines of the GetComments.vbs script contain the header information. We use *Option Explicit* to force us to declare all the variables utilized in the script. This helps to ensure that you spell the variables correctly as well as understand the logic. *On Error Resume Next* is rudimentary error handling. It tells VBScript to go to the next line in the script when there is an error. There are times, however, when you do not want this behavior, such as when you copy a file to another location prior to performing a delete operation. It would be disastrous if the copy operation failed but the delete worked.

The third and fourth lines of the GetComments.vbs script define two constants, *For-Reading* and *ForWriting*, which make the script easier to read. (You learned about constants in Chapter 2.) You'll use them when you open the DisplayComputerNames.vbs file and the Comments.txt file. You could have just used the numbers 1 and 2 in your command and skipped the two constants; however, someone reading the script needs to know what the numbers are doing. Defining the constants will make future modifications easier.

After you define the two constants, you define the variables. Listing variables on individual lines makes commenting the lines in the script easier, and the commenting lets readers of the script know why the variables are being used. In reality, it doesn't matter where you define variables, because the compiler reads the entire script prior to executing it. This means you can spread constant and variable declarations all over the script any way you want—such an approach would be hard for humans to read, but it would make no difference to VBScript.

## Reference Information

In the Reference Information section of the script, you assign values to several of the variables previously declared. Listing *scriptFile* in this manner makes it easy to modify the script later so that you can either point it to another file or make the script read all the scripts in an entire folder. In addition, you could make the script use a command-line option that specifies the name of the script to parse for comments. However, by assigning a variable to the script filename, you make all those options possible without a whole lot of rewriting. This is also where you name the file used to write the comments into—the aptly named Comments.txt file.

You also use the *Set* command three times, as shown here:

```
Set objFSO = CreateObject("Scripting.FileSystemObject")
Set objScriptFile = objFSO.OpenTextFile _
    (scriptFile, ForReading)
Set objCommentFile = objFSO.OpenTextFile(commentFile, _
    ForWriting, True)
```

Regarding the first *Set* command, you've seen *objFSO* used several times already in Chapters 1 and 2. *ObjFSO* is a variable name, which we routinely assign to our connection to the file system, that allows us to read and write to files. You have to create the file system object (as it is technically called) to be able to open text files.

The second *Set* command uses our *objScriptFile* variable name to allow us to read the DisplayComputerNames.vbs file. Note that the *OpenTextFile* command requires only one piece of information: the name of the file. VBScript will assume you are opening the file for reading if you don't include the optional file mode information. We are going to specify two bits of information so that the script is easier to understand:

- The name of the file

- How you want to use the file—that is, read or write it

By using variables for these two parts of the *OpenTextFile* command, you make the script much more flexible and readable.

The third *Set* command follows the same pattern. You assign the *objCommentFile* variable to whatever comes back from *openTextFile* command. In this instance, however, you write to the file instead of read from it. You also used variables for the name of the comment file and for the option used to write to the file.

# Worker and Output Information

The Worker and Output information portion is the core engine of the script, where the actual work is being done. The GetComments.vbs script reads each line of the Display-ComputerNames file and checks for the presence of a single quotation mark "'". When the single quotation mark is present, the script writes the line that contains that character out to the comments.txt file.

A closer examination of the Worker and Output information section of the GetComments.vbs script reveals that it begins with a *Do While...Loop*, as shown here:

```
Do While objScriptFile.AtEndOfStream <> True
    strCurrentLine = objScriptFile.ReadLine
    intIsComment = InStr(1,strCurrentLine,"'")
    If intIsComment > 0 Then
        objCommentFile.Write strCurrentLine & vbCrLf
    End If
Loop
WScript.Echo("script complete")
objScriptFile.Close
objCommentFile.Close
```

You first heard about the *Do While* statement in Chapter 2. *ObjScriptFile* is assigned to the text that is contained in the variable named *objScriptFile*. As long as you aren't at the end of the text stream, you read the line of text and see whether it contains a single quotation mark. To check for the presence of the ' character, you use the *InStr* function, just as in the last chapter. The *InStr* function returns a zero or *null* when it does not find the character; when it does find the character, it returns the numbered location of the character.

If *InStr* finds the ' character within the line of text, the variable *intIsComment* holds a number that is larger than zero. Therefore, you use the *If…Then* construct, as shown in the following code, to write out the line to the comments.txt file:

```
If intIsComment > 0 Then
    objCommentFile.Write strCurrentLine & vbCrLf
End If
```

Notice that the condition to be evaluated is contained within *If…Then*. If the variable *intIsComment* is larger than zero, you take the action on the next line. Here you use the *Write* command to write out the current line of the DisplayComputerNames file.

## Intrinsic Constants

You use the *vbCrLf* command to perform what is called a *carriage return* and *line feed*. *vbCrLf* is an *intrinsic constant*, which means that it is a constant that is built into VBScript. Since intrinsic constants are built into VBScript, you don't need to define them as you do regular constants. You'll use other intrinsic constants as you continue to develop VBScripts in later chapters.

*vbCrLf* has its roots in the old-fashioned manual typewriter. Those things had a handle on the end that rolled the platen up one or two lines (the line feed), and then repositioned the type head (the carriage return). Like the typewriter handle, the *vbCrLf* command positions the text to the first position on the following line. It's a very useful command for formatting text in both dialog boxes and text files. The last line in our *If…Then* construct is the *End If* command. *End If* tells VBScript that we're finished using the *If…Then* command. If you don't include *End If*, VBScript complains with an error.

After using *End If*, you have the *Loop* command on a line by itself. The *Loop* command belongs to the *Do While* construct that began the Worker and Output Information section. *Loop* sends the script execution back to the *Do While* line. VBScript continues to *Loop* through, reading the text file and looking for ' marks, as long as it doesn't reach the end of the text stream. When VBScript reaches the end of the text stream from the DisplayComputerNames script, you display a message that says you're finished processing the script. This is important, because otherwise there would be no indication that the script has concluded running. You then close your two files and the script is done. In reality, you don't need to close the files because they will automatically close once the script exits memory, but closing the files is good practice and could help to avoid problems if the script hangs.

# If...Then...ElseIf

*If...Then...ElseIf* adds some flexibility to your ability to make decisions by using VBScript. *If...Then* allows you to evaluate *one* condition and take action based on that condition. By adding *ElseIf* to the mixture, you can make multiple decisions. You do this in the same way you did it using the *If...Then* command. You start out with an *If...Then* on the first line in the Worker information section, and when you are finished, you end the *If...Then* section with *End If*. If you need to make additional evaluations, add a line with *ElseIf* and the condition.

---

**Just the Steps**

▶ **To Use *If...Then...ElseIf***

1. On a new line in the script, type **If *some condition* Then**.
2. On the next line, enter the command you want to invoke.
3. On the next line, type *ElseIf* and the new condition to check, and end the line with *Then*.
4. On the next line, enter the command you want to invoke when the condition on the *ElseIf* line is true.
5. Repeat steps 3 and 4 as required.
6. On the next line, type **End If**.

---

You can have as many *ElseIf* lines as you need; however, if you use more than one or two, the script can get long and confusing. A better solution to avoid a long script is to convert to a *Select Case* type of structure, which is covered later in this chapter in the section "Select Case." To illustrate the *If...Then...ElseIf* construction, we'll use the CPUType.vbs script, which identifies the type of CPU installed on a machine. As you know, the type of CPU is normally x86, but I have found old Alpha machines, old Power PCs, and even IA64 machines running in data centers. An accurate inventory of CPU types can help forestall problems, because most computer rooms are remotely managed, with physical contact with the actual boxes being a rare occurrence. Here is the CPUType.vbs script:

```
Option Explicit
On Error Resume Next
Dim strComputer
Dim cpu
Dim wmiRoot
Dim objWMIService
Dim ObjProcessor
strComputer = "."
cpu = "win32_Processor='CPU0'"
wmiRoot = "winmgmts:\\" & strComputer & "\root\cimv2"
Set objWMIService = GetObject(wmiRoot)
Set objProcessor = objWMIService.Get(cpu)
If objProcessor.Architecture = 0 Then
```

```
    WScript.Echo "This is an x86 cpu."
ElseIf objProcessor.Architecture = 1 Then
    WScript.Echo "This is a MIPS cpu."
ElseIf objProcessor.Architecture = 2 Then
    WScript.Echo "This is an Alpha cpu."
ElseIf objProcessor.Architecture = 3 Then
    WScript.Echo "This is a PowerPC cpu."
ElseIf objProcessor.Architecture = 6 Then
    WScript.Echo "This is an ia64 cpu."
Else
    WScript.Echo "Can not determine cpu type."
End If
```

# Header Information

The Header information section contains the usual information (discussed in Chapter 1 and Chapter 2), as shown here:

```
Option Explicit
On Error Resume Next
Dim strComputer
Dim cpu
Dim wmiRoot
Dim objWMIService
Dim objProcessor
```

*Option Explicit* tells VBScript that you'll name all the variables used in the script by using the *Dim* commands, and *On Error Resume Next* turns on basic error handling. The *strComputer* variable holds the name of the computer from which we retrieve the CPU type. The *Cpu* variable tells VBScript from where in Windows Management Instrumentation (WMI) we read information. The *wmiRoot* variable allows you to perform a task you haven't performed before in previous scripts: split out the connection portion of WMI to make it easier to change and more readable. The variables *objWMIService* and *objProcessor* hold information that comes back from the Reference information section.

# Reference Information

The Reference information section is the place where you assign values to the variables you named earlier in the script. The CPUType.vbs script contains these assignments:

```
strComputer = "."
cpu = "win32_Processor='CPU0'"
wmiRoot = "winmgmts:\\" & strComputer & "\root\cimv2"
Set objWMIService = GetObject(wmiRoot)
Set objProcessor = objWMIService.Get(cpu)
```

*StrComputer* is equal to ".", which is a shorthand notation that means the local computer that the script is currently executing on. With the *cpu* variable, you define the place in WMI that contains information about processors, which is *win32_Processor*.

Since there can be more than one processor on a machine, you further limit your query to *CPU0*. It is necessary to use *CPU0* instead of *CPU1* because *win32_Processor* begins counting CPUs with 0, and although a computer always has a CPU0, it does not always have a CPU1. In this script, you're only trying to determine the type of CPU running on the machine, so it isn't necessary to identify all CPUs on the machine.

## Worker and Output Information

The first part of the script declared the variables to be used in the script, and the second part of the script assigned values to some of the variables. In the next section, you use those variables in an *If...Then...ElseIf* construction to make a decision about the type of CPU installed on the computer.

The Worker and Output information section of the CPUType.vbs script is listed here:

```
If objProcessor.Architecture = 0 Then
    WScript.Echo "This is an x86 cpu."
ElseIf objProcessor.Architecture = 1 Then
    WScript.Echo "This is a MIPS cpu."
ElseIf objProcessor.Architecture = 2 Then
    WScript.Echo "This is an Alpha cpu."
ElseIf objProcessor.Architecture = 3 Then
    WScript.Echo "This is a PowerPC cpu."
ElseIf objProcessor.Architecture = 6 Then
    WScript.Echo "This is an ia64 cpu."
Else
    WScript.Echo "Can not determine cpu type."
End If
```

To write a script like this, you need to know how *win32_Processor* hands back information so that you can determine what a 0, 1, 2, 3, or 6 means. By containing that information in an *If...Then...ElseIf* construct, you can translate the data into useful information.

The first two lines listed in the preceding script work just like a normal *If...Then* statement. The line begins with *If* and ends with *Then*. In the middle of the *If...Then* language is the statement you want to evaluate. So, if the *objProcessor* returns a zero when asked about the *Architecture*, you know the CPU is an x86, and you use *WScript.Echo* to print out that data.

If, on the other hand, *objProcessor* returns a *1*, you know that the CPU type is a MIPS. By adding into the *ElseIf* statements the results of your research into return codes for WMI CPU types, you allow the script to handle the work of finding out what kind of CPU your servers are running. After you've used all the *ElseIf* statements required to parse all the possible return codes, you add one more line to cover the potential of an unexplained code, and you use *Else* for that purpose.

---

**Quick Check**

**Q.** How many *ElseIf* lines can be used in a script?

**A.** As many *ElseIf* lines as are needed.

**Q.** If more than one or two *ElseIf* lines are necessary, is there another construct that would be easier to use?

**A.** Yes. Use a *Select Case* type of structure.

**Q.** What is the effect of using *strComputer = "."* in a script?

**A.** The code *strComputer* is shorthand that means the local computer the script is executing on. It is used with WMI.

---

# If...Then...Else

It is important to point out here that you can use *If...Then...Else* without the intervening *ElseIf* commands. In such a construction, you give the script the ability to make a choice between two options.

---

**Just the Steps**

▶ **To use *If...Then...Else***

1. On a new line in the script, type **If *some condition* Then**.

2. On the next line, enter the command you want to invoke.

3. On the next line, type **Else**.

4. On the next line, type the alternate command you want to execute when the condition is not true.

5. On the next line, type **End If**.

---

The use of *If...Then...Else* is illustrated in the following code:

```
Option Explicit
On Error Resume Next
Dim a,b,c,d
a = 1
b = 2
c = 3
d = 4
If a + b = d Then
    WScript.Echo (a & " + " & b & " is equal to " & d)
Else
    WScript.Echo (a & " + " & b & " is equal to " & c)
End If
```

In the preceding IfThenElse.vbs script, you declare your four variables on one line. You can do this for simple scripts such as this one. It can also be done for routine variables that are associated with one another, such as *objWMIService* and *objProcessor* from your earlier script. The advantage of putting multiple declarations on the same line is that it makes the script shorter. Although this does not really have an impact on performance, it can at times make the script easier to read. You'll need to make that call—does making the script shorter make the script easier to read, or does having each variable on a separate line with individual comments make the script easier to read?

When you do the *WScript.Echo* command, you're using a feature called *concatenation*, which puts together an output line by using a combination of variables and string text. Notice that everything is placed inside the parentheses and that the variables do not go inside quotation marks. To concatenate the text into one line, you can use the ampersand character (&). Since concatenation does not automatically include spaces, you have to put in the appropriate spaces inside the quotation marks. By doing this, you can include a lot of information in the output. This is one area that requires special attention when you're modifying existing scripts. You might need to change only one or two variables in the script, but modifying the accompanying text strings often requires the most work.

## Select Case

When I see a *Select Case* statement in a VBScript, my respect for the script writer goes up at least one notch. Most beginning script writers can figure out the *If...Then* statement, and some even get the *If...Then...Else* construction down. However, few master the *Select Case* construction. This is really a shame, because *Select Case* is both elegant and powerful. Luckily for you, I love *Select Case* and you will be masters of this construction by the end of this chapter!

---

**Just the Steps**

▶ **To use *Select Case***

1. On a new line in the script, type **Select Case** and a variable to evaluate.
2. On the next line, type **Case 0**.
3. On the next line, assign a value to a variable.
4. One the next line, type **Case 1**.
5. On the next line, assign a value to a variable.
6. On the next line, type **End Select**.

---

In the following script, you again use WMI to obtain information about your computer. This script is used to tell us the role that the computer plays on a network (that is, whether it's a domain controller, a member server, or a member workstation). You need to use *Select Case* to parse the results that come back from WMI, because the answer is returned in the form of 0, 1, 2, 3, 4, or 5. Six options would be too messy for an *If...Then...ElseIf* construction. The text of computerRoles.vbs is listed here:

```
Option Explicit
On Error Resume Next
Dim strComputer
Dim wmiRoot
Dim wmiQuery
Dim objWMIService
Dim colComputers
Dim objComputer
Dim strComputerRole
strComputer = "."
wmiRoot = "winmgmts:\\" & strComputer & "\root\cimv2"
wmiQuery = "Select DomainRole from Win32_ComputerSystem"
Set objWMIService = GetObject(wmiRoot)
Set colComputers = objWMIService.ExecQuery _
    (wmiQuery)
For Each objComputer In colComputers
    Select Case objComputer.DomainRole
        Case 0
            strComputerRole = "Standalone Workstation"
        Case 1
            strComputerRole = "Member Workstation"
        Case 2
            strComputerRole = "Standalone Server"
        Case 3
            strComputerRole = "Member Server"
        Case 4
            strComputerRole = "Backup Domain Controller"
        Case 5
            strComputerRole = "Primary Domain Controller"
    End Select
    WScript.Echo strComputerRole
Next
```

## Header Information

The Header information section of computerRoles.vbs is listed in the next bit of code. Notice that you start with the *Option Explicit* and *On Error Resume Next* statements, which are explained earlier in this chapter and in detail in Chapter 1. Next, you declare seven variables that are recycled from the CPUType.vbs script discussed in the previous section. The variables *strComputer*, *wmiRoot*, and *objWMIService* are exactly the same as those used in CPUType.vbs.

*WmiQuery* is, however, a different variable. You'll use it in the Reference information section in which you assign a WMI query string to it. By declaring a variable and listing it separately, you can change the WMI query without having to rewrite the entire script.

*ObjWMIService* is used to hold your connection to WMI, and the name of *colComputers* is actually a little misleading. *ColComputers* sounds like it would hold a collection of computer names or objects, but in reality it holds the domain roles that come back. It too is a recycled variable name, but as long as you know what it does, you'll be fine. *StrComputerRole* holds the friendly description of the actual computer role and is used by *WScript.Echo* to print out the results of your script. *ObjComputer* is used simply to count through the results and is also a recycled variable name.

```
Option Explicit
On Error Resume Next
Dim strComputer
Dim wmiRoot
Dim wmiQuery
Dim objWMIService
Dim colComputers
Dim objComputer
Dim strComputerRole
```

## Reference Information

The Reference information section assigns values to many of the variables named in the Header information part of ComputerRoles.vbs. ComputerRoles.vbs is a very environmentally friendly script because so much of it is recycled! *StrComputer, wmiRoot,* and *objWMIService* are all recycled from earlier scripts. The Reference information section of the script is listed here:

```
strComputer = "."
wmiRoot = "winmgmts:\\" & strComputer & "\root\cimv2"
wmiQuery = "Select DomainRole from Win32_ComputerSystem"
Set objWMIService = GetObject(wmiRoot)
Set colComputers = objWMIService.ExecQuery _
    (wmiQuery)
```

There are two variables that are unique to this script, the first of which is *wmiQuery*. In the ListHardDrives script, you embedded the WMI query in the *GetObject* command, which makes for a long line. By bringing *Query* out of the *GetObject* command and assigning the query the *wmiQuery* variable, you make the script easier to read and modify in the future. Next, you use the *colComputers* variable and assign it to what happens when you actually execute the WMI query.

---

**Quick Check**

**Q. How is *Select Case* implemented?**

**A.** *Select Case* begins with the *Select Case* command and a variable to be evaluated. However, it is often preceded by a *For Each* statement.

**Q. How does *Select Case* make decisions?**

**A.** *Select Case* is used to parse the results that come back from a query.

**Q. What is the advantage of assigning a WMI query to a variable?**

**A.** It provides the ability to easily use the VBScript to query additional information from WMI.

---

## Worker and Output Information

As mentioned earlier, WMI often returns information in the form of a collection (we talked about this in Chapter 2), and to work your way through a collection, you need to use the *For Each…Next* command structure to pull out specific information. In the Worker information section of ComputerRoles.vbs, you begin with *For Each*. As seen in the next script, for each item that exists in the collection named *colComputers*, you're going to use *Select Case* to evaluate it. Examine the following *Select Case* statement and notice that the *Select Case* command begins with specifying where the information comes from—which in this case is the *DomainRole* portion of the variable *objComputer*. Here is the Worker information and the Output information part of the script:

```
For Each objComputer In colComputers
    Select Case objComputer.DomainRole
        Case 0
            strComputerRole = "Standalone Workstation"
        Case 1
            strComputerRole = "Member Workstation"
        Case 2
            strComputerRole = "Standalone Server"
        Case 3
            strComputerRole = "Member Server"
        Case 4
            strComputerRole = "Backup Domain Controller"
        Case 5
            strComputerRole = "Primary Domain Controller"
    End Select
    WScript.Echo strComputerRole
Next
```

To find out how the *DomainRole* field is structured, you need to reference the Platform SDK for Microsoft Windows Server 2003. Once you do that, you find the value descriptions shown in Table 3-1.

**Table 3-1    WMI Domain Roles from *Win32_ComputerSystem***

| Value | Meaning |
| --- | --- |
| 0 | Standalone Workstation |
| 1 | Member Workstation |
| 2 | Standalone Server |
| 3 | Member Server |
| 4 | Backup Domain Controller |
| 5 | Primary Domain Controller |

The first line of the *Select Case* command actually has *Select Case* in it and points to the part of the connection that has the information we need. Each successive statement is in the form shown here:

```
Case 0
    strComputerRole = "Standalone Workstation"
```

The case that is evaluated is the form that comes back from the *Select Case* part of the construct. The *strComputerRole = "Standalone Workstation"* code is our assignment to a new variable. You use *strComputerRole* to echo out the role of the computer in the domain after you use *End Select* for the *Select Case* construction.

You end the *Select Case* construction with *End Select*, similarly to the way you ended the *If...Then* statement with *End If*. After you use *End Select*, you use the *WScript.Echo* command to send the value of *strComputerRole* out to the user. Remember that the entire purpose of the *Select Case* construction in ComputerRoles.vbs is to find and assign the DomainRole value to the *strComputerRole* variable. After this is accomplished, you use the *Next* command to feed back into the *For Each* loop used to begin the script.

# Summary

In this chapter, you added decision making to your tool set by using two basic constructions: *If...Then* and *Select Case*. You also looked at two variations on the basic theme of *If...Then*: *If...Then...Else* and *If...Then...ElseIf*. The *If...Then...ElseIf* construction allows the evaluation of three or more situations but can get cumbersome and hard to read. For situations that require the evaluation of more than four parameters, it is almost always easier to use *Select Case*. Because we were looking at *If...Then* and *Select Case*, I also threw in the concept of intrinsic constants such as *vbCrLf*, which can be used to format output by starting a new line. You also looked at using variables to streamline WMI queries and connection strings.

# Quiz Yourself

**Q.** *If...Then* **requires the condition to be evaluated to be placed where?**

**A.** *If...Then* requires the condition to be evaluated to be contained within the words *If...Then*.

**Q.** **To evaluate two conditions, what construction would you use?**

**A.** To evaluate two conditions, you would use *If...Then...Else*.

**Q.** **How do you end an** *If...Then...Else* **construction?**

**A.** You end an *If...Then...Else* construction with the words *End If*.

**Q. What is an intrinsic constant?**

**A.** An intrinsic constant is a constant that is built into VBScript and therefore does not require assignment of a specific value prior to use.

**Q. To evaluate three conditions, what construction can be used?**

**A.** To evaluate three conditions, you can use either *If…Then…ElseIf* or *Select Case*.

**Q. If you have four or more conditions to evaluate, why is it better to use *Select Case* in most instances?**

**A.** If you have four or more conditions to evaluate, you should use *Select Case* because it is usually more compact and much easier to read and maintain.

# On Your Own

# Lab 5 Modifying CPUType.vbs

In this lab, you will modify CPUType.vbs so that it uses a *Select Case* format instead of multiple *If…Then…ElseIf* statements.

## Lab Instructions

1.  Open CPUType.vbs and save it as lab5.vbs.

2.  Turn off *On Error Resume Next* by commenting out the line.

3.  Turn the *If…Then* line into a *Select Case* statement. The only element you must keep out of this line is *objProcessor.Architecture* because it is hard to type. When you are finished, your Select Case line looks like the following:

    ```
    Select Case objProcessor.Architecture
    ```

4.  Start your case evaluation. If *objProcessor.Architecture = 0*, you know that the processor is an x86. So your first case is *Case 0*. That is all you put on the next line. It looks like this:

    ```
    Case 0
    ```

5.  Leave the *WScript.Echo* line alone.

6.  *ElseIf objProcessor.Architecture = 1* becomes *Case 1*, which is an MIPS CPU. Delete the entire *ElseIf* line and enter **Case 1**.

7.  Leave the WScript.Echo line alone.

    *ElseIf objProcessor.Architecture = 2* becomes simply *Case 2*, as you can see here:

    ```
    Case 2
    ```

    Up to this point, your *Select Case* configuration looks like the following:

```
Select Case objProcessor.Architecture
Case 0
    WScript.Echo "This is an x86 cpu."
Case 1
    WScript.Echo "This is a MIPS cpu."
Case 2
    WScript.Echo "This is an Alpha cpu."
```

8. Modify the "*ElseIf objProcessor.Architecture = 3 Then*" line so that it becomes *Case 3*.

9. Leave the WScript.Echo line alone.

   The next case *is not* case 4 but rather case 6, because you modify the following line: "*ElseIf objProcessor.Architecture = 6 Then*". The *Select Case* construction now looks like the following:

```
Select Case objProcessor.Architecture
    Case 0
        WScript.Echo "This is an x86 cpu."
    Case 1
        WScript.Echo "This is a MIPS cpu."
    Case 2
        WScript.Echo "This is an Alpha cpu."
    Case 3
        WScript.Echo "This is a PowerPC cpu."
    Case 6
        WScript.Echo "This is an ia64 cpu."
```

10. You have one more *Case* to evaluate, and it will take the place of the *Else* command, which encompasses everything else that has not yet been listed. You implement *Case Else* by changing the *Else* to *Case Else*.

11. Leave the line *WScript.Echo "Can not determine cpu type"* alone.

12. Change *End If* to *End Select*. Now you're finished with the conversion of *If…Then…ElseIf* to *Select Case*.

13. Save the file and run the script.

# Lab 6 Modifying ComputerRoles.vbs

In this lab, you'll modify ComputerRoles.vbs so that you can use it to turn on DHCP on various workstations.

## Scenario

Your company's network was set up by someone who really did not understand DHCP. In fact, the people who set up the network probably could not even spell DHCP, and as a result every workstation on the network is configured with a static IP address. This was bad enough when the network only had 100 workstations, but now the network has grown to over 300 workstations in the last couple of years. The Microsoft Excel spreadsheet that used to keep track of the mappings between computer names and IP addresses is woefully out of date, which in the past month alone has resulted in nearly 30 calls to the help desk that were traced back to addressing conflicts. To make matters worse, some of the helpful administrative assistants have learned to change the last octet in TCP/IP properties, which basically negates any hope of ever regaining a managed network. Your task, if you should choose to accept it, is to create a script (or scripts) that will do the following:

- Use WMI to determine the computer's role on the network and to print out the name of the computer, the domain name (if it is a member of a domain), and the user that belongs to the computer.

- Use WMI to enable DHCP on all network adapters installed on the computer that use TCP/IP.

Your research has revealed that you can use *Win32_ComputerSystem* WMI class to obtain the information required in the first part of the assignment.

### Part A

1. Open up the ComputerRoles.vbs file and save it as **lab6a.vbs**.

2. Comment out *On Error Resume Next* so that you will receive some meaningful feedback from the WSH run time.

3. *Dim* new variables to hold the following items:

   ❑ *strcomputerName*

   ❑ *strDomainName*

   ❑ *strUserName*

4. Modify *wmiQuery* so that it returns more than just the *DomainRole* from *Win32_ComputerSystem*. Hint: change *DomainRole* to a wildcard such as *.

   ```
   wmiQuery = "Select DomainRole from Win32_ComputerSystem"
   ```

   The new line looks like this:

   ```
   "Select * from Win32_ComputerSystem"
   ```

5. Because *colComputers* is a collection, you can't directly query it. You'll need to use *For Each Next* to give yourself a single instance to work with. Therefore, the assignment of your new variables to actual items will take place inside the *For Each Next* loop. Assign each of your new variables in the following manner:

   ❑ *strComputerName = objComputer.name*

   ❑ *strDomainName = objComputer.Domain*

   ❑ *strUserName = objComputer.UserName*

6. After the completion of the *Select Case* statement (*End Select*) but before the *Next* command at the bottom of the file, use *WScript.Echo* to return the four items required by the first part of the lab scenario. Use concatenation (by using the ampersand) to put the four variables on a single line. Those four items are declared as follows:

- ❏ *Dim strComputerRole*
- ❏ *Dim strcomputerName*
- ❏ *Dim strDomainName*
- ❏ *Dim strUserName*

7. Save the file, and run it.

8. Modify the script so that each variable is returned on a separate line. Hint: use the intrinsic constant *vbCrLf* and the ampersand to concatenate the line. It will look something like this:

```
strComputerRole & vbCrLf & strComputerName
```

9. Save and run the file.

10. Use *WScript.Echo* to add and run a complete message similar to the following:

```
WScript.Echo("all done")
```

11. Save and run the file.

## Part B

1. Open up the ComputerRoles.vbs file and save it as **lab6b.vbs**.

2. Comment out "*On Error Resume Next*" so that you will receive some meaningful feedback from the WSH run time.

3. *Dim* new variables to hold the new items required for this script. Hint: You can rename the following items:

- ❏ *Dim colComputers*
- ❏ *Dim objComputer*
- ❏ *Dim strComputerRole*

4. The new variables are listed here:

- ❏ *colNetAdapters*
- ❏ *objNetAdapter*
- ❏ *DHCPEnabled*

5. Modify the *wmiQuery* so that it looks like the following:

```
wmiQuery = "Select * from Win32_NetworkAdapterConfiguration where IPEnabled=TRUE"
```

6. Change the following *Set* statement:

```
Set colComputers = objWMIService.ExecQuery (wmiQuery)
```

Now, instead of using *colComputers*, the statement uses *colNetAdapters*. The line will look like the following:

```
Set colNetAdapters = objWMIService.ExecQuery (wmiQuery)
```

7. Delete the *Select Case* construction. It begins with the following line:

```
Select Case objComputer.DomainRole
```

And it ends with *End Select*.

8. You should now have the following:

```
For Each objComputer In colComputers
    WScript.Echo strComputerRole
Next
```

9. Change the *For Each* line so that it reads as follows:

```
For Each objNetAdapter In colNetAdapters
```

10. Assign *DHCPEnabled* to *objNetAdapter.EnableDHCP( )*. You can do it with the following:

```
DHCPEnabled = objNetAdapter.EnableDHCP()
```

11. Use *If...Then...Else* to decide whether the operation was successful. If DHCP is enabled, *DHCPEnabled* will be *0*, and you want to use *WScript.Echo* to echo out that the DHCP is enabled. The code looks like the following:

```
If DHCPEnabled = 0 Then
    WScript.Echo "DHCP has been enabled."
```

12. If *DHCPEnabled* is not set to 0, the procedure does not work. So you have your *Else* condition. It looks like the following:

```
Else
    WScript.Echo "DHCP could not be enabled."
End If
```

13. Conclude the script by using the *Next* command to complete the *If...Then...Next* construction. You don't have to put in a closing echo command, because you're getting feedback from the *DHCPEnabled* commands.

14. Save and run the script.

# 4 The Power of Many

In this chapter, you'll look at two very important concepts: passing arguments and working with arrays.

## Before You Begin

**To complete this chapter, you'll need to be familiar with the following concepts:**

- The *For Each* command
- The *Do Until* command
- The *For...Next* command

**After completing this chapter you will be familiar with the following:**

- Use command-line arguments
- Use a text file in place of arguments
- Create a useful error message when arguments are missing
- Use named arguments
- Create an array

## Passing Arguments

Passing arguments might sound like a technique to help people get along, but in reality it's a way to get additional information into a script. *Command-line arguments* are words or phrases that follow the name of the script when it is run from the command line. In this section, you'll look at two methods for obtaining runtime information: command-line arguments and text file data. You can use these two sources of information to modify the way a script runs. Let's first look at command-line arguments and see how to change the behavior of a script.

## Command-Line Arguments

Command-line arguments provide you with the ability to modify the execution of a script prior to running it.

**Just the Steps**

▶ **To implement command-line arguments**

1. On a new line, assign a variable to *WScript.Arguments.Item(0)*.

2. Use the variable assigned to *WScript.Arguments.Item(0)* as a normal variable.

In the Ping.vbs script, which you examined in Chapter 2, "Getting in the Loop," and which appears in the next code listing, you use the variable *strMachines* to hold the target of the ping command. To ping other computers on the network, you have to modify the values within the quotation marks (*s1* and *s2* in this instance). Modifying the values might be an acceptable solution when you always ping the same computers, but when you want the flexibility of the normal command-line ping, a better script is clearly called for—enter the command-line argument.

```
strMachines = "s1;s2"
aMachines = Split(strMachines, ";")
For Each machine In aMachines
    Set objPing = GetObject("winmgmts:")._
    ExecQuery("select * from Win32_PingStatus where address = '" _
        & machine & "'")
    For Each objStatus In objPing
        If IsNull(objStatus.StatusCode) Or objStatus.StatusCode<>0 Then
            WScript.Echo("machine " & machine & " is not reachable")
        Else
            WScript.Echo("reply from " & machine)
        End If
    Next
Next
```

## Making the Change

To modify the ping.vbs script to accept multiple computer names prior to running, you need to make two modifications:

- In the first line, delete "*s1;s2*".

- After *strMachines =*, add *WScript.Arguments.Item(0)*.

That's all you need to do. The new script, named PingMultipleComputers.vbs, is shown here:

```
strMachines = WScript.Arguments.Item(0)
aMachines = Split(strMachines, ";")
For Each machine In aMachines
    Set objPing = GetObject("winmgmts:")._
```

```
ExecQuery("select * from Win32_PingStatus where address = '"_
    & machine & "'")
For Each objStatus In objPing
    If IsNull(objStatus.StatusCode) Or objStatus.StatusCode<>0 Then
        WScript.Echo("machine " & machine & " is not reachable")
    Else
        WScript.Echo("reply from " & machine)
    End If
Next
Next
```

## Running from the Command Prompt

To run the script, you go to the command prompt and type the following:

```
Cscript pingMultipleComputers.vbs s1;s2;s3
```

You use this syntax because of the Split command you used on the second line, which expects a *";"* to separate the computer names. If you change the *";"* on the second line into a *","* as seen in the next code line, you can use the comma character to separate the machine names and have a slightly more orthodox command.

```
aMachines = Split(strMachines, ",")
```

Once this modification is made, the command-line syntax looks like the following:

```
Cscript pingMultipleComputers.vbs s1,s2,s3
```

---

**Quick Check**

**Q.** **To implement command-line arguments, what action needs to be performed?**

**A.** Assign a variable to the command *WScript.Arguments.Item(0)*.

**Q.** **What is the function of the *Split* command?**

**A.** The *Split* command can be used to parse a line of text based on a delimiter of your choosing.

---

## No Arguments?

If a script tries to read unnamed arguments not provided by the user, you get a Microsoft Visual Basic Script runtime error that makes a rather vague reference to "subscript out of range." This error is illustrated in Figure 4-1.

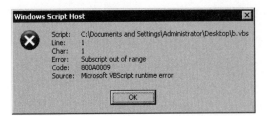

**Figure 4-1**    When a VBScript tries to read an unnamed argument that was not supplied, you get a "subscript out of range" error message

If another administrator is running your script and gets the "subscript out of range" error, that administrator will have a hard time determining the cause of the message. A quick search at *http://support.microsoft.com* returns, maybe, 25 support articles referencing "subscript out of range," but none of them tell you that the VBScript requires command-line arguments. It behooves you to make sure users of your VBScripts are not presented with such unfriendly error messages. Let's look at handling that now.

## Creating a Useful Error Message

When you supply command-line arguments for your scripts, the VBScript run time (called the Windows Scripting Host, or WSH for short) stores the arguments in an area of memory that is referenced by the *WshArguments* collection. This is cool because this storage location allows you to see how many command-line arguments are in there. Why is this important? It's important because when you know where the arguments are stored, and you know that they're kept in a collection, you can count the contents of that collection. For your script to run properly, there must be at least one argument supplied on the command line. You can make sure there is at least one argument by using the *WScript.Arguments.Count* method and putting it in an *If...Then...Else* construction. If the value is equal to zero, use *WScript.Echo* to send a message to the user that at least one argument is required. Once you make these modifications, ping-MultipleComputers.vbs looks like the following:

```
If WScript.Arguments.Count = 0 Then
    WScript.Echo("You must enter a computer To ping")
Else
    strMachines = WScript.Arguments.Item(0)
    aMachines = Split(strMachines, ",")
    For Each machine In aMachines
        Set objPing = GetObject("winmgmts:")._
        ExecQuery("select * from Win32_PingStatus where address = '"_
            & machine & "'")
        For Each objStatus In objPing
            If IsNull(objStatus.StatusCode) Or objStatus.StatusCode<>0 Then
                WScript.Echo("machine " & machine & " is not reachable")
            Else
                WScript.Echo("reply from " & machine)
```

```
            End If
        Next
    Next
End If
```

**Quick Check**

**Q.** What is a possible cause of the "subscript out of range" error message in the preceding script?

**A.** The error message could be caused by trying to run a VBScript that requires command-line arguments without supplying them.

**Q.** List one method of creating useful error messages to trap the "subscript out of range" error.

**A.** You can use an *If...Then...Else* construct to test *WScript.Arguments.Count* for the presence of a command-line argument. If none is present, you can then use the *Else* part to display a meaningful error to the user. In addition, it is important to note, you cannot always rely on the user putting in meaningful data. To solve this problem, you must parse the input data to ensure it meets the criteria for correct input.

# Using Multiple Arguments

In pingMultipleComputers.vbs, you use only one argument, which you assigned to the variable *strMachines* by using this command:

```
strMachines = WScript.Arguments.Item(0)
```

When you look at the command, you see that it's made up of several parts:

| Variable | = | WScript.Arguments.Item | Item # |
|---|---|---|---|
| strMachines | = | WScript.Arguments.Item | (0) |

If you need to use multiple arguments or multiple items (whichever term you prefer), you simply add another line and increment the item number contained within the parentheses.

**Just the Steps**

▶ **To implement multiple command-line arguments**

1. On a new line, assign a variable to *WScript.Arguments.Item(0)*.
2. On a new line, assign a variable to *WScript.Arguments.Item(1)*.
3. Use the variable from step 1 as you would any variable.
4. Use the variable from step 2 as you would any variable.

Remember that the index values for the *WScript.Arguments* collection are *zero-based*, which means that the first item counted will be zero, as used in the PingMultipleComputers script. The following script (ArgComputerService.vbs) illustrates how you handle zero-based index values. In *argComputerService*, you use two arguments. The first one is a computer name, and the second argument is the name of a service. To run this script, type the following command:

```
Cscript argComputerService.vbs computer1 lanmanserver
```

By using this command, the status of the lanmanserver server service on computer1 is returned to you. Lanmanserver is the name of the server service when it is registered in the registry. This is the name you must use when running the following script, ArgComputerService.

```
Option Explicit
On Error Resume Next
Dim computerName
Dim serviceName
Dim wmiRoot
Dim wmiQuery
Dim objWMIService
Dim colServices
Dim oservice

computerName = WScript.Arguments(0)
serviceName = WScript.Arguments(1)
wmiRoot = "winmgmts:\\" & computerName & "\root\cimv2"
Set objWMIService = GetObject(wmiRoot)
wmiQuery = "Select * from Win32_Service" &_
    " where name = " & "'" & ServiceName & "'"
Set colServices = objWMIService.ExecQuery _
    (wmiQuery)
For Each oservice In colServices
    WScript.Echo (serviceName) & " Is: "&_
    oservice.Status & (" on: ") & computerName
Next
```

## Header Information

In the ArgComputerService script is the standard Header information. It begins with *Option Explicit*, which tells VBScript that you're going to specifically name all the variables you'll be using. If you fail to list a variable here, you get an error from VBScript. The variables used in argComputerService.vbs are listed in Table 4-1.

**Table 4-1   Variables used in ArgComputerService.vbs**

| Variable name | Use |
| --- | --- |
| *computerName* | Holds the first command-line argument |
| *serviceName* | Holds the second command-line argument |

**Table 4-1   Variables used in ArgComputerService.vbs**

| Variable name | Use |
|---|---|
| *wmiRoot* | Holds the namespace of WMI |
| *wmiQuery* | Holds the query issued to WMI |
| *objWMIService* | Holds the connection into WMI |
| *colServices* | Holds the result of the WMI query |
| *oservice* | Holds each service in *colServices* as you walk through the collection |

## Reference Information

In the Reference information section, you assign variable names to specific values to make the script work properly. By changing reference assignments, you can modify the script to perform other actions. The variable *computerName* is used to hold the first command-line argument. If the first item entered on the command line is not the name of a valid computer on the network, the script fails. In this particular script, you haven't taken steps to ensure the script will end normally. The variable *serviceName* is used to hold the value of the second item from the command line. In the same way that *computerName* must be the name of a valid computer on the network, *serviceName* must be the name of a valid installed service on the target computer. The service name is not the same as the display name that is used in the services application, rather it is the name assigned within the registry when the service is created. The script could be modified to provide a list of installed services on the target machine and then allow the user to pick one of those services.

## Worker and Output Information

Once again, the Worker and Output information sections of the script are quite simple:

```
For Each oservice In colServices
    WScript.Echo (serviceName) & " Is: " & _
    oservice.Status & (" on: ") & computerName
Next
```

Because WMI returns service information in a collection (even when the collection has only a single value), you must use a *For Each Next* loop to walk through each item in the collection to obtain your information. A *For Each Next* loop is the engine that drives your script. The variable *colServices* contains every service that was returned by the *wmiQuery*. The variable *oservice* holds each individual service and is used as the "hook" for asking for certain information via WMI. In this instance, you're interested only in the status information, and so you echo out the *oservice.status* information. If you modified the *wmiQuery* variable, you'd be able to echo any of the information that is held within the *Win32_Service* part of WMI.

> **See Also** To find out more information about Win32_Service, search in the WMI platform SDK.

The only other interesting aspect of the Worker and Output information sections of the script is the use of concatenation, which was talked about in Chapter 3, "Adding Intelligence." Notice how the ampersand character (&) is used to glue two parts of the output line together. The other use of the ampersand is in conjunction with the underscore character (_). The underscore character signals to VBScript that the line is continued onto the next line. The ampersand character is often used with the line continuation character because the underscore breaks up the long line, and the ampersand is used to glue pieces together. Because a line might be in parts anyway, the line continuation character is a convenient place for breaking the script. The continuation character is primarily used to make a script more readable (both on screen and on paper).

Earlier in this section, you learned that ArgComputerService requires two command-line arguments: the first must be the name of a target computer, and the second must be the name of a valid service on the target computer. How would the user of the Arg-ComputerService script know about this requirement? If the script failed, the user could open the script in Microsoft Notepad to see which argument is required. A second solution might be to modify the script so that when it failed, it would echo the correct usage to the user. There is, however, a third choice—the use of named arguments—which is the subject of the next section.

# Tell Me Your Name

One of the rules I learned as a network administrator and as a consultant was to keep things simple. I'd therefore use short computer names and basic network designs as much as possible, because at some point, I'd be using ping.exe, tracert.exe, nslookup.exe, and so forth from the command line. As you know, I hate to type, so "the shorter the better" is my motto. This being the case, I am in somewhat of a quandary with this next section, because it will make the command-line implementation longer.

## Reasons for Named Arguments

Despite additional typing, there are valid reasons to use named arguments. One of the biggest reasons is the way VBScript handles unnamed arguments. For instance, in the ArgComputerService script, you must use command-line syntax such as this:

```
Cscript argComputerService.vbs computer1 lanmanserver
```

Suppose you happen to forget in which order the commands get entered, and you type the following:

```
Cscript argComputerService.vbs lanmanserver computer1
```

The script would fail unless you happen to have a server named lanmanserver on your network *and* unless a service named computer1 is running on lanmanserver. Don't laugh! I've seen stranger happenings. (For example, static DNS entries can point to the wrong machine. A ping would in fact work—it would just go to the wrong computer. Those are always fun.) Therefore, in keeping with my philosophy of trying to make things simple, let's explore how to create named arguments. You'll thank me, your boss will thank me, and even your mom will thank me (because stuff will run so well, and you'll be able to make it home for the holidays).

Named arguments can be used to make the order of command-line arguments irrelevant. This can make correct usage of running the script easier, especially when three or more distinct arguments are being used with a script that does not intuitively suggest a particular order.

---

**Just the Steps**

▶ **Implementing Named Arguments**

1. On a new line, use the *Set* command to assign a variable to *WScript.Arguments.Named*.
2. On the next line, assign a variable to the one defined in step 1 and define the name to be used for the first argument.
3. On the next line, assign a variable to the one defined in step 1 and define the name to be used for the second argument.
4. Use the variables defined in steps 2 and 3 as you would regular variables.

---

## Making the Change to Named Arguments

To modify the previous script to require named arguments instead of unnamed arguments, you need to modify only four lines of code. The first change is to add an additional variable that will be used to hold the named arguments from the command line. The second modification will take place in the references section, in which you will assign the new variable to the named arguments collection, and the last two changes will take place as you assign the variables to hold the server name and the service names in the script. The revised script follows:

```
Option Explicit
On Error Resume Next
Dim computerName
Dim ServiceName
Dim wmiRoot
```

```
Dim wmiQuery
Dim objWMIService
Dim colServices
Dim oservice
Dim colNamedArguments

Set colNamedArguments = WScript.Arguments.Named
computerName = colNamedArguments("computer")
serviceName = colNamedArguments("service")
wmiRoot = "winmgmts:\\" & computerName & "\root\cimv2"
Set objWMIService = GetObject(wmiRoot)
wmiQuery = "Select * from Win32_Service" &_
    " where name = " & "'" & ServiceName & "'"
Set colServices = objWMIService.ExecQuery _
    (wmiQuery)
For Each oservice In colServices
    WScript.Echo (servicename) & " Is: "&_
    oservice.status & (" on: ") & computerName
Next
```

The four lines that were changed in the preceding script are listed here:

```
Dim colNamedArguments
Set colNamedArguments = WScript.Arguments.Named
computerName = colNamedArguments("computer")
serviceName = colNamedArguments("service")
```

Because you added a variable for named arguments in the Reference section, you'll need to *Dim* that variable in the Header section. Declare *colNamedArguments* in the Header information section of the script. In the next line, you make *colNamed-Arguments* equal to the named arguments by using the *Set* command. You now give the names to the named arguments by using the same variables *computerName* and *serviceName*. This time, instead of simply referencing the *WScript.Arguments* element by index number, you are referencing the *WScript.Arguments* element using the *col-NamedArguments* variable. Instead of simply using a *0* or a *1*, you tell VBScript the name to expect from the command line.

## Running a Script with Named Arguments

To supply data to a script with named arguments, you type the name of the script at the command prompt and use a forward slash (/) with the name of the argument you are providing, separated by a colon and the value you assign to the argument. The preceding script is named NamedArgCS.vbs, and it takes two arguments: *computer* and *service*. The command to launch this script is run against a computer named S2 and queries the lanmanserver service on that machine:

```
cscript namedargcs.vbs /computer:s2 /service:lanmanserver
```

> **Quick Check**
>
> **Q.** What is one reason for using named arguments?
>
> **A.** With named arguments, when you have multiple command-line arguments, you don't need to remember in which order to type the arguments.
>
> **Q.** How do you run a script with named arguments?
>
> **A.** To run a script with named arguments, you use a forward slash and then enter the name of the argument. You follow this with a colon and the value you want to use.

# Working with Arrays

Since we have discussed collections, you might find it easy at this point to think of *arrays* as collections that you create and can control. There are several cool aspects of arrays; for example, you can populate them with information for later use in the script. In addition, you can create an array dynamically during the execution of the script. You'll explore each of these concepts in this section.

> **Just the Steps**
>
> ▶ **To create an array**
>
> **1.** On a new line, use the *Dim* command to declare the name to use for the array.
>
> **2.** Populate the array by assigning values to the name declared in the first line by using the array command and enclosing the values in parentheses.

One way to create an array is to use the *Dim* command to declare a regular, or normal, variable. You then use the variable to populate the array with computer names and use a *For Each...Next* loop to walk through the array. Remember, an array is basically a collection, and you therefore need to use a *For Each...Next* loop to walk through it. The following script creates an array with the names of three computers. The variable *i* is used as a counter to allow you to walk through the collection. Since an array is zero-based (that is, it begins counting at zero), you set *i* to an initial value of zero. Next, you populate the array with your computer names, making sure to enclose the names in quotation marks; and you use a comma to separate the values. The collection of computer names is placed inside the parentheses. You use a *For Each...Next* loop to walk through and echo the computer names to the screen. You then increment the counter *i* to the next number, and go back into the *For Each...Next* loop. This script, Basic-Array.vbs, follows:

```
Option Explicit
On Error Resume Next
```

```
Dim arComputer
Dim computer
Dim i
i = 0
arComputer = Array("s1", "s2", "s3")
For Each computer In arComputer
    WScript.Echo(arComputer(i))
    i = i+1
Next
```

# Moving Past Lame Arrays

I will admit the previous script was pretty lame. But because the construction of an array is very finicky, I wanted you to have a reference for the basic array (you will need it for your labs).

In the next script (ArrayReadTxtFile.vbs), you open up a text file, parse it line by line, and write the results into an array. You can use this line-parsing tactic later as a way to feed information into a more useful script. Right now, all you're doing with the array after it is built is echoing its contents out to the screen.

```
Option Explicit
On Error Resume Next
Dim objFSO
Dim objTextFile
Dim arrServiceList
Dim strNextLine
Dim i
Dim TxtFile
Const ForReading = 1
TxtFile = "c\scripts\ServersAndServices.txt"
Set objFSO = CreateObject("Scripting.FileSystemObject")
Set objTextFile = objFSO.OpenTextFile _
    (TxtFile, ForReading)
Do Until objTextFile.AtEndofStream
    strNextLine = objTextFile.Readline
    arrServiceList = Split(strNextLine , ",")
    WScript.Echo "Server name: " & arrServiceList(0)
    For i = 1 To UBound(arrServiceList)
        WScript.Echo "Service: " & arrServiceList(i)
    Next
Loop
WScript.Echo("all done")admit
```

## Header Information

The Header information section of your script incorporates the standard bill of fare. You use *Option Explicit* to ensure all variables are specifically declared, which prevents the misspelling of variable names during the development phase of the script. *On Error*

*Resume Next* is a rudimentary error suppression that tells VBScript to skip a line containing an error and proceed to the next line in the script. This is best turned off during development. After using *On Error Resume Next*, you declare six variables and a constant. The first variable, *objFSO*, is used to hook the file system object (which allows you to access files and folders from the script). The next variable, *objTextFile*, is used as the connection to the text file itself. The variable *arrServiceList* is used to refer to the array of services and servers that you build from the text file. The variable *strNextLine* holds the text of the next line in the text file. The *i* variable is simply a counter that gets incremented on each loop through the text file. The last variable is *TxtFile*. It holds the location inside the file system that points to the specific text file with which you will work. The constant *ForReading* is set to *1*, which tells VBScript that you are going to read a text file (as opposed to write to the file).

```
Option Explicit
On Error Resume Next
Dim objFSO
Dim objTextFile
Dim arrServiceList
Dim strNextLine
Dim i
Dim TxtFile
Const ForReading = 1
```

## Reference Information

The Reference information section of the script is used to point certain variables to their required values. The text file used as input into the array is defined with the variable *TxtFile*. By using a variable for input into ArrayReadTxtFile.vbs, you make changing the location of the file easy. The ServersAndServices text file needs only to be defined in this location, and the variable *TxtFile* is left untouched—wherever it might be used within the script. You must first connect to *FileSystemObject* to be able to read the text file. You do this by using the variable *objFSO*. You set *objFSO* equal to what happens when you create the object *Scripting.FileSystemObject*. Once you know how to talk to the File System Object, you define the variable *objTextFile* to be the result of opening the *TxtFile* so that you can read it.

```
TxtFile = "c\scripts\ServersAndServices.txt"
Set objFSO = CreateObject("Scripting.FileSystemObject")
Set objTextFile = objFSO.OpenTextFile _
    (TxtFile, ForReading)
```

## Worker and Output Information

In the Worker and Output information section of ArrayReadTxtFile.vbs, you're finally going to settle down and do something worthwhile. To work with the array, you need to implement some type of looping construction. This is where *Do Until...Next* excels.

You defined *objTextFile* to be equal to opening the ServersAndServices text file so that you could read the file. Since you can look inside and read the file by using *objTextFile*, you now say that you'll continue to read the file *until* you reach the end of the stream of text. This is a most excellent use of *Do Until...Next*. What is the script going to do until it reaches the end of the text file? It's going to read each line and assign that line of text to the variable *strNextLine*. After it's made that assignment, it will look for commas and then split the text up into pieces that are separated by those commas. Each piece of text will then be assigned to your array. You're still using a single dimension array. (A *single dimension array* is an array that has only one element.) Interestingly enough, you're actually creating a new array after you echo out the server names and the services present in the text file. The cool part is that you can include as many services as you need to use by adding a comma and the service *on the same line*. Once you go to another line in the text file, you have a new array.

The array portion of ArrayReadTxtFile.vbs is not really created until you get to the Worker and Output information section of the script. In the Header information section, when you declared the variable *arrServiceList*, you really didn't know whether it was a regular variable or something else. This is why it was given the prefix *arr*—it sort of looks like array (and requires less typing). You could have just as easily called it *arrayServiceList*, but doing so would have made your script longer. When you use the *WScript.Echo* command and the *(0)* and *(i)*, VBScript knows you want to create an array. The Worker and Output information sections of the script follow:

```
Do Until objTextFile.AtEndofStream
    strNextLine = objTextFile.Readline
    arrServiceList = Split(strNextLine , ",")
    WScript.Echo "Server name: " & arrServiceList(0)
    For i = 1 To UBound(arrServiceList)
        WScript.Echo "Service: " & arrServiceList(i)
    Next
Loop
```

## What Does *UBound* Mean?

Did you notice that I didn't explain the *For...Next* construction embedded in the *Do Until Loop*? The goal was to make ArrayReadTxtFile.vbs as flexible as possible, and therefore I didn't want to limit the number of services that could be input from the text file. To make sure you echo through all the services that could be listed in the Servers-AndServices.txt file, you need to use the *For...Next* loop to walk through the array. You can find out how many times you need to do *For...Next* by using *UBound*. Think of *UBound* as standing for the upper boundary of the array. As you might suspect, because there is an upper boundary, there is also a lower boundary in the array, but because the lower boundary is always zero, *LBound* isn't needed in this particular script.

When you run ArrayReadTxtFile.vbs, the *i* counter in *For i = 1 To UBound(arrService-List)* changes with each pass through the list of services. To track this progress, and to illustrate how *UBound* works, I've modified the ArrayReadTxtFile.vbs script to echo out the value of *UBound* each time you read a new line from the ServersAndServices text file. The modified script is called ArrayReadTxtFileUBound.vbs, and its Worker section follows:

```
Do Until objTextFile.AtEndofStream
    boundary = UBound(arrServiceList)
    WScript.Echo "upper boundary = " & boundary
    strNextLine = objTextFile.Readline
    arrServiceList = Split(strNextLine , ",")
    WScript.Echo "Server name: " & arrServiceList(0)
    For i = 1 To UBound(arrServiceList)
        WScript.Echo "Service: " & arrServiceList(i)
    Next
Loop
```

To track changes in the size of the upper boundary of the array by looking at the value of *UBound*, it was necessary to assign the value of our new variable "boundary" after the *Do Until* command but prior to entry into the *For...Next* construction. At this location in the script, the new line of text has been read from the ServersAndServices.txt file, and the script will continue to do this until it reaches the end of the file.

---

**Quick Check**

**Q.** How did we declare an array in the previous example?

**A.** We declared a regular variable—you use the *Dim* command.

**Q.** How can the population of an array be automated?

**A.** You can automate populating an array by using the *For...Next* command.

**Q.** If you do not know in advance how many elements are going to be in the array, how can you automate populating the array?

**A.** You can automate populating an array with an unknown number of elements by using the *For...Next* command in conjunction with *UBound*.

---

# Two-Dimensional Arrays

A *two-dimensional array* gives you the ability to store related information in much the same way you would store it in a Microsoft Excel spreadsheet. To visualize a two-dimensional array, it is helpful to think of a spreadsheet that contains both rows and columns.

---

**Just the Steps**

▶ **To create an array**

**1.** On a new line, use the *Dim* command to declare the name to use for the array, followed by parentheses and the number of elements to be used for each dimension, separated by a comma.

**2.** Populate the array by assigning values to the name declared in line 1 by using the array name and associating a value with each element.

---

To create a two-dimensional array, include both dimensions when you declare the variable used for the array, as illustrated here:

```
Dim a (3,3)
```

All you've really done is include the extra dimension inside the parentheses. The Array just listed contains two dimensions, each holding four elements for a total of 16 elements. Each dimension of the array is separated by a comma within the parentheses. Remember that the array begins numbering with a zero, and thus *Dim a (3,3)* states that the array *a* has four rows numbered from zero to 3, and four columns numbered from zero to 3.

The key points to remember about an array are that it resides in memory and can be used to hold information that will be used by the script. With a two-dimensional array, you have a matrix (not *The* Matrix—but a matrix nonetheless). *Dim a (3,3)* would look like the matrix in Table 4-2.

**Table 4-2  Two-dimensional array**

| 0,0 | 0,1 | 0,2 | 0,3 |
|-----|-----|-----|-----|
| 1,0 | 1,1 | 1,2 | 1,3 |
| 2,0 | 2,1 | 2,2 | 2,3 |
| 3,0 | 3,1 | 3,2 | 3,3 |

Each square in the array in Table 4-2 can hold a single piece of information. However, by using concatenation (putting strings together by using the ampersand) or by manipulating the string in other ways, you can get quite creative with the array.

## Mechanics of Two-Dimensional Arrays

In the next script (workWith2DArray.vbs), a two-dimensional array is created. The script then populates each of the 16 elements with the string *"Loop"* concatenated with the loop number. In this way, you can keep track of where you are within the matrix as you echo out the value contained within the elements.

```
Option Explicit
Dim i
Dim j
Dim numLoop
Dim a (3,3)
numLoop = 0
For i = 0 To 3
    For j = 0 To 3
        numLoop = numLoop+1
        WScript.Echo "i = " & i & " j = " & j
        a(i, j) = "loop " & numLoop
        WScript.Echo "Value stored In a(i,j) is: " & a(i,j)
    Next
Next
```

Let's look at the script in a little more detail.

## Header Information

The Header information section of the script follows the normal procedure of beginning with *Option Explicit* (which forces the declaration of each variable used in the script by using the *Dim* command). Next, two variables (*i* and *j*) are declared that will each be used to count from 0 to 3 within a *For...Next* construction. The variable *numLoop* is used to keep track of the 16 passes that are required to work through all 16 elements contained in the array. The last item in the Header information section of the WorkWith2DArray.vbs script specifically declares our two-dimensional array: *Dim a (3,3)*.

## Reference Information

The Reference information section of our script consists of one line: *numLoop = 0*. Because you use *numLoop* to keep track of how many loops are made through the array, it is important to set it to zero. Later, you'll reassign the value of *numLoop* to be equal to its current value in the loop plus 1. By incrementing the *numLoop* counter, you can easily know exactly where you are within the array.

## Worker and Output Information

The Worker and Output information section of the script (shown in the next code listing) begins immediately with a pair of nested *For...Next* constructions. The reason for nesting the *For...Next* in this section of the script is to have a separate value for both the variable *i* and the variable *j*.

### Using the *For...Next* Construction

Because the array was declared as *Dim a (3,3)* and you happen to know that the array is zero-based, you use *i = 0 to 3* in the *For...Next* loop, as shown in the first line of the following script. You next increment the *numLoop* counter and echo the current values contained in the variables *i* and *j*. Once you know your location in the array, you assign the word *"loop"* concatenated with the current value held in the *numLoop* counter to the particular array element that is currently described by *a(i,j)*. If, for instance, the script is in its first loop, the value of *i* is *0* and the value of *j* is *0*, and when you get down to the *WScript.Echo* commands, the value of *numLoop* has already been incremented. So, you would *echo "i = 0 j = 0"*. Look closely at the following script portion to make sure you understand what is happening in the first four lines:

```
For i = 0 To 3
    For j = 0 To 3
        numLoop = numLoop+1
        WScript.Echo "i = " & i & " j = " & j
        a(i, j) = "loop " & numLoop
        WScript.Echo "Value stored In a(i,j) is: " & a(i,j)
    Next
Next
```

### Assigning Values to Each Element

Once the loop counter (*numLoop*) is incremented, it's time to assign a value to each element within the array. Rather than typing a whole series of *a(0,0) = "loop" & numLoop* lines, you instead dynamically build the value of *a(i,j)* by using the two *For...Next* loops. Thus, prior to assigning the value *"loop"* and *numLoop* to the array element, the element is empty.

> **Tip**   To assign a value to an element within an array, you specify the element number, followed by the equal sign, and then specify the value. If, however, you use a *For...Next* loop, you can in many instances automate the process.

After you assign values to the array, you use one final *WScript.Echo* command to echo out the values that are contained within the array. This is where you'd do the actual work if this were a real script. You close out the script with a pair of *Next* commands: one for each *For* introduced earlier in the script.

# Summary

In this chapter, you examined two basic concepts: passing command-line arguments and working with arrays. These two vital tools are heavily utilized on a daily basis in enterprise scripts. To make a script more flexible, for example, avoiding having to edit a script just to enable it to run against various servers on the network, you use command-line arguments. Arrays are used to make scripts more powerful, efficient, and robust. By storing multiple values in memory, you avoid having to make multiple calls to either the file system or to another source of information. Indeed, all you need to do is store your configuration information within an array, and you're ready to go.

# Quiz Yourself

**Q. What are the two categories WScript uses for arguments?**

**A.** Two categories that WScript uses for arguments are named and unnamed.

**Q. What is one consideration when using multiple unnamed command-line arguments?**

**A.** When using multiple unnamed command-line arguments, the biggest consideration is getting the arguments mixed up. For instance, you could be trying to ping a server named S2 three times. But if you get the unnamed arguments mixed up, you might be trying to ping a server named 3 S2 times.

**Q. What is an advantage of named command-line arguments?**

**A.** Named command-line arguments have the advantage of being easier on both the scripter and the user. For instance, *a /server:s2* means you're aiming the command at a server named s2, and *a /numberTimes:3* means you want to perform the command three times. It does not matter in which order you put the named arguments.

**Q. Why would you want to bring input in from a text file?**

**A.** Using a text file makes it easy to run the script against any number of servers. In addition, because a text file does not require a command-line argument, script execution can be fully automated.

**Q. What is the advantage of an array?**

**A.** An array provides convenient storage inside memory to control operation of a script. It is like a collection that you have complete control over. It enables quick operation (because it is in memory) and efficient programming.

# On Your Own

# Lab 7 Working with Passing Arguments

In this lab, you'll work with passing arguments by modifying a script that uses WMI to list all the services associated with a particular process on the machine. This is in fact a very useful script. While we are at it, we will simplify the script a little to make it easier to read.

## Lab Instructions

1. Open the servicesProcess.vbs script and save it as **lab7.vbs**.

2. Add the *Option Explicit* command at the top of the script.

3. Declare each variable used in the script. This would include the following:

```
Dim objIdDictionary
Dim strComputer
Dim objWMIService
Dim colServices
Dim objService
Dim colProcessIDs
Dim i
```

4. Save the script, and run it to ensure you have all the variables defined. If you missed a variable, *Option Explicit* will cause the "variable is undefined" error and list the line number containing the undefined variable.

5. Add a declaration for *wmiRoot* by adding **Dim wmiRoot** under the line that says *Dim colProcessIDs*.

6. Under the line that says *strComputer = "."*, add the following:

```
wmiRoot = "winmgmts:\\" & strComputer & "\root\cimv2"
```

The preceding line shortens the following line:

```
Set objWMIService = GetObject("winmgmts:" _
    & "\\" & strComputer & "\root\cimv2")
```

7. Edit the *Set objWMIService = GetObject* line by deleting everything after the *GetObject* command. Inside the open parenthesis, type **wmiRoot** and add a close parenthesis. The line should now look like the following:

```
Set objWMIService = GetObject(wmiRoot)
```

What you have done is created shorthand for the long *winmgmts* string. In addition, you deleted some stuff you didn't need (which we'll discuss in detail when we talk about WMI in Chapter 5, "The Power of Many More"). The script is now much easier to read.

8. Run the script—it should work fine to this point. If it does not, compare it with lab7pt1.vbs and see where your code needs tweaking. Your script must run correctly at this point to complete the lab.

9. If everything is groovy, look at the following line:

```
Set colServices = objWMIService.ExecQuery _
    ("Select * from Win32_Service Where State <> 'Stopped'")
```

You'll make this line easier to read by placing the *"Select * from Win32_Service Where State <> 'Stopped'"* line into a variable, which we unceremoniously call *wmiQuery*. To do this, you must adjust the code in two ways. First, you must declare the variable *wmiQuery* by typing the following after the *wmiRoot* declaration:

```
Dim wmiQuery
```

Your second adjustment is much trickier and therefore much more critical. You must define *wmiQuery* to be equal to the *Select* statement listed in step 9. You handle this under the following line:

```
Set objWMIService = GetObject(wmiRoot)
```

To define *wmiQuery*, copy the *Select* statement from the *Set colServices* line, making sure to include the quotation marks with your copy. The *wmiQuery* line now looks like the following:

```
wmiQuery = "Select * from Win32_Service Where State <> 'Stopped'"
```

After you add the *wmiQuery* line above the *Set colServices* line, you delete the *Select* statement from the *Set colServices* line. In place of the *Select* statement, you use the variable *wmiQuery*. The modified line looks like this:

```
Set colServices = objWMIService.ExecQuery _
    (wmiQuery)
```

10. Save the file and run the script. It should still work properly. If it does not, compare it with the lab7pt2a.vbs file to see whether you can optimize your code.

11. Now you will perform the same kind of adjustments to the second half of the script. Look at the following code (which starts around line 44):

```
For i = 0 To objIdDictionary.Count - 1
    Set colServices = objWMIService.ExecQuery _
        ("Select * from Win32_Service Where ProcessID = '" & _
            colProcessIDs(i) & "'")
```

You want to put the *Select* statement into a *wmiQuery* variable. Recall from our discussion in Chapter 1, "Starting from Scratch," that you can reuse variables whenever you want to. To illustrate this point, you will reuse the variable name *wmiQuery*. You define *wmiQuery* to be equal to the *Select* statement. To do this, you must define it prior to the line where you'll need to use it. This will be below the *For i = 0* line and above the *Set colServices* line. After you do this, you replace the *Select* statement with the variable *wmiQuery*. The modified code looks like the following:

```
For i = 0 To objIdDictionary.Count - 1
    wmiQuery = "Select * from Win32_Service Where ProcessID = '" & _
        colProcessIDs(i) & "'"
    Set colServices = objWMIService.ExecQuery _
        (wmiQuery)
```

12. Run your script. If it does not run, compare it with lab7pt3.vbs.

13. One aspect of your script that you might find annoying is that it doesn't indicate when it is finished running. Let's fix this by adding a *WScript.Echo* command to let us know the script is done. You just do something like the following:

```
WScript.Echo "all done"
```

**14.** To modify the script to accept a command-line argument, simply edit *strComputer* = "." so that the variable *strComputer* is assigned to be whatever comes in from the command line, not "."., which means this local computer. The revised line looks like the following:

```
strComputer = WScript.Arguments(0)
```

By doing this, you now will run the script against any computer whose name is placed on the command line at the time you run the script.

**15.** Save your script. You can compare it with lab7pt4.vbs. To run the script, go to the directory where you have been saving your work, and open a command prompt. You will want to run the script under CScript, and you will need to include the name of a reachable computer on your network. The command line for mine looks like this:

```
C:\scriptingBook\ch4\lab7>cscript lab7pt4.vbs s1
```

**16.** What happens when you try to include two server names? What happens when you try to run the script without a command-line argument? Let's now modify the script so that it will provide a little bit of help when it is run. As it stands now, when the script is run without a command-line argument, you simply get a "sub-script out of range" error. In addition, when you try to include several computer names from the command line, the first one is used and the others are ignored.

**17.** To add some help, check to ensure that the person running the script added a command-line argument when they executed the script. To do this, check *WScript.Arguments.UnNamed.Count* and make sure it is not zero. Use an *If...Then...Else* construction to perform this check. This construction needs to follow the Header information section of the script. The code looks like the following:

```
If WScript.Arguments.UnNamed.Count = 0 Then
    WScript.Echo("You must enter a computer name")
Else
```

**18.** Since you're using an *If...Then...Else* construction, you must end the *If* statement. To do this, simply place the command *End If* at the bottom of the script. The script to this point is saved as lab7pt5.vbs.

**19.** Now use the *Split* function so that you can enter more than one computer name from the command line. Doing this will be a little tricky. First you must declare two new variables, listed here:

```
Dim colComputers
Dim computer
```

Because *strComputer* is used to hold the command-line arguments, and you want to be able to run the script against multiple computers, you'll need to be able to hold a collection of names. *ColComputers* is used to hold the collection of computer names you get after you parse the command-line input and "split" out the computer names that are separated by commas. Since you now have a collection, you have to be able to iterate through the collection. Each iterated item will be stored in the variable computer.

**20.** Under the *strComputer = WScript.Arguments (0)* line, add the *colComputers* line in which you use the split command to parse the command-line input. Then use a *For Each* line to iterate through the collection. The two new lines of code are listed here:

```
strComputer = WScript.Arguments(0)
colComputers = Split(strComputer, ",")

For Each computer In colComputers
```

**21.** Because you're modifying the input into the script, you need to change your *wmiRoot* statement so that it points to the parsed line that comes from the split command. To do this, you use the following line of code just after the *For Each* command in the *colComputers* line:

```
wmiRoot = "winmgmts:\\" & Computer & "\root\cimv2"
```

**22.** Add an additional *Next* statement near the end of the script. Since you are doing a *For Each Next* construction, you need to add another *Next* command. The bottom section of the script now looks like the following:

```
            For Each objService In colServices
                    WScript.Echo VbTab & objService.DisplayName
            Next
        Next
    Next

        WScript.Echo "all done"
End If
```

The script starts to get confusing when you wind up with a stack of *Next* commands. You might also notice that in the lab7pt6.vbs script, I indented several of the lines to make the script easier to read. If you're careful, you can use the Tab key to line up each *For Each* command with its corresponding *Next* command.

**23.** Save your script, and try to run it by separating several computer names with a comma on the command line. Compare your script with mine, which is saved as lab7pt6.vbs.

You've completed Lab 7. For extra credit, you might want to consider the following modifications: improve the spacing between runs of the script when it is run against other computers. Include the name of the computer at the beginning of each listing.

# Lab 8 Building Arrays

In this lab, you explore building arrays. To help you, you'll take a few ideas from the script in Lab 7 and use them in a starter file.

## Lab Instructions

1. Open the Lab8Starter.vbs file, and save it as **lab8.vbs**. Note that Lab8Starter.vbs will not run. It is provided to save you some typing so that you can spend more time working with arrays.

2. You first need to declare your arrays. The first array you need to declare is *array1*. It is initialized without a specific number of elements, and so you use the format: *Dim array1()*.

3. Declare the second array: *array2*. Because *array2* is created automatically when you use the filter command, you just simply use the format *Dim array2*.

4. Initialize the variables *a* and *i*, which are used for counting the elements in the array. In fact, in this script you'll be creating two arrays. The code goes under the series of *Dim* statements, which are used to declare the variables used in this script.

```
a = 0
i = 0
```

5. Now you come to the first of the *For Each* statements in this script:

```
For Each objService In colServices
    ReDim Preserve array1(i)
    array1(i) = objService.ProcessID
    i = i + 1
Next
```

Here you are creating a *For Each...Next* loop that you'll use to *add* elements into the first array, which is called *array1*. Recall our discussion about arrays: because you wanted to add information to the array and keep the existing data, and because you didn't know how many elements you'd have in the array, you used the format *array1()* when you declared it. Now you want to keep the information you put into the array, so you must use the *ReDim Preserve* command. Then you add items to each element of the array by using the following command:

```
array1(i) = objService.ProcessID
```

Once you add the process ID into the array, you increment the counter and go to the beginning of the *For Each* loop.

6. Save the script. Compare your script with the lab8pt1.vbs file. If you try to run it, you will still get an error.

**7.** Now you populate *array2*, once again using a *For Each Next* loop. The significant item in the code in this step is the *Filter* command. If you didn't create a second array, when you ran the script, you'd get pages of junk because the looping would create duplicate process IDs. (Remember, you're performing a query for process IDs that are associated with services, and so that behavior is to be expected.)

Since there is no unique command or method for arrays, you have to create a second array—named *array2*—by using the *Filter* command, and use a comparison filter as you add elements into it. The input into the filter is *array1*. You are matching the *ProcessID*s from *objService*. (This is actually rather sloppy coding. Because you used *objService.ProcessID* several times, you could have created an alias for it.) The *false* in the last position of the command tells VBScript that the item is brought into the array only if a match is *not* found, which gets rid of our duplicate problem. You might want to change this value to *true* and see what happens to your script!

```
For Each objService In colServices
    array2 = Filter(array1,objService.processID, false)
    a = a + 1
Next
```

**8.** Save the script (mine is called lab8pt2.vbs). At this point, the script should run. (It doesn't run very far, but it should run.)

**9.** You need to put a *For...Next* loop around the bottom WMI query. Since you're working with an array, determine the upper element in the array by using the *UBound* command, as shown in the following code:

```
For b = 0 To UBound(array2)
```

This line will be used by the second array. What you are doing now is running a second WMI query against only the unique elements that reside in the second array. Make sure you add the last *Next* command. The completed section of script, called lab8pt3.vbs, looks like the following:

```
For b = 0 To UBound(array2)
    wmiQuery = "Select * from Win32_Service Where ProcessID = '" & _
        array2(b) & "'"
    Set colServices = objWMIService.ExecQuery _
        (wmiQuery)
    WScript.Echo "Process ID: " & array2(b)
    For Each objService In colServices
        WScript.Echo VbTab & objService.DisplayName
    Next
Next
```

**10.** Run the script. The script should now run as intended. If it doesn't, compare your script with lab8pt3.vbs.

# Lab 9 Modifying a Script

You are the network administrator of a medium-sized company, and you have been studying scripting. You recently learned how to write a pretty cool script that will tell you which services are running in a process. You have been noticing some strangeness in the processor utilization on some of your servers, and you think you have traced it down to the way services run inside processes. To further investigate the issue, you want to modify a script you recently wrote (Lab 7) so that it can be fully automated.

## Lab Instructions

1. Open the Lab9Starter.vbs file, and save it as **lab9.vbs**.

2. Edit the list of variables. Remove *strComputer* and *colComputers* because they won't be used in the new script.

3. Since you're going to feed a text file, you won't need the code that references the *Arguments* collection. Therefore, remove the following lines of code:

```
If WScript.Arguments.count = 0 Then
    WScript.Echo("You must enter a computer name")
Else
    strComputer = WScript.Arguments(0)
    colComputers = Split(strComputer, ",")
```

Make sure you leave the line that is used to create the dictionary object. In addition, do not forget to get rid of the *End If* line at the bottom of the script. See lab9pt1.vbs to make sure you removed the correct lines of code.

4. Add code to accept a command-line text file. You'll need to create a variable named *txtFile* for the text file and then point the variable to a valid text file on your computer. Inside the text file, you need a list of only those computer names reachable on your network, separated by a comma. (Refer to my servers.txt file for a sample, or simply edit it to your needs.)

Next you create a constant called *ForReading* and set it equal to *1*. This is a good way to simplify accessing the file. Now create the *filesystem* object by using the *CreateObject("Scripting.FileSystemObject")* command, which you set equal to the *objFSO* variable.

After you do that, open the text file by setting the *objTextFile* variable to be equal to *objFSO.OpenTextFile*—we feed this the variable for our text file and also the constant *ForReading*. Code for accomplishing all this follows. You place this code right below the *Dim* commands. You will need to add *Dim* commands for the following variables as well: *TxtFile*, *objFSO*, and *objTextFile*. This code is saved as lab9pt2.vbs.

```
TxtFile = "c:\scriptingBook\bookScripts_vbscript\ch4\lab9\Servers.txt"
Const ForReading = 1
Set objFSO = CreateObject("Scripting.FileSystemObject")
Set objTextFile = objFSO.OpenTextFile _
    (TxtFile, ForReading)
```

**5.** Go into the text file and parse out each line so that you know where to look for services and processes. To do this, use a *Do Until* loop. The interesting thing about this section of the code is that the loop is rather large, because you want to work with one computer at a time and query its services and processes *prior* to making another round of the loop. Therefore, placement of the outside *Loop* command is vital. In addition, you need to change the variable used in the *For Each* computer line, which follows the outside loop. Change *Colcomputers* to be *arrServerList*. Also, add a variable for *strNextLine* and *arrServerList* to the Header information section of your script.

```
Do Until objTextFile.AtEndofStream
    strNextLine = objTextFile.Readline
    arrServerList = Split(strNextLine , ",")
```

**6.** Save your file. You can compare your file with lab9pt3.vbs. This file now runs.

**7.** To keep track of how the script runs, add the following line just above the *wmiRoot = "WinMgmts:\\* line:

```
WScript.Echo" Processes and services on " & (computer)
```

**8.** To control the creation of the dictionary, move the line *set objIdDictionary = CreateObject("Scripting.Dictionary")* inside the *For Each computer In arrServerList* line. Save your file and compare it with lab9pt4.vbs, if you want to.

**9.** Add a new variable called *j*.

**10.** Change *i* to **j** in the following line: *For i = 0 To objIdDictionary.Count − 1*. This gives us a new counter the second time the script is run. In addition, edit two other lines and change *colProcesses(i)* to **j** as well.

**11.** To make sure you don't reuse dictionary items the second time the script runs, remove all items from the dictionary by employing the *objIdDictionary.RemoveAll* command. You need to do this outside the *For j* loop but inside the *For Each* computer loop. The completed section looks like the following:

```
For j = 0 To objIdDictionary.Count - 1
        wmiQuery = "Select * from Win32_Service Where ProcessID = '" & _
            colProcessIDs(j) & "'"
    Set colServices = objWMIService.ExecQuery _
        (wmiQuery)
    WScript.Echo "Process ID: " & colProcessIDs(j)
     For Each objService In colServices
        WScript.Echo VbTab & objService.DisplayName
    Next
```

```
                objIdDictionary.RemoveAll
         Next
      Next
Loop
WScript.Echo "all done"
```

This completes the lab. This section is saved in lab9pt5.vbs.

# 5 The Power of Many More

In this chapter, you'll look at two very important concepts: dynamically creating arrays and creating dictionaries. Both of these techniques will enable you to create enterprise-class scripts that will quickly instantiate themselves into your day-to-day network operations.

## Before you Begin

**In order to work through the material presented in this chapter, you need to be familiar with the following concepts from earlier chapters:**

- Creating single dimension arrays

- Creating two-dimensional arrays

- Implementing the *For Next* construction

- Implementing *Select Case* construction

**After completing this chapter you will be familiar with the following:**

- Converting text files into arrays

- Converting delimited strings into arrays

- Working with dictionaries

## Strings and Arrays

In this section, you'll use text files as an input into your script to dynamically create an array that you'll use to do real work. Why is this topic important? Even though we all know about the event log in Microsoft Windows Server 2003, many network administrators and consultants are unaware of the literally hundreds of other log files lying about on the hard disk drives of their networks. Indeed, lying about is an appropriate state for the vast majority of these log files because they contain little in the way of operational guidance for the enlightened network administrator. However, some are veritable fountains of elocution and erudition (or maybe not). The following list summarizes uses for converting a text file into an array construction:

- Import existing log files for ease of manipulation

- Import comma-separated value (CSV) lists for ease of script operation

- Import CSV files to control script execution

> **Just the Steps**
>
> ▶ **To convert a text file into an array**
>
> 1. Implement a text file for the source.
>
> 2. Use the *InStr* function to parse the data.
>
> 3. Use the file system object to connect to a data source.
>
> 4. Use a dynamic array to hold the data.
>
> 5. Use *LBound* and *UBound* to iterate through the array.

# Parsing Passed Text into an Array

In this example, you work through a script that creates a dynamic array used to hold information parsed from the Windows 2003 setup log file, Setuplog.txt. One issue to note: if you're working on an upgraded version of Windows 2003, your Setuplog.txt file is contained in the WINNT directory. If you're working with a fresh installation, the Setuplog.txt file is contained in the Windows directory. The reason for this is that beginning with Microsoft Windows XP, the name of the default Windows directory was changed from WINNT to Windows. However, in an upgrade, the Windows directory cannot be renamed without breaking a whole bunch of applications.

In our script called SearchTXT.vbs (which is on the companion CD), you create a dynamic array and set the initial size to zero. You next make a connection to the file system object and open the Setuplog.txt file, contained in the Windows directory, for reading. Once the Setuplog.txt file is opened for reading, you define a search string of "Error" and use the *InStr* command to look through each line. If the string "Error" is found on the line being examined, the line with the error is written into the array. You then increment the next element in the array in case you find another line with the string "Error" in it. After you go through the entire text file, you use a *For...Next* loop and echo out each element of the array. The script concludes with a friendly "all done" message. The code for SearchTXT.vbs follows:

```
Option Explicit
On Error Resume Next
Dim arrTxtArray()
Dim myFile
Dim SearchString
Dim objTextFile
Dim strNextLine
Dim intSize
Dim objFSO
Dim i
intSize = 0
myFile = "c:\windows\setuplog.txt"
SearchString = "Error"
Const ForReading = 1
Set objFSO = CreateObject("Scripting.FileSystemObject")
```

```
Set objTextFile = objFSO.OpenTextFile _
    (myFile, ForReading)
Do Until objTextFile.AtEndofStream
    strNextLine = objTextFile.ReadLine
    If InStr (strNextLine, SearchString) Then
        ReDim Preserve arrTxtArray(intSize)
        arrTxtArray(intSize) = strNextLine
        intSize = intSize +1
    End If
Loop
objTextFile.close
For i = LBound(arrTxtArray) To UBound(arrTxtArray)
    WScript.Echo arrTxtArray(i)
Next
WScript.Echo("all done")
```

## Header Information

The Header information section of SearchTXT.vbs contains few surprises at this juncture. The important aspect in this section is the listing of all the variables contained in SearchTXT.vbs. This declaring of the variables provides a blueprint for understanding the script. Each variable and its use is listed in Table 5-1. The Header information section of the script is listed here:

```
Option Explicit
On Error Resume Next
Dim arrTxtArray()
Dim myFile
Dim SearchString
Dim objTextFile
Dim strNextLine
Dim intSize
Dim objFSO
Dim i
```

**Table 5-1   Variables Declared in SearchTXT.vbs**

| Variable | Use |
| --- | --- |
| *arrTxtArray()* | Declares a dynamic array |
| *myFile* | Holds the file to open up |
| *SearchString* | Holds the string to search for |
| *objTextFile* | Holds the connection to the text file |
| *strNextLine* | Holds the next line in the text stream |
| *intSize* | Holds the initial size of the array |
| *objFSO* | Holds the connection to the file system object |
| *i* | Used to increment *intSize* counter |

## Reference Information

The Reference information section of the script is used to assign values to many of the variables that are declared in the Header information section. The Reference information section of SearchTXT.vbs follows:

```
intSize = 0
myFile = "c:\windows\setuplog.txt"
SearchString = "Error"
Const ForReading = 1
Set objFSO = CreateObject("Scripting.FileSystemObject")
Set objTextFile = objFSO.OpenTextFile _
    (myFile, ForReading)
```

*IntSize* is used to hold the value of the initial size of the dynamic array used in this script. It is set to zero because you do not know how many items you will have in your dynamic array. You start with the value of zero, and then you later increase the array to the required size as you read through the log file. A different approach would be to create an array that is much larger than you think you'd need, and then populate the array with the items gathered from the log file. However, there are at least two problems with this approach:

- Creating an array that is too large wastes memory resources.

- Creating an array that is too large results in too many elements that have a zero value.

The *myFile* variable is assigned to the physical location of the log file you want to parse. In this instance, you are looking at the Windows Server 2003 setup log file contained in the Windows directory. This is one modification you will need to make to your script—changing the location and name of the log file you want to parse. By creating a variable called *myFile*, and by assigning it to a log file in the Reference information section of the script, you make it easy to modify the script for future use. By simply changing the file you want to parse, you can use this script to peruse many different log files.

*SearchString* is the variable that holds the string of letters you want to glean from the log file. As the script currently stands, you are searching for the word "Error" in the Windows Server 2003 setup log file. By searching for "Error," you create an array that holds all the errors that occurred during the installation of the Windows Server 2003 server.

Create a constant called *ForReading* and set it to the value of *1*. Then create a *FileSystemObject* and use the *ForReading* constant to open the log file. When you open a text file using a *FileSystemObject*, you must tell VBScript whether you're going to open the file and read from it, or open the file and write to it. In your script, you need only to be able to read from the file to find the lines containing the word "Error."

> **See Also**   For more information about creating and using constants, refer to Chapter 2, "Getting in the Loop."

You now use the *Set* command to assign the variable *objTextFile* to be equal to the command that opens the text file for reading. Here is the syntax for this command:

| Set | New variable | Command | Filename | Read or write |
|-----|-------------|---------|----------|---------------|
| *Set* | *objTextFile* | *objFSO.OpentextFile* | *myFile* | *ForReading* |

## Worker Information

The Worker information section of the SearchTXT.vbs script, shown in the following code, is where you create a text-processing engine. This engine is made up of the following components:

- *Do Until...Loop*
- *If...Then* loop
- *ReDim Preserve*

```
Do Until objTextFile.AtEndofStream
    strNextLine = objTextFile.ReadLine
    If InStr (strNextLine, SearchString) Then
        ReDim Preserve arrTxtArray(intSize)
        arrTxtArray(intSize) = strNextLine
        intSize = intSize +1
    End If
Loop
objTextFile.Close
```

The *Do Until...Loop* is used to walk through the text stream that comes from the connection to our setup log file. The *Do Until* structure controls the entire process and will continue working until it comes to the end of the data stream (which incidentally occurs when you reach the bottom of the text file).

The variable *strNextLine* is assigned to the line of text that comes from the text file when you use the *ReadLine* command on *objTextFile*. (Remember that you defined *objTextFile* to be the handle you get back from the setup log file. You do this by using the read-only version of the *OpenTextFile* command in the Reference information section of the script.)

You use an *If...Then* structure to look through *strNextLine* for the value contained in the variable you called *SearchString*. In the Reference section, you assigned the value of "Error" to the variable *SearchString*. You use the *InStr* command to search *strNext-Line* for the text string "Error." The *InStr* command has the following syntax:

| InStr | Starting position (optional) | String being searched | String searched for | Compare mode (optional) |
|---|---|---|---|---|
| InStr | | strNextLine | SearchString | |

When using *InStr*, the starting position is the first character in the text string to be searched. It is important to remember that the *InStr* command is not zero-based. A position that is actually 38 spaces away will be reported as 38. The optional starting position field of the *InStr* command is quite useful when parsing certain log files that begin each line with a time stamp or other information that makes the file difficult to parse. By skipping past the time stamp, you can parse the line more easily.

> **Note**   Many of the commands you use in VBScript are, for whatever reason, zero-based, which means that you start counting at zero. OK, that's groovy. But now you come to *InStr*, which is *not* zero-based. A position that is 12 spaces away will be reported as 12. Forget this fact, and your scripts will act really strange.

If the *InStr* command finds the search text in the search string, you use *ReDim Preserve* to expand the array by one element. *ReDim Preserve* actually performs two tasks. The first is to resize the array, and the second is to make sure you don't lose any data when the array is resized. The *arrTxtArray(intSize) = strNextLine* line adds the value contained in *strNextLine* to the *arrTxtArray* element identified by the *intSize* variable. The *intSize = intSize +1* construct increases the *intSize* variable by 1. You'll use this variable to add one more element to your array when the *InStr* command finds an additional line containing the word "Error" in the text string.

When you reach the end of the data string, you use *End If* to end the *If* loop and the *objTextFile.Close* command to close the text file. This step is not really required, because the text file automatically closes when the program quits; however, this step is considered good practice and can prevent potential file-locking problems in the future.

## Output Information

After you load the array with the information gathered from the setup log file, you really have accomplished only half of the task. This is because constructing an array and not using it is pretty well useless. In this script, you're going to simply echo out the lines found that contain the word "Error" in them. In many cases, echoing the errors out is sufficient. In later chapters, you'll learn how to save this information to a text file for future manipulation if desired. Because your script is modular in its design, you could easily replace this output information section with one that saves to a text file or creates a Web page, or one that creates and sends an e-mail.

You use a *For...Next* loop to work through the lower boundary and the upper boundary of your dynamic array. Once you get to each new element in the array, you use the *WScript.Echo* command to print to the screen the data contained in that element of the array. Then use the *Next* command to go back and read the next element in the array. You continue to do this *Until* reaching the upper boundary of the array. Once you reach the end of the array, you use *WScript.Echo* to let yourself know that the script completed successfully. This section of the script is listed here:

```
For i = LBound(arrTxtArray) To UBound(arrTxtArray)
    WScript.Echo arrTxtArray(i)
Next
WScript.Echo("all done")
```

---

**Quick Check**

**Q.** **What is the advantage of using a dynamic array?**

**A.** You can expand a dynamic array when a new element is needed. This saves memory and is more efficient.

**Q.** **How is *ReDim Preserve* used?**

**A.** *ReDim Preserve* is used to resize a dynamic array while saving the data that is contained in the element.

---

# Parsing Passed Text

One cool thing you can do with arrays is use them to hold the results of parsing a comma-separated value (CSV) file. With Windows Server 2003, you can easily create a CSV file from the event viewer. Right-click the log you are interested in, select Save As from the menu, and choose CSV File. Now, suppose you have a file such as a CSV (I included an application log from one of my test machines), and you're trying to find out about MSI installer errors on that server. Well, you can try to weed through all those long lines of text or you can open it up in Microsoft Excel, or you can use a script to do the heavy lifting.

**Just the Steps**

▶ **To convert a CSV file into an array**

**1.** Implement a CSV file for the source.

**2.** Use the *InStr* function to parse the data.

**3.** Use the file system object to connect to a data source.

**4.** Use a dynamic array to hold the data.

**5.** Use *LBound* and *UBound* to iterate through the array.

**6.** Use the *Split* function to break the text line into elements.

**7.** Add the new elements into a multidimensional array.

The ParseAppLog.vbs script follows:

```
Option Explicit
On Error Resume Next
Dim arrTxtArray()
Dim appLog
Dim SearchString
Dim objTextFile
Dim strNextLine
Dim intSize
Dim objFSO
Dim i
Dim ErrorString
Dim newArray
intSize = 0
appLog = "C:\scriptingBook\BookScripts_VbScript\ch5\applog.CSV"
SearchString = ","
ErrorString = "1004"
Const ForReading = 1
Set objFSO = CreateObject("Scripting.FileSystemObject")
Set objTextFile = objFSO.OpenTextFile _
    (appLog, ForReading)
Do Until objTextFile.AtEndofStream
    strNextLine = objTextFile.ReadLine
    If InStr (strNextLine, SearchString) Then
        If InStr ( strNextLine, ErrorString) Then
            ReDim Preserve arrTxtArray(intSize)
            arrTxtArray(intSize) = strNextLine
            intSize = intSize +1
        End If
    End If
Loop
    objTextFile.Close
For i = LBound(arrTxtArray) To UBound(arrTxtArray)
    If InStr (arrTxtArray(i), ",") Then
    newArray = Split (arrTxtArray(i), ",")
        WScript.Echo "Date: " & newArray(0)
```

```
            WScript.Echo "Time: " & newArray(1)
            WScript.Echo "Source: " & newArray(2)& " "& newArray(3)
            WScript.Echo "Server: " & newArray(7)
            WScript.Echo "Message1: " & newArray(8)
            WScript.Echo "Message2: " & newArray(9)
            WScript.Echo "Message3: " & newArray(10)
            WScript.Echo " "
        End If
Next
WScript.Echo("all done")
```

## Header Information

The Header information section in ParseAppLog.vbs is similar to the Header section in the previous script. The variables utilized are listed in Table 5-2.

**Table 5-2   Variables Declared in ParseAppLog.vbs**

| Variable | Use |
| --- | --- |
| arrTxtArray() | Declares a dynamic array |
| *appLog* | Holds the file to open |
| *SearchString* | Holds the string to search for |
| *objTextFile* | Holds the connection to the text file |
| *strNextLine* | Holds the next line in the text stream |
| *intSize* | Holds the initial size of the array |
| *objFSO* | Holds the connection to the file system object |
| *i* | Used to increment the *intSize* counter |
| *ErrorString* | Holds the second search string used |
| *newArray* | New array created to sort the output |

## Reference Information

The Reference information section is where you assign values to certain variables and define constants that are used in the script. Here is the Reference information section of the script:

```
intSize = 0
appLog = "C:\scriptingBook\BookScripts_VbScript\ch5\applog.CSV"
SearchString = ","
ErrorString = "1004"
Const ForReading = 1
Set objFSO = CreateObject("Scripting.FileSystemObject")
Set objTextFile = objFSO.OpenTextFile _
    (appLog, ForReading)
```

*Applog* is used to point to the CSV file you want to parse. You use *SearchString* to specify that you want to look for commas. The *ErrorString* you are looking for in this script is 1004, which is an error from MSI installer. By changing the error message ID, you can use the script to look for everything from dropped IP packets from the ISA server to bad logon attempts from Windows Server 2003.

> **Important**    This technique won't perfectly parse every CSV file in the world. Some are very complex and include commas and even line feeds within single pieces of data.
>
> Although special rules for advanced parsing are beyond the scope of this chapter, you are unlikely to encounter this problem with normal application setup logs (and you definitely won't see this in CSV files exported from the Event Viewer).

## Worker Information

In the Worker information section of the script, things start to get a little interesting. You begin by using a *Do Until* construction that looks for the end of the read-only text string coming from *objTextFile*. You then define *strNextLine* to be equal to what comes back from the *readline* command that we used on *objTextFile*. The magic begins when you use the *InStr* command to look for commas in the line-by-line streams of text. After you find a comma in a line, you look for the error message ID of 1004, which indicates a problem with an MSI installer package. By nesting a pair of *If Then* statements and using *InStr*, you easily filter only the desired messages. As a result, the size of the array is smaller and less memory is required. You haven't implemented error handling here, which could easily be accomplished by using the *Else* command.

```
Do Until objTextFile.AtEndofStream
    strNextLine = objTextFile.ReadLine
    If InStr (strNextLine, SearchString) > 0 Then
        If InStr ( strNextLine, ErrorString) > 0 Then
            ReDim Preserve arrTxtArray(intSize)
            arrTxtArray(intSize) = strNextLine
            intSize = intSize + 1
        End If
    End If
Loop
objTextFile.Close
```

## Output Information

After the array *arrTxtArray* is created, each element of the array contains an entire event message from the event log. You could just print out each line, but a more functional approach is to organize the data so that it is more comprehensible. To this end, you create a multidimensional array that holds specific elements of the event message. You begin the Output information section by using *For...Next* to walk from the lower boundary of the single dimensional array *arrTxtArray* to the upper boundary of *arrTxtArray*. You then look for commas in each line contained in the elements incremented by using the *i* counter. Once this is done, you build the multidimensional array and echo out only the elements that contain information you're interested in seeing. The script ends by echoing out an "all done" message.

```
For i = LBound(arrTxtArray) To UBound(arrTxtArray)
    If InStr (arrTxtArray(i), ",") Then
        newArray = Split (arrTxtArray(i), ",")
        WScript.Echo "Date: " & newArray(0)
        WScript.Echo "Time: " & newArray(1)
        WScript.Echo "Source: " & newArray(2)& " "& newArray(3)
        WScript.Echo "Server: " & newArray(7)
        WScript.Echo "Message1: " & newArray(8)
        WScript.Echo "Message2: " & newArray(9)
        WScript.Echo "Message3: " & newArray(10)
        WScript.Echo " "
    End If
Next
```

---

**Quick Check**

**Q.** **What is the simplest way to break up a CSV data stream to populate an array?**

**A.** You need to use the *Split* command and look for commas.

**Q.** **What is the *InStr* command used for?**

**A.** The *InStr* command is used to look for character combinations in a stream of text.

**Q.** **What construct can be used to hold data records that are separated by commas?**

**A.** A multidimensional array can be used to hold this type of data.

---

# Working with Dictionaries

I don't know about you, but I always think about using a dictionary to check the spelling of a word or to find a definition. In Windows Scripting, however, a dictionary has nothing to do with either of these concepts, although its use is just as important, perhaps more so. So what is a dictionary in our context? Well, a *dictionary* is kind of like an array, only easier to work with. It is a place to hold data. Just like an array can be used to hold data in a convenient place for use within the script, a dictionary also holds data. A dictionary works like a single dimension array. You can store only one column worth of data in your dictionary. On the other hand, a dictionary is kind of like an array that uses names instead of numbers for the index. However you want to look like it, you are only going to be able to store one column's worth of data in your dictionary.

Because enterprise scripts have to get information from other places (a command-line argument, a text file, or an ADSI query), it is convenient to store the information locally to avoid repeated calls to the outside source. Once the information is local, you can manipulate it into a more manageable form. In Chapter 4, "The Power of Many," and earlier in this chapter, you looked at using arrays to store information locally. In certain situations, you can use a dictionary to perform the same type of activity—that is, for convenience, you can stash working information in the dictionary object.

As mentioned earlier, the dictionary works like an array in that each item in the dictionary is stored with its associated key. Inside the dictionary is a key and the item itself. The dictionary offers a couple of advantages over arrays. The first advantage is that you can retrieve any specific item from the dictionary simply by knowing the index item, whereas with an array, you need to know the array index number. The second advantage is that a dictionary doesn't require any specific size configuration. With an array, you must either know its exact size or resize it.

## Using the Dictionary

To use the VBScript dictionary, you need to first create it. (In technical terms, the dictionary is a COM object and therefore gets instantiated via *CreateObject*.)

---

**Quick Check**

**Q.** **What are the advantages of using a dictionary rather than an array?**

**A.** The dictionary allows retrieval of specific items from the dictionary without knowledge of the index number. In addition, the dictionary is automatically dynamically sized.

**Q.** **Since a dictionary is a COM object, how does it get instantiated?**

**A.** A dictionary gets instantiated by using the *CreateObject* command.

---

### Compare Mode

The dictionary allows us to configure only one property: the compare mode. This is actually part of what makes the dictionary easy to use (the lack of configurable properties, not the compare mode itself). In reality, most of the time, the default compare mode (which is binary mode) is fine. Compare mode actually does what it implies: it allows you to configure the way in which the dictionary compares items when used to search for previously added items. The other compare mode (besides binary) is text mode. Text mode is case-insensitive. In binary mode, server1 and Server1 are two different computers, whereas in text mode they would be the same machine. It is important to remain aware of these differences.

> **Note**   If you want to change the compare mode from binary to text mode, you must do this before you add any information to the dictionary.

## Adding Items to the Dictionary

After you create the dictionary, you add items to it. (It's basically useless without information, just like a real dictionary containing only blank pages.) So how do you add information to the dictionary? You guessed it—using the *Add* method. You use this method to populate both the key name and the item value, as illustrated in the following script:

```
Set objDictionary = CreateObject("Scripting.Dictionary")
objDictionary.Add "comp1", "server1"
WScript.Echo objDictionary.Item ("comp1")
```

In the preceding script, you first create the dictionary and assign it to the variable *objDictionary*. You used this variable because you use the *CreateObject* command to make a dictionary, and the name *objDictionary* tells us that the variable is an object that is a dictionary. You then add one item to the dictionary, called *server1*, which is assigned to a key called *comp1*. From this code, you can see the syntax is *add key item*, as illustrated here:

| Command | Key | Item |
|---|---|---|
| *objDictionary.Add* | *Comp1* | *Server1* |

## Summary

In this chapter, you examined converting delimited strings into arrays. You found that by using the *InStr* command, you could parse incoming text streams and pull out only the items needed. You then created a new array by using the *Split* command to look for commas. In addition, you worked with dictionaries. You found that for many applications, the dictionary is both quicker to set up and easier to use than an array.

# Quiz Yourself

**Q.  What is the advantage of using a string to populate an array?**

**A.**  The advantage of using a string to populate an array is that strings are available from many places (such as Excel). In addition, since an array resides in memory, it is quicker than making multiple trips to read in the string.

**Q.  What is required to resize a dynamic array?**

**A.**  To resize a dynamic array, you must use the *ReDim* command. This will allow you to change the size of the array and permit the addition of elements in the array. Note that if you do not include the Preserve option, when you *ReDim* your array, you will lose all existing data.

**Q.  The dictionary allows you to configure which property?**

**A.**  The dictionary allows you to configure the compare mode property.

**Q.  How is a dictionary created?**

**A.**  A dictionary is created by using the *CreateObject* command.

# Own Your Own

# Lab 10a Implementing Basics for the *InStr* Command

In this lab, you play with the *InStr* command to become familiar with the basic features of its implementation. Because this is a short script, you don't need to implement a full Header information section.

## Lab Instructions

1. Open Notepad.exe.

2. Create a variable called *searchString* and set it equal to *5*. Your line will look like the following:

   ```
   searchString = "5"
   ```

3. Create another variable called *textSearched* and set it equal to *123456789*. Your second line will look like this:

   ```
   textSearched = "123456789"
   ```

4. Create a third variable called *InStrReturn* and set it equal to the following *InStr* command: *InStr (textSearched, searchString)*. This line will look like the following:

   ```
   InStrReturn = InStr (textSearched, searchString)
   ```

5. Use the *WScript.Echo* command to print out the results of the *InStr* command. This line will look like the following:

```
WScript.Echo (InStrReturn)
```

6. Save the file and call it **lab10a.vbs**.

7. Run the lab10a.vbs file by double-clicking it. You should see a dialog box with the number 5 printed in it. This indicates that search string 5 was found in the fifth position of the script.

# Lab 10b Understanding Advanced Features of the *InStr* Command

In this lab, you use the *InStr* command to become familiar with the advanced features of its implementation. This short script does not need a full Header information section.

## Lab Instructions

1. Open Notepad.exe

2. Create a variable called *searchString* and set it equal to *5*. Your line will look like the following:

```
searchString = "5"
```

3. Create another variable called *textSearched* and set it equal to *123456789*. Your second line will look like this:

```
textSearched = "123456789"
```

4. Create a third variable called *InStrReturn* and set it equal to the following *InStr* command: *InStr (1, textSearched, searchString, 0)*. This line will look like the following:

```
InStrReturn = InStr (1, textSearched, searchString, 0)
```

5. Use the *WScript.Echo* command to print out the results of the *InStr* command. This line will look like the following:

```
WScript.Echo InStrReturn
```

6. Save the file and call it **lab10b.vbs**.

7. Run lab10b.vbs by double-clicking it. You should see a dialog box with the number 5 printed in it. This indicates that the search string 5 was found in the fifth position of the script when you started looking from the first position of the search string.

8. Change the 1 to a **5** in your *InStrReturn* line. It will look like the following:

```
InStrReturn = InStr(5, textSearched, searchString, 0)
```

9. Save your work.

10. Run lab10b.vbs by double-clicking it. You should see a dialog box with the number 5 printed in it. This indicates that the search string 5 was found in the fifth position of the script when you started looking from the fifth position of the search string.

11. Change the 5 to a **6** in your *InStrReturn* line. It will look like the following:

```
InStrReturn = InStr(6, textSearched, searchString, 0)
```

12. Save your work.

13. Run lab10b.vbs by double-clicking it. You should see a dialog box with the number 0 printed in it. This indicates that the search string 5 was not found in the search string when you started looking from the sixth position of the search string.

# Lab 11 Creating a Dictionary

In this lab, you create a dictionary and then populate it with a list of filenames provided by the file system object.

## Lab Instructions

1. Open Notepad.exe.

2. On the first line, type **Option Explicit**.

3. Declare the following variables by using the *Dim* command:

```
Dim objDictionary
Dim objFSO
Dim objFolder
Dim colFiles
Dim objFile
Dim colItems
Dim colKeys
Dim strKey
Dim strItem
```

4. Use *CreateObject* to create the dictionary:

```
Set objDictionary = CreateObject("Scripting.Dictionary")
```

5. Create the file system object and assign it to the variable *objFSO*:

```
Set objFSO = CreateObject("Scripting.FileSystemObject")
```

6. Use the *GetFolder* method and assign it to the variable *objFolder*:

```
Set objFolder = objFSO.GetFolder("C:\scriptingBook")
```

Select a folder available on your machine.

**7.** Use the file command of the *GetFolder* method and assign it to *colFiles*:

```
Set colFiles = objFolder.Files
```

**8.** Use *For Each* to iterate through *colFiles*:

```
For Each objFile In colFiles
```

**9.** Use the *Add* method of the dictionary object to add the filename and the file size to the dictionary:

```
objDictionary.Add objFile.Name, objFile.Size
```

**10.** Close out the *For Each...Next* loop:

```
Next
```

**11.** Assign *colItems* to the *Items* collection of the dictionary:

```
colItems = objDictionary.Items
```

**12.** Assign *colKeys* to the *Keys* collection of the dictionary:

```
colKeys = objDictionary.Keys
```

**13.** Use *For Each* to iterate through the collection of keys:

```
For Each strKey In colKeys
```

**14.** Nest another *For Each* to iterate through the collection of items:

```
For Each strItem In colItems
```

**15.** Echo out the filename and the file size:

```
WScript.Echo "filename: " & strKey & " size: " & strItem
```

**16.** Close out the two *For Each...Next* constructions by typing **Next** on two separate lines.

**17.** Use the *Count* method to echo out the number of files in the folder:

```
WScript.Echo "***there are " & objDictionary.Count & " files"
```

# Part 2
# Basic Windows Administration

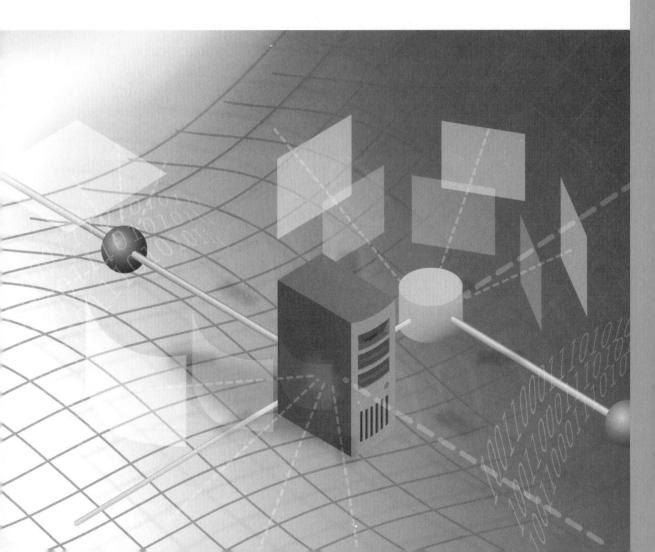

# 6  Working with the File System

In this chapter, you'll look at two very important concepts: dynamically creating arrays and dynamically creating dictionaries. Both of these techniques will enable you to create enterprise-class scripts that will quickly instantiate themselves into your day-to-day network operations.

## Before You Begin

**The material presented in this chapter requires you to be familiar with the following concepts from earlier chapters:**

- Using the *For Each...Next* construction
- Applying *Select Case* constructions
- Adopting constants
- Implementing intrinsic VBScript properties such as *VbTab* and *Now*
- Employing *If...Then...Else*

**After completing this chapter you will be familiar with the following:**

- How to create a *FileSystemObject* instance
- How to use the *FileSystemObject* to list files
- How to use the *FileSystemObject* to create files
- How to use the *FileSystemObject* to verify the existence of files
- How to use the *FileSystemObject* to work with file properties
- How to use the *FileSystemObject* to work with file attributes

## Creating File System Object

To talk to the file system, the script needs to make a connection to it so that it can read files and folders. The tool used with Microsoft Visual Basic Script (VBScript) is called the *file system object*. Once you create an instance of the file system object, you can leverage its power to perform some or all of the following tasks:

- Create files and folders
- Copy files and folders
- Move files and folders

- Delete files and folders

- List properties of files and folders

---

**Just the Steps**

▶ **To enumerate a list of files**

1. Use *CreateObject* to create the *FileSystemObject*.

2. Define the folder to be searched by using *GetFolder*.

3. Use the *Files* command to list files.

4. Use a *For Each* construct to walk through the folder.

---

# File It Under Files

In your first file system script, Listfiles.vbs, you connect to *FileSystemObject*, attach it to a folder defined by the variable *FolderPath*, and then use the *Files* command to enable the *For Each* loop to echo out each file in the folder. This is just the beginning of what you can do with this script. Continue to think of ways to expand upon this script so that you can perform some really useful network administration tasks.

```
Option Explicit
On Error Resume Next
Dim FolderPath ' folder to be searched for files
Dim objFSO
Dim objFolder
Dim colFiles
Dim objFile

FolderPath = "C:\scriptingBook\BookScripts_VbScript"
Set objFSO = CreateObject("Scripting.FileSystemObject")
Set objFolder = objFSO.GetFolder(FolderPath)
Set colFiles = objFolder.Files

For Each objFile In colFiles
    WScript.Echo objFile.Name, objFile.Size
Next
```

## Header Information

In the Header information section of Listfiles.vbs are the normal *Option Explicit* and *On Error Resume Next* commands. These are used to specify the declaration of all variables and to provide rudimentary error suppression. Next, you declare five variables that are used in the script. A description of the variables is listed in Table 6-1.

**Table 6-1   Variables Used in Listfiles.vbs**

| Variable name | Use |
| --- | --- |
| *FolderPath* | Defines the folder to be searched in the script. |
| *objFSO* | Creates *FileSystemObject*. |
| *objFolder* | Holds the connection to the folder by using the *FolderPath* variable and the *GetFolder* method of *FileSystemObject*. |
| *colFiles* | Holds the collection of files returned by using the *files* command. |
| *objFile* | Holds individual files as the script iterates through the collection of files by using the *For Each* construction. |

> **See Also**   For more information about using the *Option Explicit* and *On Error Resume Next* commands, see Chapter 1, "Starting from Scratch."

## Reference Information

The Reference information section of the Listfiles.vbs script is different from some of the earlier scripts in this book because you make the connection to *FileSystemObject*, which enables you to work with file and folders. You also define the *FolderPath* variable created in the Header information section. The *FolderPath* variable is utilized to make the script easier to modify in the future. By changing the path contained in the *FolderPath* variable, the script can list files on any machine. In addition, *FolderPath* provides a great deal of flexibility. With just a little work, you can modify Listfiles.vbs to take command-line input or to find the value for *FolderPath* by reading a list of paths from a text file.

*ObjFSO* is used to hold the reference that comes back from the *CreateObject* command. By using the *CreateObject("Scripting.FileSystemObject")* command, you can work with the file system to enumerate all the files in the folder.

The folder from which files are listed is defined by using the *GetFolder* method. The code *objFSO.GetFolder(FolderPath)* is set equal to *objFolder*, which is the variable used to address the folder defined in the *FolderPath* variable.

Once you can talk to the folder, you use the *Files* command to get a list of files contained in the folder. You assign this list of files to the *colFiles* variable by using the following code: *Set colFiles = objFolder.Files*. The complete Reference information section follows:

```
FolderPath = "C:\scriptingBook\BookScripts_VbScript"
Set objFSO = CreateObject("Scripting.FileSystemObject")
Set objFolder = objFSO.GetFolder(FolderPath)
Set colFiles = objFolder.Files
```

## Worker and Output Information

The Worker and Output Information section of the Listfiles.vbs script uses a *For Each...Next* loop to walk through the collection of files returned by the *Files* command in the Reference information section of the script. The *Wscript.Echo* command is used to display the filename and the file size:

```
For Each objFile In colFiles
    WScript.Echo objFile.Name, objFile.Size
Next
```

---

**Quick Check**

**Q.** What is required to talk to the file system by using *FileSystemObject*?

**A.** You use *FileSystemObject* by using a *CreateObject* command, assigning to a variable the hook that comes back.

**Q.** Why do you want a hook for *FileSystemObject*?

**A.** You want a hook for *FileSystemObject* because it allows you to work with files and folders.

---

# File Properties

*Name* and *Size* (used in the preceding *WScript.Echo* command) are just two file properties that can be listed by using *FileSystemObject*. A *file property* describes aspects of the file such as when it was created, when it was last accessed, when it was modified, its path, its size, and its type. The intrepid network administrator can enumerate various file properties, which can be used for both security purposes and user data management. For example, as shown in the following code, you can add a couple of lines to the Listfiles.vbs script to retrieve additional data—in this case, the date the file was created and the date it was last modified. The *vbTab* constant is added to make the output easier to read. The completed script is saved as ListfilesExtProperties.vbs on the companion CD. Here are the additional lines:

```
    WScript.Echo vbTab & "created: " & objFile.DateCreated
    WScript.Echo vbTab & "modified: " & objFile.DateLastModified
```

Additional file object properties can be retrieved in the same manner. All are listed in Table 6-2.

**Table 6-2   File Properties**

| Property | Use |
|---|---|
| *Attributes* | Bitmask representation of the file attributes such as read-only and hidden. |
| *DateCreated* | Date the file was created. |
| *DateLastAccessed* | Date the file was last accessed. |
| *DateLastModified* | Date the file was last modified. |
| *Drive* | The drive letter representing where the file is stored, followed by a colon (for example, C:). |
| *Name* | The name of the file, not including the path information (for example, ListFiles.vbs). The name does include the extension. |
| *ParentFolder* | The folder in which the file is located (not including subfolders). For example, the parent folder of C:\windows\system32\logfile.txt is Windows. |
| *Path* | The full path of the file (for example, C:\windows\system32\log-file.txt). |
| *ShortName* | 8.3 (MS-DOS format) version of the filename. For example: MyLong-FileName.txt would become MyLong~1.txt. |
| *ShortPath* | 8.3 (MS-DOS style) version of the path. For example, C:\MyLong-Path\MyLongFileName.txt would become C:\MyLong~1\MyLong~1.txt. |
| *Size* | The size of the file in bytes. |
| *Type* | The type of file as recorded in the registry. For example, a .doc file is listed as a Microsoft Word document. |

# File Attributes

*File attributes* are aspects such as read-only, hidden, system, and archive that are used to configure how a file can be utilized by the operating system. These are the same attributes you can set via the *attrib.exe* command or the Properties Action menu in Explorer.exe. These attributes are not hidden from ordinary users (they are easily read in Explorer.exe), and they are used to control how backups run and to prevent acci-dental overwriting of important configuration and system files. This fact makes file attributes of interest to network administrators. A file attribute is stored as a bitmask value to conserve space. When you query the file attribute, only a single number is returned. When a file is hidden, VBScript returns a *2*. When a file is a system file, VBScript returns a *4*. When, however, a file is both a hidden file and a system file, VBScript return a *6*. The numbers are arranged so that each attribute or combination of attributes returns a single and unique number. There are a number of possible combinations, each of which would need to be tested in a script returning these attributes. The bits representing each attribute value are listed in Table 6-3.

**Table 6-3  File Attributes and Bitmask Values**

| Attribute | Bitmask value | Meaning |
| --- | --- | --- |
| Normal | 0 | No attributes set. |
| Read-Only | 1 | File can be read but not changed. |
| Hidden | 2 | File cannot be seen in default view of Microsoft Windows Explorer. |
| System | 4 | File is used by the OS. |
| Archive | 32 | File changed since last backup. |
| Alias | 64 | File is a shortcut to another file. |
| Compressed | 2048 | File has been compressed. |

---

**Just the Steps**

▶ **To access file attributes**

1. Create an instance of *FileSystemObject*.
2. Use the *GetFile* method to bind to the file.
3. Use the *Attributes* method to return the bitmask value.

---

## Implementing the *Attributes* Property

In the FileAttributes.vbs script, you first use *CreateObject* to create an instance of the *FileSystemObject*. Once the instance is created, you use *GetFile* to provide a reference to a specific file (in this case, the boot.ini file). After you have a reference to the boot.ini file, you echo out the filename and also the attribute number by using the *Attributes* property in conjunction with the *WScript.Echo* command. Finally, you use a *Select Case* construction to match the attribute number and display the appropriate text.

**See Also**   For a detailed explanation of *Select Case*, see Chapter 3, "Adding Intelligence."

```
Option Explicit
On Error Resume Next
Dim objFSO
Dim objFile
Dim Target
```

```
Target = "C:\boot.ini"
Set objFSO = CreateObject("Scripting.FileSystemObject")
Set objFile = objFSO.GetFile(Target)

WScript.Echo "The file Is: " & target
WScript.Echo "bitmask number Is: " & (objFile.Attributes)

Select Case objFile.Attributes
    Case 0
        WScript.Echo "No Attributes Set"
    Case 1
        WScript.Echo "Read-Only"
    Case 2
        WScript.Echo "Hidden File"
    Case 3
        WScript.Echo "Read-Only, Hidden File"
    Case 4
        WScript.Echo "System File"
    Case 6
        WScript.Echo "Hidden, System File"
    Case 7
        WScript.Echo "Read-Only, Hidden, System File"
    Case 32
        WScript.Echo "Archive bit Set"
    Case 64
        WScript.Echo "Link or Shortcut"
    Case 2048
        WScript.Echo "Compressed file"
End Select
```

## Setting File Attributes

You have to use a rather strange operator—the *Xor* operator—to set the file attributes, because the bitmask values are actually ones and zeros, and you therefore are going to do a simple Boolean operation to flip the bit. This sounds more complicated than it is. You just need to know how to spell *Xor* to use it in your script. In the following script, you look for an attribute of *1*, which you know from the previous discussion is equal to the *read-only* attribute. In Boolean math, 1 *And* 1 11 1 is equal to 1, which indicates the file is read-only. 1 *And* any other combination of numbers is equal to zero, so if the file is not marked read-only, when it is *And*'ed with 1, it yields a zero and therefore is *Xor*'ed to make it into a *read-only* attribute.

```
Set objFSO = CreateObject("Scripting.FileSystemObject")
Set objFile = objFSO.GetFile("C:\scripts\test.txt")

WScript.Echo "Beginning attribute is " & objfile.attributes

If (objFile.attributes AND 1) = 0 Then
    objFile.Attributes = (objFile.Attributes Xor 1)
Else
```

```
        WScript.Echo("File attributes are unchanged: ")
    End If

    WScript.Echo "End File Attribute Is: " & objFile.Attributes
```

# A File, a File, I Need to Create a File

There are literally thousands of times when a network administrator needs to create a file. The most common occurrence is when output needs to be captured from a command prompt or from the running of a script. By the time you finish this chapter, you'll have a section of code that you can reuse again and again. Once you know how to create files, you can use this code section instead of the *WScript.Echo* command to direct output to either the command prompt or a dialog box. (Later on in Chapter 14, "Configuring Network Components," you'll learn how to automatically invoke Notepad.exe to facilitate reading of the output.) So what is involved in creating a file? The "Just the Steps" section explains the process at a high level.

---

**Just the Steps**

▶ **To create a file**

1. Use *CreateObject* to create an instance of *FileSystemObject*.

2. Use the *CreateTextFile* method.

3. Include the full path and the name of the desired file.

---

As you can see from the preceding steps, the creation of a text file via VBScript is a very easy and straightforward process. In fact, it can be accomplished with just two lines of code, as seen in the listing for CreateTextFile.vbs.

```
Set objFSO = CreateObject("Scripting.FileSystemObject")
Set objFolder = objFSO.CreateTextFile("C:\FSO.txt")
```

# Writing to a Text File

Creating text files using VBScript is cool but rather useless unless you can also add information to them. Writing information to a text file gives you a way to save information. In addition, it's a good way to create a log file to track the progress of various automated administrative tasks. You use the *WriteLine* method to write to a text file.

---

**Just the Steps**

▶ **To write to a text file**

1. Create an instance of *FileSystemObject*.

2. Use the appropriate parameter to indicate that you are going to either overwrite the file (2) or append data to the file (8).

3. Use either the *Write*, *WriteLine*, or *WriteBlankLines* method to write to the file.

4. Close the text file.

---

## How Shall I Write Thee? Let Me Count the Ways...

There are actually three different ways you can write to files, which are described in Table 6-4.

**Table 6-4   Methods Used to Write to Files**

| Method | Use |
| --- | --- |
| *Write* | Writes to the file without appending the carriage return. (The carriage return, you might recall, is when the insertion point is moved to the beginning of the next line.) |
| *WriteLine* | Writes to the file and includes a carriage return at the end of the line. |
| *WriteBlankLines(n)* | Writes blank lines to the file. The placeholder *(n)* specifies the number of lines to write. |

## Overwriting a File

You use the constant *ForWriting* in conjunction with the *Write* method to overwrite to a file. I use this when I want to track the progress of an operation in a log file. By looking in the file, I can see when the operation last ran, as illustrated in the BasicLog.vbs script.

```
LogFile = "C:\fso\fso.txt"
Const ForWriting = 2
Set objFSO = CreateObject("Scripting.FileSystemObject")
Set objFile = objFSO.OpenTextFile(LogFile, ForWriting)
objFile.WriteLine "beginning process " & Now
objFile.WriteLine "working on process " & Now
objFile.WriteLine "Process completed at " & Now
objFile.Close
```

The script begins by defining the variable *LogFile* and assigning a text file to it. You do this to make it easier to reuse the code and to make it easier to change the file you want to write to. You then define the constant *ForWriting* and set it equal to *2*, which is the number that tells VBScript to overwrite any data found in the text file that might have been previously written to. The variable *objFSO* is then set to be equal to the object returned by the *CreateObject* command that is used to create an instance of *File-SystemObject*. In the next line, the variable *objFile* is set to be equal to the handle to *LogFile* that is obtained. You use the *OpenTextFile* command and specify that you want to open the file for writing. All the preceding steps are overhead for the write operation. Once you have the *ForWriting* handle to the log file, you have completed the Reference information section of the script. You're now ready for the Output information section, which is the section of the script that actually does work. In the Output section, you use the *WriteLine* method.

---

**Quick Check**

**Q.  What are three ways to write to files?**

**A.  You can write to files using the *Write*, *WriteLine*, and *WriteBlankLines* methods.**

**Q.  If you want to overwrite a file, what do you need to do?**

**A.  You need to specify the constant *ForWriting*.**

---

In a logging situation, the dauntless network administrator is looking for two salient pieces of information: what operation completed and when it completed. Armed with this information, a network administrator can judge the success or failure of various procedures. In the BasicLog.vbs script, you can easily glean this information by incorporating the *WriteLine* method inside the *For...Next* loop of any working script. This is exactly the type of thing I do in a lab to estimate how long a certain script will take to complete. If, for instance, a certain WMI script needs 5 minutes to complete, you might not want to launch it on 100 servers at the same time because doing so could have an adverse impact on the computing environment.

In the CheckAdminTools_logged.vbs file, you merge BasicLog.vbs with the Check-AdminTools.vbs file from Chapter 1. This script simply checks when the script begins and when it ends. You could add an extra line of code to compute the run time of the script (if you were so inclined). By consulting the log entries, you can estimate how long it will take to obtain the desired information.

```
LogFile = "C:\fso\fso.txt"
Const ForWriting = 2
Set objFSO = CreateObject("Scripting.FileSystemObject")
Set objFile = objFSO.OpenTextFile(LogFile, ForWriting)
```

```
Set objShell = CreateObject("Shell.Application")
Set colTools = objShell.Namespace(47).Items

objFile.WriteLine "beginning process " & Now
For Each objTool in colTools
    WScript.Echo objTool
Next
objFile.WriteLine "Process completed at " & Now
objFile.Close
```

# Existential File Approaches

Although the approach to file management just discussed might seem laid back and groovy, in many environments, you need to take a more existential approach. In other words, you must first determine whether the file exists, and if it does, you want to append to the file (not overwrite it); if it does not exist, you want to create it. This ensures that your log file is present on each server running your script.

To check for the existence of a particular file, you use the *FileExists* method of *FileSystemObject*. Although it's true that this method complicates the script a little, it's also true that by checking for and creating a particular file as required, you add an order of magnitude to the flexibility of the script. Without further ado, take a look at the VerifyFileExists.vbs:

```
LogFile = "C:\FSO\fso.txt"
Const ForWriting = 2
Const ForAppending = 8
Set objFSO = CreateObject("Scripting.FileSystemObject")

If objFSO.FileExists(LogFile) Then
    Set objFile = objFSO.OpenTextFile(LogFile, ForAppending)
    objFile.Write "appending " & Now
Else
    Set objFile = objFSO.CreateTextFile(LogFile)
    objFile.Close
    Set objFile = objFSO.OpenTextFile(LogFile, ForWriting)
    objfile.Write "writing to new file " & Now
End If
objFile.Close
```

Notice that this script uses code that is very similar to the BasicLog.vbs script mentioned earlier in this chapter in that you define your *logfile* and create *FileSystemObject* via the *CreateObject* command. However, that is where the most obvious similarity ends.

In this script, you define two constants, *ForWriting* and *ForAppending*, because you might want to perform one of these operations depending on whether the log file exists. After you create *FileSystemObject*, you move into an *If...Then...Else* loop. Notice the way in which the *FileExists* construct is implemented:

```
If objFSO.FileExists(LogFile) Then
```

To look for the existence of a file, you use the handle to *FileSystemObject* that you obtained and call the *FileExists* method of that object. The only required parameter is the name of the file for which you want to test existence. In this case, it is the file you set equal to the variable called *LogFile*.

If the file does exist, you use the *opentextFile* method of *FileSystemObject* and specify *logfile*, and then add to the file by using the *ForAppending* constant. Remember, when you open a file by using the *OpenTextFile* command, you have to specify whether you are opening it in read-only mode, appending mode, or overwriting mode. After you specify the manner in which you are opening the file, you then use the *Write* command to write a line to the log file. The *Now* function simply writes out the current date and time in a long format.

If the file is not present, you want to create the log file. This is done by using the *CreateTextFile* method of *FileSystemObject*, as shown in the following code:

```
Set objFile = objFSO.CreateTextFile(LogFile)
```

It's necessary to follow this command up with *objFile.Close* because you want to write to the file. If you don't close the file and try to write to it, you'll get an "access denied" error because the previous command has access to the file. After the *Close* command, you use the *openTextFile* command and specify the *ForWriting* constant. Then you use the *Write* command to write out to the file. In reality, you could have specified *ForAppending* and appended to the new file, but by using *ForWriting*, you make it a little easier to know what is actually contained in the file.

# Summary

In this chapter, you examined the use of *FileSystemObject* to list and create files. You also saw how to use *FileSystemObject* to access file properties and attributes. This discussion was followed up with a look at three different ways to write to files, and the chapter concluded with a section on how to verify the existence of a file prior to attempting to write to it.

# Quiz Yourself

**Q. What are the three ways to write to a file?**

**A.** You can write to a file using the *Write*, *WriteLine*, and *WriteBlankLines* methods.

**Q. What is the difference between *Write* and *WriteLine*?**

**A.** The difference between *Write* and *WriteLine* is that *WriteLine* includes a line termination.

**Q. When using <FSO>, what is a method available for checking the existence of a file?**

**A.** To check for the existence of a file, you need to use the *FileExists* method.

**Q.** **File attributes are stored in what type of a configuration?**

**A.** File attributes are stored in a bitmask type of construction.

**Q.** **What effect does the storage mechanism used by file attributes have on your ability to successfully query the attributes?**

**A.** Because the file attributes are stored in a bitmask type of construction, you have to use *And* to test for their existence and *Xor* to set them.

**Q.** **What is the difference between a file property and a file attribute?**

**A.** A file attribute is an item such as read-only, hidden, system, and archive. A file property describes aspects of the file such as when it was created, when it was last accessed, when it was modified, its path, its size, and its type.

**Q.** **To enumerate a list of files in a folder, what type of construction is required?**

**A.** To enumerate a list of files in a folder, you must create some kind of a collection and iterate through it by using a construction like a *For Each...Next* loop.

# On Your Own

# Lab 12 Creating Files

In this lab, you will practice creating files. The result of this practice is essentially a code block that you can employ in other scripts to write information to a file instead of merely echoing it to the screen.

1. Open Notepad.exe.

2. Use *Option Explicit* and declare the following variables: *logfile*, *objFSO*, and *objFile*.

3. Create an assignment for the variable *logfile* that will hold the name and path of your log file. The code will look like the following:

```
LogFile = "C:\FSO\fso.txt"
```

4. Open Windows Explorer and create a folder called FSO and a text file called Fso.txt on your C drive.

5. Create a constant called *ForWriting* and set it equal to *2*.

6. Use *CreateObject* to create an instance of the *FileSystemObject*. Set it equal to a variable called *objFSO*. Your code will look like the following:

```
Set objFSO = CreateObject("Scripting.FileSystemObject")
```

7. Use the *OpenTextFile* method of *objFSO* to open your log file for writing. Set it equal to a variable called *objFile*. Your code will look like the following:

```
Set objFile = objFSO.OpenTextFile(LogFile, ForWriting)
```

8. Use the *WriteLine* method and the *Now* function to write a line to a text file called Fso.txt that indicates you are beginning your logging. The code will look like the following:

```
objFile.WriteLine "beginning logging " & Now
```

9. Use the *WriteLine* method and the *Now* function to write a line to the text file called Fso.txt that indicates your process is continuing. Your code will look similar to this line:

```
objFile.WriteLine "working on process " & Now
```

10. Use the *WriteLine* method and the *Now* function to indicate the logging is complete. Your code will look like the following:

```
objFile.WriteLine "Logging completed at " & Now
```

11. Use the *Close* command to close out your log file. The code will look like the following:

```
objFile.Close
```

12. Add remarks to each of the variables (*logfile*, *objFSO*, and *objFile*) that were added in step 2 to indicate their use in the script. Here is an example:

```
Dim logfile ' holds path to the log file
Dim objFSO ' holds connection to the fileSystemObject
Dim objFile 'used by OpenTextFile command to allow writing to file
```

13. Do not delete the folder or the file because you will use them in the next lab.

# Lab 13 Creating a Log File

In this lab, you are going to modify the script created in Lab 12 to check for the existence of the log file. If the file exists, you will overwrite it. If it does not exist, you will create it.

1. Open Notepad.exe.

2. Use *Option Explicit* and declare the following variables: *LogFile*, *objFSO*, and *objFile*.

3. Create an assignment for the variable *logfile* that will hold the name and path of your log file. The code will look like the following:

```
LogFile = "C:\FSO\fso.txt"
```

4. Use Windows Explorer and create a folder called FSO and a text file called Fso.txt on your C drive.

5. Create a constant called *ForWriting* and set it equal to *2*.

6. Create a constant called *ForAppending* and set it equal to *8*.

7. Use *CreateObject* to create an instance of *FileSystemObject*. Set it equal to a variable called *objFSO*. Your code will look the following:

```
Set objFSO = CreateObject("Scripting.FileSystemObject")
```

8. Use an *If…Then…Else* loop to implement the *FileExists* method of *FileSystemObject*. In this loop, test for the existence of *LogFile*. If the *LogFile* exists, append to it a line of text that indicates you appended to it, and use the *Now* function so that you know when it ran. Your code will look like the following:

```
If objFSO.FileExists(LogFile) Then
    Set objFile = objFSO.OpenTextFile(LogFile, ForAppending)
    objFile.Write "appending " & Now
Else
```

9. If the file does not exist, use the *CreateTextFile* command to create the log file. Assign the new file to the variable *objFile*. Your code will look like the following:

```
Set objFile = objFSO.CreateTextFile(LogFile)
```

10. Use the *Close* method to close the *LogFile* variable you just created. The code will look like the following:

```
objFile.Close
```

11. Use the *OpenTextFile* method to open the *LogFile* variable for writing. Set this equal to *objFile*. The following code illustrates this:

```
Set objFile = objFSO.OpenTextFile(LogFile, ForWriting)
```

12. Use the *Write* method of *objFile* to write to the *LogFile* variable. Use the *Now* function to write the date and time this occurred. Use the following code as an example:

```
objfile.write "writing to new file " & Now
```

13. End the *If* loop. Use *End If* to do this.

14. Close the log file. Use *objFile.Close* for this purpose.

# 7  Fun with Folders

In this chapter, you look at folders. Building on your work in Chapter 6, "Working with the File System," you take the next step toward writing bulletproof scripts that examine the environment into which they are thrust, check for the existence of files and folders, and create what is needed when the requisite materials are absent. When you finish this chapter, you'll be able to create folders, delete folders, and copy folders all from within a single VBScript. This ability in turn leads to greater network uptime, because you eradicate the various avenues of confusion.

## Before You Begin

**To work through the material presented in this chapter, you need to be familiar with the following concepts from earlier chapters:**

- Utilizing the *FileSystemObject*

- Using the *For Each...Next* construction

- Implementing constants

- Applying *Select Case* constructions

**After completing this chapter you will be familiar with the following:**

- How to use the *FileSystemObject* class to create folders

- How to use the *FileSystemObject* class to list folders

- How to use the *FileSystemObject* class to delete folders

- How to use the *FileSystemObject* class to verify the existence of folders

## Working with Folders

In your day-to-day life as a network administrator, you must create folders hundreds of times if for no other reason than to hold a bunch of files. In my life as a consultant, I am constantly creating folders that hold project data for my clients. During the year I wrote this book, I had to create more than two dozen folders to organize the support materials, labs, and scripts so that I could keep track of them and maintain versioning information.

---

**Just the Steps**

▶ **To create a folder**

1. Create a file system object by using *CreateObject*.

2. Use the *CreateFolder* command to create the folder.

---

## Creating the Basic Folder

Creating your basic folder requires only two lines of code. The first line of code creates an instance of the *FileSystemObject* class by using the *CreateObject* method. Set the handle returned by *CreateObject* to a variable, which is used in turn to invoke the *CreateFolder* method of *FileSystemObject*. The only items required by *CreateFolder* are the path and name of the folder to be created. This process is illustrated in the following code:

```
Set objFSO = CreateObject("Scripting.FileSystemObject")
Set objFolder = objFSO.CreateFolder("c:\fso")
```

Suppose you need to create some folders for a number of temporary users. You decide to call the users tempUser1 through tempUser10. It would actually take a while to create these folders for the users. However, by making some changes to the CreateBasic-Folder.vbs script, you can easily accomplish this task. The revised script, called CreateMultiFolders.vbs, follows:

```
Option Explicit
Dim numFolders
Dim folderPath
Dim folderPrefix
Dim objFSO
Dim objFolder
Dim i

numFolders = 10
folderPath = "C:\"
folderPrefix = "TempUser"

For i = 1 To numFolders
    Set objFSO = CreateObject("Scripting.FileSystemObject")
    Set objFolder = objFSO.CreateFolder(folderPath & folderPreFix & i)
Next
WScript.Echo(i - 1 & " folders created")
```

**Caution** FSO will not create a folder unless its parent folder already exists. Thus, an attempt to create C:\tmp\tmpusers\tmpuser1 will fail unless C:\tmp\tmpusers already exists.

## Header Information

The Header information section of CreateMultiFolder.vbs begins with *Option Explicit* to ensure that no variables are misspelled or mistakenly introduced. You then declare six variables that are used in the script. The first variable, *numFolders*, holds the number of folders you want to create. The next variable, *folderPath*, points to the location in which you will create the folders. In this instance, you are going to create 10 folders off the root of the C drive, but these values aren't assigned until the Reference section. The next variable is *folderPrefix*. In this script, you assign a word or a set of characters that VBScript will use to begin the creation of the folders. The beauty of this arrangement is that you can later change the prefix easily. The variable *objFSO* holds the connection to *FileSystemObject*, and *objFolder* holds the handle to the *CreateFolder* command. The last variable declared is *i*, which is used simply as a counter.

As you can see, we did *not* use *On Error Resume Next*. When actually modifying or moving data, it is a good idea to allow errors to cause the script to fail so that data is not harmed if something goes wrong.

## Reference Information

The Reference information section of the script assigns values to some of the variables declared in the Header information section. *NumFolders* holds the number of folders you want to create. *FolderPath* is used by the *CreateFolder* command when it comes time to create the folders. *FolderPrefix* is set to *TempUser*, which is the folder prefix you will use for each folder that gets created.

## Worker Information

The Worker information section of the script begins with a *For...Next* loop. In this section we use the counter *i* to keep track of how many folders you want to create. The number of folders created is stored in the value *numFolders*. At any given time, you have created *i* number of folders. This counting continues for each number between *1* and *numFolders* (inclusive).

On the second line of the Worker information section of the script, you use the *Create-Object* command to create an instance of the *FileSystemObject*. This line is exactly the same as all the scripts written in Chapter 6. In every situation in which you must create an instance of the *FileSystemObject* class, the syntax will be exactly the same: *Create-Object("Scripting.FileSystemObject")*. In most of your scripts, you'll set the handle to *FileSystemObject* equal to *objFSO* (although the variable can be named anything).

The third line of the Worker information section of the CreateMultiFolder.vbs script is used to actually create the folders. Note the syntax of this command:

```
CreateFolder (folderPath)
```

In the script, you concatenate *folderPath* with *folderPrefix* and a counter number. This enables you to reuse the script for a multitude of purposes. In our example, you'll create 10 folders, named TempUser1 through TempUser10. You could just as easily change *folderPrefix* to *ch* and then create folders labeled ch1 though ch10. In a school setting, you might want to change *folderPrefix* to *student*, and thus create folders labeled student1 through student10. If you change the value of *i*, you can create 10,000 or more folders just as easily as you can create 10. As you can see, it is really easy to create folders using the *FileSystemObject* class. It can also shave hours off of lengthy setup procedures. The best thing, however, is that once the script is written and tested, you get repeatable results. It is done right every single time.

```
For i = 1 To numFolders
    Set objFSO = CreateObject("Scripting.FileSystemObject")
    Set objFolder = objFSO.CreateFolder(folderPath & folderPreFix & i)
Next
```

## Output Information

After you create the folders, you want confirmation that the task completed successfully. In this script, you use *WScript.Echo* to let you know that the script completed successfully. The reason you need to use *i-1* in our count is that the value of *i* gets incremented prior to the *Echo* command. This is shown in the following code:

```
WScript.Echo(i - 1 & " folders created")
```

> **Quick Check**
>
> **Q.  What is required to create a folder?**
>
> **A.**  A connection to *FileSystemObject* is required.
>
> **Q.  Which command is used to create a folder?**
>
> **A.**  The *CreateFolder* command is used to create a folder.

# Automatic Cleanup

One cool way to use the script for creating folders is to reuse it and modify it to delete folders. The idea here is that when you use scripts to create folders and then use them to delete folders, you have basically enabled automatic cleanup after your operations are complete.

> **Just the Steps**
>
> ▶ **To delete a folder**
>
> **1.** Implement *FileSystemObject* by using *CreateObject*.
>
> **2.** Use the *DeleteFolder* command to delete the folder.

# Deleting a Folder

Deleting a folder requires a connection to *FileSystemObject*. Once the connection to *FileSystemObject* is established, you use the *DeleteFolder* command to delete the folder. This is illustrated in the following script, DeleteBasicFolder.vbs. Notice that the big difference between creating a folder and deleting a folder is that the line in which the folder is deleted does not begin with *Set*. Rather than include *Set*, you simply include *objFSO* with the *DeleteFolder* command and then the path to the folder you will delete.

```
Set objFSO = CreateObject("Scripting.FileSystemObject")
objFSO.DeleteFolder("c:\fso")
```

# Deleting Multiple Folders

It is just as easy to delete multiple folders as a single folder because the syntax is the same: make a connection to *FileSystemObject*, and then call the *DeleteFolder* method. In the DeleteMultiFolders.vbs script that follows, to make the script clean up after itself, you had to make only three changes to CreateMultiFolders.vbs. Imagine how easy it would be to run CreateMultiFolders.vbs when your school year begins—and then when the school year ends, run DeleteMultiFolders.vbs with three minor modifications. What are the modifications? There are no modifications in either the Header information or the Reference information section of the script. In the Worker information section of the script, you delete *"Set objFolder = "* and then change *CreateFolder* to *DeleteFolder*. In the Output information section of the script, you change *folders created* to read *folders deleted*.

```
Option Explicit
Dim numFolders
Dim folderPath
Dim folderPrefix
Dim objFSO
Dim objFolder
Dim i

numFolders = 10
folderPath = "C:\"
folderPrefix = "TempUser"

For i = 1 To numFolders
Set objFSO = CreateObject("Scripting.FileSystemObject")
```

```
objFSO.DeleteFolder(folderPath & folderPreFix & i)
Next
WScript.Echo(i - 1 & " folders deleted")
```

---

**Quick Check**

- **Q. To delete a folder, what two components are required?**
- **A.** You need a connection to *FileSystemObject*, and you need to use the *Delete-Folder* method.

- **Q. What is the nice aspect of deleting folders programmatically?**
- **A.** The nice aspect of deleting folders programmatically is that you can do so by easily modifying the script used to create the folders.

- **Q. What are two situations in which creating folders and deleting folders programmatically would be useful?**
- **A.** Creating folders programmatically is useful for schools that need to create a lot of student home folders at the beginning of the school year and then delete them at the end of the year. The same technique is useful for companies when they bring in temporary workers.

---

# Binding to Folders

To gain information about the properties or attributes of a folder, you must first bind to the folder. Because the File System Object represents folders as COM (Component Object Model) objects, you must create a reference to them prior to connecting to them—that is, you must *bind* to them. You already know that to create or delete a folder, you have to create an instance of *FileSystemObject*. After you do that, you use the *GetFolder* method to connect to the folder.

---

**Just the Steps**

▶ **To bind to a folder**

1. Implement the *FileSystemObject* by using *CreateObject*.
2. Specify the path to the folder.
3. Use the *Set* keyword to assign the path to a variable.

---

In the following script, you implement *FileSystemObject* by using *CreateObject*. Next, you use the *GetFolder* method to bind to the folder called fso found in the C drive.

```
Set objFSO = CreateObject("Scripting.filesystemobject")
Set objFolder = objFSO.getfolder("c:\fso")
WScript.Echo("folder is bound")
```

## Does the Folder Exist?

Binding to a folder in and of itself is rather boring, but what if the folder does not exist? If you try to bind to a folder that does not exist, you generate an error message, and your script might fail. The "path not found" error can be prevented from occurring by using the *FolderExists* method. In the CreateBasicFolder_checkFirst.vbs script, you check for the existence of a folder prior to creating a new one.

By incorporating the *FolderExists* method into the script to create new folders, you gain the ability to delete the previous folder prior to creating a new one. The scenario for this would be creating new student folders at the beginning of a new school year. In addition, this approach could be used to create a folder for logging on a workstation. If a previous logging folder was found, that folder could be deleted to make room for a new folder. If you don't want to delete the folder, if that folder exists, you simply omit the *DeleteFolder* command from the script and modify the message displayed to the user.

```
Set objFSO = CreateObject("Scripting.FileSystemObject")
If objFSO.FolderExists ("C:\fso") Then
    WScript.Echo("folder exists and will be deleted")
    objFSO.DeleteFolder ("C:\fso")
    WScript.Echo("clean folder created")
    Set objFolder = objFSO.CreateFolder("c:\fso")
Else
    WScript.Echo("folder does not exist and will be created")
    Set objFolder = objFSO.CreateFolder("c:\fso")
End if
```

# Copying Folders

Copying folders is a fundamental task in network administration. It is important for backups and for ease of management. Often the suave network administrator consolidates files and folders prior to backing them up. This allows for both a more accurate backup, and in many instances a quicker backup. In many organizations, the so-called backup window is nearly closed, and getting everything backed up during the time allotted is a constant struggle. Consolidating folders can help with that problem.

You use the *CopyFolder* method of *FileSystemObject* to copy folders. It is important to realize that this method also copies subfolders (even empty ones). The syntax of the *CopyFolder* method follows:

| Command | Required | Required | Optional |
| --- | --- | --- | --- |
| *CopyFolder* | Source folder | Destination folder | *overwrite* |

> **Tip**    Both the source folder and the destination folder can be specified as either a local path or a UNC (Universal Naming Convention) path. The *overwrite* parameter is optional and will overwrite the destination folder if it is set to *True*.

In the following script, you copy a folder called fso that resides on the C drive to a folder called fso1 on the C drive. It is important to note that the folder does not need to exist in order for the copy process to succeed.

```
Set objFSO = CreateObject ("scripting.fileSystemObject")
objFSO.CopyFolder "c:\fso","C:\fso1"
```

You can make the script a little easier to use by creating variables to hold both the source and the destination folders. In the next script, CopyFolderExtended.vbs, you do exactly that. In addition, you create a constant called *overwriteFiles* that you set to *True*. Note that in this next script, the destination folder, called *dFolder*, is located on a network share. The CopyFolderExtended.vbs script could be used by a network administrator to copy user data from the local machine to a network drive for consolidated backup. One bad aspect of the *CopyFolder* command is that it does not indicate that it is working or that it is done. To give yourself a little bit more information, you use the *Now* command and *WScript.Echo* to indicate when the command begins. In addition, after the copy operation is complete, you receive another echo with the statement that the copy ended and the time.

```
Const OverWriteFiles = True
WScript.Echo(" beginning copy " & Now)
sFolder = "C:\Documents and Settings"
dFolder = "\\s2\fileBu"

Set objFSO = CreateObject ("scripting.fileSystemObject")
objFSO.CopyFolder sFolder, dFolder , OverWriteFiles
WScript.Echo("ending copy " & Now)
```

## Moving On Up

Copying folders is a very safe operation because nothing happens to the original data. Copy operations are often used for presenting a consolidated view of data (such as copying log files) or for creating redundant data for backup purposes (as in the case of VBScript book manuscripts). Moving folders, on the other hand, can be used to free up disk space, or can be used simply because two copies of the data are neither required nor desired. If a copy operation fails halfway through, you simply end up with an extra copy of half your data. If, on the other hand, a move operation fails halfway through, to have even one complete set of information, you have to go to the destination machine and move your data back. As a result, with important data, I always copy, verify, and then delete. For stuff I am not concerned about, I perform a move.

To perform a move operation, use the *MoveFolder* method of *FileSystemObject*. The next script you look at, MoveFolder.vbs, illustrates the *MoveFolder* method. Unlike the *CopyFolder* method, *MoveFolder* has only two parameters: the source and the destination. The *overwrite* parameter, which enables overwriting an existing folder during a move operation, is not implemented. It's common to move folders between drives, but you can also use the *MoveFolder* method to move folders on the same drive, and in effect, you get the ability to rename a folder. In MoveFolder.vbs, you do exactly that. You begin with a source folder called c:\fso, and the destination folder is c:\fso1. The *MoveFolder* operation deletes the old folder, and once the operation completes, it works just like a rename operation.

```
Set objFSO = CreateObject ("scripting.fileSystemObject")
objFSO.MoveFolder "c:\fso","c:\fso1"
```

# Summary

In this chapter, you examined working with folders. You began by examining the importance of *FileSystemObject* to give you a handle to talk to the file system. After you established the handle, you learned to use the *CreateFolder* method to create folders. To delete folders, you simply use the *DeleteFolder* method. Errors can be avoided by calling the *FolderExists* method prior to either deleting a folder or creating a folder.

# Quiz Yourself

**Q.  To prevent errors when either creating or deleting folders, what should you do prior to executing the command?**

**A.**  You should always check for the existence of the folder prior to trying to either delete or create the folder. To do this, use the *FolderExists* command inside an *If...Then...Else* construction.

**Q.  What is used to bind to a folder?**

**A.**  To bind to a folder, you use the *GetFolder* method.

**Q.  Why do you need to bind to a folder?**

**A.**  You must bind to a folder because folders are COM objects, and prior to accessing the properties of the folder, you need an object reference. Creating this reference is called binding.

**Q.  What command is used to create a folder?**

**A.**  The *CreateFolder* command is used to create a folder.

**Q.  What command is used to delete a folder?**

**A.**  The *DeleteFolder* command is used to delete a folder.

> **Q.** What is the main difference between the way *DeleteFolder* is used and the way *Create-Folder* is used?
>
> **A.** When you use *DeleteFolder*, you do not begin the line with the *Set* command. With *CreateFolder*, you begin the line with a *Set* command.

# On Your Own

# Lab 14 Creating Folders

In this lab, you are going to practice creating folders. The result of this practice will be a script that can be used for creating multiple folders for a variety of occasions.

1. Open Notepad.exe.

2. At the top of the script, set *Option Explicit*.

3. Declare variables for the following: *numFolders, folderPath, folderPrefix, objFSO, objFolder*, and *i*. The Header section of your script will look like the following:

```
Option Explicit
Dim numFolders
Dim folderPath
Dim folderPrefix
Dim objFSO
Dim objFolder
Dim i
```

4. Assign *numFolders* to be equal to *10*.

5. Assign *folderPath* to be "C:\" or some other local drive on your machine. (Note that the quotation marks are required.)

6. Assign *folderPrefix* to be equal to "Student". (The quotation marks are required.) The Reference section of the script will look like the following:

```
numFolders = 10
folderPath = "C:\"
folderPrefix = "Student"
```

7. Implement a *For...Next* loop that begins like this:

```
For i = 1 To numFolders
```

8. Implement *FileSystemObject* and set it equal to *objFSO*. The code will look like the following:

```
Set objFSO = CreateObject("Scripting.FileSystemObject")
```

9. Use the *FolderExists* method to check for the existence of the folder prior to creating it. If the folder exists, echo out the path and state that it is not created. The code for this will look like the following:

```
If objFSO.FolderExists(folderPath & folderPrefix & i) Then
    WScript.Echo(folderPath & folderPrefix & i & " exists." _
        & " folder not created")
```

**10.** If the folder does not exist, you will need to create it. To do this, build the path and the prefix, and increment the *i* counter. The code will look like the following:

```
Else
    Set objFolder = objFSO.CreateFolder(folderPath & folderPreFix & i)
```

**11.** Echo out the folder path, prefix, and counter, and state that the folder was created. The code will look like the following:

```
WScript.Echo(folderPath & folderPrefix & i & " folder created")
```

**12.** Use *End If* to close out the *If...Then* section.

**13.** Use *Next* to close out the *For...Next* loop.

The completed code follows:

```
Option Explicit
Dim numFolders
Dim folderPath
Dim folderPrefix
Dim objFSO
Dim objFolder
Dim i
numFolders = 10
folderPath = "C:\"
folderPrefix = "Student"

For i = 1 To numFolders
    Set objFSO = CreateObject("Scripting.FileSystemObject")
    If objFSO.FolderExists(folderPath & folderPrefix & i) Then
        WScript.Echo(folderPath & folderPrefix & i & " exists." _
            & " folder not created")
    Else
        Set objFolder = objFSO.CreateFolder(folderPath & folderPreFix & i)
        WScript.Echo(folderPath & folderPrefix & i & " folder created")
    End If
Next
```

# Lab 15 Deleting Folders

In this lab, you are going to delete the folders created in Lab 14.

**1.** Open Notepad.exe.

**2.** Open your solution to Lab 14, or open **Lab14Solution.vbs** from the companion CD.

**3.** Copy all the Header information section from Lab 14. The code will look like the following:

```
Option Explicit
Dim numFolders
Dim folderPath
Dim folderPrefix
Dim objFSO
Dim objFolder
Dim i
```

4. Copy the Reference section of the script from Lab 14. The code will look like the following:

```
numFolders = 10
folderPath = "C:\"
folderPrefix = "Student"
```

5. Implement a *For...Next* loop, using the variable *i* that goes to the variable *numFolders*. You can copy the following line from Lab 14 as well:

```
For i = 1 To numFolders
```

6. Create an instance of *FileSystemObject*. Use the *CreateObject* method, and assign it to the variable *objFSO*. This line is also in Lab 14 and looks like the following:

```
Set objFSO = CreateObject("Scripting.FileSystemObject")
```

7. Use an *If...Then* loop that incorporates the *folderExists* method to determine whether the folder is present prior to deleting it. If the folder does exist, echo out the path. This code is present in Lab 14 and looks like the following:

```
If objFSO.FolderExists(folderPath & folderPrefix & i) Then
    WScript.Echo(folderPath & folderPrefix & i & " exists.")
```

8. Use the *DeleteFolder* method of *FileSystemObject* to delete the folder if it is present on the system. You will need to build the name of the folder by using the *folderPath* variable, *folderPrefix*, and the counter *i*. The code to do this looks like the following:

```
    objFSO.DeleteFolder(folderPath & folderPrefix & i)
```

9. Use *WScript.Echo* to echo out that the folder was deleted, as illustrated here:

```
    WScript.Echo(folderPath & folderPrefix & i & " was deleted")
```

10. The *Else* clause implements a simple *WScript.Echo* command that indicates the folder does not exist on the system. The code for this looks like the following:

```
Else
    WScript.Echo(folderPath & folderPrefix & i & " does not exist")
```

11. End your *If...Then* loop by using *End If*.

12. End the *For...Next* loop by using *Next*.

Completed code for Lab 15 looks like the following:

```
Option Explicit
Dim numFolders
Dim folderPath
Dim folderPrefix
Dim objFSO
Dim objFolder
Dim i

numFolders = 10
folderPath = "C:\"
folderPrefix = "Student"

For i = 1 To numFolders
    Set objFSO = CreateObject("Scripting.FileSystemObject")
    If objFSO.FolderExists(folderPath & folderPrefix & i) Then
        WScript.Echo(folderPath & folderPrefix & i & " exists.")
        objFSO.DeleteFolder(folderPath & folderPrefix & i)
        WScript.Echo(folderPath & folderPrefix & i & " was deleted")
    Else
        WScript.Echo(folderPath & folderPrefix & i & " does not exist")
    End If
Next
```

# 8 Why Windows Management Instrumentation?

The discussion in the first few chapters of our book focused on what you can do with Microsoft Visual Basic Script (VBScript). From a network management perspective, many useful tasks can be accomplished using just VBScript, but to truly begin to unleash the power of scripting, you need to bring in additional tools. This is where Windows Management Instrumentation (WMI) comes into play. WMI was designed to provide access to many powerful ways of managing Microsoft Windows systems. In Windows Server 2003, WMI was expanded to include management of many aspects of server operations, including both configuration and reporting capabilities of nearly every facet of the server. Some of the tasks you can perform with WMI follow:

- Report on drive configuration
- Report on available memory, both physical and virtual
- Back up the event log
- Modify the registry
- Schedule tasks
- Share folders
- Switch from a static to a dynamic IP address

## Before You Begin

**The material presented in this chapter assumes you are familiar with the following concepts from earlier chapters:**

- Implementing a dictionary
- Implementing the *For...Next* construction
- Implementing *Select Case* constructions

**After completing this chapter you will be familiar with the following:**

- Connecting to the WMI provider
- Navigating the WMI namespace
- Running queries to retrieve information from WMI
- Sending the output of a WMI query to a dictionary

# What Is WMI?

WMI is sometimes referred to as a *hierarchical namespace*, in which the layers build upon one another like an LDAP directory used in Active Directory, or the file system structure on your hard disk drive. Although it is true that WMI is a hierarchical namespace, the term doesn't really convey the richness of WMI. The WMI model has three sections that you need to be aware of:

- **WMI resources**   Resources include anything that can be accessed by using WMI—the file system, networked components, event logs, files, folders, disks, Active Directory, and so on.

- **WMI infrastructure**   The infrastructure comprises three parts: the WMI service, the WMI repository, and the WMI providers. Of these parts, WMI providers are most important because they provide the means for WMI to gather needed information.

- **WMI consumers**   A consumer "consumes" the data from WMI. A consumer can be a VBScript, an enterprise management software package, or some other tool or utility that executes WMI queries.

## An Object in Any Other Namespace...

Let's go back to the idea of a namespace introduced earlier in this chapter. You can think of a *namespace* as a way to organize or collect data related to similar items. Visualize an old-fashioned filing cabinet. Each drawer can represent a particular namespace. Inside this drawer are hanging folders that collect information related to a subset of what the drawer actually holds. For example, at home in my filing cabinet, I have a drawer reserved for information related to my woodworking tools. Inside this particular drawer are hanging folders for my table saw, my planer, my joiner, my dust collector, and so on. In the folder for the table saw is information about the motor, the blades, and the various accessories I purchased for the saw (such as an over-arm blade guard).

The WMI namespace is organized in a similar fashion. (However, you will not necessarily find a table saw folder.) Rather, namespaces contain objects, and these objects contain properties you can manipulate (and as Will Rogers once said, "manipulation is good"). Let's use a WMI script, ListWmiNameSpaces.vbs, to illustrate just how the WMI namespace is organized.

```
strComputer = "."

Set objSWbemServices = GetObject("winmgmts:\\" & strComputer & "\root")
Set colNameSpaces = objSWbemServices.InstancesOf("__NAMESPACE")

For Each objNameSpace In colNameSpaces
    WScript.Echo objNameSpace.Name
Next
```

On a Windows 2003 Server, the results would look like the following:

```
SECURITY
perfmon
RSOP
Cli
MSCluster
WMI
CIMV2
MicrosoftActiveDirectory
Policy
MicrosoftDNS
MicrosoftNLB
Microsoft
DEFAULT
directory
subscription
```

So what does all this mean, you ask? It means that on a Windows 2003 server, there are more than a dozen different namespaces from which you could pull information about our server. Understanding that the different namespaces exist is the first step to being able to navigate in WMI to find the information you need. Often, students and people new to VBScript work on a WMI script to make the script perform a certain action, which is a great way to learn scripting. However, what they often do not know is which namespace they need to connect to so that they can accomplish their task. When I tell them which namespace to work with, they sometimes reply, "It is fine for you, but how do I know that the such and such namespace even exists?" By using the ListWMInamespaces.vbs script, you can easily generate a list of namespaces installed on a particular machine, and armed with that information, search on MSDN to see what information it is able to provide.

Let's discuss the preceding script, ListWmiNameSpace.vbs, because it's similar to many other WMI scripts. The first line sets the variable *strComputer* equal to *"."*. This construction (period in quotation marks) means that the script will operate against this computer only. The period therefore is a wildcard character that allows the script to run locally on many computers without you needing to define or change the name included in the script.

The next line of the script is used to define the variable *objsWebmServices* and set it equal to the handle that is returned by using the *getObject* method to connect to *WinMgmts* and access the root namespace on the local computer. (The connection string in WMI is sometimes referred to as a *moniker*. The word moniker comes from Gaelic and simply means nickname, or familiar name.) We will discuss the WMI moniker in much more detail in Chapter 9, "WMI Continued." These first two lines of the script can be reused time and again in many WMI scripts. In the third line of the script, you use the *Set* command to assign *colNameSpaces* to be equal to a collection represented by the instances of the command that query for the presence of the word "*_NameSpace*". The

Worker information section of the script simply uses a *For Each...Next* loop to iterate through the collection of namespaces returned by the query and to echo them out to the screen.

> **Tip** Although in the ListWMInamespaces.vbs script, I used all lowercase in code for the *win-mgmts* name. There really is no requirement for name case with this particular moniker, and in the Microsoft Platform SDK you will find nearly every possible combination: *winmgmts*, *WinM-mgmts*, *WINMGMTS*, and I bet even *winMgmts*.
>
> Keep in mind, however, that name case *does* matter with some monikers such as *"WinNT:"*.

## More Than Just a Name

Knowing the default namespaces gives some information, and though helpful, to better map out the WMI namespace, you'll want information about the subnamespaces as well. You'll need to implement a recursive query so that you can gain access to the subnamespace data. The next script, RecursiveListWmiNameSpace.vbs, is similar to ListWmiNameSpace.vbs except that it utilizes a subroutine to enable it to perform a re-entrant query. On some computers, this script might seem to perform a little slowly during the first running, so I included a *WScript.Echo (Now)* command at the beginning and at the end of the script. This allows the network administrator to determine how long the script takes to run.

As with the previous script, RecursiveListWmiNameSpace.vbs uses *strNameSpace* with a "." to indicate the script is run against the local computer. It then calls the subroutine named *EnumNameSpaces* and starts with the "root" namespace. Subroutines are discussed in detail in Chapter 15, "Subs and Other Round Things," but I wanted to use one in this script, because it adds a lot of power and flexibility.

> ### Subroutines
> Basically, a *subroutine* is a section of a script that you can get to from anywhere inside the script. All we need to do is call the subroutine by name to jump to a particular part of the script. You use a subroutine in this script rather than code that is sequential (as all our other scripts have used so far) because you need to execute the commands that make up the subroutine as a group. When you are finished, you exit out. You can easily identify a subroutine because it begins with the word *Sub* followed by the name of the subroutine, and it ends with the *end sub* command. When you exit a subroutine (via the *end sub* command), you go back to the line after the one that caused you to enter the subroutine.

Once you enter the subroutine, you echo *strNameSpace*, which on the first pass is simply the root. Next you use *GetObject* to make a connection to the WMI namespace that is identified by the subroutine *strNameSpace* argument. In the first pass, you are connected to the root. The subroutine then retrieves all namespaces that are immediately below the one it is currently connected to. You then use a *For Each...Next* construction to loop through all the namespaces below the currently connected one. In doing so, you also concatenate the names to provide a fully qualified name to the namespace. You take the newly constructed name, pass it to *EnumNameSpaces*, and work through the namespace one more time.

```
WScript.Echo(Now)
strComputer = "."
Call EnumNameSpaces("root")

Sub EnumNameSpaces(strNameSpace)
    WScript.Echo strNameSpace
    Set objSWbemServices = _
        GetObject("winmgmts:\\" & strComputer & "\" & strNameSpace)
    Set colNameSpaces = objSWbemServices.InstancesOf("__NAMESPACE")
    For Each objNameSpace In colNameSpaces
        Call EnumNameSpaces(strNameSpace & "\" & objNameSpace.Name)
    Next
End Sub
WScript.Echo("all done " & Now)
```

# Providers

Understanding the namespace assists the network administrator with judiciously applying WMI scripting to his or her network duties. However, as mentioned earlier, to access information via WMI, you must have access to a WMI provider. Once the provider is implemented, you can gain access to the information that is made available.

The following script, ListWmiProviders.vbs, enumerates all the WMI providers instrumented on the machine. This information can lead the network administrator to MSDN or some other place to find details about the methods supported by the provider.

```
strComputer = "."

Set objSWbemServices = _
    GetObject("winmgmts:\\" & strComputer & "\root\cimv2")
Set colWin32Providers = objSWbemServices.InstancesOf("__Win32Provider")

For Each objWin32Provider In colWin32Providers
    WScript.Echo objWin32Provider.Name
Next
```

When you run the script on Windows 2003 Server, you get the following output:

```
Win32_WIN32_TSLOGONSETTING_Prov
MS_NT_EVENTLOG_PROVIDER
Win32_WIN32_TSENVIRONMENTSETTING_Prov
SCM Event Provider
ProviderSubSystem
VolumeChangeEvents
NamedJobObjectLimitSettingProv
HiPerfCooker_v1
WMIPingProvider
Win32_WIN32_TSNETWORKADAPTERSETTING_Prov
SystemConfigurationChangeEvents
Win32_WIN32_TERMINALSERVICE_Prov
MSVDS__PROVIDER
Win32_WIN32_TSREMOTECONTROLSETTING_Prov
Win32_WIN32_TSNETWORKADAPTERLISTSETTING_Prov
Win32_WIN32_COMPUTERSYSTEMWINDOWSPRODUCTACTIVATIONSETTING_Prov
Win32_WIN32_TSSESSIONDIRECTORY_Prov
CmdTriggerConsumer
Standard Non-COM Event Provider
SessionProvider
WBEMCORE
RouteEventProvider
WhqlProvider
Win32_WIN32_TSSESSIONSETTING_Prov
Win32_WIN32_TERMINALTERMINALSETTING_Prov
Win32_WIN32_TSCLIENTSETTING_Prov
Win32_WIN32_TERMINALSERVICESETTING_Prov
WMI Kernel Trace Event Provider
Win32_WIN32_PROXY_Prov
NamedJobObjectProv
MS_Shutdown_Event_Provider
SECRCW32
Win32ClockProvider
MSVSS__PROVIDER
MS_Power_Management_Event_Provider
Win32_WIN32_WINDOWSPRODUCTACTIVATION_Prov
RouteProvider
Cimwin32A
Msft_ProviderSubSystem
Win32_WIN32_TERMINALSERVICETOSETTING_Prov
NamedJobObjectSecLimitSettingProv
Win32_WIN32_TSSESSIONDIRECTORYSETTING_Prov
Win32_WIN32_TSPERMISSIONSSETTING_Prov
Win32_WIN32_TSACCOUNT_Prov
Win32_WIN32_TERMINAL_Prov
DskQuotaProvider
Win32_WIN32_TSGENERALSETTING_Prov
CIMWin32
NamedJobObjectActgInfoProv
NT5_GenericPerfProvider_V1
WMI Self-Instrumentation Event Provider
DFSProvider
MS_NT_EVENTLOG_EVENT_PROVIDER
```

# Adding a Touch of Class

In addition to working with namespaces, the inquisitive network administrator will also want to explore the concept of classes. In WMI parlance, you have core classes and you have common classes. *Core classes* represent managed objects that apply to all areas of management. These classes provide a basic vocabulary for analyzing and describing managed systems. Two examples of core classes are parameters and the *systemSecurity* class. *Common classes* are extensions to the core classes and represent managed objects that apply to specific management areas. However, common classes are independent from a particular implementation or technology. The *CIM_Unitary-ComputerSystem* is an example of a common class. Core and common classes are not used as much by network administrators because they serve as templates from which other classes are derived. Therefore, most of the classes stored in *root\cimv2* are abstract classes and are used as templates. However, a few classes in *root\cimv2* are dynamic classes used to hold actual information. The important aspect to remember about *dynamic classes* is that instances of a dynamic class are generated by a provider and are therefore more likely to retrieve "live" data from the system.

A *property* in WMI is a value that is used to indicate a characteristic (something describable) about a class. A property has a name and a domain that is used to indicate the class that actually owns the property. Properties can be viewed in terms of a pair of functions: one to set the property value and another to retrieve the property value.

In addition to properties are methods. As you've learned in earlier chapters, a *method* answers the question "what does this thing do." In many cases, the answer is "well, it does nothing." However, the cool thing about WMI is that it's constantly evolving—and in Windows Server 2003, more methods have been added than ever before. Like a property, a method also has a name and a domain. And just like a property, the method's domain refers back to the owning class. One slightly confusing feature of a WMI method is that it can have an overriding relationship with a method from another class. Remember when I said that the domain points to the ownership of a method? Well, ownership can be overridden when the domain from the overridden method is a *SuperClass*. It gets even worse.

**Note**   Just because a class has a method does not guarantee that the method is implemented. You must verify that the implemented qualifier is attached to the method to ensure the method actually works. (You can do this by looking the method up in the Platform SDK. It will simply say "implemented.") This is the only way you can ensure that the implementation is actually available for the class. I will admit that I have actually wasted several hours trying to make a particular method work, only to find out it was not even implemented.

The following script, ListWmiClasses.vbs, returns a list of classes found in the *root\cimv2* namespace.

```
strComputer = "."
nSpace = "\root\cimv2"
Set objSWbemServices = _
    GetObject("winmgmts:\\" & strComputer & nSpace)
Set colClasses = objSWbemServices.SubclassesOf()

For Each objClass In colClasses
    WScript.Echo objClass.Path_.Path
Next
```

# Querying WMI

In most situations, when you use WMI, you are performing some sort of query. Even when you're going to set a particular property, you still need to execute a query to return a dataset that enables you to perform the configuration. (A *dataset* is the data that comes back to you as the result of a query, that is, it is a set of data.) In this section, you'll look at the methods used to query WMI.

---

**Just the Steps**

▶ **To query WMI**

1. Specify the computer name.
2. Define the namespace.
3. Connect to the provider using *GetObject*.
4. Issue the query.
5. Use *For Each...Next* to iterate through collection data.

---

One of the problems with Windows Server 2003 for the small to medium enterprise is Windows Server 2003 product activation. Although the larger customers have the advantage of "select" keys that automatically activate the product, smaller companies often are not aware of the advantages of volume licensing and as a result do not have access to these keys. In addition, I've seen larger customers that use the wrong key—you can easily forget to activate the copy of Windows Server 2003. Many customers like to monitor the newly built machine prior to actual activation because of the problems resulting from multiple activation requests. As is often the case with many IT departments, emergencies arise, and it is easy to forget to make the trek back to the server rooms to activate the machines. This is where the power of WMI scripting can come to the rescue. The following script uses the new *Win32_WindowsProductActivation* WMI class to determine the status of product activation:

```
Option Explicit
On Error Resume Next
dim strComputer
dim wmiNS
dim wmiQuery
dim objWMIService
dim colItems
Dim objItem

strComputer = "."
wmiNS = "\root\cimv2"
wmiQuery = "Select * from Win32_WindowsProductActivation"
Set objWMIService = GetObject("winmgmts:\\" & strComputer & wmiNS)
Set colItems = objWMIService.ExecQuery(wmiQuery)

For Each objItem In colItems
    WScript.Echo "ActivationRequired: " & objItem.ActivationRequired
    WScript.Echo "IsNotificationOn: " & objItem.IsNotificationOn
    WScript.Echo "ProductID: " & objItem.ProductID
    WScript.Echo "RemainingEvaluationPeriod: " & _
        objItem.RemainingEvaluationPeriod
    WScript.Echo "RemainingGracePeriod: " & objItem.RemainingGracePeriod
    WScript.Echo "ServerName: " & objItem.ServerName
Next
```

## Header Information

The Header information section of DisplayWPAstatus.vbs contains the two normal items, *Option Explicit* and *On Error Resume Next*. (If you are unfamiliar with these commands, refer to Chapter 1, "Starting from Scratch.") Next, you declare six variables to be used in this script. Because you are writing a WMI script, you make up some new variable names. Table 8-1 lists the variables and their intended use in this script.

**Table 8-1   Variables Used in DisplayWPAstatus.vbs**

| Variable name | Variable use |
| --- | --- |
| *strComputer* | Holds the name of the computer the query will target at run time |
| *wmiNS* | Holds the namespace that the WMI query will target |
| *wmiQuery* | Holds the WMI query |
| *objWMIService* | Holds the connection to the WMI service |
| *colItems* | Holds the collection of items returned by the WMI query |
| *objItem* | Holds the individual item from which the properties will be queried |

## Reference Information

The Reference information section of the script is used to assign value to some of the variables declared in the Header information section. The first variable used in the Reference information section is *strComputer*, whose value is set to *"."*. In WMI shorthand,

*"."* is used to mean "this computer only." So the WMI query will operate on *localhost*. The second variable assigned a value is *wmiNS*, which is used to hold the value of the WMI namespace you query. You could include the namespace and the query on the same line of the script; however, by breaking the namespace and the query out of the connection string, you make it easier to reuse the script. *WmiQuery* is the next variable, which receives the value of *"Select * from Win32_WindowsProductActivation."* You can easily change the query to ask for other information. You are asking for everything that is contained in the local computer from the *Win32_WindowsProduct-Activation* namespace.

You use the *Set* command to set *objWMIService* to the handle that is obtained by the *GetObject* command. The syntax for this command is very important because it is seminal to working with WMI. When making a connection using *winmgmts://*, the use of *winmgmts* is called a moniker. A *moniker* works in the same way that the phrase "abracadabra" used to work in the old movies. It's a shortcut that performs a lot of connection work in the background. Remember the magic phrase, because it will do much of the work for you, including opening the door to the storehouse of valuable WMI data. The last item in the Reference information section is the assignment of the variable *collItems* to the handle returned by the *ExecQuery* method. The Reference information section follows:

```
strComputer = "."
wmiNS = "\root\cimv2"
wmiQuery = "Select * from Win32_WindowsProductActivation"
Set objWMIService = GetObject("winmgmts:\\" & strComputer & wmiNS)
Set colItems = objWMIService.ExecQuery(wmiQuery)
```

## Worker and Output Information

The Worker information section is the part of the script that works through the collection of data returned and produces the WPA information. This section is always going to be customized for each WMI script you write, because each query or each provider used returns customized data.

Because WMI returns data in the form of a collection, you need to use a *For Each...Next* loop to iterate through the items in the collection. This loop is required—even when WMI returns only one item, WMI still returns that item in a collection. Your question at this point is probably "how do I know what to request from WMI?" I looked that up in the Platform SDK (Software Development Kit). (The Platform SDK contains tons of detailed information about the operating system and is downloadable for free from Microsoft.com. In addition to selecting the core SDK, you should also download the WMI SDK for Windows Server 2003.) By looking in the SDK for *Win32_WindowsProductActivation*, you learn that several fields are available as properties from which you can return information. The SDK also tells you that the fields are all read-only (which would prevent us from flipping the ActivationRequired field to false). The Worker and Output information section of this script follows:

```
For Each objItem In colItems
    WScript.Echo "ActivationRequired: " & objItem.ActivationRequired
    WScript.Echo "IsNotificationOn: " & objItem.IsNotificationOn
    WScript.Echo "ProductID: " & objItem.ProductID
    WScript.Echo "RemainingEvaluationPeriod: " & _
        objItem.RemainingEvaluationPeriod
    WScript.Echo "RemainingGracePeriod: " & objItem.RemainingGracePeriod
    WScript.Echo "ServerName: " & objItem.ServerName
Next
```

The most interesting information in *Win32_WindowsProductActivation* is listed in Table 8-2.

**Table 8-2   Properties of Win32_WindowsProductActivation**

| Property | Meaning |
|---|---|
| *ActivationRequired* | If *0*, activation is not required. If *1*, the system must be activated within the number of days indicated by the *RemainingGracePeriod* property. |
| *IsNotificationOn* | If *0*, notification reminders and the activation icon are disabled. If not equal to *0* and product activation is required, notification reminders (message balloons) are enabled, and the activation icon appears in the notification tray. |
| *ProductID* | A string of 20 characters separated by hyphens. This is the same product ID that is displayed on the General tab of the System Properties dialog box in Control Panel. |
| *RemainingEvaluationPeriod* | If beta or evaluation media, this returns the number of days remaining before expiration. If retail media, this field is set to the largest possible unsigned value. |
| *RemainingGracePeriod* | Numbers of days remaining before activation is required if *ActivationRequired* is equal to *1*. |
| *ServerName* | Name of the system being queried. This could also be the IP address of the system. |

# Summary

In this chapter, you looked at WMI on Windows Server 2003. You learned about the concept of the namespace and examined several of the default namespaces available in a default installation of Windows Server 2003. In addition, you looked at the concept of classes and how they are utilized within WMI. You examined the concept of providers and saw how they are used to enable WMI to access various parts of the information contained within the different namespaces. You learned about querying WMI and about the use of monikers to abstract some of the complexity of connecting to WMI.

# Quiz Yourself

**Q. What is the default WMI namespace on Windows Server 2003?**

**A.** The default WMI namespace on Windows Server 2003 actually depends on how you define *default*. Many of the WMI tools will connect to *root\cimv2*, which contains a lot of very useful information for managing Windows Server 2003. You could also say that root is the default namespace as well because it is at the top of the tree.

**Q. You want to find a class in WMI that will tell you how much memory is installed on a server. How do you go about finding this class?**

**A.** There are several approaches to this task. You could download the WMI SDK, which includes the WMI browser. After you launch the WMI browser, you could look around and see what you find. You could also do a search in the WMI SDK for the term "WMI memory," which would return the *Win32_PhysicalMemory* class, and from this class you could return several pieces of information about installed memory.

**Q. Why do many scripts set the computer variable equal to "."?**

**A.** When a script sets the computer variable equal to ".", the writer wants the script to run against the local machine.

**Q. What is a moniker?**

**A.** A moniker is a connection shortcut that hides much of the complexity of connecting to WMI from the scripter.

# On Your Own

# Lab 16 Retrieving Hotfix Information

In this lab, you use the *Win32_QuickFixEngineering* provider to retrieve information about hotfixes installed on your server. This lab incorporates techniques learned in earlier chapters into the information about WMI discussed in this chapter.

## Lab Instructions

**1.** Open Notepad.exe.

**2.** Turn on *Option Explicit* by typing **Option Explicit** on the first line of the script.

**3.** Declare variables to be used in the script. There are six variables to be used: *strComputer*, *objWmiService*, *wmiNS*, *wmiQuery*, *objItem*, and *colItems*.

**4.** Assign the value of "." to the variable *strComputer*. The code will look like the following:

```
strComputer = "."
```

5. Assign the value of *"\root\cimv2"* to the variable *wmiNS*. The code will look like the following:

```
wmiNS = "\root\cimv2"
```

6. Assign the query *"Select * from Win32_QuickFixEngineering"* to the variable *wmiQuery*. The code will look like the following:

```
wmiQuery = "Select * from Win32_QuickFixEngineering"
```

7. Use the *winmgmts* moniker and the variable *objWMIService* as well as the *GetObject* method to make a connection to WMI. Use the *strComputer* and the *wmiNS* variables to specify the computer and the namespace to use. The code will look like the following:

```
Set objWMIService = GetObject("winmgmts:\\" & strComputer & wmiNS)
```

8. Set the variable *colItems* to be equal to the connection that comes back from WMI when it executes the query defined by *wmiQuery*. Your code should look like the following:

```
Set colItems = objWMIService.ExecQuery(wmiQuery)
```

9. Use a *For Each...Next* construction to iterate through the collection called *colItems*. Assign the variable called *objItem* to each of the items returned from *colItems*. Your code should look like this:

```
For Each objItem In colItems
```

10. Use *WScript.Echo* to echo out items such as the caption, *CSName*, and description. You can copy the following items, or use the WMI SDK to look up *Win32_QuickFixEngineering* and choose items of interest to you.

```
WScript.Echo "Caption: " & objItem.Caption
WScript.Echo "CSName: " & objItem.CSName
WScript.Echo "Description: " & objItem.Description
WScript.Echo "FixComments: " & objItem.FixComments
WScript.Echo "HotFixID: " & objItem.HotFixID
WScript.Echo "InstallDate: " & objItem.InstallDate
WScript.Echo "InstalledBy: " & objItem.InstalledBy
WScript.Echo "InstalledOn: " & objItem.InstalledOn
WScript.Echo "Name: " & objItem.Name
WScript.Echo "ServicePackInEffect: " & objItem.ServicePackInEffect
WScript.Echo "Status: " & objItem.Status
```

11. Close out your *For Each...Next* loop with the *Next* command.

12. Save your file as **lab16.vbs**.

# Lab 17 Echoing the Time Zone

In this lab, you modify the script from Lab 16 so that it echoes out the time zone configured on the computer.

## Lab Instructions

1. Open Notepad.exe.

2. Open Lab16Solution.vbs, and save it as **lab17.vbs**.

3. Edit the *wmiQuery* so that it points to *Win32_TimeZone*. The code will look like the following:

   ```
   wmiQuery = "Select * from Win32_TimeZone"
   ```

4. Inside the *For Each objItem In colItems* loop, delete all but one of the *WScript.Echo* statements so that the code looks like the following:

   ```
   For Each objItem In colItems
       WScript.Echo "Caption: " & objItem.Caption
   Next
   ```

5. Save and run the file. You are now pointing to the Caption field of *Win32_TimeZone*. No further changes are required for this lab.

# 9 WMI Continued

In this chapter, you'll continue working with WMI. You'll build upon the concepts learned in Chapter 8, "Why Windows Management Instrumentation?" and see different ways to leverage your investment in WMI to assist in day-to-day network administrative tasks.

## Before You Begin

**To work through the material presented in this chapter, you need to be familiar with the following concepts from earlier chapters:**

- Connecting to the default WMI namespace
- Accessing properties of dynamic WMI classes
- Implementing the *For...Next* construction
- Implementing a WMI query

**After completing this chapter you will be familiar with the following:**

- Alternative ways of configuring the WMI moniker
- Querying WMI
- Setting impersonation levels
- Defining the WMI object path
- Navigating the WMI namespace

## Alternate Ways of Configuring the WMI Moniker

In this section, you are going to look at different ways of constructing the WMI moniker string. There are essentially three parts to the moniker. Of the three parts, only one is mandatory. These parts are listed here:

- The prefix *WinMgmts:* (This is the mandatory part.)
- A security settings component
- A WMI object path component

> **Just the Steps**
>
> ▶ **To construct the moniker**
>
> **1.** Use the prefix *WinMgmts:*.
>
> **2.** Define the security settings component, if desired.
>
> **3.** Specify the WMI object path component, if desired.

# Accepting Defaults

Several fields are optional in constructing a finely tuned WMI moniker, and there are clearly defined defaults for those optional fields. The defaults are stored in the following registry location: HKEY_LOCAL_MACHINE\SOFTWARE\Microsoft\WBEM\Scripting. There are two keys: impersonation level and default namespace. Impersonation level is set to a default of *3*, which means that WMI impersonates the logged-on user. The default namespace is set to *root\cimv2*. In reality, these are pretty good defaults. The default computer is the local machine, so you don't need to specify the computer name when you're simply running against the local machine. All this means is that you can simplify your connection string to WMI. A default moniker would just be *"winmgmts:\\"*. When using the *getObject* method, you can use the default connection string as follows:

```
Set objWMIService = GetObject("winmgmts:\\")
```

By using a default moniker and omitting the Header information, you come up with a rather lean script. You can still shorten it even more, as you'll learn in a bit, but the SmallBIOS.vbs script that follows is a shorter script than the DetermineBIOS.vbs script, which is included on the companion CD-ROM. (The Header information of Small-BIOS.vbs is omitted.)

```
wmiQuery = "Select * from Win32_BIOS"

Set objWMIService = GetObject("winmgmts:\\")
Set colItems = objWMIService.ExecQuery(wmiQuery)

For Each objItem in colItems
    strBIOSVersion = Join(objItem.BIOSVersion, ",")
    WScript.Echo "BIOSVersion: " & strBIOSVersion
    WScript.Echo ": " & objItem.caption
    WScript.Echo ": " & objItem.releaseDate
Next
```

## Reference Information

The Reference information section of the script comprises three lines. Two of the lines would be consistent among many WMI scripts; the first line in the Reference information section would change depending upon what query you wanted to run. For the script to return information about the BIOS on the server, you need to connect to the *Win32_BIOS* namespace. Your WMI query does nothing fancy—it simply tells WMI that you want to select everything contained in the *Win32_ BIOS* namespace. The actual query looks like the following:

```
wmiQuery = "Select * from Win32_BIOS"
```

The two standard lines in the Reference section are the connection to WMI that uses the *GetObject* method and the moniker. The short version of the moniker follows:

```
Set objWMIService = GetObject("winmgmts:\\")
```

Once you have the connection into WMI, you can begin to perform tasks with it. In this case, you want to issue a query and hold the results of that query in a variable called *collItems*. So you use the following line:

```
Set collItems = objWMIService.ExecQuery(wmiQuery)
```

By removing the contents of the WMI query from the line that uses the *ExecQuery* method, you won't normally need to change this line of the script. The same is true for the WMI connection string—as long as you are running the script on your local machine and working in the *root\cimv2* namespace, you don't need to modify that line either. Now you can see why in our earlier WMI scripts we specified the computer by using *strComputer*—it gave us the ability to modify the value of that variable without having to change the rest of the script.

## Worker and Output Information

The Worker and Output information section of the script is used to iterate through the collection that is returned by *wmiQuery*. After that information is loaded into the collection of items (*collItems*), you use a *For Each...Next* construction to walk through the collection and return the desired information. The code for this section of script follows:

```
For Each objItem in collItems
    strBIOSVersion = Join(objItem.BIOSVersion, ",")
    WScript.Echo "BIOSVersion: " & strBIOSVersion
    WScript.Echo ": " & objItem.caption
    WScript.Echo ": " & objItem.releaseDate
Next
```

Each item in the collection is assigned to the variable *objItem*. In this particular situation, only one BIOS can be queried from *Win32_BIOS*; however, the nature of WMI is to return single items as a collection. Display the requested information by using the *For Each...Next* construction. Only one item is in the collection, so you make only one loop through.

### Working with Multivalue Properties

Most of the items in the Output information section are obvious to readers at this point. You use *WScript.Echo* to output specific values. However, the first item, *strBIOS-Version*, is unique because you use the VBScript *Join* method to echo out the information. (We talk about the *Join* method in two paragraphs, so for now, let's think of a *Join* as a "black box tool.") This *Join* is necessary because the data contained in the *BIOS-Version* property is stored as an array. Recall from earlier chapters that you can think of an array as multiple cells in a spreadsheet, each of which can contain a certain amount of data. The *BIOSVersion* property of *Win32_BIOS* contains several fields of information, but you can't simply do a *WScript.Echo objItem.BIOSVersion* because *WScript* won't know which field you want returned and, consequently, the command would fail. As you learned in your previous discussion of arrays, you could use something like *objItem.BIOSVersion(0)*, and if you knew which field in the array contained the most salient information, this would be a valid approach. However, short of running the script multiple times and changing the array value an arbitrary number of times, you need to take a better approach.

> **See Also** For more information about arrays, refer to Chapter 4, "The Power of Many."

One cool way to deal with the multivalue property problem is to use the *Join* technique demonstrated in our earlier script. Let's see how that works. First you need to use a new variable that will hold the result of your *Join* statement:

```
strBIOSVersion = Join(objItem.BIOSVersion, ",")
```

The *Join* statement should be old hat to readers who are familiar with T-SQL. An executed *Join* takes two arguments. It's saying, "I want to join the first thing with the second thing." This is actually quite sophisticated. In the preceding *Join* statement, you join each field from *BIOSVersion* with a comma. You assign the result of the operation to the variable *strBIOSVersion*, and you're ready to echo it out in the next line of your script. Keep in mind that the default query language into WMI is WQL. Now WQL is pronounced "weequil" and SQL is pronounced "seaquil"—they not only sound alike but are alike in that many of the tasks you can perform in SQL can also be accomplished in WQL. The *Join* technique is very important, and you'll use it again when you come across other arrayed properties. Wondering how I knew that *BIOSVersion* was an array? The Platform SDK told me.

---

**Quick Check**

Q. **Why do you need a moniker for WMI?**

A. The WMI moniker gives you the ability to connect to WMI in an easier fashion.

Q. **What construction is required to return property data stored in an array?**

A. You need to either specify the element you're interested in, or simply use a *Join* function with a comma to give you a string to work with.

Q. **What part of the WMI moniker is required?**

A. The required part of the WMI moniker is the prefix, *WinMgmts:*.

Q. **What are the two optional parts to the WMI moniker?**

A. The two optional parts of the WMI moniker are the security settings and the WMI object path.

---

# Moniker Security Settings

In many cases, the default security settings work just fine for the WMI moniker. In many example scripts, you will see the line *impersonationLevel=impersonate* in a script. This line is often not needed, because the default security setting for Microsoft Windows 2000, Windows XP, and Windows Server 2003 is set to the impersonation level to be equal to impersonate.

**Note**   When I first started using WMI in my scripting, I noticed lots of scripts had *impersonationLevel=impersonate* set, and it made me curious. After a lot of searching I found the other levels. However, when I tried to change the security settings, the script failed. The reason? You cannot specify security settings when running local. They work only when you are connecting remotely to another computer.

But what does that really mean? Why are there options we would not normally utilize? You can use four levels of impersonation: Anonymous, Identify, Impersonate, and Delegate. By default, WMI uses the Impersonate permission, which allows a WMI call to utilize the credentials of the caller. When the person calling the WMI script is a domain administrator, the script runs with domain administrator privileges. You can also use other impersonation levels, as described in Table 9-1.

**Table 9-1   Impersonation Levels**

| Moniker | Meaning | Registry value |
|---------|---------|----------------|
| Anonymous | Hides the credentials of the caller. Calls to WMI might fail with this impersonation level. | *1* |
| Identify | Allows objects to query the credentials of the caller. Calls to WMI might fail with this impersonation level. | *2* |
| Impersonate | Allows objects to use the credentials of the caller. This is the recommended impersonation level for Scripting API for WMI calls. | *3* |
| Delegate | Allows objects to permit other objects to use the credentials of the caller. This impersonation will work with Scripting API for WMI calls but might constitute an unnecessary security risk. | *4* |

If you decide to specify the impersonation level of the script, the code would look like the following:

```
Set objWMIService=GetObject("winmgmts:{impersonationLevel=impersonate}")
```

Because Impersonate is the default impersonation level for WMI, the addition of the curly braces and *impersonationLevel=impersonate* code is redundant. If you want to keep your moniker nice and clean, and yet you feel the need to modify the impersonation level, you can do this easily by defining the impersonation level of the *SWbemSecurity* object. In practice, your code might look like the following:

```
Set objWMIService=GetObject("winmgmts:\\" & strComputer & wmiNS)
objWMIService.Security_.ImpersonationLevel = 4
```

In this code, the first line contains the normal moniker to make the connection to WMI. You use *strComputer* and *wmiNS* to specify target computers and the target namespace, respectively. Because you haven't specified an impersonation level, you're using the default Impersonate security setting. On the next line, you use the handle that came back from the *GetObject* command that was assigned to *objWMIService*, and you define the *impersonationLevel* to be equal to *4*. (Impersonation values are listed in Table 9-1.) Obviously, you could define a constant and set it to a value of *4* and then substitute the constant value for *4* in the script. *ImpersonationLevel* is a property of *Security_. Security_* is a property of the *SWbemSecurity* object. The *SWbemSecurity* object is used to read or set security settings for other WMI objects such as *SWbemServices*, which is actually the object created when you use *GetObject* and the WMI moniker. Understanding this "gobbledygook" is not necessary for writing WMI scripts; however, having a feel for some of it is useful if you're going to do much reading in the Platform SDK for WMI.

# *WbemPrivilege* Has Its Privileges

To add elevated privileges, you need to add a privilege string in the space immediately following the impersonation level. These privilege strings correspond to the *Wbem-PrivilegeEnum* constants, which are documented in the Platform SDK. Some of the more useful privilege strings for network administrators are listed in Table 9-2. (There are 26 defined privileges in the Platform SDK, most of which are of interest only to developers writing low-level WMI applications.)

**Table 9-2   Privilege Strings**

| Privilege | Value | Meaning |
|-----------|-------|---------|
| *SeCreateTokenPrivilege* | 1 | Required to create a primary token. |
| *SeLockMemoryPrivilege* | 3 | Required to lock physical pages in memory. |
| *SeMachineAccountPrivilege* | 5 | Required to create a computer account. |
| *SeSecurityPrivilege* | 7 | Required to perform a number of security-related functions, such as controlling and viewing audit messages. This privilege identifies its holder as a security operator. |
| *SeTakeOwnershipPrivilege* | 8 | Required to take ownership of an object without being granted discretionary access. This privilege allows the owner value to be set only to those values that the holder might legitimately assign as the owner of an object. |
| *SeSystemtimePrivilege* | 11 | Required to modify the system time. |
| *SeCreatePagefilePrivilege* | 14 | Required to create a paging file. |
| *SeShutdownPrivilege* | 18 | Required to shut down a local system. |
| *SeRemoteShutdownPrivilege* | 23 | Required to shut down a system using a network request. |
| *SeEnableDelegationPrivilege* | 26 | Required to enable computer and user accounts to be trusted for delegation. |

As you can see from Table 9-2, some of these privileges are rather interesting. This being the case, how do you request them? Well, this is where your work gets a little interesting. If you're requesting the privilege in a moniker string, you use the privilege string listed in Table 9-2, but you have to drop the *Se* part and the *Privilege* part of the string. For example, if you want to request the *SeShutdownPrivilege* in a moniker, you would specify the privilege as *Shutdown*, as illustrated in the following WMI connection string:

```
Set objWMIService=GetObject("winmgmts:{impersonationlevel=impersonate, (Shutdown)}")
```

# Summary

In this chapter, you examined the construction of the WMI moniker. You looked at various ways in which the moniker can be built and the ways in which it can be utilized. In addition, you studied the defaults that are configured on a Windows Server 2003 machine, and saw different ways of modifying that behavior. You then spent quite a bit of time looking at security surrounding the WMI connection. You looked at both impersonation features and individual security settings. Finally, the chapter concluded with a discussion of *WbemPrivilegeEnum* constants and an exploration of how to convert *WbemPrivilegeEnum* constants into Windows NT and Windows 2000 strings.

# Quiz Yourself

**Q.** **What is the WMI moniker, and why should you care?**

**A.** The WMI moniker is used to simplify the connection into WMI. It includes both default security and default namespace configuration information to the amount of scripting involved.

**Q.** **What are impersonation levels?**

**A.** Impersonation levels control allowed privileges when connecting to a remote WMI namespace.

**Q.** **What are the four impersonation levels available to WMI?**

**A.** The four impersonation levels available to WMI are Anonymous, Identify, Impersonate, and Delegate.

**Q.** **In Windows Server 2003, what is the default impersonation level?**

**A.** In Windows Server 2003, the default impersonation level is Impersonate.

**Q.** **How do you use a *WbemPrivilegeEnum* privilege constant in constructing the WMI moniker?**

**A.** To use the *WbemPrivilegeEnum* privilege constant in constructing a WMI moniker, you drop the initial *Se* and the trailing privilege parts of the constant. For example, if you want to have the *SeRemoteShutdownPrivilege* when connecting to a remote WMI namespace, you would simply use the *RemoteShutdown* portion of the privilege name in your moniker, like this: *impersonationLevel= RemoteShutdown*.

# On Your Own

# Lab 18a Using the Default WMI Moniker

In this lab, you will practice using the default WMI moniker. To do this, you write a cute little script that enumerates all the programs listed in the Add/Remove Programs dialog box, available from Control Panel.

## Lab Instructions

1. Open Notepad.exe.

2. On the first line, type **Option Explicit** to ensure you declare all variables used in the script.

3. Declare the following variables: *objWMIService*, *collItems*, and *objItem*. Add comments following each declaration to specify what each variable is used for.

4. Set *objWMIService* equal to what comes back from the *GetObject* method when used in conjunction with the WMI moniker. Your code will look like the following:

   ```
   Set objWMIService = GetObject("winmgmts:\\")
   ```

5. Set *collItems* equal to what comes back from issuing the WQL statement *"Select * from AddRemovePrograms"* as you use the *execQuery* method. Your code will look like the following:

   ```
   Set colItems = objWMIService.ExecQuery("SELECT * FROM AddRemovePrograms")
   ```

6. Use a *For Each...Next* loop to iterate through *collItems* as you look for the following properties of the *AddRemovePrograms* object: *displayName*, *Publisher* and *Version*. Use the variable *objItem* to assist you in iterating through the collection. Make sure you close out the *For Each...Next* loop with the *Next* command. Your code could will look like the following:

   ```
   For Each objItem In colItems
        WScript.Echo "DisplayName: " & objItem.DisplayName
        WScript.Echo "Publisher: " & objItem.Publisher
        WScript.Echo "Version: " & objItem.Version
        WScript.Echo
   Next
   ```

7. Save your file as Solution18-1.vbs.

8. Make sure you run this program in CScript by going to a command prompt and typing **cscript *pathtoyourfile*\solution18-1.vbs**. (More than likely, you have a lot of programs in Add/Remove Programs. If you run the program by double-clicking it, and it runs under WScript, you will have tons of pop-up dialog boxes to close unless you open Task Manager and kill the WScript.exe process.)

# Lab 18b Invoking the WMI Moniker to Display the Machine Boot Configuration

In this lab, you explore an alternate method of invoking the WMI moniker. In so doing, you write a WMI script that displays the boot configuration of a machine.

## Lab Instructions

1. Open Notepad.exe.

2. On the first line, specify **Option Explicit** to ensure all variables utilized are declared.

3. Declare three variables (using the same variables we declared in Lab 18a). The variables are *objWMIService*, *colItems*, and *objItem*.

4. Set *objWMIService* equal to what comes back from the *GetObject* method when used in conjunction with the WMI moniker. In addition, define an impersonation level of Anonymous. Your code will look like the following:

```
Set objWMIService = GetObject("winmgmts:{impersonationLevel=anonymous}")
```

5. Set *colItems* equal to what comes back from issuing the WQL statement *"Select * from Win32_BootConfiguration"* as you use the *execQuery* method. Your code will look like the following:

```
Set colItems = objWMIService.ExecQuery("SELECT * FROM Win32_BootConfiguration")
```

6. Use a *For Each...Next* loop to iterate through *colItems* as you look for the following properties of the *Win3_BootConfiguration* object: *BootDirectory*, *Caption*, *ConfigurationPath*, *Description*, *LastDrive*, *Name*, *ScratchDirectory*, *SettingID*, and *TempDirectory*. Use the variable *objItem* to assist you in iterating through the collection. Make sure you close out the *For Each...Next* loop with the *Next* command. Your code will look like the following:

```
For Each objItem In colItems
    WScript.Echo "BootDirectory: " & objItem.BootDirectory
    WScript.Echo "Caption: " & objItem.Caption
    WScript.Echo "ConfigurationPath: " & objItem.ConfigurationPath
    WScript.Echo "Description: " & objItem.Description
    WScript.Echo "LastDrive: " & objItem.LastDrive
    WScript.Echo "Name: " & objItem.Name
    WScript.Echo "ScratchDirectory: " & objItem.ScratchDirectory
    WScript.Echo "SettingID: " & objItem.SettingID
    WScript.Echo "TempDirectory: " & objItem.TempDirectory
    WScript.Echo
Next
```

7. Save your work as Solution_18a.vbs.

8. Use CScript to run the script. *It will fail!* Why does the script fail? Hint: Check the impersonation level.

9. Change the line containing the WMI moniker. Set the impersonation level to Identify.

10. Save your work as Solution_18b.vbs.

11. Use CScript to run the script. *It will fail!*

12. Why does the script fail? Hint: Check the impersonation level.

13. Change the line containing the WMI moniker. Set the impersonation level to Impersonate.

14. Save your work as Solution_18c.vbs.

15. Use CScript to run the script. It works just fine. Why does the script work?

16. Change the line containing the WMI moniker. Set the impersonation level to Delegate.

17. Save your work as Solution_18d.vbs.

18. Use CScript to run the script. It works just fine. What does this tell you about using the different impersonation levels on Windows Server 2003?

# Lab 18c Including Additional Security Permissions

In this lab, you will modify the WMI moniker to include the specification of additional security permissions. You will use a script that displays information about the display.

## Lab Instructions

1. Open Notepad.exe.

2. On the first line, specify **Option Explicit** to ensure variables are declared and spelled correctly.

3. On the next line, declare the following variables: *objWMIService*, *colItems*, and *objItem*. These are the same variables you used in previous scripts in this chapter.

4. Set *objWMIService* equal to what comes back from the *GetObject* method when used in conjunction with the WMI moniker. In addition, you want to define an impersonation level of Impersonate as well as the special debug privilege. Your code will look like the following:

```
Set objWMIService = GetObject("winmgmts:{impersonationLevel=impersonate, (debug)}"
)
```

5. Set *colItems* equal to what comes back from issuing the WQL statement *"Select * from Win32_DisplayConfiguration"* as you use the *execQuery* method. Your code will look like the following:

```
Set colItems = objWMIService.ExecQuery("SELECT * FROM Win32_DisplayConfiguration")
```

6. Use a *For Each...Next* loop to iterate through *colItems* as you look for the following properties of the *Win32_DisplayConfiguration* object: *BitsPerPel, Caption, Description, DeviceName, DisplayFlags, DisplayFrequency, DriverVersion, LogPixels, PelsHeight, PelsWidth, SettingID*, and *SpecificationVersion*. Use the variable *objItem* to assist you in iterating through the collection. Make sure you close out the *For Each...Next* loop with the *Next* command. Your code will look like the following:

```
For Each objItem in colItems
    WScript.Echo "BitsPerPel: " & objItem.BitsPerPel
    WScript.Echo "Caption: " & objItem.Caption
    WScript.Echo "Description: " & objItem.Description
    WScript.Echo "DeviceName: " & objItem.DeviceName
    WScript.Echo "DisplayFlags: " & objItem.DisplayFlags
    WScript.Echo "DisplayFrequency: " & objItem.DisplayFrequency
    WScript.Echo "DriverVersion: " & objItem.DriverVersion
    WScript.Echo "LogPixels: " & objItem.LogPixels
    WScript.Echo "PelsHeight: " & objItem.PelsHeight
    WScript.Echo "PelsWidth: " & objItem.PelsWidth
    WScript.Echo "SettingID: " & objItem.SettingID
    WScript.Echo "SpecificationVersion: " & objItem.SpecificationVersion
Next
```

7. Save your program as Solution18-3.vbs.

8. Modify the WMI connection string to include not only the debug privilege, but also the shutdown privilege. Your code will look like the following:

```
Set objWMIService = GetObject("winmgmts:{impersonationLevel=impersonate, (debug, shutdown)}")
```

9. Modify the connection string from line 8 to indicate that the WMI connection should attach to the local host machine. This WMI connection string is starting to be rather long, so break the line after *impersonationlevel*. Your code will look like the following:

```
Set objWMIService = GetObject("winmgmts:{impersonationLevel=impersonate," _
& "(debug, shutdown)}\\localhost")
```

10. Save your work.

11. Modify the connection in the preceding string to indicate that you want WMI to make a connection to the *\root\cimv2* namespace on the computer called *localhost*. Your code will look like the following:

```
Set objWMIService = GetObject("winmgmts:{impersonationLevel=impersonate," _
    & "(debug, shutdown)}\\localhost\root\cimV2")
```

12. Save your work, and then use CScript to run the script.

# Lab 19 Using *Win32_Environment* and VBScript to Learn About WMI

In this lab, you use *Win32_Environment* and VBScript to learn about both WMI and the environment settings on your server.

## Lab Instructions

1. Open Notepad.exe.

2. On the first line, type **Option Explicit**.

3. Use the *Dim* command to declare the following variables: *objWMIService*, *colItems*, *objItem*, *wmiQuery*, and *strComputer*.

4. Use *WScript.Echo* and the *Now* function to indicate the script is beginning its run.

5. Assign the value of *"."* to the variable *strComputer*.

6. Assign the query *"Select * from Win32_Environment"* to the variable *wmiQuery*.

7. Set *objWMIService* = to the handle that comes back from the *GetObject* function with the *winmgmts:* moniker. Incorporate the variable *strComputer* to tell WMI which computer to use to execute the connection.

8. Use a *For Each...Next* Loop to iterate through the collection called *colItems*. For each *objItem* in *colItems*, echo out the following properties: *caption*, *description*, *installDate*, *Name*, *Status*, *SystemVariable*, *UserName*, and *VariableValue*.

9. Close out the *For Each...Next* loop.

10. Echo a line indicating the script is finished, and use the *Now* function to print out the time.

11. Save your work as lab19.vbs.

12. Run the script in CScript.

# 10 Using WMI Queries

In the last two chapters, you looked at Windows Management Instrumentation (WMI). So far, you examined connecting to WMI, the structure of WMI, and various ways of obtaining results. Now you are going to look at ways to make your information gathering more efficient, more powerful, and more directed. Learning about WMI queries accomplishes more than just reducing network traffic or helping you be more directed—a well-crafted WMI Query Language (WQL) statement can make your script easier to write and the returned data easier to manipulate.

## Before you Begin

**To work through the material presented in this chapter you need to be familiar with the following concepts from earlier chapters:**

- Creating the WMI moniker
- Implementing the *For...Next* construction
- Navigating the WMI namespace
- Implementing *GetObject*
- Implementing the *ExecQuery* method

**After completing this chapter you will be familiar with the following:**

- Return all properties from all instances of a class
- Return some properties from all instances of a class
- Return all properties from some instances of a class
- Return some properties from some instances of a class

## Tell Me Everything About Everything!

When novices first write WMI scripts, they nearly all begin by asking for every property about all instances of a class that are present on a particular system. (This is also referred to as the infamous "select * query".) As you have no doubt found out, this approach can often return an overwhelming amount of data, particularly when you are querying a class such as installed software, or processes and threads. Rarely would you need to have so much data. Typically, when you query for installed software, you're looking for information about a *particular* software package.

There are, however, several occasions when I want to use the "tell me everything about all instances of a particular class" query:

- During development of a script to see representative data

- When troubleshooting a more directed query, for example, when I'm possibly trying to filter on a field that does not exist

- When the returned data is so small that being more precise doesn't make sense

---

**Just the Steps**

▶ **To return all information from all instances**

1. Make a connection to WMI.

2. Use the *Select* statement to choose everything: *Select \**.

3. Use the *From* statement to indicate the class from which you wish to retrieve data. For example, *From Win32_Share*.

---

In the next script, you make a connection to the default namespace in WMI and return all the information about all the shares on a local machine. This is actually good practice, because in the past numerous worms have propagated via unsecured shares, and you might have unused shares around—a user might create a share for a friend and then forget to delete it. (As I was writing this script, I found four shares on my laptop that I didn't know were present!) In the script that follows, called ListShares.vbs, you print out all the information about shares that are present on the machine.

```
Option Explicit
On Error Resume Next
dim strComputer
dim wmiNS
dim wmiQuery
dim objWMIService
dim colItems
dim objItem

strComputer = "."
wmiNS = "\root\cimv2"
wmiQuery = "Select * from Win32_Share"
Set objWMIService = GetObject("winmgmts:\\" & strComputer & wmiNS)
Set colItems = objWMIService.ExecQuery(wmiQuery)

For Each objItem In colItems
    WScript.Echo "AccessMask: " & objItem.AccessMask
    WScript.Echo "AllowMaximum: " & objItem.AllowMaximum
    WScript.Echo "Caption: " & objItem.Caption
    WScript.Echo "Description: " & objItem.Description
    WScript.Echo "InstallDate: " & objItem.InstallDate
    WScript.Echo "MaximumAllowed: " & objItem.MaximumAllowed
    WScript.Echo "Name: " & objItem.Name
```

```
WScript.Echo "Path: " & objItem.Path
WScript.Echo "Status: " & objItem.Status
WScript.Echo "Type: " & objItem.Type
WScript.Echo
```

# Next

## Header information

The Header information section of ListShares.vbs contains all the standard information. You use *Option Explicit* to force the declaration of all variables. This is followed by *On Error Resume Next* to make sure the script goes to the next line of code if it encounters an error.

> **Note**   In Chapter 1, "Starting from Scratch," we talked about the pros and cons of using *On Error Resume Next*. Most of the time, when you are working with WMI, you are displaying property values, which is a harmless activity. Using *On Error Resume Next* helps the script to run, even when the script encounters an error. This is largely a good thing with WMI.

These two standard lines are followed by the same variable names declared in previous WMI scripts: *strComputer*, *wmiNS*, *wmiQuery*, *objWMIService*, *colItems*, and *objItem*. The variable *strComputer* assigns the target computer, *wmiNS* assigns the target WMI namespace, *wmiQuery* holds the value of the query to be executed, and *colItems* holds the collection of items that are returned by the query. The variable *objItem* is used by the *For Next…Each* loop to iterate through the collection.

## Reference Information

The Reference information section of the script is used to assign values to five of the six variables. The variable *strComputer* is assigned the value of *"."*, which indicates the script will run against the local computer. The variable *wmiNS* is assigned to *\root\CIMV2*, which is the default WMI namespace. The variable *wmiQuery* is set to *"Select * from Win32_Share"*. This is the query you want to execute against the default WMI namespace. *Select * * tells WMI that you want to retrieve all properties from the *Win32_Share* object. Note that this query doesn't display all the properties; it simply displays all the properties from the *Win32_Share* object. What you do with the returned data depends on your current needs. Unless you need it, returning all the data might not be a very efficient use of networking resources. It is, however, very easy to construct such a query.

The variable *objWMIService* is used to connect to WMI and uses the WMI moniker to do so. You utilize two variables to assist in this operation: *strComputer* and *wmiNS*. The *colItems* variable holds the handle that comes back from the *execQuery* method that is used to execute your WMI query against the *Win32_Share* class.

# Worker and Output Information

The Worker information section of the ListShare.vbs script simply uses *WScript.Echo* to write the various properties and their associated values to the command line (if run in CScript) or to a pop-up dialog box (if run in WScript, which is not a really good idea when you have lots of shares). The most convenient listing of all the available properties for a particular class is contained in the platform SDK. A quick search for *Win32_Share* reveals the properties listed in Table 10-1.

**Table 10-1    *Win32_Share* Properties**

| Data type | Property | Meaning |
|-----------|----------|---------|
| Boolean | *AllowMaximum* | Allow maximum number of connections? True or False. |
| string | *Caption* | Short, one-line description. |
| string | *Description* | Description. |
| datetime | *InstallDate* | When the share was created (optional). |
| uint32 | *MaximumAllowed* | Number of concurrent connections allowed. Only valid when *AllowMaximum* is set to *False*. |
| string | *Name* | Share name. |
| string | *Path* | Physical path to the share. |
| string | *Status* | Current status of the share: degraded, OK, or Failed. |
| uint32 | *Type* | Type of resource shared: disk, file, printer, and so on. |

---

**Quick Check**

**Q.** What is the syntax for a query that returns all properties of a given object?

**A.** *Select* * returns all properties of a given object.

**Q.** What is one reason for using *Select* * instead of a more directed query?

**A.** In troubleshooting, *Select* * is useful because it returns any available data. In addition, *Select* * is useful in trying to characterize the data that might be returned from a query.

# Selective Data from All Instances

The next level of sophistication (from using *Select \**) is to return only the properties you are interested in. This is a more efficient strategy. For instance, in the previous example, you did a *Select \** and returned a lot of data you weren't necessarily interested in. Suppose you wanted to know only what shares are on each machine. With a simple change to the *wmiQuery* variable and by deleting a few *WScript.Echo* commands, you can modify your script to get exactly what you want.

---

**Just the Steps**

▶ **To select specific data**

1. Make a connection to WMI.

2. Use the *Select* statement to choose the specific property you are interested in, for example, *Select name*.

3. Use the *From* statement to indicate the class from which you want to retrieve data, for example, *From Win32_Share*.

---

You need to make only two small changes in the ListShares.vbs script to enable garnering specific data via your WMI script. In place of the asterisk in the *Select* statement assigned in the Reference information section of the script, you substitute the property you want. In this case, you want only the name of the shares.

The second change is to eliminate all unused properties from the Output section. This is very important because the script *could* fail if you try to echo out a property that is not selected in the *Select* statement. I said it *could* fail as opposed to *would* fail, because if you include *On Error Resume Next*, the script will work. If you don't include this error handling, the script fails with an "object does not support this property or method" error. Because this error message is rather confusing, you should be able to recognize it! It is important that you select each item for which you want to return information. In this way, WQL acts just like SQL. If you don't select a property, you can't do anything with the property, because to the program, the object doesn't exist. Here is the modified ListShares.vbs script:

```
strComputer = "."
wmiNS = "\root\cimv2"
wmiQuery = "Select Name from Win32_Share"
Set objWMIService = GetObject("winmgmts:\\" & strComputer & wmiNS)
Set colItems = objWMIService.ExecQuery(wmiQuery)

For Each objItem In colItems
    WScript.Echo "Name: " & objItem.Name
Next
```

# Selecting Multiple Properties

If you're interested in only a certain number of properties, you can use *Select* to specify that. All you have to do is separate the properties by a comma. Suppose you run the preceding script and find a number of undocumented shares on one of the servers—you might want a little bit more information such as the path to the share and how many people are allowed to connect to it. By default, when a share is created, the "maximum allowed" bit is set, which basically says anyone who has rights to the share can connect. This can be a problem, because if too many people connect to a share, they can degrade the performance of the server. To preclude such an eventuality, I always specify a maximum number of connections to the server.

> **Note**    I occasionally see people asking whether spaces or namecase in the property list matters. In fact, when I first started writing scripts and they failed, I often modified spacing and capitalization in feeble attempts to make the script work. Spacing and capitalization *do not matter* for WMI properties.

Your revised script now looks like the following (excluding the Header information section, which hasn't changed):

```
strComputer = "."
wmiNS = "\root\cimv2"
wmiQuery = "Select Name, Path, AllowMaximum from Win32_Share"
Set objWMIService = GetObject("winmgmts:\\" & strComputer & wmiNS)
Set colItems = objWMIService.ExecQuery(wmiQuery)

For Each objItem In colItems
    WScript.Echo "Name: " & objItem.Name
    WScript.Echo "Path: " & objItem.path
    WScript.Echo "AllowMaximum: " & objItem.AllowMaximum
    WScript.Echo

Next
```

You can use this technique of specifying using just the properties you're interested in with any of the supported properties from *Win32_Share* listed in Table 10-1. Interestingly enough, you don't really need to include the *Name* property on the *Select* line, because for *Win32_Share*, *Name* is the *key* property. The *key* property in WMI works just like the Key column in a database: it is used to uniquely identify a row, and it is often the column or property that is indexed to make searching easier. This is just like the key to a house or to a car. The key provides entry into the house or car so that you can access the property inside. The *key* property is always returned, even when it isn't specifically mentioned on the *Select* line.

**Quick Check**

- **Q.** To select specific properties from an object, what do you need to do on the *Select* line?
- **A.** You need to separate the specific properties of an object with a comma on the *Select* line of the *execQuery* method.

- **Q.** To avoid error messages, what must be done when selecting individual properties on the *Select* line?
- **A.** Errors can be avoided if you make sure each property used is specified in the select line. For example, the WMI query is just like a paper bag that gets filled with items that are picked up by using the select statement. If you do not put something in the paper bag, you cannot pull anything out of the bag. In the same manner, if you do not "select" a property, you cannot later print or sort on that property. This is exactly the way that a SQL *Select* statement works.

- **Q.** What can you check for in your script if it fails with an "object does not support this method or property" error?
- **A.** If you are getting "object does not support this method or property" error messages, you might want to ensure you have referenced the property in your *Select* statement prior to trying to work with it in an Output section.

# Specifying Specifics

In many situations, you will want to limit the data you return to a specific instance of that class in the data set. If you go back to your query and add a *Where* clause to the *Select* statement, you'll be able to greatly reduce the amount of information returned by the query. Notice that in the value associated with the *wmiQuery*, you added a dependency that indicated you wanted only information with share name *C$*. This value is not case-sensitive, but it must be surrounded with single quotation marks, as you can see in the *wmiQuery* string in the following script. These single quotation marks are important because they tell WMI that the value is a string value and not some other programmatic item. Because the addition of the *Where* statement was the only thing you really added to the ListShares.vbs, we're not going into a long discussion of the ListShares.vbs script.

```
strComputer = "."
wmiNS = "\root\cimv2"
wmiQuery = "Select Name, path, allowMaximum from Win32_Share where name = 'C$'"
Set objWMIService = GetObject("winmgmts:\\" & strComputer & wmiNS)
Set colItems = objWMIService.ExecQuery(wmiQuery)
```

```
For Each objItem In colItems
    WScript.Echo "Name: " & objItem.Name
    WScript.Echo "Path: " & objItem.path
    WScript.Echo "AllowMaximum: " & objItem.AllowMaximum
    WScript.Echo

Next
```

---

**Just the Steps**

▶ **To limit specific data**

1. Make a connection to WMI.

2. Use the *Select* statement to choose the specific property you are interested in, for example, *Select name*.

3. Use the *From* statement to indicate the class from which you want to retrieve data, for example, *From Win32_Share*.

4. Add a *Where* clause to further limit the data set that is returned. Make sure the properties specified in the *Where* clause are first mentioned in the *Select* statement, for example, *where name*.

5. Add an evaluation operator. You can use the equal sign, or the less than or greater than symbols, for example, *where name = 'C$'*.

---

# Smooth Operator

One of the cool things you can do is use greater than and less than operators in your evaluation clause. What is so cool about greater than? you might ask. It makes working with alphabetic characters and numeric characters easy. If you work on a server that hosts home directories for users (which are often named after their user names), you can easily produce a list of all home directories from the letters T through Z by using the $> S$ operation. This is illustrated in the following script:

```
strComputer = "."
wmiNS = "\root\cimv2"
wmiQuery = "Select Name, path, allowMaximum from Win32_Share where name > 's'"
Set objWMIService = GetObject("winmgmts:\\" & strComputer & wmiNS)
Set colItems = objWMIService.ExecQuery(wmiQuery)

For Each objItem In colItems
    WScript.Echo "Name: " & objItem.Name
    WScript.Echo "Path: " & objItem.path
    WScript.Echo "AllowMaximum: " & objItem.AllowMaximum
    WScript.Echo

Next
```

There are many other available operators in VBScript as well. These operators are listed in Table 10-2.

**Table 10-2   VBScript Operators**

| Operator | Description |
|----------|-------------|
| = | Equal to |
| < | Less than |
| > | Greater than |
| <= | Less than or equal to |
| >= | Greater than or equal to |
| != | Not equal to |
| <> | Not equal to (both != and <> mean not equal to) |

# Where Is the Where Clause?

To more easily modify the *Where* clause in a script, substitute the *Where* clause with a variable. This configuration can be modified to include command-line input as well.

```
strComputer = "."
wmiNS = "\root\cimv2"
vWhere = " name = 'c$'"
wmiQuery = "Select Name, path, allowMaximum from Win32_Share where " & vWhere
Set objWMIService = GetObject("winmgmts:\\" & strComputer & wmiNS)
Set colItems = objWMIService.ExecQuery(wmiQuery)

For Each objItem In colItems
    WScript.Echo "Name: " & objItem.Name
    WScript.Echo "Path: " & objItem.path
    WScript.Echo "AllowMaximum: " & objItem.AllowMaximum
    WScript.Echo

Next
```

Let's return to our scenario in which you are looking for shares that have not been limited by the number of connections. You can modify the *vWhere* variable to look for *AllowMaximum = 'true'*. It would look like the following:

```
strComputer = "."
wmiNS = "\root\cimv2"
vWhere = " AllowMaximum = 'true'"
wmiQuery = "Select Name, path, allowMaximum from Win32_Share where " & vWhere
Set objWMIService = GetObject("winmgmts:\\" & strComputer & wmiNS)
Set colItems = objWMIService.ExecQuery(wmiQuery)

For Each objItem In colItems
    WScript.Echo "Name: " & objItem.Name
    WScript.Echo "Path: " & objItem.path
```

```
WScript.Echo "AllowMaximum: " & objItem.AllowMaximum
WScript.Echo
```

```
Next
```

---

**Quick Check**

**Q.** To limit the specific data returned by a query, what WQL tool can be utilized?

**A.** The *Where* clause is very powerful in limiting the specific data returned by a query.

**Q.** What are three possible operators that can be employed in creating powerful *Where* clauses?

**A.** The equal sign and the greater than and the less than symbols can be used to evaluate the data prior to returning the data set.

---

# Summary

In this chapter, you examined how to use the WMI query language to return data from servers via WMI. By constructing a judicious WMI query, you can both limit the amount of data sent across the wire and reduce the amount of time required to process the query. There are essentially three ways to employ WQL techniques in your scripts. The first one involves limiting the number of properties from which data is returned by specifically adding them to the *Select* line. The second approach involves utilizing the *Where* clause to limit the number of instances that are returned when querying a particular object. The third approach involves simply using an asterisk (*) in the *Select* line and not having a *Where* clause.

# Quiz Yourself

**Q.** What method is used to execute a WMI query?

**A.** The *execQuery* method is employed to execute a WMI query.

**Q.** What is the WQL construction that will limit the number of instances that are returned in response to a query?

**A.** You can limit the number of instances that are returned in response to a query by employing a *Where* clause.

**Q.** The specific *Select* construction in which named properties are listed in the *Select* statement is utilized to control data returned in what manner?

**A.** By using a specific *Select* construction in which named properties are listed, you are able to limit the number of properties returned from the object but not the number of instances that are returned.

**Q.** If you want only specific data about a specific item, how do you construct your WMI query?

**A.** A query that returns only specific data about a specific item must use both a specific *Select* clause and a *Where* clause.

# On Your Own

# Lab 20 Writing an Informative WMI Script

In this lab, you are going to write a WMI script that returns a lot of information about processes. This will be used as the starter script in Lab 21.

## Lab Instructions

1. Open Notepad.exe.

2. On the first line, type **Option Explicit** to ensure you declare all variables used in the script.

3. Declare the following variables: *objWMIService*, *colItems*, *objItem*, and *wmiQuery*. Add comments following each declaration specifying what each variable is used for.

4. Assign *wmiQuery* to be equal to a WQL *Select* statement that returns everything from the *win32_Process*. Your code will look like the following:

```
wmiQuery = "Select * from Win32_Process"
```

5. Set *objWMIService* equal to what comes back from the *GetObject* method when used in conjunction with the WMI moniker. Your code will look like the following:

```
Set objWMIService = GetObject("winmgmts:\\")
```

6. Set *colItems* equal to what comes back from issuing the WQL statement held by the variable *wmiQuery* as you use the *execQuery* method. Your code will look like the following:

```
Set colItems = objWMIService.ExecQuery(wmiQuery)
```

7. Use a *For Each…Next* loop to iterate through *colItems* as you look for the standard properties of the *Win32_Process* class. Instead of typing all the properties in your script, open the student resource CD and copy For Each Next Loop from the Lab20Starter—For Each Next Loop.vbs script. Save your work as Lab20Solution.vbs. Your completed script will look like the following:

```
Option Explicit
On Error Resume Next
dim wmiQuery
dim objWMIService
dim colItems
dim objItem
```

```
wmiQuery = "Select * from Win32_Process"
Set objWMIService = GetObject("winmgmts:\\")
Set colItems = objWMIService.ExecQuery(wmiQuery)

For Each objItem In colItems
    WScript.Echo "Caption: " & objItem.Caption
    WScript.Echo "CommandLine: " & objItem.CommandLine
    WScript.Echo "CreationClassName: " & objItem.CreationClassName
    WScript.Echo "CreationDate: " & objItem.CreationDate
    WScript.Echo "CSCreationClassName: " & objItem.CSCreationClassName
    WScript.Echo "CSName: " & objItem.CSName
    WScript.Echo "Description: " & objItem.Description
    WScript.Echo "ExecutablePath: " & objItem.ExecutablePath
    WScript.Echo "ExecutionState: " & objItem.ExecutionState
    WScript.Echo "Handle: " & objItem.Handle
    WScript.Echo "HandleCount: " & objItem.HandleCount
    WScript.Echo "InstallDate: " & objItem.InstallDate
    WScript.Echo "KernelModeTime: " & objItem.KernelModeTime
    WScript.Echo "MaximumWorkingSetSize: " & objItem.MaximumWorkingSetSize
    WScript.Echo "MinimumWorkingSetSize: " & objItem.MinimumWorkingSetSize
    WScript.Echo "Name: " & objItem.Name
    WScript.Echo "OSCreationClassName: " & objItem.OSCreationClassName
    WScript.Echo "OSName: " & objItem.OSName
    WScript.Echo "OtherOperationCount: " & objItem.OtherOperationCount
    WScript.Echo "OtherTransferCount: " & objItem.OtherTransferCount
    WScript.Echo "PageFaults: " & objItem.PageFaults
    WScript.Echo "PageFileUsage: " & objItem.PageFileUsage
    WScript.Echo "ParentProcessId: " & objItem.ParentProcessId
    WScript.Echo "PeakPageFileUsage: " & objItem.PeakPageFileUsage
    WScript.Echo "PeakVirtualSize: " & objItem.PeakVirtualSize
    WScript.Echo "PeakWorkingSetSize: " & objItem.PeakWorkingSetSize
    WScript.Echo "Priority: " & objItem.Priority
    WScript.Echo "PrivatePageCount: " & objItem.PrivatePageCount
    WScript.Echo "ProcessId: " & objItem.ProcessId
    WScript.Echo "QuotaNonPagedPoolUsage: " & objItem.QuotaNonPagedPoolUsage
    WScript.Echo "QuotaPagedPoolUsage: " & objItem.QuotaPagedPoolUsage
    WScript.Echo "QuotaPeakNonPagedPoolUsage: " & _
        objItem.QuotaPeakNonPagedPoolUsage
    WScript.Echo "QuotaPeakPagedPoolUsage: " & objItem.QuotaPeakPagedPoolUsage
    WScript.Echo "ReadOperationCount: " & objItem.ReadOperationCount
    WScript.Echo "ReadTransferCount: " & objItem.ReadTransferCount
    WScript.Echo "SessionId: " & objItem.SessionId
    WScript.Echo "Status: " & objItem.Status
    WScript.Echo "TerminationDate: " & objItem.TerminationDate
    WScript.Echo "ThreadCount: " & objItem.ThreadCount
    WScript.Echo "UserModeTime: " & objItem.UserModeTime
    WScript.Echo "VirtualSize: " & objItem.VirtualSize
    WScript.Echo "WindowsVersion: " & objItem.WindowsVersion
    WScript.Echo "WorkingSetSize: " & objItem.WorkingSetSize
    WScript.Echo "WriteOperationCount: " & objItem.WriteOperationCount
    WScript.Echo "WriteTransferCount: " & objItem.WriteTransferCount
    WScript.Echo " *******************************"

Next
```

# Lab 21a Obtaining More Direct Information

In this lab, you modify the Lab20Solution.vbs file to return a bit more directed information.

## Lab Instructions

1. Open Notepad.exe.

2. Open the Lab21Starter.vbs file or your completed Lab20Solution.vbs file and save it as **Lab21Solution.vbs**.

3. Under the list of declared variables, add a new declaration for a variable called *vWhere*.

4. Insert a new line above the line defining the *wmiQuery*.

5. Save and run the script from a command line using CScript.

6. Identify no more than five "interesting properties" for inclusion in your new script. I decided to use the following: *Name*, *CommandLine*, *MaximumWorkingSetSize*, *QuotaPeakNonPagedPoolUsage*, *ProcessID*, and *ThreadCount*. I chose *CommandLine* rather than the executable path because many times, programs will launch with a command-line parameter (or switch), which does not show up in the executable path variable. In addition, when something is running in the *svcHost*, the command-line parameter enables you to see what is actually running in that service host. Your *For Each...Next* loop might look something like this code:

```
For Each objItem In colItems
    WScript.Echo "CommandLine: " & objItem.CommandLine
    WScript.Echo "PID: " & objItem.ProcessID
    WScript.Echo "MaximumWorkingSetSize: " & objItem.MaximumWorkingSetSize
    WScript.Echo "QuotaPeakNonPagedPoolUsage: " & _
        objItem.QuotaPeakNonPagedPoolUsage
    WScript.Echo "ThreadCount: " & objItem.ThreadCount
    WScript.Echo " *******************************"
Next
```

7. Save your work.

8. Above the *wmiQuery* line, define the *vWhere* variable to be equal a *Where* clause that specifies the number of threads as greater than 10. Make sure you encase the entire *Where* clause in a set of double quotation marks. In addition, make sure that the number is also encased in single quotation marks. That will entail a *'10'"* at the end of your *Where* clause. Your code might look like the following:

```
vWhere = " where threadCount > '10'"
```

9. Save your work.

10. Modify the *wmiQuery* to utilize the *vWhere* variable. This is rather simple in that all you need to do is insert a space at the end of the query inside the double quotation marks, and then use the ampersand and type the *vWhere* variable name. The code will look like the following:

```
wmiQuery = "Select * from Win32_Process " & vWhere
```

11. Save your script as Lab21aSolution.vbs.

# Lab 21b Using a More Complicated *Where* Clause

In this lab, you modify the Lab21aSolution.vbs file to use a more complicated *Where* clause.

## Lab Instructions

1. Open Notepad.exe.

2. Open the Lab21aSolution.vbs file, and save it as **Lab21bSolution.vbs**.

3. Modify the *vWhere* clause to include the requirement that the PID (Process ID) is greater than 100. Your completed *vWhere* line might look like the following:

```
vWhere = " where threadCount > '10' and ProcessID >100"
```

4. Save your script, and run it in CScript. Notice how many lines of data are returned.

5. Modify the *vWhere* clause so that the PID must be greater than 1000. Your code will look like the following:

```
vWhere = " where threadCount > '10' and ProcessID >1000"
```

6. Save the script, and run it in CScript. Notice how the data set has been trimmed.

7. Now change the thread count so that it is 50. Your code will look like the following:

```
vWhere = " where threadCount > '50' and ProcessID >1000"
```

8. How many lines of data are returned now? On my machine there are none.

9. Now you are going to switch operators. Change the *and* to an *OR*. The line will now look like the following:

```
vWhere = " where threadCount > '50' or ProcessID >1000"
```

10. Look through the data that is returned. You will see data in which the thread count is greater than 50, and you will see data in which the *processID* is greater than 1000, but you will probably not see both in a single data set (that is what we did in step 7).

11. Save your script.

# Part 3
# Advanced Windows Administration

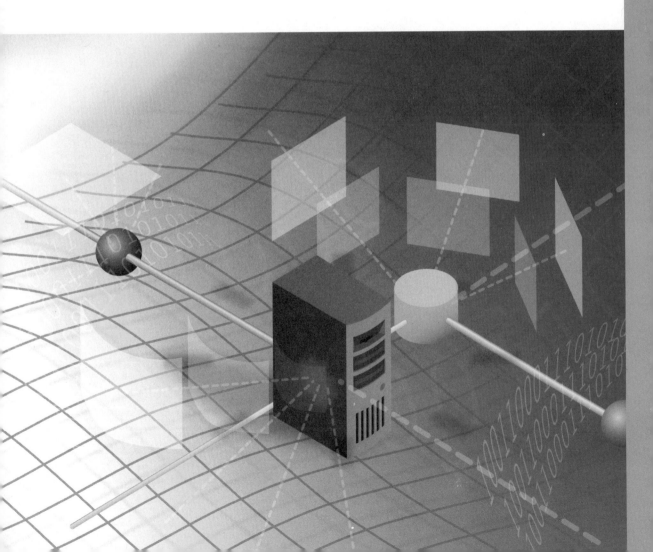

# 11 Introduction to Active Directory Service Interfaces

In this chapter, you're introduced to Active Directory Service Interfaces (ADSI). Notice that two concepts are presented in its name: Active Directory and service interfaces. To effectively use Microsoft Visual Basic Script (VBScript) to perform directory operations, you need to understand both concepts. A full discussion of the Active Directory directory service is beyond the scope of this book, but you'll look at how to use ADSI to automate, anticipate, and obviate routine tasks.

## Before you Begin

**The material presented in this chapter assumes you are familiar with the following concepts from earlier chapters:**

- Creating arrays
- Outputting data to text files
- Reading information contained in text files
- Implementing the *For…Next* construction
- Implementing *Select Case* constructions

**After completing this chapter you will be familiar with the following:**

- Connecting to Active Directory
- ADSI providers
- Working with Active Directory namespaces
- Creating organizational units (OUs) in Active Directory
- Creating users in Active Directory

## Working with ADSI

In this section, you use ADSI and VBScript to perform basic network administration tasks. The following list summarizes some high-level uses:

- Importing a list of names and creating user accounts
- Importing a list and changing user passwords

- Importing a list and creating an entire organizational unit (OU) structure following an upgrade to Microsoft Windows Server 2003

- Reading the Microsoft Exchange 5.x directory and setting the display name in Active Directory with the value from Exchange 5.x

- Reading the Exchange 5.x directory for a default personalized SMTP address and setting it in Active Directory

- Reading the computer name or IP address and mapping local printers to users

- Creating personalized shortcuts for users at logon time based on group memberships

- Mapping drives based upon OU membership

---

**Just the Steps**

▶ **To connect to Active Directory**

1. Implement a connection to Active Directory.

2. Use the appropriate provider.

3. Specify the path to the appropriate object in Active Directory.

4. Use *SetInfo* to write changes to Active Directory.

---

In a basic fashion, the following script, CreateOU.vbs, utilizes each of the four steps in the preceding Just the Steps sidebar. To maintain readability, the Header information section of the script is left out so that you can focus only on the steps involved in connecting to Active Directory and creating an OU. CreateOU.vbs uses variables for each of the four main steps to maintain portability.

```
provider = "LDAP://"
OU = "ou=hiring, ou=hr,"
domain = "dc=a,dc=com"
oClass = "organizationalUnit"
oOU = "ou="
oOUname = "myOU"

Set objDomain = GetObject(provider & OU & domain)
Set objOU = objDomain.create(oClass, oOU & oOUname)

objOU.SetInfo

WScript.Echo("OU " & oOUname & " was created")
```

# Reference Information

The Reference information section of the script configures the connection to Active Directory and specifies the path and target of the operation. The first decision you need to make is which provider to use. Let's talk about ADSI providers prior to looking at the remainder of the Reference information section.

# ADSI Providers

Table 11-1 lists four providers available to users of ADSI. Connecting to a Microsoft Windows NT 4 system requires using the special *WinNT* provider. During Active Directory migrations, consultants often write a script that copies users from a Windows NT 4 domain to a Microsoft Windows Server 2003 Active Directory OU or domain. In some situations (such as with customized naming schemes), writing a script is easier than using the Active Directory Migration Tool (ADMT).

**Table 11-1   ADSI Supported Providers**

| Provider | Purpose |
| --- | --- |
| *WinNT:* | To communicate with Windows NT 4.0 Primary Domain Controllers (PDCs) and Backup Domain Controllers (BDCs), and with local account databases for Windows 2000 and newer workstations. |
| *LDAP:* | To communicate with LDAP servers, including Exchange 5.x directory and Windows 2000 Active Directory. |
| *NDS:* | To communicate with Novell Directory Services servers. |
| *NWCOMPAT:* | To communicate with Novell NetWare servers. |

The first time I tried using ADSI to connect to a machine running Windows NT, I had a very frustrating experience because of the way the provider was implemented. You *must* type the *WinNT* provider name *exactly* as shown in Table 11-1. You cannot type it using all lowercase letters or all uppercase letters. You type all other provider names in all uppercase letters, but the *WinNT* name is Pascal-cased, that is, it is partially uppercase and partially lowercase. Remembering this will save you a lot of grief later. In addition, you don't get an error message telling you that your provider name is "spelled wrong"—rather, the bind operation simply fails to connect.

Once you specify the ADSI provider, you need to specify the path to the directory target. This is where a little knowledge of Active Directory comes in handy because of the way the hierarchical naming space is structured. When you connect to an LDAP (Lightweight Directory Access Protocol) service provider, you must specify where in the LDAP database hierarchy to make the connection, as the hierarchy is a structure of the database itself and not the protocol or the provider. For instance, in the CreateOU.vbs script, you create an OU that resides inside the hiring OU, which is in the HR OU. This can get confusing, until you realize that the HR OU is contained in a domain that is called *a.com*. It is vital, therefore, that you understand the hierarchy with which you are working. One tool you can use to make sure you understand the hierarchy of your domain is ADSI Edit.

> **Note** Perhaps the hardest part of using ADSI is finding out what things are called in the directory. This is because the names often bear no relationship to the display names you see in tools such as Active Directory Users and Computers. To see an example of this, refer to Appendix B, "ADSI Documentation."

ADSI Edit is included in the support tools on the Windows Server 2003 disk. It is in the support\tools directory and is installed by clicking Suptools.msi. Installation requires Help and other programs to be closed. The installation takes only a couple of minutes and does not require a reboot. After the support tools are installed, you open a blank MMC console and add the ADSI Edit snap-in. After you install the snap-in, right-click the ADSI Edit icon, select Connect To, and specify your domain using the drop-down box, as illustrated in Figure 11-1.

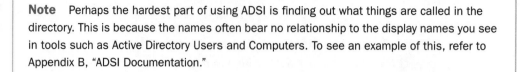

**Figure 11-1** Exploring the hierarchy of a forest to ensure correct path information for your script

## LDAP Names

When specifying the OU and the domain name, you have to use the LDAP naming convention in which the namespace is described as a series of naming parts called *relative distinguished names* (RDNs). The relative distinguished name will always be a name part that assigns a value by using the equal sign. When you put together all the relative distinguished names, and the RDNs of each of the ancestors all the way back to the root, you end up with a single globally unique distinguished name.

The relative distinguished names are usually made up of an attribute type, an equal sign, and a string value. Table 11-2 lists some of the attribute types you will see when working with Active Directory.

**Table 11-2   Common Relative Distinguished Name Attribute Types**

| Attribute | Description |
| --- | --- |
| *DC* | Domain Component |
| *CN* | Common Name |
| *OU* | Organizational Unit |
| *O* | Organization Name |
| *Street* | Street Address |
| *C* | Country Name |
| *UID* | User ID |

## Worker Information

The Worker information section of the script includes two lines of code: the first line performs the binding, and the second creates the OU. To perform these tasks, you need to build the distinguished name, which entails creating the OU after connecting to the appropriate container in Active Directory.

In the CreateOU.vbs script, the distinguished name is a concatenation of two separate variables. The variables and their associated values are listed here:

```
OU = "ou=hiring, ou=hr,"
domain = "dc=a,dc=com"
```

You can verify that you are connecting to the correct OU by using ADSI Edit. To do this, right-click the target OU, select Properties, and choose Distinguished Name from the list of available properties. A dialog box like the one shown in Figure 11-2 appears.

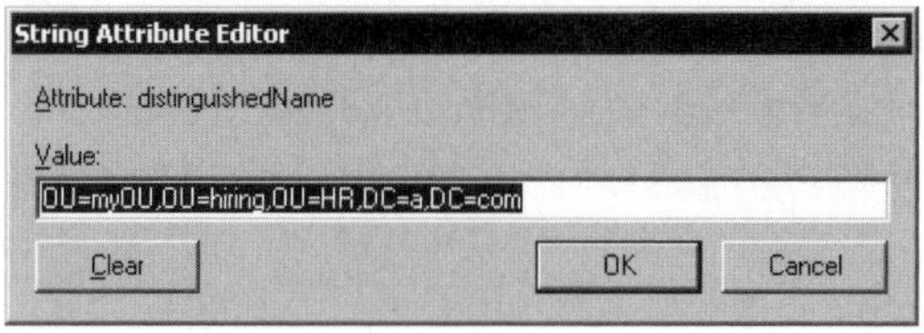

**Figure 11-2**   Using the string attribute editor in ADSI Edit to quickly verify the distinguished name of a potential target for ADSI scripting

The next line in the Reference information section specifies the object class you are working with. When you use the *Create* method, you need to specify what type of object you are creating. In CreateOU.vbs, you implement code that looks like the following line:

```
oClass = "organizationalUnit"
```

### IADsContainer

In your script, you are actually using the *Create* method of a well-known interface called *IADsContainer*. It is used to enable an ADSI container object to create, delete, or otherwise manage ADSI objects. All container objects in Active Directory implement *IADsContainer*. *IADsContainer* supports five methods, listed in Table 11-3, that you can use on any ADSI container object in Active Directory. You will use each of these methods in scripts later in this book.

**Table 11-3    *IADsContainer* Methods**

| Method | Meaning |
|---|---|
| *GetObject* | Binds the directory item with the specified *ADsPath* to a named variable. |
| *Create* | Creates a new object of a specified class in the current container. |
| *Delete* | Removes an object of the specified class from the current container. |
| *CopyHere* | Creates a copy of the object with a specified *ADsPath* in the current container. Be aware that the object must be in the same directory namespace. For example, you cannot copy an object from an *LDAP:* namespace to a *WinNT:* namespace. |
| *MoveHere* | Moves the object with a specified *ADsPath* from its original location to the current container. The same namespace restrictions that apply to the *Copy-Here* method also apply to the *MoveHere* method. |

In the CreateOU.vbs script, you implement the *IADsContainer Create* method to create the OU. You use two variables to do this. The first variable is called *oOU*, and it holds the class of the object you want to create. This time, no surprises here—you set *oOU* to equal *OU*. The second variable you use is called *oOUname*; it looks like it could hold the name of the OU because it does. You use the variable *objOU* to hold the connection to the *Create* method once you implement the connection using the *Set* command, as shown in this line of code:

```
Set objOU = objDomain.create(oClass, oOU & oOUname)
```

### Binding

Whenever you want to do anything with ADSI, you must connect to an object in Active Directory, a process also known as *binding*. Think of binding as being like tying a rope around an object to enable you to work with it. (In Texas, they'd call it lassoing.) Before you can do any work with an object in Active Directory, you must supply binding information. The *binding string* enables you to use various ADSI elements including methods and properties. The target of the proposed action is specified as a computer, a domain controller, a user, or another element that resides within the directory structure. A binding string consists of five parts. These parts are illustrated in the following binding string from the CreateOU.vbs script:

| Keyword | Variable | Command | Provider | ADsPath |
|---------|----------|---------|----------|---------|
| *Set* | *objDomain* | *GetObject* | *LDAP://* | *OU=hiring, OU=hr, dc=a, dc=com* |

> **Note**   Avoid a mistake I made early on: make sure that when you finish connecting and creating, you actually commit your changes to Active Directory. Changes to Active Directory are transactional in nature, so your change will roll back if you don't commit it. Committing the change requires you to use the *SetInfo* method, as illustrated in the following line from the CreateOU.vbs script: *objOU.SetInfo*.

## Output Information

By default, this script would not have any output information. However, to illustrate that the script is actually doing something, I implemented a simple *WScript.Echo* command to echo out the name of the container that was created. Because the OU to be created is held in the variable named *oOUname*, it was a simple proposition to echo out the contents of the variable, as illustrated in the following code snippet, which comes from the now famous CreateOU.vbs script:

```
WScript.Echo("OU " & oOUname & " was created")
```

> **Quick Check**
>
> **Q.** What is the process of connecting to Active Directory called?
>
> **A.** The process of connecting to Active Directory is called binding.
>
> **Q.** When specifying the target of an ADSI operation, what is the target called?
>
> **A.** The target of the ADSI operation is called the *ADsPath*.
>
> **Q.** An LDAP name is made up of several parts. What do you call each part separated by a comma?
>
> **A.** An LDAP name is made up of multiple parts that are called relative distinguished names.

# Creating Users

One cool trick you can do using ADSI is create users. Although using the GUI to create a single user is easy, using the GUI to create a dozen or more users would certainly not be. In addition, as you'll see, because there is a lot of similarity among ADSI scripts, deleting a dozen or more users is just as simple as creating them. And because you can use the same input text file for all the scripts, ADSI makes creating temporary accounts for use in a lab or school a real snap.

---

**Just the Steps**

▶ **To create users**

1. Use the appropriate provider for your network.

2. Connect to the container for your users.

3. Specify the domain.

4. Specify the *User* class of the object.

5. Bind to Active Directory.

6. Use the *Create Method* to create the user.

7. Use the *Put* method to at least specify the *sAMAccountName* property.

8. Use *SetInfo* to commit the user to Active Directory.

---

The CreateUser.vbs script, which follows, is very similar to the CreateOU.vbs script. In fact, CreateUser.vbs was created from CreateOU.vbs, so a detailed analysis of the script is unnecessary. The only difference is that *oClass* is equal to the "*User*" class instead of to an "*organizationalUnit*" class.

```
provider = "LDAP://"
OU = "ou=hiring, ou=hr,"
domain = "dc=a,dc=com"
oClass = "User"
oCN = "CN="
oUname = "myuser"

Set objDomain = GetObject(provider & OU & domain)
Set objUser = objDomain.create(oClass, oCN & oUname)
objUser.Put "sAMAccountName", oUname
objUser.SetInfo

WScript.Echo("User " & oUname & " was created")
```

## Reference Information

The Reference information section is where you assign values to the variables that would normally be declared in a script of this type. The provider in this case is *LDAP://*. Remember that the provider name is case-sensitive—all caps is a requirement. You next specify the OU you'll use in the *ADsPath* portion of the binding string. You are targeting an OU called *hiring* that resides within another OU called *hr*. The domain name is made up of two *domain components*, or DCs, separated by commas. The domain name is *a.com*, so the first component is *dc=a*, and the second is *dc=com*.

You must specify the user class when creating user accounts. When creating a user account, the user name is separated by a *"cn="* prefix. In Table 11-2, you learned that *cn* actually stands for *common name*. For users, you must specify the common name property of the user object.

The user will at least need a *sAMAccountName* to be able to log on to the network. The *sAMAccountName* can be the same as the common name property, and in many cases it is. You are taking the defaults for everything else, including leaving the account disabled. In the lab, you'll create a better user, but for illustrative purposes, this suffices.

## Worker Information

In the Worker information section of the script, the script starts to depart from other scripts you have looked at thus far. In this script are four lines of code, which follow:

```
Set objDomain = GetObject(provider & OU & domain)
Set objUser = objDomain.create(oClass, oCN & oUname)
objUser.Put "sAMAccountName", oUname
objUser.SetInfo
```

The binding to ADSI is exactly the same as in the previous script. You even use the same variable name. In the next line, however, when you call the *Create* method, you use different variables because you create a *User* instead of an *OU*. The *oClass* is equal to *User*, *oCN* is equal to *"CN="*, and *oUname* holds the value of the user to be created.

You now utilize the *Put* method to specify the *sAMAccountName* property. In this script, you use the *CN* name of *oUname* and use that variable for the *sAMAccountName* as well. Once all that work is done, you call *SetInfo* and write the data to Active Directory.

## Output Information

After creating the user, it would be nice to have some type of feedback. You use the same methodology as in the previous script by calling *WScript.Echo* to echo out the *oUname* variable with a note that indicates the user was created.

---

**Quick Check**

**Q.** **To create a user, which class must be specified?**

**A.** You need to specify the *User* class to create a user.

**Q.** **What is the *Put* method used for?**

**A.** The *Put* method is used to write additional property data to the object that it is bound to.

# Summary

In this chapter, you examined the use of ADSI to connect to Active Directory and create both OUs and users. You looked at the process of binding to Active Directory and saw the components that make up the binding construction. You looked at the different providers that can be employed for ADSI and learned about how you would use them. In addition, you learned that they're case-sensitive. You looked at the *Create* method that is used to create objects in Active Directory and examined the process for creating both users and OUs. You reviewed the additional properties available for the *User* object and saw how to use the *Put* method to change the values contained in different properties of the *User* object. You also learned about using the *setInfo* command to write data to Active Directory.

# Quiz Yourself

**Q.  What is the purpose of an ADSI provider?**

**A.**  The purpose of an ADSI provider is that it knows the complexities of the directory it is talking to, and it hides this from you. Each of the providers is utilized in a similar manner to standardize the scripting process.

**Q.  What are the four ADSI providers included in the box?**

**A.**  The four ADSI providers are *LDAP*, *WinNT*, *NDS*, and *NWCOMPAT*.

**Q.  What does the LDAP relative distinguished name attribute *CN* stand for?**

**A.**  The LDAP relative distinguished name attribute *CN* stands for common name.

**Q.  How is the *IADsContainer* method named *GetObject* utilized?**

**A.**  The *IADsContainer* method *GetObject* is used to bind the directory object with the specified ADsPath to a named variable.

# On Your Own

# Lab 22 Creating OUs

In this lab, you are going to practice creating OUs. The result of this will eventually become a subroutine that you can employ in other scripts when you need OUs.

## Lab Instructions

1. Open Notepad.exe.

2. On the first line, type **Option Explicit**.

3. Declare the following variables: *provider*, *domain*, *oClass*, *oOU*, *objDomain*, *objOU*, *oOUname*, and *oDescription*.

4. Assign the LDAP provider to the variable called *provider*. Your code will look like the following:

```
provider = "LDAP://"
```

5. Assign the variable domain to a domain that is accessible on the network, such as *a.dom*. Split each section of the domain name into domain components. This will look like the following:

```
domain = "dc=a,dc=com"
```

6. Assign the variable to the *organizationalUnit* class. Make sure you encase the class name in quotation marks, as shown here:

```
oClass = "organizationalUnit"
```

7. Assign a value to the variable used to hold the *OU* name. In this case, the variable is *oOUname* and the value is *Lab22*. The code will look like the following:

```
oOUname = "Lab22"
```

8. Assign an appropriate description to the *oDescription* variable. It will look something like the following:

```
oDescription = "For Lab 22 Use"
```

9. Use the *Set* command to set the variable *objDomain* equal to the handle that comes back from using the *GetObject* function when fed the provider variable and the domain variable. The code will look like the following:

```
Set objDomain = GetObject(provider & domain)
```

10. Use the *Set* command to set the variable *objOU* equal to the handle that comes back from using the *Create* method when fed the *oClass*, *oOU*, and *oOUname* variables. The code will look like the following:

```
Set objOU = objDomain.create(oClass, oOU & oOUname)
```

11. Use the *Put* method to put the data contained in the *oDescription* variable into the field designated as *Description*. Separate the variable from the field name with a comma. The code will look like the following:

```
objOU.Put "description", oDescription
```

12. Use the *SetInfo* method to commit the changes to Active Directory. The code will look like the following:

```
objOU.SetInfo
```

13. Conclude your script by using *WScript.Echo* to echo out the name of the *oOUname* and an appropriate description of the action that was taken. I used the following code to do this:

```
WScript.Echo("OU " & oOUname & " was created")
```

14. Save the script as **Lab22Solution.vbs**.

15. Run the script. For this script, it doesn't matter whether you run it in CScript or from WScript. It's probably easier to just double-click the script and let it run in WScript.

16. Open Active Directory Users and Computers to verify the presence of the Lab22 OU.

17. Right-click the Lab22 OU and choose Properties from the Action menu. On the General tab, verify that the description you assigned in step 11 is present in the Description field.

18. Close everything out. Do not delete the Lab22 OU because you'll use it in the next lab.

# Lab 23 Creating Multi-Valued Users

In this lab, you are going to practice creating users. You'll place the user in the OU created in Lab 22. The result of this will eventually become a subroutine that you can employ in other scripts when you need to use *Users*.

## Lab Instructions

1. Open Notepad.exe.

2. On the first line, type **Option Explicit**.

3. Declare the following variables: *provider, ou, domain, oClass, oCN, objDomain, objUser, oUname,* and *oDescription*.

4. Assign the LDAP provider to the variable provider. It will look like the following:

```
provider = "LDAP://"
```

5. Assign the Lab22 OU to the *OU* variable. It will look like the following:

```
OU = "ou=lab22,"
```

6. Assign the domain used in step 5 of Lab 22 to the domain variable. This domain should be the one on your local network and the one you created in the Lab22 OU. Your code will look something like the following:

```
domain = "dc=a,dc=com"
```

7. Assign the *User* class to the *oClass* variable. It will look like the following:

```
oClass = "User"
```

8. Assign the "*CN=*" value to the *oCN* variable, as shown here:

```
oCN = "CN="
```

9. Assign to the *oUname* variable the name of the user to be created. In the solution file, you create a user called *labUser*:

```
oUname = "labUser"
```

10. Assign an appropriate description for the new user. This entails assigning a value to the *oDescription* variable:

```
oDescription = "created for lab22 use"
```

11. Use the *Set* command to set the variable *objDomain* equal to the handle that comes back from using the *GetObject* function when fed the provider variable, *OU* variable, and the *domain* variable. The code looks like the following:

```
Set objDomain = GetObject(provider & OU & domain)
```

12. Use the *Set* command to set the variable *objUser* equal to the handle that comes back from using the *Create* method when fed the *oClass*, *oCN*, and *oUname* variables. The code will look like the following:

```
Set objUser = objDomain.Create(oClass, oCN & oUname)
```

13. Use the *Put* method to put the data contained in the *oUname* variable into the field designated as *sAMAccountName*. Separate the variable from the field name with a comma. The code looks like the following:

```
objUser.Put "sAMAccountName", oUname
```

14. Use the *Put* method to put the data contained in the *oUname* variable into the field designated as *DisplayName*. Separate the variable from the field name with a comma. The code looks like the following:

```
objUser.Put "DisplayName", oUname
```

15. Use the *Put* method to put the data contained in the *oDescription* variable into the field designated as *description*. Separate the variable from the field name with a comma. The code looks like the following:

```
objUser.Put "description", oDescription
```

16. Use the *SetInfo* method to commit the changes to Active Directory. The code will look like the following:

```
objUser.SetInfo
```

17. Conclude your script by using *WScript.Echo* to echo out the name of the *oUname* and an appropriate description of the action that was taken. I used the following code to do this:

```
WScript.Echo("User " & oUname & " was created")
```

18. Save the script as **Lab23Solution.vbs**.

19. Run the script. For this script, it doesn't matter whether you run it in CScript or from WScript. It's probably easier to just double-click the script and let it run in WScript.

20. Open Active Directory Users and Computers to verify the presence of the new user. The user will be contained in the Lab22 OU.

21. Right-click on the new user and choose Properties from the Action menu. On the General tab, verify that the display name and description you assigned earlier are present.

22. Close everything out.

# 12 Reading and Writing for ADSI

In this chapter, you'll look at several very important concepts such as deleting users and creating groups. You'll learn about ways to use Microsoft Visual Basic Script (VBScript) to modify user information in Active Directory—a fundamental task that consultants need to perform during upgrades and domain reorganization. You might also need to modify information in Active Directory to make global changes, such as when introducing a User Principal Name (UPN).

> **Note** One of the cool things you can do in both Microsoft Windows Server 2003 and Windows 2000 Server is abstract the complexity of the domain environment from your users. In Active Directory, you can store a logon name that can be used anywhere in the forest. It is called a *User Principal Name* and looks like an e-mail address. It is not an e-mail address, but it can be the same as the user's e-mail address, making remembering the name easy for the user.

## Before You Begin

**To work through the material presented in this chapter you need to be familiar with the following concepts from earlier chapters:**

- Binding to Active Directory
- Creating users in Active Directory
- Creating organizational units (OUs) in Active Directory
- Implementing ADSI providers
- Working with Active Directory namespaces
- Implementing constants

**After completing this chapter you will be familiar with the following:**

- Deleting users in Active Directory
- Deleting OUs in Active Directory
- Modifying users in Active Directory
- Creating groups in Active Directory

# Working with Users

In this section, you will use ADSI to modify user properties stored in Active Directory. The following list summarizes a few of the items you can change or configure:

- Office and telephone contact information

- Mailing address information

- Department, title, manager, and direct reports (people who report to the user inside the "chain of command")

User information that is stored in Active Directory can easily replace several pieces of disparate information in a single swoop. For instance, you might have an internal website that contains a telephone directory; you can put the phone number into Active Directory as an attribute of the user object. You might also have a website containing a social roster that includes employees and their hobbies; you can put hobby information in Active Directory as a custom attribute. You can also add to Active Directory information such as an organizational chart. The problem, of course, is that during a migration, information such as a user's title is the last thing the harried mind of the network administrator thinks about. To leverage the investment in Active Directory, you need to enter this type of information because it quickly becomes instrumental in the daily lives of demure users. This is where the power of ADSI and VBScript really begins to shine. We can update hundreds or even thousands of records easily and efficiently using scripting. Such a task would be unthinkable using conventional point-and-click methods.

---

**Just the Steps**

▶ **To modify user properties in Active Directory**

1. Implement the appropriate protocol provider.

2. Perform binding to Active Directory.

3. Specify the appropriate *ADsPath*.

4. Use the *Put* method to write selected properties to users.

5. Use *SetInfo* method to commit changes to Active Directory.

---

## General User Information

One of the more confusing issues when you use VBScript to modify information in Active Directory is that the names displayed on the property page do not correspond with the ADSI nomenclature. This was not done to make your life difficult; rather, the names you see in ADSI are derived from LDAP standard naming conventions. Although this naming convention makes traditional LDAP programmers happy, it does nothing for the network administrator who is a casual scripter. This is where the following script, ModifyUserProperties.vbs, comes in handy. The LDAP properties corresponding to each field in Figure 12-1 are used in this script. Some of the names make sense, but others appear to be rather obscure. Notice the series of *objUser.Put* statements. Each lines up with the corresponding fields in Figure 12-1. Use the values to see which display name maps to which LDAP attribute name.

```
provider = "LDAP://"
OU = "ou=lab22,"
domain = "dc=a,dc=com"
oCN = "CN="
oUname = "labUser,"

Set objUser = GetObject(provider & oCN & oUname & OU & domain)

objUser.Put "givenName", "fred"
objUser.Put "initials", "f."
objUser.Put "sn", "flintstone"
objUser.Put "DisplayName", "labUser"
objUser.Put "description", "funny looking dude"
objUser.Put "physicalDeliveryOfficeName", "RQ2"
objUser.Put "telephoneNumber", "999-222-1111"
objUser.Put "mail", "fff@hotmail.com"
objUser.Put "wwwHomePage", "http://www.fred.msn.com"

objUser.SetInfo

WScript.Echo("User " & oUname & " was modified")
```

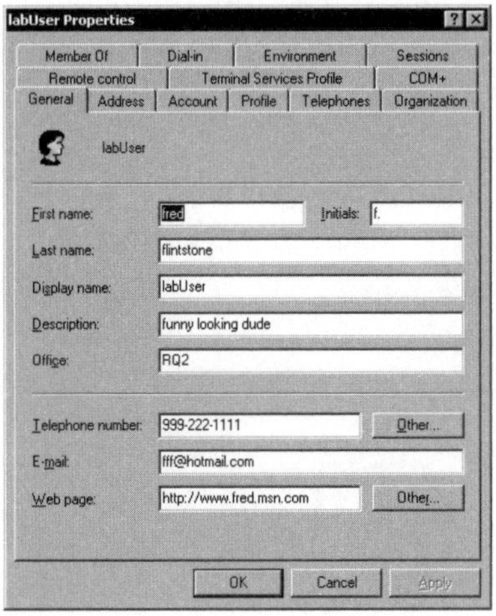

**Figure 12-1**   All the General User Properties can be set by using ADSI and VBScript

**On the CD**    The Header information section of ModifyUserProperties.vbs has been omitted for clarity. This section does, however, exist in the original script on the companion CD.

## Reference Information

The Reference information section of the script assigns values to the variables used in the script. Here you assign the LDAP provider to the provider variable. You then assign the entire OU path to the *OU* variable. The variable called *Domain* gets assigned both of the domain components that are used for constructing a fully qualified name. These domain components are the *"DC="* sections of the code. You use *oCN* to hold the *CN=* reference, and you end the section by equating *oUname* to the user name you plan to modify. If you were using a text file to supply the variable, you could still use this variable. The Reference section follows:

```
provider = "LDAP://"
OU = "ou=lab22,"
domain = "dc=a,dc=com"
oCN = "CN="
oUname = "labUser,"
```

## Worker Information

The Worker information section of the ModifyUserProperties.vbs script contains a lot of code because it modifies all the properties contained on the General tab of the user properties in Microsoft Windows Server 2003. The first line in the Worker information section performs the binding to Active Directory. In this instance, you bind not to an OU but to a specific user, as shown here:

```
Set objUser = GetObject(provider & oCN & oUname & OU & domain)
```

You assign *"CN"* to the variable *oCN* to keep it separate from the user name portion. In this way, you can more easily make changes to multiple users. In our particular situation, you connect to the OU created in the previous chapter, and the Lab 22 OU is off the root in the Active Directory hierarchy. If the OU was nested, you could still use the script, and in the Reference section specify something like *OU = "ou=level1, ou=level2, ou=level3"* (or whatever the actual namespace consisted of). The domain variable holds the entire domain component. *CN, UserName, Ou,* and *Domain* make up the *ADsPath* portion of the binding string.

Once you have the binding to Active Directory, you are ready to begin modifying user information. The cool part about using the *Put* method is that it overwrites any information already present in that property of the cached copy of the *User* object. You will see the effect only on the particular property being *Put* until you call *SetInfo* to write the changes to Active Directory. If you don't specify a particular piece of information (that is, you leave the space between the quotation marks empty), you'll be greeted with an error message. Figure 12-2 shows this friendly message.

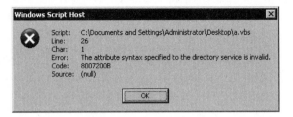

**Figure 12-2**   Error message received when a property value is left out of a *Put* command

To write information to a specific user property, use the *Put* method. This entails specifying both the ADSI field name and the desired value. The pertinent Worker information section of the ModifyUserProperties.vbs script follows:

```
objUser.Put "givenName", "fred"
objUser.Put "initials", "f."
objUser.Put "sn", "flintstone"
objUser.Put "DisplayName", "labUser"
objUser.Put "description" , "funny looking dude"
objUser.Put "physicalDeliveryOfficeName", "RQ2"
objUser.Put "telephoneNumber", "999-222-1111"
objUser.Put "mail", "fff@hotmail.com"

objUser.Put "wwwHomePage", "http://www.fred.msn.com"
```

The last item in the Worker information section is the *SetInfo* command. If *SetInfo* isn't called, the information isn't written to Active Directory. The information simply does not exist. There will be no error message—merely an absence of data. The ModifyUser-Properties.vbs script uses the following *SetInfo* line to ensure changes are written to Active Directory:

```
objUser.SetInfo
```

## Output Information

Once all the changes are loaded into Active Directory, you include an output statement to let you know that the changes have been made to Active Directory. In the Modify-UserProperties.vbs script, you use a simple *WScript.Echo* statement. This echo statement is listed here:

```
WScript.Echo("User " & oUname & " was modified")
```

---

**Quick Check**

Q. **What is the field name for the user's first name?**

A. The field for the user's first name is called "*GivenName*". You can find field mapping information in the Platform SDK.

Q. **Why do you need to do a *SetInfo* command?**

A. Without a *SetInfo* command, all changes introduced during the script are lost because the changes are made to a cached set of attribute values for the object being modified. Nothing is committed to Active Directory until you call *SetInfo*.

---

# Creating the Second Page

One of the more useful tasks you can perform with Active Directory is exposing address information. This ability is particularly important when a company has more than one location and more than a few hundred employees. I remember when one of the first uses for an intranet was to host a centralized list of employees. Such a project quickly paid for itself because companies no longer needed an administrative assistant to modify, copy, collate, and distribute hundreds of copies of the up-to-date employee directory—potentially a full-time job for one person. Once an intranet site was in place, personnel at each location were given rights to modify the list. With Active Directory, you avoid this duplication of work by keeping all information in a centralized location. The "second page" in Active Directory Users and Computers is the address page, shown in Figure 12-3.

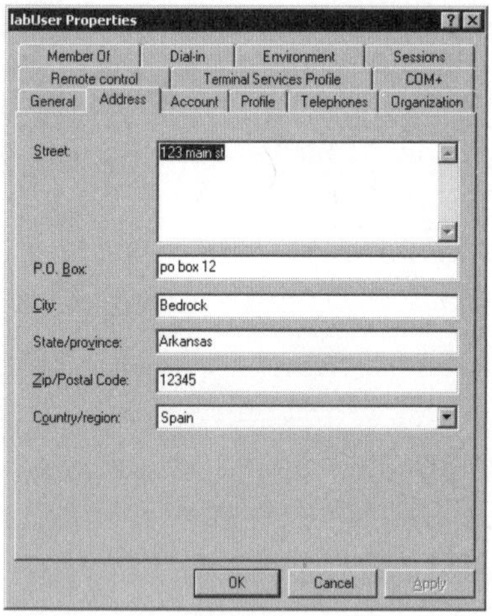

**Figure 12-3**   Every item on the Address tab in Active Directory Users and Computers can be filled in via ADSI and VBScript

In the ModifyUserSecondPage.vbs script, you use ADSI to set the street, post office box, city, state, zip code, and country values for the *User* object. Table 12-1 lists the

Active Directory attribute names and their mappings to the Active Directory Users and Computers (ADUC) management tool "friendly" display names.

**Table 12-1   Address Page Mappings**

| Active Directory Users and Computers label | Active Directory attribute name |
| --- | --- |
| Street | *streetAddress* |
| P.O. Box | *postOfficeBox* |
| City | *l* (Note that this is lowercase.) |
| State/Province | *st* |
| Zip/Postal Code | *postalCode* |
| Country/Region | *c* |

```
provider = "LDAP://"
OU = "ou=lab22,"
domain = "dc=a,dc=com"
oCN = "CN="
oUname = "labUser,"

Set objUser = GetObject(provider & oCN & oUname & OU & domain)

objUser.Put "streetAddress", "123 main st"
objUser.Put "postOfficeBox", "po box 12"
objUser.Put "l", "Bedrock"
objUser.Put "st", "Arkansas"
objUser.Put "postalCode" , "12345"
objUser.Put "c", "RO"


objUser.SetInfo

WScript.Echo("User " & oUname & " was modified")
```

# Reference Information

The Reference information section assigns values to the variables declared in the script. In this section, you assign the LDAP provider to the provider variable. You then build the entire OU path to the *OU* variable. The domain variable gets assigned both domain components and constructs a fully qualified name. You use *oCN* to hold the *CN=* reference, and then conclude the Reference information section by equating *oUname* to the user name you plan to modify.

# Worker Information

The Worker information section begins by performing an Active Directory binding:

```
Set objUser = GetObject(provider & oCN & oUname & OU & domain)
```

The hardest part of the Worker information section of this script is figuring out how to make the country assignment show up in ADUC. I will admit that it took me a bit of time before I realized that the country codes have to be entered in accordance with ISO standard 3166. If you use the c field, you use the two-letter country code. If you use ISO standard 3166-1, which contains two-letter country codes that have been officially assigned, you will be in fine shape. However, 3166-1 also contains country number assignments and short text names. The alternate forms of country codes do not work with the c field. The ISO 3166 is actually divided into three different parts and is updated on a regular basis to keep up with political changes in the global environment. In compliance with ISO 3166, country codes can actually be entered in three different ways. The easiest to deal with uses the letter c as the field and a two-letter country code as the property.

Although the ISO 3166-1 specifies all the country codes as uppercase letters, ADSI seems to be case-agnostic for this field, so "us" or "US" will both cause the field to display the name of United States. (One interesting thing about the ISO 3166-1 codes is that they are the same as the national top-level domain names.) A sample two-letter country code sheet based on ISO 3166-1 is listed in Table 12-2. The full table is available at *http://www.iso.org*.

**Table 12-2  ISO 3166-1 Country Codes**

| Country code | Country name |
| --- | --- |
| AF | AFGHANISTAN |
| AU | AUSTRALIA |
| EG | EGYPT |
| LV | LATVIA |
| ES | SPAIN |
| US | UNITED STATES |

### Staying Put

Filling out the second page of the Active Directory Users and Computers user address properties entails modifying a lot of fields. To do this you use the *Put* command, as shown in the following code:

```
objUser.Put "streetAddress", "123 main st"
objUser.Put "postOfficeBox", "po box 12"
objUser.Put "l", "Bedrock"
objUser.Put "st", "Arkansas"
objUser.Put "postalCode" , "12345"
objUser.Put "c", "RO"
```

Most of the fields are self-explanatory. The only two that do not make much sense are the small letter "*l*" for *city* and the country code because of the way you fill it in, which you learned about earlier. Unfortunately, you're not always presented with an error; the script just does not seem to update, so you are left (or at least I am left) clicking the Refresh button in Active Directory Users and Computers as you wait for replication to take place.

> **Note**   Do not forget to use the *SetInfo* method to commit your changes to Active Directory. If I seem to harp on this, it's because I've forgotten to do so on occasion, and I want to spare you the mental agony. This is one occasion when it is easy to commit. You just use this code: *objUser.SetInfo*.

## Output Information

After creating all those lovely updates, I for one want to see something to let me know the script has completed running. Obviously, if you were running this in the scheduler, you wouldn't want to present a message box (although you might want to write something to the event log). In your script, you use a simple *WScript.Echo* box to let you know the script completed. Note that even though the script says the updates took place, it only *assumes* they worked—it does not perform any verification. *WScript.Echo* could just as easily say "go jump in a lake," although that wouldn't be the friendliest message to display. The output code follows:

```
WScript.Echo("User " & oUname & " was modified")
```

> **Quick Check**
>
> **Q.** To set the country name on the address page for Active Directory Users and Computers, what is required?
>
> **A.** To update the country name on the address page for Active Directory Users and Computers, you must specify the c field and feed it a two-letter code that is found in ISO publication 3166.
>
> **Q.** What field name in ADSI is used to specify the city information?
>
> **A.** You set the city information by assigning a value to the "l" (lowercase *l*) field after making the appropriate connection to Active Directory.
>
> **Q.** If you put an inappropriate letter code in the c field, what error message is displayed?
>
> **A.** No error message is displayed. The update simply fails to display in ADUC. If, however, you go into ADSI Edit, you will see the value stored there. The Active Directory Users and Computers tool is smart enough to not display codes it does not understand.

# Deleting Users

There are times when you need to delete user accounts, and with ADSI you can very easily delete large numbers of users with the single click of a mouse. Some reasons for deleting user accounts follow:

- To clean up a computer lab environment, that is, to return machines to a known state.

- To clean up accounts at the end of a school year. Many schools delete all student-related accounts and files at the end of each year. Scripting makes it easy to both create and delete the accounts.

- To clean up temporary accounts created for special projects. If the creation of accounts is scripted, their deletion can also be scripted, ensuring no temporary accounts are left lingering in the directory.

---

**Just the Steps**

▶ **To delete users**

1. Perform the binding to the appropriate OU.

2. Use *GetObject* to make a connection.

3. Specify the appropriate provider and *ADsPath*.

4. Call the *Delete* method.

5. Specify object class as *User*.

6. Specify the user to delete by CN.

---

To delete a user, call the *Delete* method after binding to the appropriate level in the Active Directory namespace. Then specify both the object class, which in this case is *User*, and the CN of the user to be deleted. This can actually be accomplished in only two lines of code:

```
Set objOU = GetObject("LDAP://ou=management,dc=fabrikam,dc=com")
objOU.Delete "User", "cn=myerken"
```

If you modify the CreateUser.vbs script, you can easily transform it into a DeleteUser.vbs script, which follows. Notice that the Reference information section is basically the same. It holds the path to the OU and the path to the user in the variables, enabling you to modify the script more easily. The main change is in the Worker section of the script. The binding string is the same as seen earlier. However, you use the connection that was made in the binding string, and call the *Delete* method. You specify the class of the object in the *oClass* variable in the Reference section of the script. You also list the *oUname* and *CN=* parts as well. The syntax is *Delete(Class, target)*. The deletion takes effect immediately. No *SetInfo* command is required.

```
provider = "LDAP://"
OU = "ou=Lab22,"
domain = "dc=a,dc=com"
oClass = "User"
oCN = "CN="
oUname = "labUser"

Set objDomain = GetObject(provider & OU & domain)
objDomain.Delete oClass, oCN & oUname

WScript.Echo("User " & oUname & " was deleted")
```

# Summary

In this chapter, you examined modifying user properties in Active Directory by using ADSI. To modify these properties, you match the UI names with the names that are utilized in Active Directory. Once the properties are mapped to the user interface, you can use the *Put* method to write the changes. Writing changes to Active Directory is transactional in nature, so once changes are made, you must call the *SetInfo* method to write them. Country properties of users can present a special challenge because they aren't intuitive; you have to use the two-letter codes maintained by ISO 3166. This chapter concluded by looking at the process of deleting a user. In many cases, it takes only one or two changes to modify a script that creates a user into a script that deletes a user. One important issue to keep in mind when using scripts to delete users is that no *SetInfo* command is required. When the command completes, the user is deleted. No additional steps are required to delete users.

# Quiz Yourself

**Q.** **What is the main advantage of deleting users via a script?**

**A.** The advantage of deleting users via a script is that in many cases, you can use the creation script and make only a few changes to it. This makes for a nice life cycle solution.

**Q.** **What is the command required to commit the deletion of users in Active Directory?**

**A.** To commit the deletion of users in Active Directory, no special command is required. Users are deleted as soon as the *Delete* method is called.

**Q.** **In which publication are the country codes used to fill in the country section of the User Address tab in Active Directory Users and Computers found?**

**A.** The country codes used to fill in the country section of the user address tab in Active Directory Users and Computers are found in ISO 3166.

**Q.** **How is the user's first name modified in Active Directory via ADSI?**

**A.** A user's first name is modified by using the *Put* command to add a value to the Given-Name field. Once the value is written, you must use the *SetInfo* command to write the change to Active Directory.

**Q.** When using the *Put* method to write to a cached value, what happens when data already exists in the field being written to?

**A.** When using the *Put* method to write to Active Directory, any data already existing in the field is overwritten without prompting. This means you need to be careful when using scripting to modify user information in Active Directory. Such scripts should always be tested prior to being run in production.

# On Your Own

# Lab 24 Deleting Users

In this lab, you will practice deleting users. You begin with a starter file that was used to create the user. This is a good practice because you can ensure that all created users get deleted when the time comes. While working on your script, if you need to run the script several times, you can use the Lab24Starter.vbs file to create your user prior to deleting the user. If the user isn't present when you try deletion, you get an error.

## Lab Instructions

1. Open Notepad.exe.

2. Open Lab24Starter.vbs.

3. Delete the declaration for the variable *objUser*.

4. Delete three of the four lines that call *objUser* in the Worker information section of the script. These lines look like the following:

```
objUser.Put "sAMAccountName", oUname
objUser.Put "DisplayName", oUname

objUser.SetInfo
```

5. Locate the *Set objUser* line used to create the user initially so that the line now deletes the user instead. The original line looks like the following:

```
Set objUser = objDomain.create(oClass, oCN & oUname)
```

6. Remove the *Set objUser* portion of the line. It will look like the following:

```
objDomain.create(oClass, oCN & oUname)
```

7. Change the method called in the preceding line from *Create* to *Delete*. The line will now look like the following:

```
objDomain.Delete(oClass, oCN & oUname)
```

8. Save your work. If you try to run the script now, you'll get an error because you need to remove the parentheses. Once removed, the code looks like the following:

```
objDomain.Delete oClass, oCN & oUname
```

9. Change the output message so that it says *deleted* instead of *created*. It looks like the following once the change is implemented:

```
WScript.Echo("User " & oUname & " was deleted")
```

10. Save your work.

11. Open Active Directory Users and Computers to verify that *LabUser* was deleted.

12. Run the script. If it fails, run the starter script to ensure there is a user on the server. After this is done, run the script to see whether it works. When it does, run the starter script again, because you'll need the user for the next lab.

# Lab 25 Using the Event Log

In this lab, you modify the delete user script from Lab 24 and write the resulting output to the event log instead of to a pop-up dialog box. This gives us an enterprise type of solution because the script could be scheduled, or the script might delete a large number of users, in which case writing output to a dialog box or even to a command prompt would be impractical. The event log always exists, so it is a convenient place to log information. Only three lines of code are required to implement writing to the event log.

## Lab Instructions

1. Open Notepad.exe.

2. Open the **Lab25Starter.vbs** file, and save it as **Lab25Solution.vbs**. This will ensure you have a fresh working copy of the script and will give you a fallback option if required.

3. Delete the *WScript.Echo* line that is at the bottom of the script. This line looks like the following:

```
WScript.Echo("User " & oUname & " was deleted")
```

4. Add two new variables. The first variable is *objShell* and is used to hold the connection to the scripting shell object. The second variable is *oMessage* and holds the text of the message you write to the event log. These two declarations look like the following:

```
Dim objShell ' holds connection to scripting shell
Dim oMessage ' holds text of the message we write.
```

5.  Now define a constant called *EVENT_SUCCESS* and set it equal to *0*. The code to do this looks like the following:

    ```
    Const EVENT_SUCCESS = 0
    ```

6.  Save your work.

7.  At the bottom of the script where the *WScript.Echo* command used to reside, use the *CreateObject* method to create an instance of the scripting shell. Set the handle equal to *objShell*. The code to do this looks like the following:

    ```
    Set objShell = CreateObject("WScript.Shell")
    ```

8.  Use the *LogEvent* method to write your message to the event log. You're interested in only a return code of *0*, which indicates a success. (Complete information on *LogEvent* is available in the WSH 5.6 help file.) The code looks like the following:

    ```
    objShell.LogEvent EVENT_SUCCESS, oMessage
    ```

9.  Save the script and run it.

10. Notice that there is no feedback. However, if you open the application log on the machine running the script, you see the event message. This is quite useful because the event message allows you to log updates as well as to audit them. The log looks like the one in Figure 12-4.

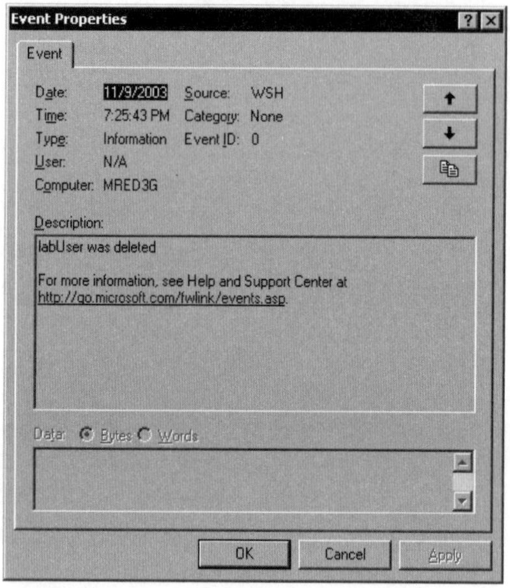

**Figure 12-4**   Using the *LogEvent* method to write scripts that provide notification and don't require user intervention

11. Open Active Directory Users and Computers to verify the user was deleted.

# 13 Searching Active Directory

In this chapter, you'll look at two very important concepts: searching Active Directory and making configuration changes. Searching might not sound like a very exciting topic; however, once you see how easily cords of crucial configuration information is returned, you might very well begin to carol the capabilities of ADSI.

## Before You Begin

**To work through the material presented in this chapter you need to be familiar with the following concepts from earlier chapters:**

- ADSI binding operations
- ADSI namespace
- Creating a dictionary object
- Implementing *For Each...Next* constructions
- Implementing *Select Case* constructions
- Implementing the *While Not Wend* construction

**After completing this chapter you will be familiar with the following:**

- Connecting to Active Directory to perform a search
- Controlling the way data is returned

## Connecting to Active Directory to Perform a Search

In this section, you are going to use a special query technique to search Active Directory. You'll be able to use the results returned by that custom query to perform additional tasks. For example, you could search Active Directory for all users who don't have telephone numbers assigned to them. You could then send that list to the person in charge of maintaining the telephone numbers. Even better, you could modify the search so that it returns the user names and their managers' names. You could then take the list of users with no phone numbers that is returned and send e-mail to the managers to get the phone list in Active Directory updated. The functionality incorporated in your scripts is primarily limited by your imagination. The following summarizes uses for search technology:

- Query Active Directory for a list of computers that meet a given search criterion
- Query Active Directory for a list of users who meet a given search criterion

- Query Active Directory for a list of printers that meet a given search criterion

- Use the data returned from the preceding three queries to perform additional operations

---

**Just the Steps**

▶ **To search Active Directory**

1. Create a connection to Active Directory by using ADO.

2. Use the *Open* method of the object to access Active Directory.

3. Create an ADO command object and assign the *ActiveConnection* property to the connection object.

4. Assign the query string to the *CommandText* property of the command object.

5. Use the *Execute* method to run the query and store the results in a *RecordSet* object.

6. Read information in the result set using properties of the *RecordSet* object.

7. Close the connection by using the *Close* method of the connection object.

---

The following script, BasicQuery.vbs, illustrates how to search using Active Directory. This script follows the steps detailed in the "Just the Steps: To search Active Directory" section.

```
Option Explicit
On Error Resume Next
Dim oQuery
Dim objConnection
Dim objCommand
Dim objRecordSet

oQuery = "<LDAP://dc=a,dc=com>;;name;subtree"
Set objConnection = CreateObject("ADODB.Connection")
Set objCommand = CreateObject("ADODB.Command")
objConnection.Open "Provider=ADsDSOObject;"
objCommand.ActiveConnection = objConnection
objCommand.CommandText = oQuery
Set objRecordSet = objCommand.Execute

While Not objRecordSet.EOF
    WScript.Echo objRecordSet.Fields("name")
    objRecordSet.MoveNext
Wend

objConnection.Close
```

In the BasicQuery.vbs script, you define your query after using the normal *Option Explicit* and *On Error Resume Next* commands. You then assign the value of the query to the variable called *oQuery*. The syntax of the query looks similar to the syntax you used to query WMI, and it follows a SQL-like formula. The aspect of this syntax that is a little unusual is assigning a search string to a command method. If you envision the procedure as stating that the command you want to execute is the query you want executed, perhaps the procedure will make a little more sense.

The query actually consists of two parts. The first part of the query is contained in angle brackets (< >) and specifies both the provider to utilize and the LDAP name of the container you want to connect to. The second part of the query lists the fields you want to return in the result set.

**Note**   The BasicQuery.vbs script query we're examining follows the same syntax you would use for an ActiveX Data Objects (ADO) search. ADO is a standard for connecting and querying different types of data sources. The basic syntax of an ADO connection is discussed in the next section, "Creating More Effective Queries," and is highlighted in Table 13-1.

## Header Information

The Header information section of the BasicQuery.vbs script contains the *Option Explicit* command as the first line as well as the *On Error Resume Next* line, which causes the script to continue executing the line after an error occurs. The following lines of the script detail all the variables that have been declared in the script:

```
Dim oQuery
Dim objConnection
Dim objCommand
Dim objRecordSet
```

## Reference Information

The Reference information section of the script is used to define the LDAP query, set up the connection to Active Directory, and execute the query, as shown in the following code:

```
oQuery = "<LDAP://dc=a,dc=com>;;name;subtree"
Set objConnection = CreateObject("ADODB.Connection")
Set objCommand = CreateObject("ADODB.Command")
objConnection.Open "Provider=ADsDSOObject;"
objCommand.ActiveConnection = objConnection
objCommand.CommandText = oQuery
Set objRecordSet = objCommand.Execute
```

The *oQuery* variable is used to define the query you will submit to Active Directory. In this instance, you're interested in the *Name* attribute, which is specified following two semicolons. The *subtree* part of the query tells VBScript the scope of your query. The *subtree* modifier means that you want to search the subtree found under the target that you specified in the LDAP portion of the query. You define the starting point of your search by using angle brackets and the LDAP syntax. In this case, you start your search at the root of *a.com*, and you're interested in returning the *Name* attribute from every object in the subtree—which means searching the entire hierarchy.

*Set ObjConnection* creates a connection object that will be used to connect to Active Directory. Specifying *ADODB* means you will use the ADSI OLE DB provider to talk to Active Directory. The *CreateObject* method actually goes ahead and creates the connection object in memory.

Now that you have a connection object resident in memory (named *ObjConnection*), you can create a command object that will be used to shuttle a query into Active Directory. You name this command object *objCommand* and set it equal to the object you get when you call *ADODB.Command*.

Having created the command object, you're now ready to open the connection to Active Directory. In this case, you use the *ADsDSOObject* provider. Because you can use ADO to talk to different data sources, you must specify which data provider to use when opening the connection. Here's an analogy to help you understand why you must specify a particular data provider when opening a connection. Think of opening a connection as being like opening a can of food in your kitchen. In most cases, the standard wheel type of can opener provides the needed leverage. At times, however, you might need a different type of can opener, such as the kind that pokes holes in the can. In the same way, depending on your data source, you might need to use a different provider. When talking to Active Directory, you will always use the *ADsDSOObject* provider.

Next, you need to define which connection to use for the command object. In this instance, you tell VBScript to use *objConnection* as the active connection. After telling VBScript to use *objConnection* as the active connection, specify the query to use by assigning the value of the *oQuery* variable as equal to *commandText*.

Now you have a query, a connection, a command, a provider, an active connection, and command text. All that is left is to execute the command, which you do by using the following code:

```
Set objRecordSet = objCommand.Execute
```

You use the *Execute* method of the command object and set the data that comes back equal to the variable called *objRecordSet*. You do this so that you can feed data into the Worker information section of the script.

## Worker and Output Information

The Worker information section of the BasicQuery.vbs script is used to iterate through the recordset that was returned when you used the *Execute* method of *objCommand*.

In this instance, you use the *While Not Wend* construction to coordinate echoing out the name field. The *While Not Wend* control structure allows you to know whether you've reached the end of the recordset file. (The end of the file is referred to as *EOF*, or end of file.) If you haven't reached the end of the file comprising the recordset (called *objRecordSet*), you echo out the name retrieved by the initial query. After you echo out the name, you move to the next record in the recordset. Here's the code that illustrates this process:

```
While Not objRecordSet.EOF
    WScript.Echo objRecordSet.Fields("name")
    objRecordSet.MoveNext
Wend
objConnection.Close
```

The Output information section of BasicQuery.vbs does a very simple *WScript.Echo* output that indicates the result of the search. In more advanced scripts, you might want to write to a text file, a database, or even a Web page. After you produce output for all your information, you close the active connection by using *objConnection.Close*.

---

**Quick Check**

**Q.** What technology is utilized to search Active Directory?

**A.** ADO is the technology that is used to search Active Directory.

**Q.** Which part of the script is used to perform the query?

**A.** The command portion of the script is used to perform the query.

**Q.** How are results returned from an ADO search of Active Directory?

**A.** The results are returned in a recordset.

---

## Creating More Effective Queries

Effective querying of Active Directory requires that you understand a little more about ADO searches. Table 13-1 lists the objects that are associated with searching Active Directory.

**Table 13-1   Objects Used to Search Active Directory**

| Object | Description |
| --- | --- |
| *Connection* | An open connection to an OLE DB data source such as ADSI. |
| *Command* | Defines a specific command to execute against the data source. |
| *Parameter* | An optional collection for any parameters to provide to the command object. |

**Table 13-1    Objects Used to Search Active Directory**

| Object | Description |
| --- | --- |
| *RecordSet* | A set of records from a table, a command object, or SQL syntax. A *RecordSet* object can be created without any underlying *Connection* object. |
| *Field* | A single column of data in a recordset. |
| *Property* | A collection of values supplied by the provider for ADO. |
| *Error* | Contains details about data access errors. Refreshed when an error occurs in a single operation. |

For ADO to talk with ADSI, two objects are required. The first object is the connection object, and the second object is *RecordSet*. The command object is used to maintain the connection, pass along the query parameters, and perform such tasks as specifying the page size and search scope and executing the query. The *Connection* object is used to load the provider and to validate the user's credentials. By default, it utilizes the credentials of the currently logged-on user. If you need to specify alternative credentials, you can use the properties listed in Table 13-2.

**Table 13-2    Authentication Properties for the *Connection* Object**

| Property | Description |
| --- | --- |
| *User ID* | A string that identifies the user whose security context is used when performing the search. (For more information about the format of the user name string, see *IADsOpenDSObject::OpenDSObject* in the Platform SDK.) If the value is not specified, the default is the logged-on user or the user impersonated by the calling process. |
| *Password* | A string that specifies the password of the user identified by *"User ID"*. |
| *Encrypt Password* | A Boolean value that specifies whether the password is encrypted. The default is *False*. |
| *ADSI Flag* | A set of flags from the *ADS_AUTHENTICATION_ENUM* enumeration. The flag specifies the binding authentication options. The default is *zero*. |

A number of search options are available to the network administrator. The use of these search options will have an extremely large impact on the performance of your queries against Active Directory. It is imperative, therefore, that you learn to use the following options. Obviously, not all options need to be specified in each situation. In fact, in many situations, the defaults will perform just fine. However, if a query is taking a long time to complete, or you seem to be flooding the network with unexpected traffic, you might want to take a look at the search properties in Table 13-3.

Note that you should specify a page size. In Windows Server 2003, Active Directory is limited to returning 1500 objects from the results of a query when no page size is specified. The *Page Size* property tells Active Directory how many objects to return at a time. When this property is specified, there is no limit on the number of returned objects Active Directory can provide. If you specify a size limit, the page size must be smaller.

**Table 13-3   ADO Search Properties**

| Property | Description |
| --- | --- |
| *Asynchronous* | A Boolean value that specifies whether the search is synchronous or asynchronous. The default is *False* (synchronous). A synchronous search blocks until the server returns the entire result (or for a paged search, the entire page). An asynchronous search blocks until one row of the search results is available, or until the time specified by the *Timeout* property elapses. |
| *Cache results* | A Boolean value that specifies whether the result should be cached on the client side. The default is *True*; ADSI caches the result set. Turning off this option might be desirable for large result sets. |
| *Chase referrals* | A value from *ADS_CHASE_REFERRALS_ENUM* that specifies how the search chases referrals. The default is *ADS_CHASE_REFERRALS_ EXTERNAL*. |
| *Column Names Only* | A Boolean value that indicates that the search should retrieve only the name of attributes to which values have been assigned. The default is *False*. |
| *Deref Aliases* | A Boolean value that specifies whether aliases of found objects are resolved. The default is *False*. |
| *Page size* | An integer value that turns on paging and specifies the maximum number of objects to return in a result set. The default is no page size. (For more information, see PageSize in the Platform SDK.) |
| *SearchScope* | A value from the *ADS_SCOPEENUM* enumeration that specifies the search scope. The default is *ADS_SCOPE_SUBTREE*. |
| *Size Limit* | An integer value that specifies the size limit for the search. For Active Directory, the size limit specifies the maximum number of returned objects. The server stops searching once the size limit is reached and returns the results accumulated up to that point. The default is *no limit*. |
| *Sort on* | A string that specifies a comma-separated list of attributes to use as sort keys. This property works only for directory servers that support the LDAP control for server-side sorting. Active Directory supports the sort control, but this control can have an impact on server performance, particularly when the result set is large. Be aware that Active Directory supports only a single sort key. The default is *no sorting*. |

**Table 13-3  ADO Search Properties**

| Property | Description |
| --- | --- |
| *Time Limit* | An integer value that specifies the time limit, in seconds, for the search. When the time limit is reached, the server stops searching and returns the results accumulated to that point. The default is *no time limit*. |
| *Timeout* | An integer value that specifies the client-side timeout value, in seconds. This value indicates the time the client waits for results from the server before quitting the search. The default is *no timeout*. |

# Searching for Specific Types of Objects

One of the best ways to improve the performance of Active Directory searches is to limit the scope of the search operation. Fortunately, searching for a specific type of object is one of the easiest tasks to perform. For example, to perform a task on a group of computers, limit your search to the computer class of objects. To work with only groups, users, computers, or printers, specify the *objectClass* or the *objectCategory* in the search filter. The *objectCategory* attribute is a single value that specifies the class from which the object in Active Directory is derived. In other words, users are derived from an *objectCategory* called *users*. All the properties you looked at in the last chapter are contained in a template called an *objectCategory*. When you create a new user, Active Directory does a lookup to find out what properties the user class contains. Then it copies all those properties onto the new user you just created. In this way, all users have the same properties available to them. The attribute called *objectClass* is a multivalued attribute, and as you learned in the discussion of WMI, you have to use a *For...Next* type of construction to iterate all instances of values contained in the multivalued attribute. Because of this, *objectCategory* is easier to work with for filtering out types of objects.

---

**Just the Steps**

▶ **To limit the Active Directory search**

1. Create a connection to Active Directory by using ADO.

2. Use the *Open* method of the object to access Active Directory.

3. Create an ADO command object, and assign the *ActiveConnection* property to the *Connection* object.

4. Assign the query string to the *CommandText* property of the *command* object.

5. In the query string, specify the *objectCategory* of the target query.

6. Choose specific fields of data to return in response to the query.

7. Use the *Execute* method to run the query and store the results in a *RecordSet* object.

8. Read information in the result set using properties of the *RecordSet* object.

9. Close the connection by using the *Close* method of the connection object.

---

In the FilterComputers.vbs script, you use ADO to query Active Directory with the goal of returning a recordset containing selected properties from all the computers with accounts in the directory. The Header information and Worker information sections of the script are the same as in the previous script, so we won't discuss them.

```
Option Explicit
On Error Resume Next

Dim qQuery
Dim objConnection
Dim objCommand
Dim objRecordSet

qQuery = "<LDAP://dc=a,dc=com>;" & _
    "(objectCategory=computer);" & _
    "distinguishedName,name;subtree"

Set objConnection = CreateObject("ADODB.Connection")
Set objCommand = CreateObject("ADODB.Command")
objConnection.Open "Provider=ADsDSOObject;"
objCommand.ActiveConnection = objConnection
objCommand.CommandText = qQuery
Set objRecordSet = objCommand.Execute

While Not objRecordSet.EOF
    WScript.Echo objRecordSet.Fields("name")
    objRecordSet.MoveNext
Wend

objConnection.Close
```

## Reference Information

The Reference information section is basically the same as in the previous script, with the exception of the query. You call the query *qQuery* in this script, as shown here:

```
qQuery = "<LDAP://dc=a,dc=com>;" & _
    "(objectCategory=computer)" & _
    ";distinguishedName,name;subtree"
```

You can see the power of using the ADO connection to query Active Directory. You choose a couple of attributes from the dozens of available attributes associated with the computer object in Active Directory. This makes a very efficient query because you return only the desired information.

## Output Information

The studious reader will realize that we've returned data on two attributes of the computer object: the *distinguishedName* and the *name* of the computer. The Output information section of the script looks like the following:

```
WScript.Echo objRecordSet.Fields("name")
```

You returned an additional field that you didn't use. You will, however, use it in the lab. At this point, it is sufficient to illustrate how to write data from the recordset. You use the *Echo* command to send the data out, but the interesting part is you specify the field by name. It is perhaps confusing here that the field you are sending out is called *name*. To send out the *distinguishedName* field, put *distinguishedName* in quotation marks.

---

**Quick Check**

**Q.** **What is one way to limit the amount of data returned by an ADO query of Active Directory?**

**A.** To limit the amount of data returned by an ADO query of Active Directory, you can specify an *objectCategory*, which is very easy to do. In this way, you can limit searches to just computers, users, printers, or other objects in Active Directory.

**Q.** **To specify an alternate set of credentials or to encrypt the password, what must be done in your script?**

**A.** To specify an alternate set of credentials or to encrypt the password, you must use the authentication properties of the connection object.

**Q.** **What two items must be specified for ADO to talk to Active Directory?**

**A.** The two items that must be specified for ADO to talk to Active Directory are the connection string and recordset. All other fields are optional.

---

# What Is Global Catalog?

As you become more proficient in writing your scripts, and as you begin to work your magic on the enterprise on a global scale, you will begin to wonder why some queries seem to take forever and others run rather fast. After configuring some of the parameters you looked at earlier, you might begin to wonder whether you're hitting a Global Catalog server. A *Global Catalog server* is a server that contains all the objects and their associated attributes from your local domain. If all you have is a single domain, it doesn't matter whether you're connecting to a domain controller or a Global Catalog server, because the information would be the same. If, however, you are in a multiple domain forest, you might very well be interested in which Global Catalog server you are hitting. Depending on your network topology, you could be executing a query that is going across a slow WAN link. You can control replication of attributes by selecting the Global Catalog check box. You can find this option by opening the Active Directory Schema MMC, highlighting the Attributes container, and then double-clicking the attribute you want to modify. You will then be presented with the form shown in Figure 13-1.

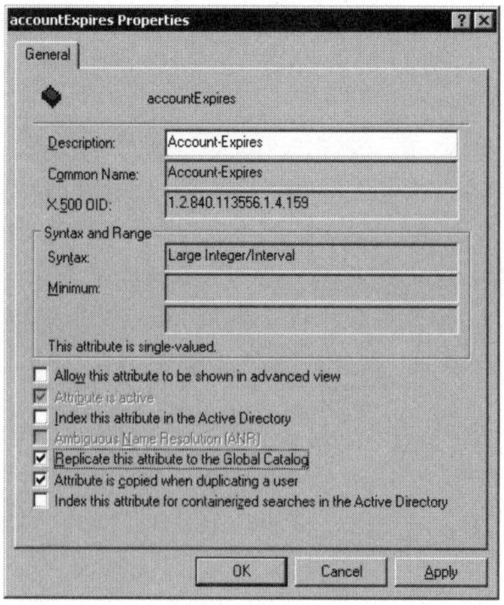

**Figure 13-1**   By indicating inclusion in the Global Catalog server, the industrious network administrator can improve query performance

In addition to controlling the replication of attributes, the erstwhile administrator might also investigate attribute indexing. (See Figure 13-2.) Active Directory already has indexes built on certain objects. However, if an attribute is heavily searched on, you might consider an additional index. You should do this, however, with caution, because an improperly placed index is worse than no index at all. The reason for this is the time spent building and maintaining an index. Both of these operations utilize processor time and disk I/O.

Suppose you create a custom attribute called *badge number* in our Active Directory. This attribute is a small number with a high degree of cardinality. *Cardinality* does not mean that all the numbers are red! It is a database term that refers to the degree of uniqueness of the data. High cardinality implies greater uniqueness. For example, in most cases, the *givenName* field in Active Directory will have a low level of cardinality because several users are likely to have the popular first names of Bob, Alice, Sally, Teresa, and Ed. On the other hand, only one user in Active Directory is associated with a particular employee number, and so therefore the employee number field has a high level of cardinality. Employee number, then, would be a good candidate for indexing.

However, just because a field is a good candidate for indexing doesn't mean it should be indexed. It simply means it *could* be indexed. Before you decide to select the check box for the *badge number* attribute, for example, decide how often you'll search on users by employee number. To help you figure this out, you could audit LDAP queries that are performed against Active Directory.

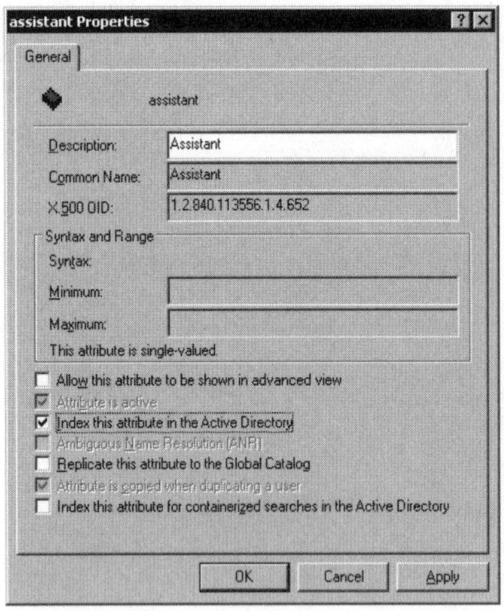

**Figure 13-2** Indexing improves query performance in situations where the indexed attribute is part of the selection criteria

---

**Quick Check**

**Q. Why would a local Global Catalog server not be used in responding to a query?**

**A.** One reason could be that the Global Catalog server does not contain the attribute you were searching for. If it does not contain the attribute, it must refer the query to another server.

**Q. What are the main questions the network administrator must answer prior to indexing an attribute in Active Directory?**

**A.** The network administrator should look at the size of the data field, the level of cardinality, and the amount of use the attribute will generate as a search criterion.

---

# Summary

In this chapter, you examined two basic concepts: searching Active Directory and controlling the way data is returned from Active Directory. When searching Active Directory, you must take several issues into consideration, including the provider you will use and the fields you will include in the query. After you address these concerns, you iterate through the recordset data and decide what to do with your information. In the examples in this chapter, we used the *Echo* command to display the information, but we could have just as easily fed it to a text file.

# Quiz Yourself

**Q.** **What provider can be used with ADO connections to Active Directory?**

**A.** *ADsDSOObject* can be used with ADO to talk to Active Directory.

**Q.** **What is the field object in ADO used for in conjunction with Active Directory queries?**

**A.** The field object in ADO is often used to hold attribute data that comes back from a query of Active Directory.

**Q.** **The ADO search property** *"Cache results"* **is used to determine which aspect of an ADO search?**

**A.** The ADO search property *"Cache results"* is used to tell VBScript whether to cache the results of the query on the client side of the connection.

**Q.** **How does** *"Cache results"* **affect an ADO search?**

**A.** *"Cache results"* defaults to caching the results of the search on the client side of the connection. With large data sets, you might not want to bring all the data down to the client.

# On Your Own

# Lab 26 Creating an ADO Query into Active Directory

In this lab, you will practice creating an ADO query into Active Directory to pull out information about computer objects.

## Lab Instructions

1. Open Notepad.exe.

2. Type **Option Explicit** on the first line to force the declaration of all variables.

3. Declare the following variables by using the *Dim* command: *qQuery, objConnection, objCommand*, and *objRecordSet*.

4. Create a query using the LDAP namespace that connects to your local Domain Controller. Specify the *objectCatagory* that is equal to *computer*. Choose the following fields: *distinguishedName, name*, and *logonCount*. Set the search dimension to *subtree*. Assign this query to a variable called *qQuery*. Your code will look like the following:

```
qQuery = "<LDAP://dc=a,dc=com>;" & _
    "(objectCategory=computer)" & _
    ";distinguishedName,name" & _
    ",operatingSystem" & _
    ",logonCount" & _
    ";subtree"
```

5. Create an ADODB connection object and set it to a variable called *objConnection*. Your code will look like the following:

```
Set objConnection = CreateObject("ADODB.Connection")
```

6. Create an ADODB command object and set it to a variable called *objCommand*. Your code will look like the following:

```
Set objCommand = CreateObject("ADODB.Command")
```

7. Open your connection object and specify the *ADsDSOObject* provider. Your code will look like the following:

```
objConnection.Open "Provider=ADsDSOObject;"
```

8. Use the *ActiveConnection* method of the *objCommand* object to specify the connection held by *objConnection* as the active connection to Active Directory. Your code will look like the following:

```
objCommand.ActiveConnection = objConnection
```

9. Use the *commandText* method to set the query represented by the variable *qQuery* to be the command text for the command object. Your code will look like the following:

```
objCommand.CommandText = qQuery
```

10. Assign the variable *objRecordSet* to be equal to the *recordset* that is returned by the execute method of *objCommand*. Your code will look like the following:

```
Set objRecordSet = objCommand.Execute
```

11. Use a *While Not Wend* construction to iterate through the recordset and echo out the following fields: *Name*, *distinguishedname*, *operatingsystem*, and *logoncount*.

12. Once you echo out these fields, use the *moveNext* method of the *objectRecordSet* object to advance to the next record. Your code will look like the following:

```
While Not objRecordSet.EOF
    WScript.Echo objRecordSet.Fields("name")
    WScript.Echo objRecordSet.Fields("distinguishedName")
    WScript.Echo objRecordSet.Fields("operatingSystem")
    WScript.Echo objRecordSet.Fields("LogonCount")
    objRecordSet.MoveNext
Wend
```

13. Close the connection. Your code will look like the following:

```
objConnection.Close
```

# Lab 27 Controlling How a Script Executes Against Active Directory

In this lab, you modify the FilterMoreComputers.vbs script to control the way it executes against Active Directory.

## Lab Instructions

1. Open the FilterMoreComputers.vbs script in Notepad.exe.

2. Save the script as **Lab27Solution.vbs**.

3. On the line following the *objCommand.CommandText = qQuery* statement, add an *objCommand* property statement that will change the default asynchronous behavior from *false* to *true*. The amended script will look like the following:

```
Option Explicit
'On Error Resume Next

Dim qQuery
Dim objConnection
Dim objCommand
Dim objRecordSet

qQuery = "<LDAP://dc=a,dc=com>;" & _
    "(objectCategory=computer)" & _
    ";distinguishedName,name;subtree"

Set objConnection = CreateObject("ADODB.Connection")
Set objCommand = CreateObject("ADODB.Command")
objConnection.Open "Provider=ADsDSOObject;"
objCommand.ActiveConnection = objConnection
objCommand.CommandText = qQuery
objCommand.properties("Asynchronous")=True
Set objRecordSet = objCommand.Execute

While Not objRecordSet.EOF
    WScript.Echo objRecordSet.Fields("name")
    WScript.Echo objRecordSet.Fields("distinguishedName")
    objRecordSet.MoveNext
Wend

objConnection.Close
```

4. Save the script.

5. Open a command prompt, and run the script in CScript by typing **cscript** before the name of the lab27.vbs script.

**6.** Turn off the caching of results by setting *Cache Results* to *false*. Do this under the *objCommand.properties("Asynchronous") = True* line you added in step 3. Your code for this command will look like the following:

```
objCommand.properties("cache results") = False
```

**7.** Save and run the script.

**8.** Set a page size of *1* to tell Active Directory to return one object at a time. This line can go below the cache results setting specified in line 6. Your code will look like the following:

```
objCommand.properties("Page Size") = 1
```

**9.** Save and run the script.

**10.** Change the page size to *10*, and set a size limit of *100* to limit the number of objects returned. The two lines of code will look like the following:

```
objCommand.properties("Page Size") = 10
objCommand.properties("Size limit") = 100
```

**11.** Set a query time limit that will limit how long the server is allowed to search for results. You will use the *Time Limit* property, as shown in the following code. Place this code below the size limit line.

```
objCommand.Properties("Time Limit") = 2
```

**12.** Save and run the script.

**13.** Set a timeout value that will limit how long the client machine waits for results from the server. This value should be lower than the time limit value, so set it to *1* second for the lab.

```
objCommand.Properties("Timeout") = 1
```

**14.** Save and run the script.

**15.** Close your work.

# 14 Configuring Networking Components

In this chapter, you'll look at some of the ways that using Microsoft Visual Basic Script (VBScript) can simplify basic networking tasks. You begin with a common task: switching from static to dynamic IP addresses. This task might seem to be a no-brainer—that is, you just open the network connection, select Properties, choose TCP/IP, and select Obtain An IP Address Automatically—but when you do it a thousand times or more while merging a remote, previously static site into your Dynamic Host Configuration Protocol (DHCP) hierarchy, the task is daunting.

 **See Also** If you are working with older clients during a migration, you might want to refer to *http://support.microsoft.com/?kbid=197424* for a sample script.

## Before You Begin

**To work through the material presented in this chapter you need to be familiar with the following concepts from earlier chapters:**

- Creating text files

- Writing to text files

- Making a connection to WMI

- Making a connection to Active Directory

- Implementing the *For…Next* construction

- Implementing the *Select Case* construction

**After completing this chapter you will be familiar with the following:**

- Using WMI to configure networking components

- Converting a text file from Active Directory into input for script

- Working with input text files

## WMI and the Network

In this section, you use WMI to configure networking components. However, instead of just dashing off a quick WMI script, you will take a step forward and begin combining several of the techniques looked at earlier in this book, such as writing to text files and reading from Active Directory. This little bit of magic will track every step of your networked operations, enabling you to avoid dire consequences should an operation fail to properly complete. The following summarizes a few uses for this configuration technique:

- Import a list of computers from an OU in Active Directory
- Import a list of users from an OU in Active Directory
- Import a list of users from a group that resides in Active Directory
- Read Active Directory and make changes on workstations
- Use a Lightweight Directory Access Protocol (LDAP) provider
- Make an ADO connection
- Execute an ADO command
- Use *While Not...Wend* to iterate through the record set
- Use WMI to make changes on desktop machines

## Making the Connection

When creating a script with multiple parts or multiple actions, taking a systematic approach vastly simplifies the process. There are five major components to the script you will examine in this chapter. As you write the script, you will test it after each portion is written to ensure it is working properly. Next, you will need to test the query syntax to ensure it is returning only the machines you want to modify. Once you have the query working properly, you will want to test the WMI portion of the script to ensure it works as planned. Lastly, you put the entire script together.

The following script is called ConnectToADou.vbs, and it connects to Active Directory using the LDAP provider, makes an ADO connection, and executes an ADO command. Lastly, it uses *While Not...Wend* to iterate through the returned recordset. It does not use WMI at this point.

```
Option Explicit
'On Error Resume Next

Dim qQuery
Dim oConnection
Dim oCommand
Dim oRecordSet
Dim oDom
Dim oProvider
Dim oOU

oProvider = "'LDAP://"
oDom = "dc=nwtraders, dc=msft'"
```

```
oOU = "ou=workstations,"
qQuery = "Select Name from " & oProvider _
    & oOU & oDom & "where objectClass='computer'"

Set oConnection = CreateObject("ADODB.Connection")
Set oCommand = CreateObject("ADODB.Command")
oConnection.Open "Provider=ADsDSOObject;"
oCommand.ActiveConnection = oConnection
oCommand.CommandText = qQuery
Set oRecordSet = oCommand.Execute

While Not oRecordSet.EOF
    WScript.Echo oRecordSet.Fields("name")
    oRecordSet.MoveNext
Wend

oConnection.Close
```

## Header Information

The Header information section of the script continues to be rather uninteresting. However, being boring doesn't mean you should ignore it (or else my wife would never talk to me). Remember, the use of *Option Explicit* means we must declare all our variables. Since all the variables get listed out, *Option Explicit* gives us a good place to document their use. By documenting the use of every variable, you perform two functions: provide a reference for future modifications, and provide a reference for others who might read the script at a point later in time. I will admit, there are scripts I did not document because at the time I understood what the script was doing. However, later, when I had to modify the script, I had to conduct a lot of additional research to figure out what I had done. The time to add documentation to a script is when it is being written, not months later. Additionally, it makes sense to document the changes you make when you modify the script. This can take the form of comments with an associated date, and you can easily incorporate these comments into a script template, as shown in the following code section:

```
'================================================
'
' VBScript:  AUTHOR: Ed Wilson , MS,  11/09/2003
'
' NAME: <ConnectToADOU.vbs>
'
' COMMENT: Key concepts are listed below:
'1. making connection to AD
'2. Controlling results by using a filter
' REVISIONS:
' 11/10/2003 connection string - split into parts
' 11/11/2003 added computer filter to query
' 11/12/2003 changed names of vars from obj to o
'================================================
```

The standard Header information is placed just below the template section, as shown here:

```
Option Explicit
'On Error Resume Next

Dim qQuery
Dim oConnection
Dim oCommand
Dim oRecordSet
Dim oDom
Dim oProvider
Dim oOU
```

# Reference Information

The Reference information section of the script is used to assign specific values to variables used in the script. One advantage of breaking the connection string into multiple parts is that the connection is easier to read and understand while also providing additional flexibility because of the ease of supplying different variables. The one issue to keep in mind when breaking up connection strings is that when the variables are concatenated back together, these variables must supply *exactly* what VBScript is expecting. Remember that with scripting, spelling counts big-time!

> **Tip**   I often find myself having to use the *WScript.Echo* command to spit out my connection string or my query after it has been put back together. More often than not, I find I've left out a semicolon, comma, or quotation mark that VBScript was expecting. This is where echoing out the query is invaluable. It takes one second to echo something out, whereas it could take hours of staring, visualizing, and imagining what the query or connection string looks like when put back together.

The variable *oProvider* is assigned to the string *'LDAP://'* and is used to tell VBScript you will be talking via LDAP to Active Directory. You use *oDOM* to hold the domain components of the connection string. Using normal LDAP language, each part of the domain name is specified: *Dc=nwtraders, dc=msft*. In this example, you don't use a .com, .net, or .org upper-level domain name; you use the .msft imaginary name. The next variable you define is *oOU*, which you set equal to the workstations' OU. After assigning values to the provider, domain, and OU variables, you're ready to create the query. You use the *qQuery* variable to hold your constructed query. Notice how the syntax looks similar to a SQL query. You are selecting the name field from *'LDAP://ou=workstations, dc=nwtraders, dc=msft'*, but you want only the name field if the object class is a computer. So you specify that in the *where* clause of our query.

The next six lines of the script make an ADO connection to Active Directory. You use *oConnection* to hold the hook that comes back from using the *CreateObject* command to give you an ADODB connection. Next, you use *oCommand* to hold the hook that comes back from using the *CreateObject* command to give us an ADODB command object. If the previous sentence seems redundant, that's because it is. This is one of the features of ADO, in fact! The developers tried very hard to make the syntax similar to reduce the learning curve. So things often seem boring and repetitive. (But hey, who wants lots of excitement when writing code?) Once you have the connection object and the command object, you can move forward with making the connection into Active Directory. You can think of building the ADO connection into Active Directory as connecting pipes. The provider is the kind of pipe you are going to run, the connection object is the path you are going to take while running the pipes, and the command is the valve that controls the flow of data through the pipes. Just as pipes are run one stick at a time, so too are each of the plumbing pieces necessary to connect to Active Directory, one at a time.

Now it's time to open the valve, but just like a water valve in your house, you need to know which valve to open and how far to turn the valve. With ADO, you specify the provider (that is, which pipe), which in this case is *ADsDSOObject*, and you specify which connection is the active connection. Next you specify the command text, which is your *qQuery* (indicates how far you will open the valve). Once everything is lined up, you execute (open the valve). But wait! At home, you need a glass or a bucket to hold the water. With ADO, you need something to hold your data flow—in this script, you use the variable called *oRecordSet* to hold the data that comes back.

```
oProvider = "'LDAP://"
oDom = "dc=nwtraders, dc=msft'"
oOU = "ou=workstations,"
qQuery = "Select Name from " & oProvider _
& oOU & oDom & "where objectClass='computer'"

Set oConnection = CreateObject("ADODB.Connection")
Set oCommand = CreateObject("ADODB.Command")
oConnection.Open "Provider=ADsDSOObject;"
oCommand.ActiveConnection = oConnection
oCommand.CommandText = qQuery
Set oRecordSet = oCommand.Execute
```

## Worker and Output Information

The Worker information section of the script is used to iterate through the record set that comes back from the *qQuery*. To do this, you use a *While Not...Wend* construction. Since you don't know in advance how many computers are in the workstation OU, you return a set of records from Active Directory and work through each record in the set until you reach the end of the file, which is designated as *oRecordSet.EOF*. As long as there are records in the record set you haven't touched, you echo out the name of the record and then move to the next record in the set. If you come to the end of the recordset, you end the *While Not...Wend* construction. You are using the *Echo* command right now as a test mechanism. After you make sure the script works as planned, you replace the *Echo* command with some WMI code to change the TCP/IP address from static to dynamic.

```
While Not oRecordSet.EOF
    WScript.Echo oRecordSet.Fields("name")
    oRecordSet.MoveNext
Wend

oConnection.Close
```

> **Quick Check**
>
> **Q.** What is an advantage of using *WScript.Echo* to display the text of a query?
>
> **A.** An advantage of using *WScript.Echo* to display the text of a query is that it makes troubleshooting a concatenated query string easy.
>
> **Q.** Why do you need to use *While Not* in the Worker information section of the script?
>
> **A.** *While Not* is used to iterate through the recordset. It gives you the ability to work with an unknown number of computers.

# Changing the TCP/IP Settings

After your script can connect to Active Directory and return a recordset of computer names, you're ready to use WMI to convert the machines from static IP addresses to DHCP-assigned addresses. You scrounge around and come up with a script that uses WMI to turn on DHCP. This script, called EnableDHCP.vbs, is shown here:

```
Target = "."
Set oWMIService = GetObject("winmgmts:\\" & Target & "\root\cimv2")
Set colNetAdapters = oWMIService.ExecQuery _
 ("Select * from Win32_NetworkAdapterConfiguration where IPEnabled=TRUE")
For Each oNetAdapter In colNetAdapters
    errEnable = oNetAdapter.EnableDHCP()
     If errEnable = 0 Then
        WScript.Echo "DHCP has been enabled."
    Else
        WScript.Echo "DHCP could not be enabled."
    End If
Next
```

> **Just the Steps**
>
> ▶ **To enable DHCP by using WMI**
>
> 1. Make a connection to *WinMgmts* on the target machine.
> 2. Connect to the *root\cimv2* namespace in WMI.
> 3. Create a collection to hold the result of the query.
> 4. Use a query to choose network adapter configurations that are enabled for IP.
> 5. Use a *For Each...Next* loop to iterate through the collection of network adapter configurations.
> 6. Use the *EnableDHCP* command on each network adapter configuration.

## Header Information

The Header information section in this script is similar to that in the previous script. The variables utilized are *Target*, *oWMIService*, *colNetAdapters*, *oNetAdapter*, and *errEnable*. When you merge the WMI script with the previous ADSI script, you need to declare each of these new variables.

## Reference Information

In the Reference information section, you assign values to the variables used in the script. The variable *oWMIService* is assigned to the hook that comes back from WMI when you use the *createObject* command. You attach to the *root\cimV2* namespace on the target machine. You use *colNetAdapters* to hold the hook that comes back from running a query against the WMI namespace. The query you run is designed to return all the network adapter configurations installed on the target computer that are IP-enabled. You do this because there is no point in trying to turn on DHCP on an IPX/SPX or AppleTalk network adapter configuration.

## Worker and Output Information

In the Worker information section of the script, you use the *oNetAadapter* variable as a placeholder by using the *For Each...Loop* to help you iterate through the collection of network adapter configurations. One cool thing you do here is use a variable called *errEnable*. You set *errEnable* to be equal to the value that is returned by VBScript when you try to turn on DHCP by using the *enableDHCP* command. If the operation is successful, the return code is 0. However, if the operation fails, you get a different return code. In this script, you're interested only in whether DHCP works. So if the return code is 0, everything is copasetic, and you echo out that DHCP was enabled. If DHCP enablement fails, you get a different error code as just mentioned, and so you use the *Else* part of the script and simply echo that DHCP failed.

---

**Quick Check**

Q. To programmatically turn on DHCP, which WMI namespace do you connect to?

A. You need to connect to *root\cimV2*.

Q. In what fashion is the network adapter returned by WMI?

A. The network adapter is returned by WMI as a collection.

Q. What return code indicates a successful WMI operation?

A. A return code of 0 indicates a successful WMI operation.

---

# Merging WMI and ADSI

Now that you know that both the ADSI script and the WMI script work as advertised, merging the two scripts is a rather easy task. By merging them, you will connect to Active Directory, perform a query of all computers in the workstation OU, take the returned data into a recordset, iterate through the recordset, and enable DHCP on each workstation in the recordset until you reach the end of the file. Along the way, echo out the results of the DHCP operation. The new script is called AdOuWmiDHCP.vbs.

You need to assign a computer name to the variable *Target*. You do this inside the *While Not…Wend* loop by using *Target = oRecordSet.Fields("name")*, because as you walk through the recordset, *Target* is the name you want to get back. The variable *Target* contains computer names retrieved from ADSI, each of which will then be used as targets of a WMI query. The rest of the WMI script is placed inside the *While Not…Wend* loop without additional alteration. Incorporating the two scripts enables you to leverage two different technologies to simplify a seemingly daunting desktop management problem. The only required changes to the ADSI script were declaring the variables utilized by WMI in the Worker information section of the script. To make it obvious which variables were added with the merger, I added all new variables to two lines in the Header information section of the script. Although the only requirement for doing this is to place a comma between the variable names, I do not normally use this technique unless I have tons of variables that need to be declared.

```
Option Explicit
'On Error Resume Next

Dim qQuery
Dim oConnection
Dim oCommand
Dim oRecordSet
Dim oDom
Dim oProvider
Dim oOU
Dim Target, oWMIService, colNetAdapters
Dim oNetAdapter, errEnable
```

```
oProvider = "'LDAP://"
oDom = "dc=nwtraders, dc=msft'"
oOU = "ou=workstations,"
qQuery = "Select Name from " & oProvider _
& oOU & oDom & "where objectClass='computer'"

Set oConnection = CreateObject("ADODB.Connection")
Set oCommand = CreateObject("ADODB.Command")
oConnection.Open "Provider=ADsDSOObject;"
oCommand.ActiveConnection = oConnection
oCommand.CommandText = qQuery
Set oRecordSet = oCommand.Execute

While Not oRecordSet.EOF
    Target= oRecordSet.Fields("name")
    Set oWMIService = GetObject("winmgmts:\\" & Target _
        & "\root\cimv2")
    Set colNetAdapters = oWMIService.ExecQuery _
        ("Select * from Win32_NetworkAdapterConfiguration" _
        & " where IPEnabled=TRUE")
    For Each oNetAdapter In colNetAdapters
       errEnable = oNetAdapter.EnableDHCP()
       If errEnable = 0 Then
            WScript.Echo "DHCP has been enabled."
       Else
            WScript.Echo "DHCP could not be enabled."
       End If
    Next
    oRecordSet.MoveNext
Wend
oConnection.Close
```

---

**Quick Check**

**Q.** What is one technique for reducing the amount of space in a script that must declare a large number of variables?

**A.** You can reduce the space taken up in a script by variables by declaring multiple variables on the same line.

**Q.** In the AdOuWmiDHCP.vbs just discussed, why was the WMI section of the script placed inside the *While Not…Wend* section?

**A.** The WMI section of the script was placed inside the *While Not…Wend* section so it could gain access to the name field in the recordset. The name then became the target of the WMI portion of the script.

---

# Win32_NetworkAdapterConfiguration

The *Win32_NetworkAdapterConfiguration* WMI class is chock-full of both properties and methods. The properties are elements containing information about the specific network adapter configuration, and the methods are used to perform a specific action on the network adapter configuration, such as enabling DHCP. Indeed, with 41 methods defined in Microsoft Windows Server 2003, it is hard to think of an operation that isn't covered. Some of the more common methods are listed in Table 14-1. You can find complete documentation by searching on *Win32_NetworkAdapterConfiguration* in the Platform SDK.

**Table 14-1    *Win32_NetworkAdapterConfiguration* Methods**

| Method | Description |
| --- | --- |
| *DisableIPSec* | Disables IP security on this TCP/IP-enabled network adapter# |
| *EnableDHCP* | Enables the Dynamic Host Configuration Protocol (DHCP) for service with this network adapter |
| *EnableDNS* | Enables the Domain Name System (DNS) for service on this TCP/IP-bound network adapter |
| *EnableIPFilterSec* | Enables IP security globally across all IP-bound network adapter configurations |
| *EnableIPSec* | Enables IP security on this specific TCP/IP-enabled network adapter |
| *EnableStatic* | Enables static TCP/IP addressing for the target network adapter |
| *EnableWINS* | Enables WINS settings specific to TCP/IP but independent of the network adapter |
| *ReleaseDHCPLease* | Releases the IP address bound to a specific DHCP-enabled network adapter |
| *ReleaseDHCPLeaseAll* | Releases the IP addresses bound to all DHCP-enabled network adapter configurations |
| *RenewDHCPLease* | Renews the IP address on specific DHCP-enabled network adapter configurations |
| *RenewDHCPLeaseAll* | Renews the IP addresses on all DHCP-enabled network adapter configurations |
| *SetDatabasePath* | Sets the path to the standard Internet database files (Hosts, LMhosts, Networks, and Protocols) |
| *SetDNSDomain* | Sets the DNS domain |
| *SetDNSServerSearchOrder* | Sets the server search order as an array of elements |
| *SetDNSSuffixSearchOrder* | Sets the suffix search order as an array of elements |
| *SetDynamicDNSRegistration* | Indicates dynamic DNS registration of IP addresses for this IP-bound adapter |
| *SetGateways* | Specifies a list of gateways for routing packets destined for a different subnet than the one this adapter is connected to |

**Table 14-1   *Win32_NetworkAdapterConfiguration* Methods**

| Method | Description |
| --- | --- |
| *SetIPConnectionMetric* | Sets the routing metric associated with this IP-bound adapter |
| *SetKeepAliveInterval* | Sets the interval separating Keep Alive Retransmissions until a response is received |
| *SetKeepAliveTime* | Sets how often TCP attempts to verify that an idle connection is still available by sending a Keep Alive packet |
| *SetTcpipNetbios* | Sets the default operation of NetBIOS over TCP/IP |
| *SetTcpMaxConnectRetransmissions* | Sets the number of attempts TCP will retransmit a connect request before aborting |
| *SetTcpMaxDataRetransmissions* | Sets the number of times TCP will retransmit an individual data segment before aborting the connection |
| *SetTcpNumConnections* | Sets the maximum number of connections that TCP might have open simultaneously |
| *SetTcpWindowSize* | Sets the maximum TCP Receive Window size offered by the system |
| *SetWINSServer* | Sets the primary and secondary Windows Internet Naming Service (WINS) servers on this TCP/IP-bound network adapter |

# Summary

In this chapter, you examined integrating WMI and ADSI into a single script. By combining these two technologies, you can fine-tune your targeting of management scripts. In addition, you looked at the *Win32_NetworkAdapterConfiguration* class in WMI and saw some of the powerful methods that are exposed through that class.

# Quiz Yourself

**Q.** What are some of the advantages of using ADSI and WMI together?

**A.** ADSI is dynamic and provides up-to-date information from Active Directory. This means that a query run against the workstation OU today could have different results than a query run against the workstation OU tomorrow, allowing for more accurate results.

**Q.** What WMI class can be used to control the behavior of NetBIOS over TCP/IP?

**A.** To control the behavior of NetBIOS over TCP/IP, you can use the *Win32_Network-AdapterConfiguration* class.

> **Q.** Which method of *Win32_NetworkAdapterConfiguration* is used to disable NetBIOS over TCP/IP?
>
> **A.** The method of *Win32NetworkAdapterConfiguration* that can be used to disable NetBIOS over TCP/IP is the *SetTcpIpNetbios* method (when assigned a value of 2, it is disabled).
>
> **Q.** How can you specify a unique domain name for a network connection?
>
> **A.** You can specify a unique domain name for a network connection by using the *SetDNS-Domain* method. It will show up in the DNS Suffix For This Connection box on the DNS tab of the Advanced TCP/IP settings sheet.

# On Your Own

# Lab 28 Using WMI to Assign Network Settings

In this lab, you will practice using WMI to set various networking configuration properties. The result of this will become the Worker information section for use in Lab 29.

## Lab Instructions

1. Open Notepad.exe.

2. Open the **EnableDHCP.vbs** script contained in lab folder 28 on the companion CD.

3. On the first line, add the *Option Explicit* command.

4. Change the variable *strComputer* to **Target** everywhere it is mentioned in the script. (The Find and Replace feature of Notepad is a good tool to use when renaming variables.)

5. Change the variable *objWMIService* to **oWMIService** everywhere it is mentioned in the script.

6. Change the variable *objNetAdapter* to **oNetAdapter** everywhere it is mentioned in the script.

7. Declare all the variables used in the script by using the *Dim* command. You will need to declare seven variables: *Target, oWMIService, oNetAdapter, colNetAdapters, DNSDomainErr, DNSsearchErr,* and *DNSserver*.

8. Modify the line *errEnable = oNetAdapter.EnableDHCP()* so that you can assign a DNS suffix for NWTraders.com. The line will look like the following:

```
DNSDomainErr = oNetAdapter.SetDNSDomain("NWTraders.com")
```

9. Delete the Output section.

10. Add a couple of DNS servers to the DNS search list. To do this, use the *SetDNS-searchOrder* method. However, because the DNS server is stored as an array, you

will need to make a couple of entries in the script. On the line below the *Target* = "." line, add the following code:

```
DNSserver = Array("128.1.2.1", "129.1.2.2")
```

**11.** Add the *SetDNSsearchOrder* method under the *SetDNSDomain* line. Your code will look like the following:

```
DNSsearchErr=objNetAdapter.SetDNSServerSearchOrder(DNSserver)
```

**12.** Add a couple of lines of code so that you know the result of your operation. To do this, you echo out the value of both *DNSsearchErr* and *DNSDomainErr* along with appropriate remarks. The code for this looks like the following:

```
WScript.Echo "DNSDomain returned " & (DNSDomainErr)
WScript.Echo "DNSsearchOrder returned " & (DNSsearchErr)
```

**13.** Save your work as **lab28.vbs**.

# Lab 29 Combining WMI and ADSI in a Script

In this lab, you combine the WMI script created in Lab 28 with an ADSI script.

## Lab Instructions

**1.** Open Notepad.exe.

**2.** Open the Lab29Starter.vbs file.

**3.** Open the ConnectToADOU.vbs file.

**4.** Save the ConnectToADOU.vbs file as **Lab29Solution.vbs**.

**5.** Copy the seven variable declarations from the Lab29Starter.vbs file and paste them into the Header information section of your Lab29Solution.vbs script. The seven variable declarations look like the following:

```
Dim target
Dim oWMIService
Dim colNetAdapters
Dim oNetAdapter
Dim DNSDomainErr
Dim DNSsearchErr
Dim DNSServer
```

**6.** In your Lab29Solution.vbs file, locate the *While Not...Wend* section of the script. Remove the *WScript.Echo* portion of the *WScript.Echo oRecordSet.Fields("name")* command.

**7.** Replace the *WScript.Echo* command with *Target* = so that the new command looks like the following:

```
Target= oRecordSet.Fields("name")
```

8. In the Lab29Starter.vbs script, copy the remaining portion of the script and paste it just below the new *Target = oRecordSet.Fields("name")* command. The new *While Not...Wend* construction looks like the following:

```
While Not oRecordSet.EOF
    Target= oRecordSet.Fields("name")
    DNSserver=Array("128.1.2.1", "129.1.2.2")
    Set oWMIService = GetObject("winmgmts:\\" & target & "\root\cimv2")
    Set colNetAdapters = oWMIService.ExecQuery _
        ("Select * from Win32_NetworkAdapterConfiguration where IPEnabled=TRUE")
    For Each oNetAdapter In colNetAdapters
        DNSDomainErr = oNetAdapter.SetDNSDomain("NWTraders.com")
        DNSsearchErr=oNetAdapter.SetDNSServerSearchOrder(DNSserver)
        WScript.Echo "DNSDomain returned " & (DNSDomainErr)
        WScript.Echo "DNSsearchOrder returned " & (DNSsearchErr)
    Next
    oRecordSet.MoveNext
Wend
```

9. Save your work.

10. Test the script. If it works, remove the comment from the *On Error Resume Next* command. If it doesn't work, compare it with Lab29Solution.vbs, which you can find on the companion CD.

# 15 Subs and Other Round Things

In this chapter, you'll examine subroutines—a very important and powerful way to make your scripts more flexible, easier to read, and easier to modify. Along the way, you'll also look at additional user and group management tricks.

## Before You Begin

**To work through the material presented in this chapter you need to be familiar with the following concepts from earlier chapters:**

- Reading text files
- Writing to text files
- Creating files
- Creating folders
- Using the *For...Next* construction
- Creating *Select Case* constructions
- Connecting to Active Directory
- Reading information from WMI

**After completing this chapter you will be familiar with the following:**

- Converting inline code into a subroutine
- Calling subroutines
- Performing Active Directory User management

## Working with Subroutines

In this section, you'll learn about how network administrators use subroutines. For many, the use of subroutines will be somewhat new territory and might even seem unnecessary, particularly when you can cut and paste sections of working code. But before we get into the *how-to* section, let's go over the *what* section.

I used to think a subroutine was getting up in the morning, eating breakfast, standing a watch, and going to bed. But I've since learned that a subroutine is a named section of code that gets run only when something in the script calls it by name. Nearly every script we've worked with thus far has been a group of commands, which have been processed from top to bottom in a consecutive fashion. Although this consecutive processing approach, which I call *linear scripting*, makes the code very easy for the network administrator to work with, it does not always make his work very efficient. In addition, when you need to perform a similar activity from different parts of the script, using the inline cut-and-paste scripting approach quickly becomes inefficient and hard to understand. This is where subroutines come into play. A subroutine is not executed when its body is defined in the code; instead, it is executed only when it is called by name. If you define a subroutine, and use it only one time, you might make your script easier to read or easier to maintain, but you will not make the script shorter. If, however, you have something you want to do over and over, the subroutine does make the script shorter. The following summarizes uses for subroutines in VBScript:

- Prevents needless duplication of code

- Makes code portable and reusable

- Makes code easier to troubleshoot and debug

- Makes code easier to read and maintain

- Makes code easier to modify

The following script (LinearScript.vbs) illustrates the problem with linear scripting. In this script are three variables: *a*, *b*, and *c*. Each of these is assigned a value, and you need to determine equality. The script uses a series of *If Then...Else* constructions to perform the evaluative work. As you can see, the code gets a little redundant.

```
Option Explicit
Dim a
Dim b
Dim c

a=1
b=2
c=3

If a = b Then
    WScript.Echo a & " and " & b & " are equal"
Else
    WScript.Echo a & " and " & b & " are not equal"
End If


If b = c Then
    WScript.Echo b & " and " & c & " are equal"
Else
    WScript.Echo b & " and " & c & " are not equal"
End If


If a + b = c Then
    WScript.Echo a + b & " and " & c & " are equal"
Else
    WScript.Echo a + b & " and " & c & " are not equal"
End if
```

OK, so the script might be a little redundant, although if you're paid to write code by the line, this is a great script! Unfortunately, most network administrators are not paid by the line for the scripts they write. This being the case, clearly you need to come up with a better way to write code. (I am telegraphing the solution to you now....) That's right! You will use a subroutine to perform the evaluation. The modified script uses a subroutine to perform the evaluation of the two numbers. This results in saving two lines of code for each evaluation performed. In this example, however, the power is not in saving a few lines of code—it's in the fact that you use one section of code to perform the evaluation. Using one section makes the script easier to read and easier to write.

> **Note**   Business rules is a concept that comes up frequently in programming books. The idea is that many programs have concepts that are not a technical requirement but still must be adhered to. These are non-technical rules. For instance, a business rule might say that when a payment is not received within 30 days after the invoice is mailed, a follow-up notice must be sent out, and a 1 percent surcharge is added to the invoice amount. Because businesses sometimes change these non-technical requirements, such rules would be better incorporated into a separate section of the code (a subroutine, for example) as opposed to sprinkling them throughout the entire program. If the business later decides to charge an additional 1 percent surcharge after 60 days, this requirement can be easily accommodated in the code.

In the script you are currently examining, your business rules are contained in a single code section, so you can easily modify the code to incorporate new ways of comparing the three numbers (to determine, for example, that they are not equal instead of equal). If conditions are likely to change or additional information might be required, creating a subroutine makes sense.

---

**Quick Check**

**Q.** To promote code re-use within a script, where is one place you can position the code?

**A.** You can place the code within a subroutine.

**Q.** To make changing business rules easier to code, where is a good place to position the rules?

**A.** You can place business rules within a subroutine to make them easier to update.

## Calling the Subroutine

In the next script you'll examine, SubRoutineScript.vbs, the comparison of *a*, *b*, and *c* is done by using a subroutine called *compare*. To use a subroutine, you simply place its name on a line by itself. Notice that you don't need to declare the name of the subroutine because it isn't a variable. So, that script works even though you specified *Option Explicit* and did not declare the name used for the subroutine. In fact, you cannot declare the name of your subroutine. If you do, you will get a "name redefined" error.

## Creating the Subroutine

Once you decide to use a subroutine, the code for creating it is very light. Indeed, all that is required is the word *Sub* followed by the name you will assign to the subroutine. In the SubRoutineScript.vbs script, the subroutine is assigned the name *compare* by the following line: *Sub Compare*. That's all there is to it. You then write the code that performs the comparison and end the subroutine with the command *End Sub*. After you do all that, you have your subroutine.

```
Option Explicit
Dim a, b, c
Dim num1, num2
a=1
b=2
c=3

num1 = a
num2 = b
compare

num1 = b
num2 = c
compare

num1 = a + b
num2 = c
compare

Sub compare
    If num1 = num2 Then
        WScript.Echo (num1 & " and " & num2 & " are equal")
    Else
        WScript.Echo(num1 & " and " & num2 & " are not equal")
    End If
End Sub
```

---

**Just the Steps**

▶ **To create a subroutine**

1. Begin the line of code with the word *Sub* followed by name of the subroutine.

2. Write the code that the subroutine will perform.

3. End the subroutine by using the *End Sub* command on a line by itself.

---

# Creating Users and Logging Results

As your scripts become more powerful, they have a tendency to become longer and longer. The next script, CreateUsersLogAction.vbs, is nearly 80 lines long. The reason for this length is that you perform three distinct actions. First, you read a text file and parse the data into an array. Then you use this array to create new users and add the users into an existing group in Active Directory. As you create users and add them to groups, you want to create a log file and write the names of the created users. All the code to perform these actions begins to add up and can make a long VBScript hard to read and understand. This is a situation in which the subroutine becomes rather useful. In fact, the subroutine used to create the log file is nearly 30 lines long itself because you need to check whether the folder exists or the log file exists. If the folder or file does not exist, you need to create it. If each is present, you need to open the file and append data to it. By placing this code into a subroutine, you are able to access it each time you loop through the input data you're using to create the users in the first place. After the user is created, you go to the subroutine, open the file, write to it, close the file, and then go back into the *Do Until...Loop* to create the next user.

**Note**   Holding the text file open might seem like an easier approach, but I prefer to close the file after each loop so that I can guarantee the consistency of the file as a log of the accounts that are being created. There are other benefits of closing the file as well. It makes the operation more modular and therefore promotes portability. Making an open and a close part of the routine hides complexity that could arise.

If you kept the file open and wrote to the log file in an asynchronous manner, your log writer could get behind, and in the event of an anomaly, your log might not be an accurate reflection of the actual accounts created on the server. Here is the Create-UsersLogAction.vbs script:

```
Option Explicit
'On Error Resume Next
Dim objOU
Dim objUser
```

```
    Dim objGroup
    Dim objFSO
    Dim objFile
    Dim objFolder
    Dim objTextFile
    Dim TxtIn
    Dim strNextLine
    Dim i
    Dim TxtFile
    Dim LogFolder
    Dim LogFile

    TxtFile = "C:\UsersAndGroups.txt"
    LogFolder = "C:\FSO"
    LogFile = "C:\FSO\fso.txt"
    Const ForReading = 1
    Const ForWriting = 2
    Const ForAppending = 8
    Set objFSO = CreateObject("Scripting.FileSystemObject")
    Set objTextFile = objFSO.OpenTextFile _
        (TxtFile, ForReading)

Do Until objTextFile.AtEndOfStream
    strNextLine = objTextFile.ReadLine
    TxtIn = Split(strNextLine , ",")
    Set objOU = GetObject("LDAP://OU=LabOU," _
        & "dc=nwtraders,dc=msft")
    Set objUser = objOU.Create("User", "cn="& TxtIn(0))
    objUser.Put "sAMAccountName", TxtIn(0)
    objUser.SetInfo

    Set objGroup = GetObject _
        ("LDAP://CN="& TxtIn(1) & ",cn=users," _
        & "dc=nwtraders,dc=msft")
    objGroup.add _
        "LDAP://cn="& TxtIn(0) & ",ou=LabOU," _
        & "dc=nwtraders,dc=msft"
    Logging
Loop

Sub Logging
    If objFSO.FolderExists(LogFolder) Then
        If objFSO.FileExists(LogFile) Then
            Set objFile = objFSO.OpenTextFile _
                (LogFile, ForAppending)
            objFile.WriteBlankLines(1)
            objFile.Writeline "Creating User " & Now
            objFile.Writeline  TxtIn(0)
            objFile.Close
        Else
            Set objFile = objFSO.CreateTextFile(LogFile)
            objFile.Close
            Set objFile = objFSO.OpenTextFile _
                (LogFile, ForWriting)
```

```
        objFile.WriteLine "Creating User " & Now
        objFile.WriteLine TxtIn(0)

        objFile.Close
     End If
  Else
     Set objFolder = objFSO.CreateFolder(LogFolder)
     Set objFile = objFSO.CreateTextFile(LogFile)
     objFile.Close
     Set objFile = objFSO.OpenTextFile _
         (LogFile, ForWriting)
     objfile.WriteLine "Creating User " & Now
     objFile.WriteLine TxtIn(0)
     objFile.Close
  End If
End Sub

WScript.Echo("all done")
```

# Header Information

The Header information section of CreateUsersLogAction.vbs is used to declare all the variables used in the script. Twelve variables are used in the script and are listed in Table 15-1.

**Table 15-1   Variables Used in CreateUsersLogAction.vbs**

| Variable | Description |
| --- | --- |
| *objOU* | Holds connection to target OU in Active Directory. |
| *objUser* | Holds hook for *Create* user command. Takes *TxtIn(0)* as input for user name. |
| *objGroup* | Holds hook for add to *Group* command. Takes *TxtIn(1)* as input for name of group and *TxtIn(0)* as name of user to add. |
| *objFSO* | Holds hook that comes back from the *CreateObject* command used to create the *FileSystemObject*. |
| *objFile* | Holds hook that comes back from the *OpenTextFile* command issued to *objFSO*. |
| *objFolder* | Holds hook that comes back from *CreateFolder* command issued to *objFSO* if the folder does not exist. |
| *objTextFile* | Holds the data stream that comes from the *OpenTextFile* command that is used to open the UsersAndGroups.txt file. |
| *TxtIn* | An array that is created from parsing *strNextLine*. Each field split by the comma becomes an element in the array. Holds user name to be created and the group that the user is to be added to. |
| *strNextLine* | Holds one line worth of data from the UsersAndGroups.txt file. |
| *TxtFile* | Holds path and name of text file to be parsed as input data. |

**Table 15-1   Variables Used in CreateUsersLogAction.vbs**

| Variable | Description |
| --- | --- |
| *LogFolder* | Holds path and name of folder used to hold logging information. |
| *LogFile* | Holds path and name of text file to be used as the log file. |

## Reference Information

The Reference information section of the script is used to assign values to some of the variables used in the script. In addition to the mundane items such as defining the path and title for the text file used to hold the users and groups, in this section, you create three constants that are used in working with text files.

> **Note**   If you create standard variable names, and you consistently use them in your scripts, you will make it easier to re-use your subroutines without any modification. For instance, if you use *objFSO* consistently for creating *FileSystemObject*, you minimize the work required to "rewire" your subroutine. Of course, using the Find and Replace feature of Notepad.exe, or any other script editor, makes it rather easy to rename variables.

These constants are *ForReading*, *ForWriting*, and *ForAppending*. The use of these constants was discussed in detail in Chapter 4, "The Power of Many." The last two tasks done in the Reference information section of the script are creating an instance of the *FileSystemObject* and using the *OpenTextFile* command so that you can read it in the list of users that need to be created and the group to which each user will be assigned. Here is the Reference information section of the script:

```
TxtFile = "C:\UsersAndGroups.txt"
LogFolder = "C:\FSO"
LogFile = "C:\FSO\fso.txt"
Const ForReading = 1
Const ForWriting = 2
Const ForAppending = 8
Set objFSO = CreateObject("Scripting.FileSystemObject")
Set objTextFile = objFSO.OpenTextFile _
    (TxtFile, ForReading)
```

## Worker Information

The Worker information section of the script is where the users are actually created and assigned to a group. To work through the UsersAndGroups.txt file, you need to make a connection to the file. This was done in a previous Reference information section of the script in which we assigned *objTextFile* to be equal to the hook that came back once the connection into the file was made. Think back to the pipe analogy (in Chapter 5, "The Power of Many More"), in which you set up a pump and pulled the text, one line at a time, into a variable called *strNextLine*. As long as data is in the text file, you can continue to pump the information by using the *ReadLine* command. However, if you reach the end of the text stream, you exit the *Do Until...Loop* construction you created.

```
Do Until objTextFile.AtEndOfStream
    strNextLine = objTextFile.ReadLine
    TxtIn = Split(strNextLine , ",")
    Set objOU = GetObject("LDAP://OU=LabOU," _
        & "dc=nwtraders,dc=msft")
    Set objUser = objOU.Create("User", "cn="& TxtIn(0))
    objUser.Put "sAMAccountName", TxtIn(0)
    objUser.SetInfo

    Set objGroup = GetObject _
        ("LDAP://CN="& TxtIn(1) & ",cn=users," _
        & "dc=nwtraders,dc=msft")
    objGroup.add _
        "LDAP://cn="& TxtIn(0) & ",ou=LabOU," _
        & "dc=nwtraders,dc=msft"
    Logging
Loop
```

## Output Information

Once you create a new user and assign that user to a group, you need to document the script changes. To do this, you call a subroutine (in our script, called *logging*) that opens a log file and writes the name of the new user that was created as well as the time in which the creation occurred. The first task the *logging* subroutine does is check for the existence of the logging folder that is defined by the variable *LogFolder*. To check for the presence of the folder, you use the *FolderExists* method. If the folder is present on the system, you next check for the existence of the logging file defined by the *LogFile* variable. To check for the presence of the *LogFile*, you use the *FileExists* method. If both of these conditions are copasetic, you open the log file by using the *OpenTextFile* command and specify that you will append to the file instead of overwriting it (which is normally what you want a log file to do). In writing to the file, you use two different methods: *WriteBlankLines* to make the log a little easier to read, and *WriteLine* to write the user name and the time that user was created in the log.

If, on the other hand, the log folder exists but the log file does not exist, you need to create the log file prior to writing to it. This is the subject of the first *Else* command present in the subroutine. You use the *CreateTextFile* command and the *LogFile* variable to create the log file. After the file is created, you must close the connection to the file; if you do not, you get an error message stating that the file is in use. After you close the connection to the log file, you reopen it by using the *OpenTextFile* command, and then you write your information to the file.

The other scenario our subroutine must deal with is if neither the folder nor the log file is in existence, in which case you have to create the folder (by using the *CreateFolder* method) and then create the file (by using the *CreateTextFile* method). Once again, it is necessary to use *objFile.Close* to close the connection to the newly created text file so that you can write your logging information to the file. Once you write to the log file, you exit the subroutine by using the *End Sub* command, and you enter the *Do Until...Loop* again. The logging subroutine is shown here:

```
Sub Logging
    If objFSO.FolderExists(LogFolder) Then
        If objFSO.FileExists(LogFile) Then
            Set objFile = objFSO.OpenTextFile _
                (LogFile, ForAppending)
            objFile.WriteBlankLines(1)
            objFile.WriteLine "Creating User " & Now
            objFile.WriteLine  TxtIn(0)
            objFile.Close
        Else
            Set objFile = objFSO.CreateTextFile(LogFile)
            objFile.Close
            Set objFile = objFSO.OpenTextFile _
                (LogFile, ForWriting)
            objfile.WriteLine "Creating User " & Now
            objFile.WriteLine  TxtIn(0)

            objFile.Close
        End If
    Else
        Set objFolder = objFSO.CreateFolder(LogFolder)
        Set objFile = objFSO.CreateTextFile(LogFile)
        objFile.Close
        Set objFile = objFSO.OpenTextFile _
            (LogFile, ForWriting)
        objfile.WriteLine "Creating User " & Now
        objFile.WriteLine  TxtIn(0)
        objFile.Close
    End If
End Sub

WScript.Echo("all done")
```

# Summary

In this chapter, you examined using subroutines to facilitate code re-use within a single script. You looked at the advantages of using subroutines: making scripts easier to read, easier to change, and easier to write. You used a real-world example to look at the use of subroutines to perform logging when creating a large number of new users and assigning those users to groups. In the script example in this chapter, all the code associated with the logging operation was placed into a subroutine. This subroutine could easily be added to several of the other scripts examined in this book. The only trick would be to make sure you were consistent with the variable naming convention used in the subroutine.

# Quiz Yourself

**Q. How do you create a subroutine?**

**A.** To create a subroutine, you begin a line with the word *Sub* followed by the name of the subroutine. You end the subroutine by using the command *End Sub* on a line following your subroutine code.

**Q. How do you call a subroutine?**

**A.** You call a subroutine by placing the name of the subroutine on a line by itself at the place in your code where you want to use the subroutine.

**Q. What are three uses for subroutines in VBScript?**

**A.** Subroutines make code more portable and easier to read and troubleshoot, and they promote code re-use.

# On Your Own

# Lab 30 Using ADSI and Subs, and Creating Users

In this lab, you will expand the script used in this chapter. Instead of creating only a user, you will add information to the user. You will use a subroutine to perform logging.

## Lab Instructions

1. Open Notepad.exe.

2. Open the CreateUsers.vbs file and save it as **Lab30Solution.vbs**.

3. Make sure you have a file called UsersAndGroups.txt, and run the Lab30Solution.vbs file. Go into Active Directory Users and Computers and delete the users that were created.

4. Cut the code used to open the text file that holds the names of users to add to Active Directory. It is under the variable declarations, in the Reference information section of the script. It is five lines long. This code looks like the following:

```
TxtFile = "C:\UsersAndGroups.txt"
Const ForReading = 1
Set objFSO = CreateObject("Scripting.FileSystemObject")
Set objTextFile = objFSO.OpenTextFile _
    (TxtFile, ForReading)
```

**5.** Paste the code after the *WScript.Echo* command at the end of the script.

**6.** Under the declarations, where the *txtFile* code used to be, type **ReadUsers**. This is the name of the new subroutine you will create. It will look like the following:

```
Dim objOU
Dim objUser
Dim objGroup
Dim objFSO
Dim objTextFile
Dim TxtIn
Dim strNextLine
Dim i
Dim TxtFile
dim boundary

ReadUsers
```

**7.** On the line before the code that reads the *txtFile* that you copied to the end of your script, use the *Sub* command to create a subroutine called *ReadUsers*.

**8.** At the end of the subroutine, add the *End Sub* command. The completed subroutine looks like the following:

```
Sub ReadUsers
    TxtFile = "C:\UsersAndGroups.txt"
    Const ForReading = 1
    Set objFSO = CreateObject("Scripting.FileSystemObject")
    Set objTextFile = objFSO.OpenTextFile _
        (TxtFile, ForReading)
End Sub
```

**9.** Save your work. Run the script to make sure it still works.

**10.** Modify the subroutine so that it is reading a text file called MoreUsersAndGroups.txt. This file is located in the lab starter files folder.

**11.** In the Worker section of the script that creates the user, use the *Put* method to add the user's first name, last name, building, and phone number. The Active Directory attributes are called *givenName*, *sn*, *physicalDeliveryOfficeName*, and *telephoneNumber*. Each of these fields is in the array that gets created, so you need to increment the array field. The completed code will look like the following:

```
Set objUser = objOU.Create("User", "cn="& TxtIn(0))
objUser.Put "sAMAccountName", TxtIn(0)
objUser.Put "givenName", TxtIn(1)
objUser.Put "sn", TxtIn(2)
objUser.Put "physicalDeliveryOfficeName", TxtIn(3)
objUser.Put "telephoneNumber", TxtIn(4)
```

**12.** Because the group membership field is the last field and you added fields to the text file, you need to increment the array index that is used to point to the group field. The new index number is 5, and the code will look like the following:

```
Set objGroup = GetObject _
    ("LDAP://CN="& TxtIn(5) & ",cn=users,dc=nwtraders,dc=msft")
```

13. Save the script and run it. After you successfully run the script, delete the users created in Active Directory.

# Lab 31 Adding a Logging Subroutine

In this lab, you add logging capability to the script you finished in Lab 30.

## Lab Instructions

1. Open Notepad.exe.

2. Open Lab31Starter.vbs and save the file as **Lab31Solution.vbs**.

3. After the *objGroup.add* command statement but before the *Loop* command, add a call to the subroutine called *LogAction*. The modification to the script will look like the following:

```
Set objGroup = GetObject _
    ("LDAP://CN="& TxtIn(5) & ",cn=users,dc=nwtraders,dc=msft")
objGroup.Add _
    "LDAP://cn="& TxtIn(0) & ",ou=LabOU,dc=nwtraders,dc=msft"
LogAction
Loop
```

4. Under the *ReadUsers* subroutine, add a subroutine called *LogAction*. This will consist of the *Sub* command and the *End Sub* command. Leave two blank lines in between the two commands. The code will look like the following:

```
Sub LogAction

End Sub
```

5. Save your work.

6. Open the CreateLogFile.vbs file and copy all the variable declarations. Paste them under the variables in your script.

7. Delete the extra *objFSO* variable.

8. Copy the three reference lines from the CreateLogFile.vbs script and paste them under the variable declarations. This section of the script now looks like the following:

```
Dim objOU
Dim objUser
Dim objGroup
Dim objFSO
Dim objTextFile
Dim TxtIn
Dim strNextLine
```

```
Dim i
Dim TxtFile
Dim objFile            ' holds hook to the file to be used
Dim message            ' holds message to be written to file
Dim objData1      ' holds data from source used to write to file
Dim objData2      ' holds data from source used to write to file
Dim LogFolder
Dim LogFile
message="Reading computer info " & Now
objData1 = objRecordSet.Fields("name")
objData2 = objRecordSet.Fields("distinguishedName")
```

9. Modify the message so that it states that the code is creating a user, and use the element *TxtIn(0)* as the user name that gets created. This modified line will look like the following:

```
message="Creating user " & TxtIn(1) & Now
```

10. Move the message line to the line after you parse *strNextLine*. You do this because you are using an element of the array that must be an assigned value before it can be used.

```
strNextLine = objTextFile.ReadLine
TxtIn = Split(strNextLine , ",")
message="Creating user " & TxtIn(1) & Now
```

11. Modify the *objData1* and *objdata2* data assignments. Use *TxtIn(0)* for the user field and *TxtIn(5)* for the group. The two lines will look like the following:

```
objData1 = TxtIn(0)
objData2 = TxtIn(5)
```

12. Copy the remainder of the script and paste it between the two lines used to create the subroutine. The completed section looks like the following:

```
Sub LogAction
    If objFSO.FolderExists(LogFolder) Then
        If objFSO.FileExists(LogFile) Then
            Set objFile = objFSO.OpenTextFile(LogFile, ForAppending)
            objFile.WriteBlankLines(1)
            objFile.Writeline message
            objFile.Writeline  objData1
            objFile.Writeline objData2
            objFile.Close
        Else
            Set objFile = objFSO.CreateTextFile(LogFile)
            objFile.Close
            Set objFile = objFSO.OpenTextFile(LogFile, ForWriting)
            objfile.WriteLine message
            objFile.WriteLine  objData1
            objFile.WriteLine objData2
            objFile.Close
        End If
    Else
        Set objFolder = objFSO.CreateFolder(LogFolder)
```

```
            Set objFile = objFSO.CreateTextFile(LogFile)
            objFile.Close
            Set objFile = objFSO.OpenTextFile(LogFile, ForWriting)
            objfile.writeline message
            objFile.WriteLine objData1
            objFile.WriteLine objData2
            objFile.Close
        End If
    End Sub
```

**13.** Save and run the script.

# 16 Logon Scripts

In this chapter, you'll look at creating logon scripts. Logon scripts have traditionally been either nonexistent or simple batch files containing a series of *net use* commands. With the power of Microsoft Visual Basic Script (VBScript), however, you can make a number of intelligent decisions in your logon scripts and bring a new level of manageability and configurability to the table.

## Before You Begin

**To work through the material presented in this chapter you need to be familiar with the following concepts from earlier chapters:**

- Using WMI
- Using ADSI
- Using the *InStr* function
- Implementing *For...Next* constructions
- Implementing *Select Case* constructions
- Implementing the file system object

**After completing this chapter you will be familiar with the following:**

- Using the *IADsADSystemInfo* interface
- Using *WshNetwork*
- Using the *Join* function
- Creating dynamic logon scripts
- Implementing logging for logon scripts

## Working with *IADsADSystemInfo*

In this section, you will use the *IADsADSystemInfo* interface to obtain data about the local computer. The *IADsADSystemInfo* interface is implemented for access to the *ADSystemInfo* class. Because this class resides in the adsldp.dll file, which is part of ADSI, it is present on Microsoft Windows Server 2003, Windows XP, and even Windows 2000. To use *IADsADSystemInfo*, you need to hook it by creating an instance of the *ADSystemInfo* class. This process is actually simple—you use the *CreateObject* command. Table 16-1 summarizes the nine properties exposed by *IADsADSystemInfo*.

**Table 16-1   Properties Exposed by *IADsADSystemInfo***

| Property | Meaning |
| --- | --- |
| *ComputerName* | Retrieves the distinguished name of the local computer |
| *DomainDNSName* | Retrieves the DNS name of the local computer's domain |
| *DomainShortName* | Retrieves the short name of the local computer's domain (the NetBIOS version of the name) |
| *ForestDNSName* | Retrieves the DNS name of the local computer's forest |
| *IsNativeMode* | Determines whether the local computer's domain is native or mixed mode |
| *PDCRoleOwner* | Retrieves the distinguished name of the DC that owns the PDC emulator role in the local computer's domain |
| *SchemaRoleOwner* | Retrieves the distinguished name of the Schema Master in the local computer's forest |
| *SiteName* | Retrieves the site name the local computer resides in |
| *UserName* | Retrieves the distinguished name of the currently logged-on user |

The advantage of using *IADsADSystemInfo* over other means of gaining user and computer information is that *IADsADSystemInfo* retrieves fully qualified domain names, which are immediately useful when working with Active Directory. In addition to the nine properties listed in Table 16-1, there are 13 methods exposed by *IADsADSystemInfo*. However, most of them duplicate the properties listed in Table 16-1, so Table 16-2 describes only the methods that provide additional information.

**Table 16-2   *IADsADSystemInfo* Methods Providing Unique Information**

| Method | Description |
| --- | --- |
| *GetAnyDCName* | Retrieves the DNS name of a domain controller in the local computer's domain. |
| *RefreshSchemaCache* | Refreshes ADSI's Active Directory schema cache on the local computer. |
| *GetTrees* | Retrieves the DNS names of all the directory trees in the local computer's forest. Returned as an array. |

The following script, called SysInfo.vbs, illustrates using the *IADsADSystemInfo* interface. In the first line, you use *objSysInfo* to hold the hook that comes back when you use *CreateObject* to create an instance of *ADSystemInfo*. After you do this, you use the *RefreshSchemaCache* method to refresh the Active Directory schema cache that is resident on the local computer. Performing this step ensures that you are working with the most recent copy of the Active Directory schema. After refreshing the schema cache on the local machine, you echo out the pertinent information. The only step that is a little tricky is the use of *For Each...Next* to walk through the array that is returned when you use the *GetTrees* method. This step is required, even when only one domain is present in the forest.

```
Set objSysInfo = CreateObject("ADSystemInfo")
objSysInfo.RefreshSchemaCache
WScript.Echo "User name: " & objSysInfo.UserName
WScript.Echo "Computer name: " & objSysInfo.ComputerName
WScript.Echo "Site name: " & objSysInfo.SiteName
WScript.Echo "Domain short name: " & objSysInfo.DomainShortName
WScript.Echo "Domain DNS name: " & objSysInfo.DomainDNSName
WScript.Echo "Forest DNS name: " & objSysInfo.ForestDNSName
WScript.Echo "PDC role owner: " & objSysInfo.PDCRoleOwner
WScript.Echo "Schema role owner: " & objSysInfo.SchemaRoleOwner
WScript.Echo "Domain is in native mode: " & objSysInfo.IsNativeMode
WScript.Echo "Active Directory DomainController: " & objSysInfo.GetAnyDCName

For Each tree In objSysInfo.GetTrees
    WScript.Echo "Domain trees: " & tree
Next
```

# Using Logon Scripts

In the old days, network administrators spent hours and hours trying to craft the perfect logon script. In the end, it was a fruitless effort, as needs were always changing, and the capabilities of logon scripts were limited. Many networks today seem to run just fine without a logon script. With the widespread adoption of Group Policy, some people might question why we need logon scripts at all. However, when using VBScript for your logon scripts, you can craft some very powerful solutions for configuring and maintaining your users' environments. In addition, because Group Policy is often handled by a separate group within enterprise networks, making a change to a logon script can be easier than talking another group into modifying its "perfect Group Policy." There are several tasks that logon scripts can be quickly called into service to perform:

■ Mapping network drives

■ Mapping printers

■ Collecting system information

■ Checking antivirus signatures

■ Checking hotfix and security updates

■ Checking security settings

> **Just the Steps**
>
> ▶ **To create powerful and flexible logon scripts**
>
> 1. Use *IADsADSystemInfo* to determine user information.
> 2. Use ADSI to query for group membership information.
> 3. Use Windows Scripting Host (WSH) to map network drives.
> 4. Use WSH to set default printers.

# Deploying Logon Scripts

Perhaps the simplest way to implement a logon script is to modify the logon script user attribute. Although you can assign logon scripts to users by using the GUI interface, you can also do this easily by using the *scriptpath* Active Directory attribute of the *user* object. I prefer, however, to use Group Policy to assign the logon script to users. However you choose to assign logon scripts to your users, once you write the script, this script will need to be saved in the sysvol share in the scripts directory. If you do this, you can link the script to multiple Group Policy Objects (GPOs). You could, of course, also save the logon script within the actual GPO itself. If you choose to save it in this way, you will not be able to reuse the script with other GPOs. In fact, you could end up deleting the script if you delete the GPO that is hosting the script.

So what does a VBScript logon script look like? The following script (Logonscript.vbs) is similar to many logon scripts I've used with customers in the past. It has several advantages over the old-fashioned batch files that many of you grew up with. We'll discuss these advantages as we examine each section that makes up LogonScript.vbs.

```
Option Explicit
Dim fServer
Dim home
Dim wshNet
Dim ADSysInfo
Dim CurrentUser
Dim strGroups
Dim GroupMember
Dim a,b,c,d
Const HR = "cn=hrgroup"
Const MARKETING = "cn=marketinggroup"
Const SALES = "cn=salesgroup"

fServer = "\\london"
home = "\\london\users"
Set wshNet = CreateObject("WScript.Network")
Set ADSysInfo = CreateObject("ADSystemInfo")
Set CurrentUser = GetObject("LDAP://" _
    & ADSysInfo.UserName)
strGroups = LCase(Join(CurrentUser.MemberOf))

wshNet.MapNetworkDrive "h:", fServer & "\Users\" _
```

```
             & wshNet.UserName
WScript.Echo(wshNet.Username & " " & strgroups)
GroupMember = True
Select Case GroupMember
    Case a = InStr(strGroups, HR)
         HRsub
    Case b = InStr(strGroups, SALES)
         SalesSub
    Case c = InStr(strGroups, MARKETING)
         MarketingSub
End Select

Sub HRsub
    WScript.Echo("made it to HR")
    wshNet.MapNetworkDrive "g:","\\london\Hr\"
    wshNet.AddWindowsPrinterConnection _
        "\\london\HrPrinter"
    wshNet.SetDefaultPrinter "\\london\HrPrinter"
End Sub

Sub SalesSub
    WScript.Echo("made it to sales")
    wshNet.MapNetworkDrive "s:", "\\london\Sales"
    wshNet.AddWindowsPrinterConnection _
        "\\london\SalesPrinter"
    wshNet.SetDefaultPrinter "\\london\SalesPrinter"
End Sub

Sub MarketingSub
    WScript.Echo("made it to marketing")
    wshNet.MapNetworkDrive "m:","\\london\Marketing\"
    wshNet.AddWindowsPrinterConnection _
        "\\london\MarketingPrinter"
    wshNet.SetDefaultPrinter _
        "\\london\MarketingPrinter"
End Sub
```

## Header Information

The Header information section of LogonScript.vbs includes the *Option Explicit* command and the declaration of several variables.

> **Tip**   You don't use *On Error Resume Next* in logon scripts because if the logon script fails, you want to hear from your user community immediately. You don't want to suppress error messages nor risk mapping only a few of the drives that the users need to be able to perform their work. I've seen situations in which the logon script messed up drive mappings for a group of users, and these users had no idea where their data was stored. We wound up having to reproduce the error in a lab to determine what drives had been mapped for which user so that we could find the work the users had "lost." Once this was done, we removed error suppression on the logon script, and although doing this might have resulted in a few more help desk calls, it vastly simplified the consequences when the logon script failed.

Seven variables are used in LogonScript.vbs and are listed in Table 16-3.

**Table 16-3  LogonScript.vbs Variables**

| Variable | Use |
| --- | --- |
| *fServer* | Holds the name of the file server. Used when mapping home directory for the user. Could be used in other mappings as well, but not implemented in this version of the script. |
| *Home* | Holds the relative path of the users' home directory share. This variable also could be expanded by using site information to point the closed file server to the users. |
| *wshNet* | Holds the hook that comes back when you create an instance of *WScript.Network*. You use this to allow the mapping of drives and printers. |
| *ADSysInfo* | Holds the hook that comes back when you create an instance of *ADSystemInfo*. This allows you to obtain current user information. |
| *CurrentUser* | Holds a connection into Active Directory using LDAP provider. |
| *strGroups* | Holds a list of all the groups the user is a member of. |
| *GroupMember* | Used by the *Select Case* construction to hold the value of the group membership. |

**Tip**  Depending on how you decide to document your scripts, creating a table of variables can be an awesome reference tool. I know some Internet administrators who print out all their production scripts and store them in a binder along with their definitive software library (DSL). Others store backup copies of production scripts on a network share, and use remarks to document the scripts. Even if you do not need a variable table for script documentation, you might find that creating one is sometimes helpful as reference when writing the script—it forces you to think about the script flow, and in a long script, it is easier to work with a table than scrolling back up to the Header information section of the script. This is a good habit to develop if you program in C# or Visual Basic .NET as well.

## Reference Information

In addition to defining the variables listed in the Header information section of the script, you also define some constants. The three constants hold the name of the groups that are searched for by using the *Instr* command. In this example, the group memberships are *HrGroup*, *MarketingGroup*, and *SalesGroup*. You assign the "*cn=*" version of the name to the constants called *Hr*, *Marketing*, and *Sales*. You do this because when you perform the query for the group memberships, the string of data returned will include the full LDAP name of the groups. However, to make the code easier to type and understand and thus easier to work with, you assign the longer names to constants. The resultant code looks like the following:

```
Const HR = "cn=hrgroup"
Const MARKETING = "cn=marketinggroup"
Const SALES = "cn=salesgroup"
```

The remainder of the Reference information section appears in the code that follows. You use a variable *fServer* to hold the name of the file server. This makes it easy to change the script if you move the shared directories to other servers. In this version of the script, no drive mappings use variable names for the server. Instead, the drive mappings use the hardcoded Universal Naming Convention (UNC) path to a specific server share. This means that when the data gets moved to a different server, the logon script must be modified in several places.

```
fServer = "\\london"
home = "\\london\users"
Set wshNet = CreateObject("WScript.Network")
Set ADSysInfo = CreateObject("ADSystemInfo")
Set CurrentUser = GetObject("LDAP://" _
    & ADSysInfo.UserName)
strGroups = LCase(Join(CurrentUser.MemberOf))
```

All the users' home directories are in a shared directory called *users*. If you move the share to a different location, you will need to modify the *home* = \\*london*\\*users* line in the script. Changing this line is easier than making a change in the Home Folder field on the Profile tab in Active Directory Users and Computers (ADUC). Change one line in the logon script, or make thousands of changes via the GUI in ADUC—seems to be a relatively painless choice!

---

**Quick Check**

**Q.** What are three ways of assigning a logon script to a user?

**A.** Three ways of assigning a logon script to a user are via the GUI interface by using Active Directory Users and Computers, via VBScript by using the *script-Path* property, or by using Group Policy.

**Q.** What are three common activities performed by logon scripts?

**A.** Three common activities performed by logon scripts are mapping to network shares, mapping to network printers, and setting default printers for users.

---

## Using the *WshNetwork* Class

The next order of business is wiring up three connections to turn on the power of VBScript in our logon script. The first of these connections is used to hold the hook that comes back from creating an instance of the *WScript.Network* class. You use the

*WScript.Network* progid to create an object that is called *WshNetwork*. *WshNetwork* allows you to connect to and disconnect from network shares and network printers. In addition, we can use *WshNetwork* to map or remove network shares or to access information about a user on a network. This said, you might be asking yourself why we decided to use *ADSystemInfo* to obtain the user name. The reason is that the user name coming from *WshNetwork* is a single-label name, for example, Bob. But to query Active Directory to obtain all your group memberships, you need the distinguished name— for example, a name like *cn=bob, ou=LabOU, dc=nwtraders,* or *dc=msft.* You can use the distinguished name to make an LDAP binding and then to query all the information you need to obtain for the logon script.

After you create an instance of the *WshNetwork,* you are ready to connect to the *IADs-ADSystemInfo* interface so that you can get information about the local computer and local user. You learned about this in detail earlier in this chapter, so I won't elaborate further here.

After you have a hook into the *ADSystemInfo* interface, you use the *UserName* command to obtain the fully qualified local user name, and then combine that with the LDAP provider and make a connection into Active Directory. The hook that comes back from Active Directory is called *CurrentUser.* You have now wired up all the connections necessary to get the logon script up and running.

You do need to define one more reference—a list of groups that the current user is a member of. To do this, you use the *MemberOf* command. The problem is that the *MemberOf* command will return with an array.

### Using the *Join* Function

Although arrays are groovy, dealing with an array will make your script just a little bit more complicated—in fact, because you are interested only in the presence of a particular string sequence, you don't need an array at all. For assistance, you use the VBScript *Join* function. The *Join* function comes back with a string that gets created by putting together (that is, joining) the data contained in the array elements. In this way, you can easily use the *InStr* command to search the string for the presence of your group membership items. You can see an example of using the *Join* function in the Join.vbs script, which you'll examine in a moment.

Notice that you begin the Join.vbs script by declaring a five-element array. You then assign a value to each element in the array. On the next-to-last line, you use the *Join* function to pull together all the elements of the array, which is called *MyArray.* You assign the string that comes from using the *Join* function to a variable called *MyString.* Because you now have a string that contains all the elements of the array, you can use *WScript.Echo* to display the value of *MyString.*

```
Dim MyString
Dim MyArray(4)
MyArray(0) = "Mr."
MyArray(1) = "Sam"
MyArray(2) = "Spade,"
MyArray(3) = "Private"
MyArray(4) = "Eye"
MyString = Join(MyArray)
WScript.Echo(MyString)
```

## Worker Information

The Worker information section of the script comprises a single *Select Case* construction. The *Select Case* statement is interesting because you are doing something new. *Group-Member* is a variable that holds the result of the cases that are being tested against. In reality, this variable is more of a placeholder than anything else, because you don't use it anywhere else in the script. Each case being evaluated is assigned a variable to hold the results of the test string. When a match is found, the variable *GroupMember* will be set to the value of the match that was made when the case was evaluated. The cool part of this *Select Case* construction happens on the other side of the equal signs. Instead of performing a simple match, you're adding a higher level of intelligence to the script and are requiring the *Select Case* construction to use the *InStr* function to search the string data contained in the variable *strGroups*. Each case is therefore tested to see whether the string represented by each constant is found in *strGroups*. When a match is found, you jump to the appropriate subroutine. This type of construction makes the Worker information section extremely easy to read and understand.

```
Select Case GroupMember
    Case a = InStr(strGroups, HR)
        HRsub
    Case b = InStr(strGroups, SALES)
        SalesSub
    Case c = InStr(strGroups, MARKETING)
        MarketingSub
End Select
```

## Output Information

Once you work through each case in the *Select Case* construction, you enter into a subroutine. Each subroutine is designed around the particular needs of various groups within your organization. The *WScript.Echo* commands let you know which subroutine is being run—these are primarily used for troubleshooting and can be either left in or deleted, depending on the type of customer experience your users are willing to put up with.

To map a network drive, you use the *MapNetworkDrive* command of a *WshNetwork* object. The important issue to keep in mind here is that assigning a drive letter requires a letter and a colon surrounded by double quotation marks. Next, a comma is required to separate the drive letter from the path statement.

When you use *WshNetwork* to map to a printer, you use the *AddWindowsPrinter-Connection* command. (Although this command name is descriptive, it could have been shortened just a tad.) The *AddWindowsPrinterConnection* command needs only a UNC path to the print server and the share name. No commas are required here. (In fact, commas put here will cause the command to fail.)

The last task our subroutine needs to perform is assigning the default Windows printer, so you use a command named *SetDefaultPrinter*. Again, the only work you need to do is include the UNC path to the print server and encase the share name in double quotation marks. Here are the subroutines for the Worker information section of the script:

```
Sub HRsub
    WScript.Echo("made it to HR")
    wshNet.MapNetworkDrive "g:","\\london\Hr\"
    wshNet.AddWindowsPrinterConnection _
        "\\london\HrPrinter"
    wshNet.SetDefaultPrinter "\\london\HrPrinter"
End Sub

Sub SalesSub
    WScript.Echo("made it to sales")
    wshNet.MapNetworkDrive "s:", "\\london\Sales"
    wshNet.AddWindowsPrinterConnection _
        "\\london\SalesPrinter"
    wshNet.SetDefaultPrinter "\\london\SalesPrinter"
End Sub

Sub MarketingSub
    WScript.Echo("made it to marketing")
    wshNet.MapNetworkDrive "m:","\\london\Marketing\"
    wshNet.AddWindowsPrinterConnection _
        "\\london\MarketingPrinter"
    wshNet.SetDefaultPrinter _
        "\\london\MarketingPrinter"
End Sub
```

# Summary

In this chapter, you examined the use of logon scripts. The chapter began with a discussion of the traditional uses of logon scripts and then looked at several methods for assigning logon scripts to users. Then you learned about *ADSysInfo* and the *Wsh-Network* scripting interfaces, and you looked at some of the useful information that can be obtained from each. You learned about using the *Join* function to put together multiple elements of an array. The chapter concluded with a detailed discussion of one way to design and write logon scripts.

# Quiz Yourself

**Q. What is the advantage of obtaining user and computer information via *ADSysInfo* as opposed to *WshNetwork*?**

**A.** The advantage of using *ADSysInfo* to obtain user and computer information is that *ADSysInfo* returns the distinguished user name, which you can use to directly bind to Active Directory to query information.

**Q. What does the *Join* function do?**

**A.** The Join function puts elements of an array together into a single string.

**Q. What are three tasks that *WshNetwork* can perform?**

**A.** *WshNetwork* is able to map to network shares, remove network shares, and map to network printers.

**Q. What does *RefreshSchemaCache* do?**

**A.** *RefreshSchemaCache* is used to refresh the local copy of the Active Directory schema on a computer.

# On Your Own

# Lab 32 Adding a Group to a Logon Script

In this lab, you will add a group to a logon script.

## Lab Instructions

1. Open Notepad.exe.

2. Open Lab32Starter.vbs and save it as **Lab32Solution.vbs**.

3. Look over the script, and add documentation to each variable that is declared in the script.

4. Under the Constants, declare a new constant called *Production*. Set it equal to *cn=productiongroup*. The completed constant section will look like the following:

```
Const HR = "cn=hrgroup"
Const MARKETING = "cn=marketinggroup"
Const SALES = "cn=salesgroup"
Const PRODUCTION = "cn=productiongroup"
```

5. Add a new *case d* to the *Select Case* construction. *Case d* is equal to finding the value assigned to the constant *Production* in the string assigned to *strGroups*. If the case is met, it should jump to a subroutine called *ProductionSub*. The new *Select Case* statement looks like the following:

```
Select Case GroupMember
    Case a = InStr(strGroups, HR)
        HRsub
    Case b = InStr(strGroups, SALES)
        SalesSub
    Case c = InStr(strGroups, MARKETING)
        MarketingSub
    Case d = InStr (strGroups, PRODUCTION)
        ProductionSub
End Select
```

**6.** At the bottom of the various subroutines, add a new subroutine called *Production-Sub*. End the subroutine with the *End Sub* command. It will look like the following:

```
Sub ProductionSub

End Sub
```

**7.** For the first line of the Production Sub subroutine, use *WScript.Echo* to inform the user that he or she is in the production subroutine. It could look like the following:

```
WScript.Echo("made it to production")
```

**8.** Use the *MapNetworkDrive* method of the *WshNetwork* object to map the drive letter *"P:"* to the production share on the London server. This line of code will look like the following:

```
wshNet.MapNetworkDrive "p:","\\london\Production\"
```

**9.** Use the *AddWindowsPrinterConnection* method of *WshNetwork* to add a connection to the *ProductionPrinter* that is set up on the London server. This line of code will look like the following:

```
wshNet.AddWindowsPrinterConnection "\\london\ProductionPrinter"
```

**10.** Set the new Production Printer to be the default printer for members of the production group. To do this, use the *SetDefaultPrinter* command of the *WshNetwork* object. This line of code will look like the following:

```
wshNet.SetDefaultPrinter "\\london\ProductionPrinter"
```

**11.** Save and test the script.

# Lab 33 Adding Logging to a Logon Script

In this lab, you add logging to the logon script that was created in Lab 32.

## Lab Instructions

**1.** Open Notepad.exe.

**2.** Open up the Lab33Starter.vbs file and save the file as **Lab33Solution.vbs**.

3. Open the Lab33Starter2.vbs file.

4. Copy the declared variables from the Lab33Starter2.vbs file, and paste them into the Header information section of the Lab33Solution.vbs file. The new Header information section of the script looks like the following:

```
Option Explicit
Dim fServer
Dim home
Dim wshNet
Dim ADSysInfo
Dim CurrentUser
Dim strGroups
Dim GroupMember
Dim objFSO            ' holds connection to file system object
Dim objFile            ' holds hook to the file to be used
Dim message            ' holds message to be written to file
Dim objData1        ' holds data from source used to write to file
Dim objData2        ' holds data from source used to write to file
Dim LogFolder
Dim LogFile
```

5. Copy the entire Reference information section of the Lab33Starter2.vbs file, including all the constants and variable assignments. Paste this under the constants in your script. The completed section looks like this:

```
Const HR = "cn=hrgroup"
Const MARKETING = "cn=marketinggroup"
Const SALES = "cn=salesgroup"
Const PRODUCTION = "cn=productiongroup"
Const ForWriting = 2
Const ForAppending = 8
LogFolder = "C:\fso"
LogFile = "C:\fso\logFile.txt"
Set objFSO = CreateObject("Scripting.FileSystemObject")
message="Reading computer info " & Now
objData1 = objRecordSet.Fields("name")
objData2 = objRecordSet.Fields("distinguishedName")
```

6. Change the message text so that it reads "Processing Logon Script ".

7. Cut the *objData1* and *objData2* variables and paste them under the *strGroups = lcase* line. This section of the script now looks like the following:

```
Set ADSysInfo = CreateObject("ADSystemInfo")
Set CurrentUser = GetObject("LDAP://" & ADSysInfo.UserName)
strGroups = LCase(Join(CurrentUser.MemberOf))
objData1 = objRecordSet.Fields("name")
objData2 = objRecordSet.Fields("distinguishedName")
wshNet.MapNetworkDrive "h:", fServer & "\Users\" & wshNet.UserName
WScript.Echo(wshNet.Username & " " & strgroups)
```

8. Assign meaningful values to *objData1* and *objData2*. Make *objData1* equal to *ADSysInfo.UserName* and *objData2* equal to *strGroups*. The two modified *objData* lines now look like the following:

```
objData1 = ADSysInfo.UserName
objData2 = strGroups
```

9. At the bottom of the subroutines in your Lab 33 solution script, create a new empty subroutine called *LoggingSub*.

10. Inside the empty *LoggingSub* subroutine, paste the entire *If…Then…End If* section from the CreateLogFile.vbs file. The completed *LoggingSub* subroutine now looks like the following:

```
Sub LoggingSub
    If objFSO.FolderExists(LogFolder) Then
        If objFSO.FileExists(LogFile) Then
            Set objFile = objFSO.OpenTextFile(LogFile, ForAppending)
            objFile.WriteBlankLines(1)
            objFile.WriteLine message
            objFile.WriteLine  objData1
            objFile.WriteLine objData2
            objFile.Close
        Else
            Set objFile = objFSO.CreateTextFile(LogFile)
            objFile.Close
            Set objFile = objFSO.OpenTextFile(LogFile, ForWriting)
            objFile.WriteLine message
            objFile.WriteLine  objData1
            objFile.WriteLine objData2
            objFile.Close
        End If
    Else
        Set objFolder = objFSO.CreateFolder(LogFolder)
        Set objFile = objFSO.CreateTextFile(LogFile)
            objFile.Close
            Set objFile = objFSO.OpenTextFile(LogFile, ForWriting)
            objfile.WriteLine message
            objFile.WriteLine  objData1
            objFile.WriteLine objData2
            objFile.Close
    End If
End Sub
```

11. Save your work.

12. In the *HrSub* subroutine, add a command to go to the *LoggingSub* subroutine after the *setDefaultPrinter* command. The new *HrSub* subroutine now looks like the following:

```
Sub HRsub
    WScript.Echo("made it to HR")
    wshNet.MapNetworkDrive "g:","\\london\Hr\"
    wshNet.AddWindowsPrinterConnection "\\london\HrPrinter"
```

```
    wshNet.SetDefaultPrinter "\\london\HrPrinter"
    Loggingsub
End Sub
```

**13.** Add the *LoggingSub* command to the *salesSub*, *marketingSub*, and *productionSub* subroutines as well. The completed subroutines look like the following:

```
Sub SalesSub
    WScript.Echo("made it to sales")
    wshNet.MapNetworkDrive "s:", "\\london\Sales"
    wshNet.AddWindowsPrinterConnection "\\london\SalesPrinter"
    wshNet.SetDefaultPrinter "\\london\SalesPrinter"
    Loggingsub
End Sub

Sub MarketingSub
WScript.Echo("made it to marketing")
    wshNet.MapNetworkDrive "m:","\\london\Marketing\"
    wshNet.AddWindowsPrinterConnection "\\london\MarketingPrinter"
    wshNet.SetDefaultPrinter "\\london\MarketingPrinter"
    Loggingsub
End Sub

Sub ProductionSub
    WScript.Echo("made it to production")
    wshNet.MapNetworkDrive "p:","\\london\Production\"
    wshNet.AddWindowsPrinterConnection "\\london\ProductionPrinter"
    wshNet.SetDefaultPrinter "\\london\ProductionPrinter"
    Loggingsub
End Sub
```

**14.** Save your work, and test it out.

# 17 Working with the Registry

In this chapter, you'll look at the registry. For many network administrators, the registry is like the island of Kauai—dark, foreboding, and yet enchanting and mystical. Just as the playful swishing and splashing of the waves upon the beach draws you closer to the island, the power of editing via Microsoft Visual Basic Script (VBScript) lures you closer to fooling with the registry. The music of the waves, however, is borne aloft by sharp jagged volcanic rocks. Keep this in mind as you explore your three main tasks when working with the registry: reading items from the registry, writing to the registry, and backing up the registry.

## Before You Begin

**To work through the material presented in this chapter you need to be familiar with the following concepts from earlier chapters:**

- Creating an instance of the *FileSystemObject* class

- Creating a connection into Microsoft Windows Management Instrumentation (WMI)

- Implementing the *For…Next* construction

- Implementing *Select Case* construction

**After completing this chapter you will be familiar with the following:**

- Implementing the *WshShell* class

- Scripting Reg.exe

- Working with the WMI *StdRegProv* class

- Working with the *WshController* object

## First You Back Up

In this section, you will use the Reg.exe program to back up the registry. Backing up is an important step, because you can make changes to the registry that would preclude Microsoft Windows Server 2003 from even loading. So before you ever make any change to the registry, you must have a backup.

> **Note** Don't be scared of working with the registry out of fear of "hosing" your machine. If you do not have a backup of the registry, and you suspect a registry change caused a problem, try booting your server and selecting "last known good" from the Startup menu. If this does not work, try booting into the recovery console off of the Microsoft Windows Server 2003 CD-ROM and using the command-line registry editor to undo the changes you previously made.

Numerous utilities can back up the registry; backing up using a script is convenient as well. By using the Reg.exe support tool via VBScript, you can perform the following operations:

- Back up a registry key prior to making modifications
- Back up a registry hive as part of maintenance
- Import a registry key as part of maintenance
- Import a registry key to restore a previous configuration

---

**Just the Steps**

▶ **To back up the registry using the Reg.exe command**

1. Create an instance of the *WshShell* class.
2. Use the *Exec* method of *WshShell* to execute the Reg.exe command.
3. Use the Reg.exe *Save* command.
4. Specify the registry key to save and the file to save it into.

---

## Creating the *WshShell* Object

To use the Reg.exe tool to back up the registry, it is necessary to create an instance of the *WshShell* class. This allows you to launch programs that are not part of Windows Scripting Host. The following program, RegBack.vbs, illustrates making a hook into *WshShell*:

```
Option Explicit
dim objShell

WScript.Echo("beginning " & Now)
Set objShell = CreateObject("WScript.Shell")
objShell.Exec "%comspec% /k reg.exe EXPORT HKLM c:\hklm.reg"
WScript.Echo("completed " & Now)
```

As you can see in RegBack.vbs, you declare a variable called *objShell* and set it equal to the hook that comes back from using *CreateObject* to create an instance of *WshShell*.

After we have this hook into the *Shell* object, you use the *Exec* method to launch a command-line interpreter with the */k* option.

> **Tip**   The */k* in this context means to leave the command window open so that you can examine anything written to the window by using the program you are executing. However, it seems the behavior of */k* and */c* (which means to close the command window after the script is finished executing) is largely dependant upon the command being executed, and it therefore could seem to be erratic and unpredictable. As always, if something is important to you, test it in a lab.

## Setting the *comspec* Variable

The way that you get the command interpreter in RegBack.vbs is by using a well-known system variable called *%comspec%*. If you are in doubt as to the value of *%comspec%* on your computer, open a system prompt and type the following:

```
Echo %comspec%
```

If you are running on a Windows Server 2003, Windows 2000, or Windows XP machine, the value returned is C:\WINDOWS\system32\cmd.exe.

## Defining the Command Line

When you use the *Exec* method of *WshShell*, the command line is placed inside the quotation marks. Because Reg.exe is a command-line program in the preceding code, there really was no need to include the *%comspec%*. Our command line could have simply been the following:

```
objShell.Exec "reg.exe EXPORT HKLM c:\hklm.reg"
```

If, on the other hand, you need to use a command line for a command that is internal to the command processor (cmd.exe or command.com), such as the *dir* command, you need to launch a command shell interpreter, either by using the *%comspec%* system variable or by using Cmd.exe, as illustrated by CmdDir.vbs, which follows. The issue of when to supply a command processor name and when not to is sometimes confusing, but this explanation should help you.

```
Option Explicit
Dim objShell
Dim objExec
Dim strLine
Dim dirTxt
Dim dirFile

dirFile = "ntuser.dat"
WScript.Echo("beginning " & Now)
```

```
Set objShell = WScript.CreateObject("WScript.Shell")
Set objExec = objShell.Exec("%comspec% /c dir /aH c:\*.dat /s")

Do Until objExec.StdOut.AtEndOfStream
    strLine = objExec.StdOut.ReadLine()
    dirTxt = Instr(strLine,dirFile)
    If dirTxt<> 0 Then
        Wscript.Echo strLine
    End If
Loop
WScript.Echo("all done " & Now)
```

> **Tip**   When using the *WshShell Exec* method, everything inside the outer quotation marks is
> executed. One quick way to make sure that you are getting the results you want and that the
> code is running properly is to paste your executable code into a Start\Run dialog box. This
> approach will not work, however, if you are using embedded quotes in strings. In this case, it
> is better to use WScript.Echo to echo out the value of your variable, enabling you to ensure
> you are sending the correct commands to VBScript.

# Connecting to the Registry

To work with the registry, you need to connect to it first. You can use the WMI *StdReg-Prov* class to make a connection and to read or write information into it. Although reading from the registry is a safe process, writing to the registry could have disastrous consequences if you don't take normal safety precautions such as making a backup of the key you intend to change and testing the script in a lab on machines that would be easily recoverable.

At times, just being able to read a listing of keys is sufficient for your needs. For instance, when the hotfix installer is run, it creates an entry under HKLM\SOFTWARE \Microsoft\Windows NT\CurrentVersion\HotFix. Realizing this, if you read this key, you can see what hotfixes have been applied to a particular machine. The following script, ReadHotFixes.vbs, does this very thing. By using the *EnumKey* method of the WMI *StdRegProv*, you can rather easily create a listing of subkeys.

```
Option Explicit
On Error Resume Next
Dim strKeyPath
Dim strComputer
Dim objReg
Dim subKey
Dim arrSubKeys

Const HKCR = &H80000000 'HKEY_CLASSES_ROOT
Const HKCU = &H80000001 'HKEY_CURRENT_USER
Const HKLM = &H80000002 'HKEY_LOCAL_MACHINE
Const HKU  = &H80000003 'HKEY_USERS
Const HKCC = &H80000005 'HKEY_CURRENT_CONFIG
```

```
strKeyPath = "SOFTWARE\Microsoft\Windows NT" _
    & "\CurrentVersion\HotFix"
strComputer = "."

Set objReg=GetObject("winmgmts:\\" &_
    strComputer & "\root\default:StdRegProv")

objReg.EnumKey HKLM, strKeyPath, arrSubKeys

    WScript.Echo("Keys under " & strKeyPath)
For Each subKey In arrSubKeys
    WScript.Echo vbTab & subKey
Next
```

# Header Information

The Header information section of ReadHotFixes.vbs consists of the *Option Explicit* and *On Error Resume Next* commands, as well as the declarations for five variables. The five variables are described in Table 17-1.

**Table 17-1   Variables Used in ReadHotFixes.vbs**

| Variable | Use |
| --- | --- |
| *strKeyPath* | The main registry that defines the entry point for the script |
| *strComputer* | Holds the name of the computer that is targeted by WMI |
| *objReg* | Holds the hook that comes back from the WMI *StdRegProv* |
| *subKey* | Holds the name of the registry key to be enumerated |
| *arrSubKeys* | Holds an array of registry keys found under the *subKey* |

# Reference Information

The Reference information section of the script is used to define constants and variables used in the operation of the script. There are several tree values defined in winreg.h that you can use to define constants and to shorten the length of your scripts. The default tree is HKEY_LOCAL_MACHINE, so in reality, specifying the tree is unnecessary. However, for clarity, and to ensure you hit the correct portion of the registry, I do not advocate relying on the default registry tree. All the hex numbers that represent the registry trees are listed in the Reference information section of this script. I normally include them in all registry scripts so that I don't have to look them up later. They don't take up too much space, and they form the basis of a nice registry script template.

The *strKeyPath* is the registry key you want to look at. In this instance, since you're using the *EnumKey* method, you'll get back only a listing of key names that reside below the *strKeyPath*. This is a pretty useful method to use when you don't know what you'll find below a particular registry key.

You make your connection to the standard registry provider by using *GetObject* to make a connection into *winmgmts*. By default, *StdRegProv* resides in the root\default namespace—it is important to note, however, that software makers can compile the Regevent.mof file used to define the *StdRegProv* into a different namespace for use in their applications. If you're working with such an application, you should connect to a different namespace.

```
Const HKCR = &H80000000 'HKEY_CLASSES_ROOT
Const HKCU = &H80000001 'HKEY_CURRENT_USER
Const HKLM = &H80000002 'HKEY_LOCAL_MACHINE
Const HKU  = &H80000003 'HKEY_USERS
Const HKCC = &H80000005 'HKEY_CURRENT_CONFIG
strKeyPath = "SOFTWARE\Microsoft\Windows NT" _
    & "\CurrentVersion\HotFix"
strComputer = "."

Set objReg=GetObject("winmgmts:\\" &_
    strComputer & "\root\default:StdRegProv")
```

## Worker and Output Information

The Worker and Output information section of the script is where you use the hook into the *StdRegProv* that you obtained to perform some work. In the ReadHotFixes.vbs file, you use the *EnumKey* method of the *StdRegProv* WMI class to read a listing of subkeys. Because the hotfix installer documents hotfixes under the hotfix registry key, this is a useful application of the *EnumKey* method. Normally, however, you would use the *EnumKey* method to find out what subkeys existed prior to performing some other action on the registry. For instance, you could use *EnumKey* to find out whether a subkey existed to determine whether a particular application had been installed on a computer. It would also be useful in finding certain types of viruses.

The *objReg.EnumKey* command uses the *HKLM* constant you defined in the Reference information section of the script as well as the *strKeyPath* variable. The information is written to a variable called *arrSubKeys*.

The subkeys are stored in an array, so you use a *For Each...Next* construction to iterate through each element in the array. You assign each new element to a variable called *subKey*. You write the information by using *WScript.Echo* and use the function *vbTab* to indent the results under the heading that was echoed out before entering the *For Each...Next* loop.

```
objReg.EnumKey HKLM, strKeyPath, arrSubKeys

WScript.Echo("Keys under " & strKeyPath)
For Each subKey In arrSubKeys
    WScript.Echo vbTab & subKey
Next
```

# Unleashing *StdRegProv*

The nice aspect of *StdRegProv* is the power it brings to a script. In Chapter 1, "Starting From Scratch," our tutorial script illustrated using *RegRead*. You could follow the same methodology and use the *RegWrite* and *RegDelete* methods of *WshShell*, but there are limitations to using *WshShell* to work with the registry: you cannot work remotely, and there is no enumeration. However, all are resolved by using *StdRegProv*. It has 16 methods defined. These methods and a description of what they can do are listed in Table 17-2.

**Table 17-2  *StdRegProv* Methods**

| Method | Description |
|---|---|
| *CheckAccess* | Verifies that the user has the specified access permissions |
| *CreateKey* | Creates a subkey |
| *DeleteKey* | Deletes a subkey |
| *DeleteValue* | Deletes a named value |
| *EnumKey* | Enumerates subkeys |
| *EnumValues* | Enumerates the named values of a key |
| *GetBinaryValue* | Gets the binary data value of a named value |
| *GetDWORDValue* | Gets the DWORD data value of a named value |
| *GetExpandedStringValue* | Gets the expanded string data value of a named value |
| *GetMultiStringValue* | Gets the multiple string data values of a named value |
| *GetStringValue* | Gets the string data value of a named value |
| *SetBinaryValue* | Sets the binary data value of a named value |
| *SetDWORDValue* | Sets the DWORD data value of a named value |
| *SetExpandedStringValue* | Sets the expanded string data value of a named value |
| *SetMultiStringValue* | Sets the multiple string values of a named value |
| *SetStringValue* | Sets the string value of a named value |

One cool task you can perform as a network administrator is to create a key in the registry that you use to keep track of certain machines. This is similar to a trick I used to use with the Microsoft Systems Management Server product, where I placed a certain text file in the root drive of the workstation and used the presence of the file in creating ad hoc collections.

> **Just the Steps**
>
> ▶ **To create a registry key**
>
> 1. Create a constant for *HKLM* and assign it the value of *&H80000002*.
>
> 2. Define variables to hold the registry path you want to create.
>
> 3. Use *GetObject* to create an instance of the WMI *StdRegProvider*.
>
> 4. Use the *CreateKey* method and feed it the *HKLM* constant and the registry path variable defined earlier.

# Creating Registry Keys

To create keys and subkeys in the registry, you use the *CreateKey* method, as illustrated in the CreateRegKey.vbs script:

```
Option Explicit
On Error Resume Next
Dim strKeyPath ' the portion of registry to read
Dim strComputer ' the target computer
Dim objReg ' holds connection to registry provider
Dim subKey ' used to enumerate throught the array
Dim arrSubKeys ' holds the sub keys
Dim ParentKey
Const HKCR = &H80000000 'HKEY_CLASSES_ROOT
Const HKCU = &H80000001 'HKEY_CURRENT_USER
Const HKLM = &H80000002 'HKEY_LOCAL_MACHINE
Const HKU  = &H80000003 'HKEY_USERS
Const HKCC = &H80000005 'HKEY_CURRENT_CONFIG

ParentKey = "SOFTWARE\EdWilson"
strKeyPath = "SOFTWARE\EdWilson\VBScriptBook"

strComputer = "."

Set objReg=GetObject("winmgmts:\\" & _
    strComputer & "\root\default:StdRegProv")


objReg.CreateKey HKLM, strKeyPath

    WScript.Echo("Created key :" & strKeyPath)
    WScript.Echo("New subkey under : " & ParentKey)

objReg.EnumKey HKLM, ParentKey, arrSubKeys
For Each subKey In arrSubKeys
    WScript.Echo vbTab & subKey
Next
```

# Header Information

The Header information section is similar to that in the script you just examined. The only new variable is *ParentKey*, which is used to hold the path to the parent key that gets created.

# Reference Information

The Reference information section is where you assign values to the variables defined in the Header information section. You assign a value to *ParentKey* of SOFTWARE\ EdWilson. You assign the value of SOFTWARE\EdWilson\VBScriptBook to the *strKey-Path*. To create the registry key and subkey, you need only the *strKeyPath* variable. However, because you intend to use *EnumKey* to verify that you successfully created the new key and subkey, you defined *ParentKey* to simplify the use of *EnumKey*. The remaining items in the Reference information section of the script are the same as in the previous script. The beauty of the *StdRegProv* is how similarly you use it through all the different methods.

```
Const HKCR = &H80000000 'HKEY_CLASSES_ROOT
Const HKCU = &H80000001 'HKEY_CURRENT_USER
Const HKLM = &H80000002 'HKEY_LOCAL_MACHINE
Const HKU  = &H80000003 'HKEY_USERS
Const HKCC = &H80000005 'HKEY_CURRENT_CONFIG

ParentKey = "SOFTWARE\EdWilson"
strKeyPath = "SOFTWARE\EdWilson\VBScriptBook"

strComputer = "."

Set objReg=GetObject("winmgmts:\\" &_
    strComputer & "\root\default:StdRegProv")
```

# Worker and Output Information

In the Worker and Output information section of the script, you create the key and sub-key and then use *EnumKey* to verify the existence of the new key. The only difference between using *CreateKey* and *EnumKey* is that *CreateKey* needs only two arguments: the registry tree constant and the key path to create. *EnumKey*, on the other hand, uses three arguments: the registry tree constant, the key path to enumerate, and the variable to hold the output.

```
objReg.CreateKey HKLM, strKeyPath

WScript.Echo("Created key :" & strKeyPath)
WScript.Echo("New subkey under : " & ParentKey)

objReg.EnumKey HKLM, ParentKey, arrSubKeys
For Each subKey In arrSubKeys
```

```
    WScript.Echo vbTab & subKey
Next
```

# Writing to the Registry

I don't know about you, but I've always thought that writing to the registry would be really difficult. However, using the appropriate method of the *StdRegProv* WMI class makes it as easy as eating pineapple on the beach in Kauai—once you sink your teeth into it, it's sweet. In the script WriteToRegKey.vbs, you use the *SetStringValue* method to write information into a key called *bookReviews* that is stored under the SOFTWARE \EdWilson\VBScriptBook subkey. When you execute the script, the key bookReviews does not exist. One nice aspect of *SetStringValue* is that it will create a key and set the value in one operation. Once you write your data, which is contained in a variable called *strData*, to the key, you use the *GetStringValue* to read the information you just wrote. The syntax of *SetStringValue* needs several arguments: the registry tree (in this case, *HKLM*); the registry key path (held in *strKeyPath*); the registry key to modify (held in *strNamedValue*); and the data to write (held in *strData*).

To verify that your changes were made as expected, use *GetStringValue* to retrieve the data you just wrote to the registry. *GetStringValue* works much like *SetStringValue* except that the last argument is the variable name you want to use to hold the data returned from the registry. With *setStringValue*, the fourth argument is the variable that holds the data you want to write to the registry. With *getStringValue*, the fourth argument is the variable that will hold the data once you read it from the registry. Everything else about the two commands is the same.

```
Option Explicit
On Error Resume Next
Dim strKeyPath ' the portion of registry
Dim strComputer ' the target computer
Dim objReg ' holds connection to registry provider
Dim subKey ' used to enumerate thought the array
Dim arrSubKeys ' holds the sub keys
Dim ParentKey
Dim strNamedValue
Dim strData
Dim strReturnValue
Const HKCR = &H80000000 'HKEY_CLASSES_ROOT
Const HKCU = &H80000001 'HKEY_CURRENT_USER
Const HKLM = &H80000002 'HKEY_LOCAL_MACHINE
Const HKU  = &H80000003 'HKEY_USERS
Const HKCC = &H80000005 'HKEY_CURRENT_CONFIG

ParentKey = "SOFTWARE\EdWilson"
strKeyPath = "SOFTWARE\EdWilson\VBScriptBook"
strNamedvalue = "book reviews"
strData = "Awesome"

strComputer = "."

Set objReg = GetObject("winmgmts:\\" & _
```

```
    strComputer & "\root\default:StdRegProv")


objReg.SetStringValue HKLM, strKeyPath, strNamedValue, strData

WScript.Echo("value set")

objReg.GetStringValue HKLM, strKeyPath, strNamedValue, strReturnValue

WScript.Echo strNamedValue & " contains " & strReturnValue
```

# Deleting Registry Information

If you need to delete a registry key, perhaps as a result of cleaning up after a virus, uninstalling software, or cleaning up after you're finished with the keys you created, you can use the *DeleteKey* method of *StdRegProv*. The next script illustrates how easy this is to do. Additional cautions about having a good backup and testing on other machines is applicable here! Be careful!

Though much of the script is similar to other registry provider scripts, a couple of items are important to note here. Notice in the Worker information section of the script that you have to delete the subkey before you can delete the parent key. The *DeleteKey* method deletes only keys. If you have a large section of the registry you need to lobotomize, you could use the *EnumKey* method and, as you iterate through the array, you could use *DeleteKey*.

```
Option Explicit
On Error Resume Next
Dim strKeyPath ' the portion of registry to read
Dim strComputer ' the target computer
Dim objReg ' holds connection to registry provider
Dim subKey ' used to enumerate throught the array
Dim arrSubKeys ' holds the sub keys
Dim ParentKey
Const HKCR = &H80000000 'HKEY_CLASSES_ROOT
Const HKCU = &H80000001 'HKEY_CURRENT_USER
Const HKLM = &H80000002 'HKEY_LOCAL_MACHINE
Const HKU  = &H80000003 'HKEY_USERS
Const HKCC = &H80000005 'HKEY_CURRENT_CONFIG

ParentKey = "SOFTWARE\EdWilson"
strKeyPath = "SOFTWARE\EdWilson\VbscriptBook"

strComputer = "."

Set objReg=GetObject("winmgmts:\\" & _
    strComputer & "\root\default:StdRegProv")


objReg.DeleteKey HKLM, strKeyPath
objReg.DeleteKey HKLM, ParentKey
```

```
If Err.Number = 0 Then
    WScript.Echo("Deleted key:" & strKeyPath)
    WScript.Echo("Deleted subKey: " & ParentKey)
Else
    WScript.Echo("Error number " & Err.Number & "occurred")
End If
```

# Summary

In this chapter, you looked at using WMI to work with the registry. The *StdRegProv* class exposes five methods for working with registry data: *GetBinaryValue, Get-DWORDvalue, GetExpandedStringValue, GetMultiStringValue,* and *GetStringValue.* These methods are required because of the different types of data that can reside in the registry. In addition to looking at the WMI provider, you also looked at the *WshShell* class and saw the power and flexibility that it brings to your VBScripts.

# Quiz Yourself

**Q.** **What object in VBScript allows you to run an external program?**

**A.** The *WshShell* object allows you to run programs that are external to VBScript.

**Q.** **What is the WMI provider that allows you to work with the registry?**

**A.** The *StdRegProv* WMI class allows you to work with the registry.

**Q.** **To write a string value to the registry, which method of the *StdRegProv* do you use?**

**A.** To write a string value to the registry, you use the *SetStringValue* method.

**Q.** **If you need to delete a key and several subkeys from the registry using the *DeleteKey* method of *StdRegProv*, what actions do you need to take?**

**A.** To delete a key and several subkeys, you need to delete the subkeys first. Then you can delete the parent key.

# On Your Own

# Lab 34 Reading the Registry Using WMI

In this lab, you will practice reading the registry by using the WMI *StdRegProv* class.

## Lab Instructions

1. Open Notepad.exe.

2. Add *Option Explicit* to the first line of your script.

**3.** Save the script as **Lab34Solution.vbs**.

**4.** Declare the following variables: *strKeyPath*, *strComputer*, *objReg*, *subKey*, and *arrSubKeys*. The Header information section of your script will look like the following:

```
Option Explicit
Dim strKeyPath
Dim strComputer
Dim objReg
Dim subKey
Dim arrSubKeys
```

**5.** Define a constant to be used for *HKLM*. Its hex value is *&H80000002*. Your code for this looks like the following:

```
Const HKLM = &H80000002
```

**6.** Assign the Software\Microsoft path to the *strKeyPath* variable. It will look like the following:

```
strKeyPath = "SOFTWARE\Microsoft"
```

**7.** Assign the value of "*.*" to the variable *strComputer*.

**8.** Set the *objReg* variable to be equal to the hook that comes back from using the *GetObject* command into the WMI *winmgmts* moniker. Connect into the *root\default:stdRegProv* namespace on the local computer. Your code to do this looks like the following:

```
Set objReg=GetObject("winmgmts:\\" &_
    strComputer & "\root\default:StdRegProv")
```

**9.** Now use the *EnumKey* method to read the subkeys found under the Software\Microsoft key. The Software\Microsoft key is located in the *HKLM* tree. Feed the results out into a variable called *arrSubKeys*. The code for this looks like the following:

```
objReg.EnumKey HKLM, strKeyPath, arrSubKeys
```

**10.** Use *WScript.Echo* to echo out the *strKeyPath*. This will be a header for the list of software contained in the Software\Microsoft key. You can use something like this:

```
WScript.Echo("Keys under " & strKeyPath)
```

**11.** Use a *For Each…Next* loop to iterate through the subkeys that are contained in the *arrSubKeys* variable. Use *WScript.Echo* to echo out the subkeys. Use the *subKey* variable as your placeholder. Your code will look like the following:

```
For Each subKey In arrSubKeys
    WScript.Echo vbTab & subKey
Next
```

**12.** Save and run the program.

# Lab 35 Creating Registry Keys

In this lab, you create a couple of registry keys that can be used to keep track of a software inventory of the workstation.

## Lab Instructions

1.  Open Notepad.exe.

2.  On the first line, type **Option Explicit**. Save your script as **Lab35Solution.vbs**.

3.  Declare the following variables: *strKeyPath*, *strComputer*, *objReg*, *subKey*, *arrSub-Keys*, and *ParentKey*. You code will look like the following:

    ```
    Option Explicit
    Dim strKeyPath
    Dim strComputer
    Dim objReg
    Dim subKey
    Dim arrSubKeys
    Dim ParentKey
    ```

4.  Define the constant for *HKLM* and set it equal to *&H80000002*. It will look like the following:

    ```
    Const HKLM = &H80000002 'HKEY_LOCAL_MACHINE
    ```

5.  Assign the value of *"SOFTWARE\INVENTORY"* to the *ParentKey* variable. It will look like the following:

    ```
    ParentKey = "SOFTWARE\INVENTORY"
    ```

6.  Assign the value of *"SOFTWARE\INVENTORY\Conducted"* to the *strKeyPath* variable. It looks like the following:

    ```
    strKeyPath = "SOFTWARE\INVENTORY\Conducted"
    ```

7.  Assign the value of *"."* to the *strComputer* variable. It looks like the following:

    ```
    strComputer = "."
    ```

8.  Set the *objReg* variable to be equal to the hook that comes back from using the *GetObject* command into the WMI *winmgmts* moniker. Connect into the *root\default:stdRegProv* namespace on the local computer. Your code to do this looks like the following:

    ```
    Set objReg=GetObject("winmgmts:\\" & _
        strComputer & "\root\default:StdRegProv")
    ```

9.  Use the *createKey* method of *objReg* to create the new registry keys. It will need both the *HKLM* constant and the *strKeyPath* for arguments. It will look like the following:

    ```
    objReg.CreateKey HKLM, strKeyPath
    ```

**10.** Use *WScript.Echo* to provide feedback to the user that the key and the subkey were created. Your code could look like the following:

```
WScript.Echo("Created key :" & strKeyPath)
WScript.Echo("New subkey under : " & ParentKey)
```

**11.** Use *EnumKey* to verify the existence of the newly created registry keys. *EnumKey* will need *HKLM*, *ParentKey*, and *arrSubKeys* as arguments. Use a *For Each…Next* loop to walk through the *arrSubKeys* variable. Echo out each subkey. Your code will look like the following:

```
objReg.EnumKey HKLM, ParentKey, arrSubKeys
For Each subKey In arrSubKeys
    WScript.Echo vbTab & subKey
Next
```

**12.** Save and run the script.

# 18 Working with Printers

In this chapter, you'll look at using Microsoft Windows Management Instrumentation (WMI) to monitor and manage printers. In the enterprise network, printers—by virtue of being mechanical devices often located in remote places—are frequently labor-intensive machines. Although it's true that most printers operate reliably for extended periods of time, it's also true that when they go bad, you're facing a high-profile issue. To alleviate some of that pain, you'll learn some of the ways in which WMI can assist you in your goal of managing and monitoring printers.

## Before You Begin

**To work through the material presented in this chapter you need to be familiar with the following concepts from earlier chapters:**

- Creating a connection into WMI

- Creating an instance of the *FileSystemObject* class

- Implementing the *For...Next* construction

- Implementing *Select Case* constructions

**After completing this chapter you will be familiar with the following:**

- Working with the *Win32_Printer* WMI class

- Converting status codes into readable text

- Working with the *Win32_PrintJob* WMI class

## Working with *Win32_Printer*

In this section, you are going to use the WMI *Win32_Printer* class. This particular WMI class is large and robust, defining over 80 properties and implementing 7 methods. Some of its more useful properties are listed in Table 18-1.

**Table 18-1   Useful *Win32_Printer* Properties**

| Property | Description |
|----------|-------------|
| *Attributes* | Attributes of a Windows printing device. Represented by a combination of flags. |
| *Availability* | Availability and status of the device. Return values are as follows: *2* = unknown, *3* = running or full power, *8* = offline. |

**Table 18-1    Useful *Win32_Printer* Properties**

| Property | Description |
|---|---|
| *AvailableJobSheets* | Array of all job sheets available on a printer. Also used to describe the banner a printer might provide. |
| *AveragePagesPerMinute* | Print rate of the printer. |
| *CharSetsSupported* | Array of available character sets for output. Strings in this property are defined in RFC 2046 (MIME part 2) and in the IANA character-set registry. Examples: *utf-8*, *us-ascii*, and *iso-8859-1*. |
| *Comment* | String that contains a comment for a print queue. Example: color printer. |
| *CurrentLanguage* | Printer language currently being used. Examples: 1 = other, 2 = unknown, 3 = PCL, 6 = PS. |
| *Default* | Boolean. If *true*, the printer is the default printer on the computer. |
| *DefaultCopies* | Number of copies that are produced for one job. |
| *DetectedErrorState* | Printer error information. Examples: *1* = unknown, *2* = other, *3* = no error, *5* = no paper, *6* = low toner, *9* = jammed, *10* = offline. |
| *Direct* | Boolean. If *true*, the print job is sent directly to the printer. If *false*, the print job is spooled. |
| *DoCompleteFirst* | Boolean. If *true*, the printer starts jobs that are finished spooling. If *false*, the printer starts jobs in the order they are received. |
| *DriverName* | String. Name of the Windows printer driver. |
| *JobCountSinceLastReset* | Number of print jobs since the printer was last reset. |
| *KeepPrintedJobs* | Boolean. If *true*, the print spooler does not delete completed jobs. |
| *LastErrorCode* | Last error code that the logical device reports. |
| *Local* | Boolean. If *true*, the printer is not attached to a network. |
| *ServerName* | String. Name of the server that controls the printer. |
| *Shared* | Boolean. If *true*, the printer is available as a shared network resource. |
| *ShareName* | String. Share name of the print device. |
| *Status* | String. Current status. Examples: ok, error, degraded, unknown, and stopping. |
| *workOffLine* | Boolean. If *true*, you can queue print jobs on the computer when the printer is offline. |

> **Just the Steps**
>
> ▶ **To use the *Win32_Printer* class to manage a printer**
>
> **1.** Create a variable to hold a WMI connection.
>
> **2.** Use *GetObject* and the WMI moniker to make a WMI connection.
>
> **3.** Assign the hook that comes back from the WMI connection to the variable in step 1.
>
> **4.** Use the *ExecQuery* method to query *Win32_Printer*.
>
> **5.** Use *For Each...Next* to iterate through the printer's collection.

# Obtaining the Status of Printers

In your first printer management script, you'll use the *Win32_Printer* WMI class to obtain information about the status of printers defined on a computer. This particular script runs on Microsoft Windows Server 2003 and on Windows XP, so it can run on a server to obtain the status of all the printers defined, or it can run as a diagnostic tool on a workstation. The MonitorPrinterStatus.vbs follows:

```
Option Explicit
'On Error Resume Next
Dim strComputer
Dim wmiNS
Dim wmiQuery
Dim objWMIService
Dim colItems
Dim objItem
Dim strStatus

strComputer = "."
wmiNS = "\root\cimv2"
wmiQuery = "Select * from Win32_Printer"
Set objWMIService = GetObject("winmgmts:\\" _
    & strComputer & wmiNS)
Set colItems = objWMIService.ExecQuery(wmiQuery)

For Each objItem In colItems
    WScript.Echo "Name: " & objItem.Name
    WScript.Echo "Location: " & objItem.Location
    subEvalStatus
    WScript.Echo "Printer Status: " & strStatus
    WScript.Echo "Server Name: " & objItem.ServerName
    WScript.Echo "Share Name: " & objItem.ShareName
    WScript.Echo
Next

Sub subEvalStatus
    Select Case objItem.PrinterStatus
        Case 1
            strStatus = "Other"
```

```
    Case 2
        strStatus = "Unknown"
    Case 3
        strStatus = "Idle"
    Case 4
        strStatus = "Printing"
    Case 5
        strStatus = "Warmup"
    Case 6
        strStatus = "Stopped Printing"
    Case 7
        strStatus = "Offline"

    End Select
End sub
```

## Header Information

The Header information section of the script does not perform any real magic. You begin with *Option Explicit* so that you're forced to keep track of your variables. Next you have *On Error Resume Next*, which is commented out, and then you have seven variables. A description of the variables appears in Table 18-2.

**Table 18-2   Variables for MonitorPrinterStatus.vbs**

| Variable | Use |
| --- | --- |
| *strComputer* | Holds the target computer. |
| *wmiNS* | Holds the WMI namespace that will be connected to. |
| *wmiQuery* | Holds the WMI query that will be executed. |
| *objWMIService* | Holds the connection into WMI. |
| *colItems* | Holds the collection that comes back as a result of the WMI query. |
| *objItem* | Placeholder that allows us to iterate through the collection of items that was returned by the WMI query. |
| *strStatus* | The status of the printer. |

## Reference Information

The Reference information section of the script is used to assign values to some of the variables that were declared in the Header information section of the script. You use the period inside a set of double quotation marks to represent the local machine and assign it to *strComputer*. If you wanted to run the script against other computers, you could substitute their names for the period. The *root\cimv2* namespace is assigned to the variable *wmiNS*. You use "*Select * from Win32_Printer*" to return everything from the *Win32_Printer*. Though easy to do, this is not the most efficient way to gather your information, which is somewhat of an issue when working with *Win32_Printer* because it is a rather large class. *ObjWMIService* is your reference to the system's WMI service. You use the *winmgmts* moniker to simplify the connection process. The last reference information that needs to be set is using the *ExecQuery* method of *objWMI-Service* to execute the query represented by the variable *wmiQuery*.

```
strComputer = "."
wmiNS = "\root\cimv2"
wmiQuery = "Select * from Win32_Printer"
Set objWMIService = GetObject("winmgmts:\\" _
    & strComputer & wmiNS)
Set colItems = objWMIService.ExecQuery(wmiQuery)
```

## Worker Information

The Worker information section of the MonitorPrinterStatus.vbs script consists of a single subroutine called *subEvalStatus*. The *subEvalStatus* routine is used to translate the status code that is returned by the *PrinterStatus* property into a more meaningful message. To do the matching, you use a *Select Case* construction that looks for a match with one of the seven possible return status codes.

```
Sub subEvalStatus
    Select Case objItem.PrinterStatus
        Case 1
            strStatus = "Other"
        Case 2
            strStatus = "Unknown"
        Case 3
            strStatus = "Idle"
        Case 4
            strStatus = "Printing"
        Case 5
            strStatus = "Warmup"
        Case 6
            strStatus = "Stopped Printing"
        Case 7
            strStatus = "Offline"
    End Select
End Sub
```

## Output Information

Once you work through matching the return status codes with a more meaningful status message, it is time to echo out the information. You use a *For Each…Next* construction to iterate through the collection of items that was returned by the WMI query. You use *WScript.Echo* to echo out a few of the more than 80 properties available via the *Win32_Printer* class. Because both the *Name* and the *Location* properties are simple string data, you can echo them out directly. However, to properly interpret the printer status code, you need to enter the *subEvalStatus* subroutine. You come out of that subroutine with a meaningful status message, and so you echo that out as well. Finally, you echo out the server name and the printer share name.

```
For Each objItem In colItems
    WScript.Echo "Name: " & objItem.Name
    WScript.Echo "Location: " & objItem.Location
    subEvalStatus
    WScript.Echo "Printer Status: " & strStatus
    WScript.Echo "Server Name: " & objItem.ServerName
    WScript.Echo "Share Name: " & objItem.ShareName
    WScript.Echo
Next
```

---

**Quick Check**

**Q.** What WMI class provides more than 80 properties for managing printers?

**A.** The *Win32_Printer* class provides more than 80 properties for managing printers.

**Q.** What is needed to obtain meaningful information from the *PrinterStatus* property?

**A.** To obtain meaningful information from the *PrinterStatus* property, you must interpret the status codes.

**Q.** When using the *Win32_Printer* class, how is the data returned?

**A.** When using the *Win32_Printer* class, the data is returned as a collection of printer objects.

---

# Creating a Filtered Print Monitor

One cool thing you can do is filter out only the information you need prior to presenting it to the screen. A Windows Server 2003 print server commonly hosts a couple of hundred printers, so weeding through all the print devices looking for one that is offline could take a long time. By making just a couple of changes to the MonitorPrinterStatus.vbs script, you can allow Microsoft Visual Basic Script (VBScript) to perform the weeding work for you.

---

**Just the Steps**

▶ **To use a filter on the *Win32_Printer* class to manage a printer**

1. Create a variable to hold a connection into WMI.

2. Use *GetObject* and the WMI moniker to make a connection into WMI.

3. Assign the hook that comes back from the WMI connection to the variable in step 1.

4. Use the *ExecQuery* method with a *Where* clause to query *Win32_Printer*. The *Where* clause should look for *1, 2,* or *7* in the *PrinterStatus* property.

5. Use the *Count* property to determine the population of the collection of printers. If the collection of printers is empty, echo a message to that effect.

6. If the collection of printers is not empty, use *For Each...Next* to iterate through the collection.

The revised printer monitor script is called FilterPrinterStatus.vbs. Only a couple of changes were made to effect filtering. The addition of the *Where* clause to the WMI query takes place in the Reference information section. The use of *If…Then…Else* in conjunction with the *Count* property takes place in the Output information section. The FilterPrinterStatus.vbs script is listed here:

```
Option Explicit
'On Error Resume Next
Dim strComputer
Dim wmiNS
Dim wmiQuery
Dim objWMIService
Dim colItems
Dim objItem
Dim strStatus

strComputer = "."
wmiNS = "\root\cimv2"
wmiQuery = "Select * from Win32_Printer" _
    & " Where PrinterStatus = 1" _
    & " or PrinterStatus = 2" _
    & " or PrinterStatus = 7"
Set objWMIService = GetObject("winmgmts:\\" _
    & strComputer & wmiNS)
Set colItems = objWMIService.ExecQuery(wmiQuery)

If colItems.Count = 0 Then
    WScript.Echo "all printers are fine"
Else
    For Each objItem In colItems
        WScript.Echo "Name: " & objItem.Name
        WScript.Echo "Location: " & objItem.Location
        subEvalStatus
        WScript.Echo "Printer Status: " & strStatus
        WScript.Echo "Server Name: " & objItem.ServerName
        WScript.Echo "Share Name: " & objItem.ShareName
        WScript.Echo
    Next
End If

Sub subEvalStatus
    Select Case objItem.PrinterStatus
        Case 1
            strStatus = "Other"
        Case 2
            strStatus = "Unknown"
        Case 3
            strStatus = "Idle"
        Case 4
            strStatus = "Printing"
        Case 5
            strStatus = "Warmup"
        Case 6
            strStatus = "Stopped Printing"
```

```
        Case 7
            strStatus = "Offline"
    End Select
End Sub
```

## Reference Information

The Reference information section is where you modify your WMI query. The only change is adding a compound *Where* clause to the value you assigned to *wmiQuery*. You are interested in only those printers that have a status of *1*, *2*, or *7*.

```
strComputer = "."
wmiNS = "\root\cimv2"
wmiQuery = "Select * from Win32_Printer" _
    & " Where PrinterStatus = 1" _
    & " or PrinterStatus = 2" _
    & " or PrinterStatus = 7"
Set objWMIService = GetObject("winmgmts:\\" _
    & strComputer & wmiNS)
Set colItems = objWMIService.ExecQuery(wmiQuery)
```

## Output Information

If you tried to iterate through a collection that had no members, you would not receive a meaningful message. To avoid this, you add an *If...Then...Else* construction around the Output information section that appeared in the earlier script. If there are no printers with an error condition, the *Count property* of *colItems* will be zero. You use *WScript.Echo* to send a message to the console that all printers are fine. If, however, the count is not zero, you echo out the information used in the previous script. The revised section looks like the following code:

```
If colItems.count = 0 Then
    WScript.Echo "all printers are fine"
Else
    For Each objItem in colItems
        WScript.Echo "Name: " & objItem.Name
        WScript.Echo "Location: " & objItem.Location
        subEvalStatus
        WScript.Echo "Printer Status: " & strStatus
        WScript.Echo "Server Name: " & objItem.ServerName
        WScript.Echo "Share Name: " & objItem.ShareName
        WScript.Echo
    Next
End If
```

> **Quick Check**
>
> **Q.** What was required in the FilterPrinterStatus.vbs script to return only selected records from the WMI query?
>
> **A.** To return selected records, a *Where* clause was added to the WMI query.
>
> **Q.** What is needed in the FilterPrinterStatus.vbs script to ensure you have printers in your collection?
>
> **A.** To ensure you have printers in your collection, you used the *Count* property of collected items in the FilterPrinterStatus.vbs script.
>
> **Q.** What does a *PrinterStatus* code of 7 mean?
>
> **A.** A *PrinterStatus* code of 7 means the printer is offline.

# Monitoring Print Queues

To understand your print environment, it is necessary to examine the way the queues on the print servers are utilized. The MonitorPrintQueue.vbs script uses the *Win32_PrintJob* WMI class to obtain useful information about the load placed on your print servers. Because MonitorPrintQueue.vbs is based on previous scripts, you will look only at the Worker and Output information section of the script. You assign *"Select * from Win32_PrintJob"* to the *wmiQuery* variable in the Reference section. That is the only change required there.

```
Option Explicit
'On Error Resume Next
Dim strComputer
Dim wmiNS
Dim wmiQuery
Dim objWMIService
Dim colItems
Dim objItem
Dim intTotalJobs
Dim intTotalPages
Dim intMaxPrintJob

strComputer = "."
wmiNS = "\root\cimv2"
wmiQuery = "Select * from win32_PrintJob"
Set objWMIService = GetObject("winmgmts:\\" _
    & strComputer & wmiNS)
Set colItems = objWMIService.ExecQuery(wmiQuery)
```

```
If colItems.count = 0 Then
    WScript.Echo("There are no print jobs at this time")
Else
    For Each objitem In colItems
        intTotalJobs = intTotalJobs + 1
        intTotalPages = intTotalPages + objitem.TotalPages
        If objitem.TotalPages > intMaxPrintJob Then
            intMaxPrintJob = objitem.TotalPages
        End If
    Next
    WScript.Echo "Total print jobs in queue: " & intTotalJobs
    WScript.Echo "Total pages in queue: " & intTotalPages
    WScript.Echo "Largest print job in queue: " & intMaxPrintJob
End if
```

## Worker and Output Information

To return meaningful information, you use the *Count property* of *colItems* just like you did in the previous script. If there are print jobs in the collection, iterate through them by using the *For Each...Next* construction. To get a count of the total number of print jobs in the queue, you use a counter called *intTotalJobs*, which gets incremented each time you loop through the collection of print jobs. For each print job in the collection, you get the *TotalPages* property and add it to the *intTotalPages* variable. By keeping a running total of pages, once you iterate through the collection, you will know the total pages left in the queue. To determine the largest print job in the queue, you use the variable called *intMaxPrintJob* and evaluate its size on each iteration through the collection of print jobs. Each time a larger print job is found, its value will be stored in *intMaxPrintJob*. At the end of the iteration, the largest print job will be stored in *intMaxPrintJob*, the total number of pages will be stored in the *intTotalPages* variable, and the total number of print jobs will be stored in the *intTotalJobs* variable.

# Summary

In this chapter, you examined printer management by using VBScript, starting by looking at the *Win32_Printer* WMI class. You wrote a couple of scripts that monitored the status of printers connected to our print servers. You looked at creating a subroutine out of a *Select Case* construction to convert cryptic printer status codes into readable text. You examined how to use the *Count* property to avoid attempting operations on an empty collection. Finally, you concluded this chapter by looking at the *Win32_PrintJobs* WMI class and using it to monitor the activity of print queues.

# Quiz Yourself

**Q.** **What is the WMI class that contains a wealth of information about printers?**

**A.** The *Win32_Printer* class contains a lot of information about printers.

**Q.** **What is the WMI class that represents a print job generated by a Windows application?**

**A.** The *Win32_PrintJobs* class represents this print job.

**Q.** **What collection property contains the number of items in the collection?**

**A.** The *Count* property contains the number of items.

**Q.** **What can be added to a WMI query to reduce the number of records returned?**

**A.** A *Where* clause can be added to the query.

# On Your Own

# Lab 36 Monitoring Print Jobs

In this lab, you will practice monitoring print jobs by using the *Win32_PrintJob* WMI class.

## Lab Instructions

1. Open Notepad.exe.

2. Set *Option Explicit*.

3. Save your script as **Lab36Solution.vbs**.

4. Declare the following variables: *strComputer, wmiNS, wmiQuery, objWMIService, colItems,* and *objItem*. Your Header information section will look like the following:

```
Option Explicit
'On Error Resume Next
Dim strComputer
Dim wmiNS
Dim wmiQuery
Dim objWMIService
Dim colItems
Dim objItem
```

5. Assign the value "." to the variable *strComputer*.

6. Assign the value "*\root\cimv2*" to the variable *wmiNS*.

7. Assign the value *"Select \* from Win32_PrintJob"* to the *wmiQuery* variable. The code for steps 5, 6, and 7 is shown here:

```
strComputer = "."
wmiNS = "\root\cimv2"
wmiQuery = "Select * from win32_PrintJob"
```

8. Set *objWMIService* equal to the hook that comes back from using the *GetObject* command to connect to the *root\cimv2* namespace on the local machine. Use the *winmgmts* moniker. Specify the target computer as *strComputer*. Your code for this will look like the following:

```
Set objWMIService = GetObject("winmgmts:\\" _
    & strComputer & wmiNS)
```

9. Set the variable *colItems* equal to the hook that comes back from the *ExecQuery* method of *objWMIService* when it executes the query contained in the variable *wmiQuery*. Your code will look like the following:

```
Set colItems = objWMIService.ExecQuery(wmiQuery)
```

10. Use the *colItems.Count* property to ensure there are print jobs in the collection. Implement an *If...Then...Else* construction to handle this. If there are no print jobs, echo a message to that effect. If there are print jobs, move into a *For Each* loop. Your code for this part looks like the following:

```
If colItems.Count = 0 Then
WScript.Echo("There are no print jobs at this time")
else
```

11. Use a *For Each...Next* construction to iterate through the print jobs contained in the *colitems* collection. Use the variable *objitem* to hold each job as you walk through the collection. Echo out the *JobId*, *JobStatus*, *Owner*, and *TotalPages* properties. Your code for this looks like the following:

```
For Each objitem In colItems
    WScript.Echo("Print job: " & objItem.JobId)
    WScript.Echo("job status: " & objItem.JobStatus)
    WScript.Echo("Owner: " & objItem.Owner)
    WScript.Echo("Remaining pages: " & objItem.TotalPages)
Next
```

12. Close out the *If...Then...Else* construction by using *End If*.

13. Save your work.

14. Run the script.

# Lab 37 Checking the Status of a Print Server

In this lab, you will check the status of a print server, and if the server is not OK, you will cancel all print jobs on the box. This script is based on the FilterPrinterStatus.vbs script, so you use a starter file.

## Lab Instructions

1. Open Notepad.exe.

2. Open the Lab37Starter.vbs file, and save it as **Lab37Solution.vbs**.

3. Delete the entire *subEvalstatus* subroutine from the bottom of the script. This subroutine looks like the following:

```
Sub subEvalStatus
    Select Case objItem.PrinterStatus
        Case 1
            strStatus = "Other"
        Case 2
            strStatus = "Unknown"
        Case 3
            strStatus = "Idle"
        Case 4
            strStatus = "Printing"
        Case 5
            strStatus = "Warmup"
        Case 6
            strStatus = "Stopped Printing"
        Case 7
            strStatus = "Offline"
    End Select
End sub
```

4. Locate the *For Each…Next* construction. Delete everything that is between the *For Each* and the *Next*. Following is the *For Each…Next* construction:

```
For Each objItem in colItems
    WScript.Echo "Name: " & objItem.Name
    WScript.Echo "Location: " & objItem.Location
    subEvalStatus
    WScript.Echo "Printer Status: " & strStatus
    WScript.Echo "Server Name: " & objItem.ServerName
    WScript.Echo "Share Name: " & objItem.ShareName
    WScript.Echo
Next
End If
```

5. Inside the *For Each...Next* construction, echo out the *objItem.Name* property with an appropriate label. It will look like the following:

```
WScript.Echo "Name: " & objItem.Name
```

6. Under the *WScript* command, assign the variable *canStatus* to be equal to *objItem.CancelAllJobs*. The *CancelAllJobs* method has a return value that you want to capture with the *canStatus* variable. This line of code looks like the following:

```
canStatus = objItem.cancelAllJobs
```

7. Use *WScript.Echo* to echo out the value of *canStatus*. The completed *For Each...Next* construction now looks like the following:

```
For Each objItem In colItems
    WScript.Echo "Name: " & objItem.Name
    canStatus = objItem.CancelAllJobs
WScript.Echo(canStatus)
Next
```

8. Add the variable *canStatus* to the declarations section of the script.

9. Save and run the script.

# Part 4
# Scripting Other Applications

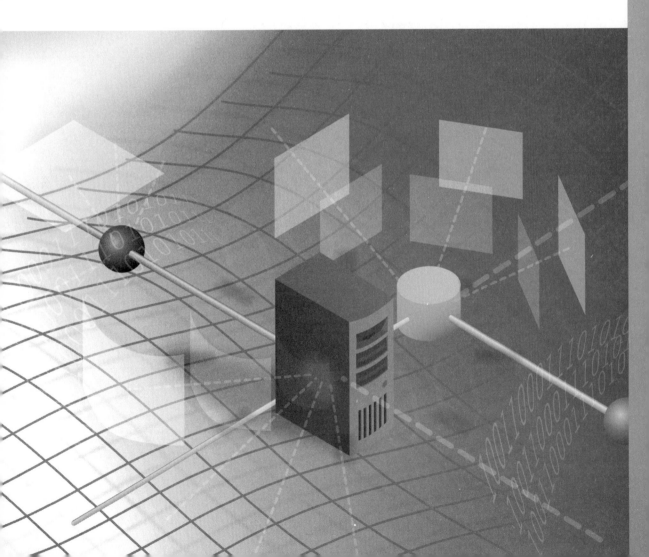

# 19 Managing IIS 6.0

In this chapter, you'll look at managing Microsoft Internet Information Services (IIS) 6.0 by using Microsoft Visual Basic Script (VBScript). IIS 6.0 is a significant improvement over previous versions in both security and manageability. The new Windows Management Instrumentation (WMI) provider for IIS 6.0 offers the network administrator tremendous flexibility and can significantly reduce the number of hands required to handle configuration when managing the servers.

## Before You Begin

**To work through the material presented in this chapter you need to be familiar with the following concepts from earlier chapters:**

- Connecting to WMI

- Connecting to Active Directory

- Implementing the *For...Next* construction

- Implementing *Select Case* constructions

- Using the *ExecQuery* method

**After completing this chapter you will be familiar with the following:**

- Connecting to the *MicrosoftIISv2* namespace

- Using the IIS WMI providers

- Working with the IIS metabase

## What's in a Name?

All classes of the IIS 6.0 WMI provider are contained in a namespace called *MicrosoftIISv2*. This namespace is made up of five different classes of elements, discussed briefly in the next few sections.

### CIM_ManagedSystemElement

The *CIM_ManagedSystemElement* class contains elements that relate to the IIS metabase schema. An example of one of these elements is the *IISWebServer*, which maps to an instance of an IIS Web server. Another element is the *IISWebVirtualDir*, which maps to an instance of a Web virtual directory. The elements in *CIM_ManagedSystemElement* are read-only. To set these types of settings, use the *CIM_Setting* class.

# CIM_Setting

The elements in the *CIM_Setting* class map closely to the elements in the *CIM_ManagedSystemElement* class. This means that the elements correspond to nodes of the IIS 6.0 metabase schema. The *CIM_Setting* class contains methods that allow you to work with the properties that match the read-only elements of the *CIM_ManagedSystemElement* class.

> **Tip**   The *IisWebServerSetting* element in the *CIM_Setting* element class allows you to make changes to your IIS Web server. To view data, you use the *IisWebServer* element in the *CIM_ManagedSystemElement* class. It is important to remember that both of these elements refer to websites on your server. *IisWebServer* is read-only, and *IisWebServerSetting* allows you to make changes.

# IIsStructuredDataClass

The *IIsStructuredDataClass* presents information that is also accessible via Active Directory Service Interfaces (ADSI). However, the *IIsStructuredDataClass* information is structured in a way that is easier to work with than the ADSI data. For instance, the *ServerBinding*'s property in ADSI is a string that consists of *IP:Port:Hostname*. If the parts are out of order or are missing colons, an error occurs. By using *IIsStructuredDataClass*, you can take advantage of the element class called *ServerBinding*, whose properties are easier to set.

# CIM_Component

*CIM_Component* is an association class that maps each element in the *CIM_ManagedSystemElement* class to other elements in the same class. It does this to mimic the way the data would be accessed via ADSI.

# CIM_ElementSetting

The *CIM_ElementSetting* class is also an association class. As such, it maps elements in the *CIM_ManagedSystemElement* class to elements in the *CIM_Setting* class. The properties of the elements contained in the *CIM_ElementSetting* class are simply references to the two associated elements.

# Using *MicrosoftIISv2*

To use the *MicrosoftIISv2* namespace, you need to understand the way the five classes represent the structure of the IIS 6.0 metabase schema. Instances of the elements in each of the classes contain current information that is viewable via the IIS Manager or the Metabase Configuration Editor.

On a default installation of IIS 6.0, the *IisWebVirtualDir* element of the *Cim_Managed-SystemElement* class contains three instances of virtual directories: W3SVC/1/Root, W3SVC/1/Root/Scripts, and W3SVC/1/Root/Printers. These three virtual directories are also represented in the *IisWebVirtualDirSetting* element of the *CIM_Setting* class. The only difference between the two is that you make changes to the virtual directories using only *IisWebVirtualDirSetting*.

---

**Just the Steps**

▶ **To connect to the *MicrosoftIISv2* namespace**

1. Define a variable to hold the hook that comes back from the connection.

2. Specify the namespace as /root/*MicrosoftIISv2*.

3. Set your variable equal to the hook that comes back from using the *GetObject* command to connect through *winmgmts* to the root/*MicrosoftIISv2* on your machine.

4. Use the *ExecQuery* method to obtain information.

---

## Making the Connection

To get an idea of the types of data accessible from the *CIM_Setting* element class, you can use the CIMSettingClass.vbs script. This script also illustrates connecting to the *MicrosoftIISv2* namespace and using WMI to query for information.

```
Option Explicit
'On Error Resume Next
Dim strComputer
Dim wmiNS
Dim wmiQuery
Dim objWMIService
Dim colItems
Dim objItem

strComputer = "london"
wmiNS = "/root/MicrosoftIISv2"
wmiQuery = "select * from CIM_Setting"
Set objWMIService = GetObject("winmgmts://" _
    & strComputer & wmiNS)
Set colItems = objWMIService.ExecQuery(wmiQuery)

For Each objItem In colItems
    WScript.Echo ": " & objItem.Name
Next
```

## Header Information

The Header information section of CimSettingClass.vbs, which follows, contains the normal *Option Explicit*, a commented-out *On Error Resume Next*, and six variables. The advantage of splitting out the variables instead of including the data on the connection string is that doing so makes the script more portable and easier to modify. Use of the variables is detailed in Table 19-1.

```
Option Explicit
'On Error Resume Next
Dim strComputer
Dim wmiNS
Dim wmiQuery
Dim objWMIService
Dim colItems
Dim objItem
```

**Table 19-1   Variables Used in CimSettingClass.vbs**

| Variable | Use |
| --- | --- |
| *strComputer* | Holds assignment of target computer name |
| *wmiNS* | Holds the WMI namespace |
| *wmiQuery* | Holds the WMI query |
| *objWMIService* | Holds the connection into the target WMI namespace |
| *colItems* | Holds the collection of items that are returned in result to the WMI query |
| *objItem* | Used to iterate through the collection |

## Reference Information

The Reference information section of the script is used to assign values to the variables that are listed in the Header information section. *StrComputer* is the target computer—the one that is running IIS 6.0 and the one from which you are trying to obtain information. In this case, you are targeting the server called London. You next use the variable *wmiNS* to hold the namespace you want to connect into. When working with IIS 6.0, you will use the /root/*MicrosoftIISv2* namespace.

You defined the target computer and the target WMI namespace. Next, you define your query. You use the generic "*Select * *" format and assign the query to the *wmiQuery* variable. The only tricky issue with querying WMI is how to know which class to target and what properties the classes support. For this information, the best tool is to use the Platform SDK, which is available at *http://www.msdn.microsoft.com*. You can download a copy of it and install it on your laptop. (It makes for great reading while you are sitting on the beach in Kauai. The only problem is keeping sand out of the keyboard.) Pursuant to our earlier discussions, you will query the *CIM_Setting* element class for names of all the read/write properties for the IIS 6.0 *admin* object.

The last task you need to complete in the Reference section is setting the *colItems* variable equal to the data that comes back from running the *ExecQuery* method when you feed it your WMI query.

```
strComputer = "london"
wmiNS = "/root/MicrosoftIISv2"
wmiQuery = "select * from CIM_Setting"
Set objWMIService = GetObject("winmgmts://" _
    & strComputer & wmiNS)
Set colItems = objWMIService.ExecQuery(wmiQuery)
```

## Worker and Output Information

The Worker and Output information section of the script is very small because most of the real work was done in the Reference information section. Since you have a collection of items that comes back from the WMI query, you need to iterate through the collection to display the information. The easiest way to iterate through the collection is to use the *For Each…Next* construction. *ObjItem* is used as a placeholder to represent the present record being worked with. Once you issue the next command, you move to the next record in the stream and assign it to the *objItem* variable. You then simply use *WScript.Echo* to echo out the name of the item in the collection.

```
For Each objItem In colItems
    WScript.Echo ": " & objItem.name
Next
```

# Creating a Website

The advantage of using WMI to create websites is that it gives you a consistent product and vastly simplifies the creation process by automating dozens of minute details. For companies that create a lot of websites, scripting makes a lot of sense.

---

**Just the Steps**

▶ **To use WMI to create a website**

1. Define the appropriate variables.

2. Use *CreateObject* to create an instance of the *WbemScripting SWbemLocator* object.

3. Use the *locator* object so that you can use the *ConnectServer* method to connect to the *MicrosoftIISv2* namespace on the target computer.

4. Use the *service* object to get an instance of "*IIsWebService='W3SVC'*".

5. Use the *server* binding object to set your bindings.

6. Use the *createNewSite* method to create the website.

---

The following code is CreateSite.vbs:

```
Option Explicit
'On Error Resume Next
Dim strComputer
Dim wmiNS
```

```
Dim siteName
Dim strSiteObjPath
Dim locatorObj
Dim providerObj
Dim objPath
Dim vDirObj
Dim serverObj
Dim serviceObj
Dim bindings
Dim strSitePath

strComputer = "London"
wmiNS = "root/MicrosoftIISv2"
siteName = "LondonWebSite"

Set locatorObj = CreateObject("WbemScripting.SWbemLocator")
Set providerObj = locatorObj.ConnectServer _
    & (strComputer, wmiNS)
Set serviceObj = providerObj.Get _
    & ("IIsWebService='W3SVC'")
Set objPath = CreateObject("WbemScripting.SWbemObjectPath")

Bindings = Array(0)
Set Bindings(0) = providerObj.Get("ServerBinding") _
    & .SpawnInstance_()
Bindings(0).IP = ""
Bindings(0).Port = "8383"
Bindings(0).Hostname = ""

strSiteObjPath = serviceObj.CreateNewSite _
    & (siteName, Bindings, "C:\Inetpub\Wwwroot")
objPath.Path = strSiteObjPath
strSitePath = objPath.Keys.Item("")
    subCheckErrors

WScript.Echo "Created " & siteName
WScript.Echo "The path/ID is " & strSitePath

Sub subCheckErrors
    If Err Then
        WScript.Echo "Error: " & Hex(Err.Number) _
            & ": " & Err.Description
        WScript.Quit(1)
    End If
End Sub
```

## Header Information

The Header information section of CreateSite.vbs includes a lot of variables. Understanding how to use these variables will further your understanding of the script. The variables used in this script are described in Table 19-2.

**Table 19-2   Variables Used in CreateSite.vbs**

| Variable | Use |
|---|---|
| *strComputer* | Holds assignment of the target computer name |
| *wmiNS* | Holds the WMI namespace |
| *siteName* | Holds the name of the new website to create |
| *strSiteObjPath* | Holds the path to the new website |
| *locatorObj* | Holds the hook that comes back from *SWbemLocator* |
| *providerObj* | Uses the hook from *locatorObj* to make a connection to the server |
| *objPath* | Holds the hook that comes back from *SWbemObjectPath* |
| *serviceObj* | Holds the hook that comes back from the *providerObj* to get an instance of *IIsWebService='W3SVC'* |
| *bindings* | Holds the elements of the array that is used for *ServerBinding* |
| *strSitePath* | Holds the key items from *objPath* |

# Reference Information

The Reference information section in CreateSite.vbs is very large. This section could be condensed somewhat by combining statements and pulling data directly into the script instead of first populating variables. However, reducing the code by a few lines would make a much less readable script. You begin the Reference information section of the script by assigning a value to *strComputer*. In previous WMI scripts, you were able to use a period inside double quotation marks to denote the local computer. This will not work with the IIS WMI provider, which requires a name. You then set the *wmiNS* variable to be equal to the root/*MicrosoftIISv2* namespace. Note that the *MicrosoftIISv2* namespace is under the root. It is not in root\\*cimv2*, as many of your WMI scripts have been. You now assign a name to the *siteName* variable, which is the name of the website you will be creating.

We set the variable *locatorObj* to be equal to the hook that comes back when you use *CreateObject* to create an instance of the *SWbemLocator* object. You need to create an instance of the *SWbemLocator* object so that you can gain access to the *ConnectServer* method. You use *ConnectServer* to connect to the root/*MicrosoftIISv2* namespace on your target server. You set *providerObj* equal to this connection.

You now set *serviceObj* equal to the hook you get when you connect to the Web service on your London server. Once you make your connection to the Web service, you need to build a binding object. The binding object is a required parameter of the *CreateNewSite* method, and because it has multiple elements, it is stored as an array. *SpawnInstance* is the WMI method used because you're creating a new instance on an object.

```
strComputer = "London"
wmiNS = "root/MicrosoftIISv2"
siteName = "LondonWebSite"

Set locatorObj = CreateObject("WbemScripting.SWbemLocator")
Set providerObj = locatorObj.ConnectServer _
    & (strComputer, wmiNS)
Set serviceObj = providerObj.Get _
    & ("IIsWebService='W3SVC'")
Set objPath = CreateObject("WbemScripting." _
    & "SWbemObjectPath")

Bindings = Array(0)
Set Bindings(0) = providerObj.Get("ServerBinding") _
    & .SpawnInstance_()
Bindings(0).IP = ""
Bindings(0).Port = "8383"
Bindings(0).Hostname = ""
```

## Worker and Output Information

In the Worker and Output information section of the script, the website is created. *StrSiteObjPath* is the variable that holds the return information from using the *CreateNewSite* method of the *IIsWebService* object. To call the *CreateNewSite* method, you have to specify the site name, the bindings, and the physical path for the files. *StrSiteObjPath* is in the format of *IIsWebServer='W3SVC/1180970907'*; therefore, to parse out the absolute path, you use the *SWbemObjectPath* WMI object.

After you complete parsing out the absolute path, you call the *subCheckErrors* subroutine. In the *subCheckErrors* subroutine, you check the *err* object and echo out both the number and description of the error.

The script ends by echoing out the completed site name as well as the path and the unique site ID number that was built by using the *strSitePath* variable.

```
strSiteObjPath = serviceObj.CreateNewSite _
    & (siteName, Bindings, "C:\Inetpub\Wwwroot")
objPath.Path = strSiteObjPath
strSitePath = objPath.Keys.Item("")
    subCheckErrors

WScript.Echo "Created " & siteName
WScript.Echo "The path/ID is " & strSitePath

Sub subCheckErrors
    If Err Then
        WScript.Echo "Error: " & Hex(Err.Number) _
            & ": " & Err.Description
        WScript.Quit(1)
    End If
End sub
```

## Summary

In this chapter, you examined the structure of the *MicrosoftIISv2* namespace, including the five different classes of elements that it consists of. In looking at the different classes, you discovered that some of the classes are read-only, whereas some allow you to set data. The data that you can discover via the *MicrosoftIISv2* namespace is the same data and configuration available via the IIS manager tool or by editing the metabase. You looked at using the IIS 6.0 WMI provider to manage IIS and saw that by making a connection into the namespace, you can discover properties or even use WMI to create new websites.

## Quiz Yourself

**Q.  What is the WMI namespace used to manage IIS 6.0?**

**A.  The WMI namespace *MicrosoftIISv2* is used to manage IIS 6.0.**

**Q.  Where does the *MicrosoftIISv2* namespace reside?**

**A.  The *MicrosoftIISv2* namespace resides directly under \root.**

**Q.  To create a new website, what method do you use?**

**A.  To create a new website, you can use the *CreateNewSite* method of the *IIsWebService* provider.**

# On Your Own

# Lab 38 Backing Up the Metabase

In this lab, you are going to practice backing up the metabase.

## Lab Instructions

1. Open Notepad.exe.

2. On the top of a blank page, set *Option Explicit*.

3. Save your file as **Lab38Solution.vbs**.

4. Declare the following variables: *strPassword*, *strFilePath*, *strMetabasePath*, *intFlags*, *locatorObj*, *providerObj*, and *computerObj*. Your completed Header information section will look like the following:

```
Option Explicit
Dim strPassword
Dim strFilePath
Dim strMetabasePath
Dim intFlags
Dim locatorObj
Dim providerObj
Dim computerObj
```

5. Define three constants to be used to control the export behavior: *EXPORT_CHILDREN = 0*, *EXPORT_INHERITED = 1*, and *EXPORT_NODE_ONLY = 2*. The *EXPORT_CHILDREN* constant is used to add the properties of child keys to the export file. The *EXPORT_INHERITED* constant is used to add inherited properties to the exported keys, and the *EXPORT_NODE_ONLY* constant does not add subkeys of the specified key to the export file. The constants section of the script will look like the following:

```
Const EXPORT_CHILDREN = 0
Const EXPORT_INHERITED = 1
Const EXPORT_NODE_ONLY = 2
```

6. Assign the password "ExportingPassw0rd" to the *strPassword* variable.

7. Specify the physical path for the exported metabase. To do this, assign the value of *"C:\exported.xml"* to the *strFilePath* variable.

8. Set the *strMetabasePath* to be equal to *"/lm/logging/custom logging"*. This is represented in the metabase.xml file.

9. Set the *intFlags* variable equal to *EXPORT_NODE_ONLY OR EXPORT_INHERITED* constants. This will tell the export command to show only the node with inherited properties. This section of the script looks like the following:

```
strPassword = "ExportingPassw0rd"
strFilePath = "C:\exported.xml"
strMetabasePath = "/lm/logging/custom logging"
intFlags = EXPORT_NODE_ONLY OR EXPORT_INHERITED
```

10. Set the *locatorObj* variable equal to the hook that comes back to the *SWbemLocator* object when you use the *CreateObject* command. This code looks like the following:

```
Set locatorObj = CreateObject("WbemScripting.SWbemLocator")
```

11. Set the *providerObj* variable equal to the hook that comes back from using the *ConnectServer* method of *SWbemLocator*. At this point, the hook will be used to connect into the London server *MicrosoftIISv2* namespace. This line of code looks like the following:

```
Set providerObj = locatorObj.ConnectServer _
    ("London", "root/MicrosoftIISv2")
```

12. Set the *computerObj* variable equal to the hook into *IIsComputer = 'LM'* when you use the *Get* command of the *providerObj*. This line of code looks like the following:

```
Set computerObj = providerObj.Get("IIsComputer = 'LM'")
```

13. Call the *export* method from the computer object. The command needs the *strPassword*, the *strFilePath*, the *strMetabasePath*, and the *intFlags*. The code looks like the following:

```
computerObj.Export strPassword, strFilePath, strMetabasePath, intFlags
```

14. Print out the results by using the *WScript.Echo* command to echo out a message that includes the *strMetabasePath* and the *strFilePath*. Your code could look like the following:

```
WScript.Echo "Exported the node at " & strMetabasePath _
    & " to " & strFilePath
```

15. Save and run the script.

# Lab 39 Importing the Metabase

In this lab, you will import the metabase that was exported in Lab 38.

## Lab Instructions

1. Open Notepad.exe.

2. On the top of a blank page, set *Option Explicit*.

3. Save your file as **Lab39Solution.vbs**.

4. Declare the following variables: *strPassword*, *strFilePath*, *strMetabasePath*, *intFlags*, *locatorObj*, *providerObj*, and *computerObj*. Your completed Header information section will look like the following:

```
Option Explicit
Dim strPassword
Dim strFilePath
Dim strSourceMetabasePath
Dim strDestinationMetabasePath
Dim intFlags
Dim locatorObj
Dim providerObj
Dim computerObj
```

5. Create four constants to control the import behavior. *CONST IMPORT_CHILDREN = 0* recursively imports the subkeys of the specified key; *CONST IMPORT_INHERITED = 1* imports the inherited properties of the keys; *CONSTANT IMPORT_NODE_ONLY = 2* does not import subkeys from the specified file. The last constant is *CONST IMPORT_MERGE = 4*, which merges the imported keys into the existing configuration instead of completely replacing what previously existed. The code for this looks like the following:

```
Const IMPORT_CHILDREN = 0
Const IMPORT_INHERITED = 1
Const IMPORT_NODE_ONLY = 2
Const IMPORT_MERGE = 4
```

6. Assign the password "ExportingPassw0rd" to the *strPassword* variable.

7. Specify the physical path for the exported metabase by assigning the value of "*C:\exported.xml*" to the *strFilePath* variable.

8. Set the *strSourceMetabasePath* to be equal to "*/lm/logging/custom logging*". This is represented in the metabase.xml file.

9. Set the *strDestinationMetabasePath* to be equal to "*/lm/logging/custom logging*". This value can be different from the *strSourceMetabasePath* if required.

10. Set the *intFlags* to be equal to *IMPORT_NODE_ONLY OR IMPORT_INHERITED*. This will import only the node with the inherited properties. This section of code looks like the following:

```
strPassword = "ExportingPassw0rd"
strFilePath = "C:\exported.xml"
strSourceMetabasePath = "/lm/logging/custom logging"
strDestinationMetabasePath = "/lm/logging/custom logging"
intFlags = IMPORT_NODE_ONLY OR IMPORT_INHERITED
```

**11.** Set the *locatorObj* variable equal to the hook that comes back to the *SWbemLocator* object when you use the *CreateObject* command. This code looks like the following:

```
Set locatorObj = CreateObject("WbemScripting.SWbemLocator")
```

**12.** Set the *providerObj* variable equal to the hook that comes back from using the *ConnectServer* method of *SWbemLocator*. The *providerObj* variable is used to connect to the London server *MicrosoftIISv2* namespace. This line of code looks like the following:

```
Set providerObj = locatorObj.ConnectServer _
    ("London", "root/MicrosoftIISv2")
```

**13.** Set the *computerObj* variable equal to the hook into *IIsComputer = 'LM'* when you use the *get* command of the *providerObj*. This line of code looks like the following:

```
Set computerObj = providerObj.Get("IIsComputer = 'LM'")
```

**14.** Call the import method from the computer object. The import method requires the *strPassword*, the *strFilePath*, the *strSourceMetabasePath*, the *strDestinationMetabasePath*, and the *intFlags*. This line of code looks like the following:

```
computerObj.Import strPassword, strFilePath, _
    strSourceMetabasePath, strDestinationMetabasePath, intFlags
```

**15.** Echo out the results. Include the *strFilePath* variable and the *strDestinationMetabasePath* variables as confirmation. Your code could look like the following:

```
WScript.Echo "Imported the node in " & strFilePath & " to " _
    & strDestinationMetabasePath
```

**16.** Save and test your file.

# 20 Working with Exchange 2003

In this chapter, you'll look at querying Microsoft Exchange 2003 by using Windows Management Instrumentation (WMI). Though much of the client configuration data is available in Active Directory via Active Directory Service Interface (ADSI), a wealth of information is also available either from the Exchange 2003 System Manager utility or by using the appropriate WMI namespace.

## Before You Begin

**In order to work through the material presented in this chapter you need to be familiar with the following concepts from earlier chapters:**

- Creating a connection into WMI
- Creating a WMI query
- Implementing the *For...Next* construction
- Implementing the *Select Case* construction

**After completing this chapter you will be familiar with the following:**

- Connecting to the *MicrosoftExchangeV2* namespace
- Querying the *Exchange_Logon* class
- Querying the *Exchange_Mailbox* class
- Querying the *Exchange_PublicFolder* class
- Querying the *Exchange_QueueSMTPVirtualServer* class

## Working with the Exchange Provider

When Exchange 2003 is installed, it creates the *MicrosoftExchangeV2* namespace that resides under the root WMI namespace. This is a very rich namespace covering a wide range of management and data issues. Changes to the *MicrosoftExchangeV2* namespace for Exchange 2003 are detailed in Table 20-1.

**Table 20-1 Changes to the Exchange WMI Namespace**

| WMI class | Changes in Exchange 2003 |
| --- | --- |
| *ExchangeClusterResource* | No changes. |
| *ExchangeConnectorState* | No changes. |
| *ExchangeLink* | No changes. Additional capabilities are provided in the new *Exchange_Link* class. |
| *ExchangeQueue* | No changes. Additional capabilities are provided in the new *Exchange_Queue* class. |
| *ExchangeServerState* | No changes. Additional capabilities are provided in the new *Exchange_Server* class. |
| *Exchange_DSAccessDC* | No changes. |
| *Exchange_FolderTree* | New class. |
| *Exchange_Link* | New class. |
| *Exchange_Logon* | New class. |
| *Exchange_Mailbox* | New class. |
| *Exchange_MessageTrackingEntry* | Additional message-tracking entry-type values were added to provide more detailed tracking of internal message-transfer events. |
| *Exchange_PublicFolder* | New class. |
| *Exchange_Queue* | New class. |
| *Exchange_QueueCacheReloadEvent* | New class. |
| *Exchange_QueuedMessage* | New class. |
| *Exchange_QueuedSMTPMessage* | New class. |
| *Exchange_QueuedX400Message* | New class. |
| *Exchange_QueueSMTPVirtualServer* | New class. |
| *Exchange_QueueVirtualServer* | New class. |
| *Exchange_QueueX400VirtualServer* | New class. |
| *Exchange_ScheduleInterval* | New class. |
| *Exchange_Server* | New class. |
| *Exchange_SMTPLink* | New class. |
| *Exchange_SMTPQueue* | New class. |
| *Exchange_X400Link* | New class. |
| *Exchange_X400Queue* | New class. |

> **Just the Steps**
>
> ▶ **To query the *Exchange_QueueSMTPVirtualServer* class**
>
> 1. Create a variable to hold the connection into the \\*root*\\*MicrosoftExchangeV2* namespace.
> 2. Use the *ExecQuery* method to select * from *Exchange_QueueSMTPVirtualServer*.
> 3. Use *For Each...Next* to iterate through the returned collection.
> 4. Use *WScript.Echo* to echo out the important properties.

# Connecting to *MicrosoftExchangeV2*

To use WMI to retrieve information from Exchange 2003, you need to make a connection into the *MicrosoftExchangeV2* namespace, which is even easier to work with than the IIS namespace. As you will soon see, the *MicrosoftExchangeV2* namespace is very logically laid out, and the scripts will rapidly become redundant. The only trick to using the namespace is finding the data you want to retrieve.

## The *Exchange_QueueSMTPVirtualServer* Class

For the first code sample (ExchangeSMTPQueue.vbs), consider the *Exchange_Queue-SMTPVirtualServer* class, which returns properties for SMTP queue virtual servers. ExchangeSMTPQueue.vbs is shown here:

```
Option Explicit
On Error Resume Next
Dim strComputer
Dim wmiNS
Dim wmiQuery
Dim objWMIService
Dim colItems
Dim objItem

strComputer = "."
wmiNS = "\root\MicrosoftExchangeV2"
wmiQuery = "Select * from Exchange_QueueSMTPVirtualServer"
Set objWMIService = GetObject("winmgmts:\\" & strComputer & wmiNS)
Set colItems = objWMIService.ExecQuery(wmiQuery)


For Each objItem In colItems
    WScript.Echo "Caption: " & objItem.Caption
    WScript.Echo "Description: " & objItem.Description
    WScript.Echo "GlobalActionsSupported: " _
        & objItem.GlobalActionsSupported
    WScript.Echo "GlobalStop: " & objItem.GlobalStop
    WScript.Echo "InstallDate: " & objItem.InstallDate
    WScript.Echo "Name: " & objItem.Name
```

```
        WScript.Echo "ProtocolName: " & objItem.ProtocolName
        WScript.Echo "Status: " & objItem.Status
        WScript.Echo "VirtualMachine: " & objItem.VirtualMachine
        WScript.Echo "VirtualServerName: " & objItem.VirtualServerName
        WScript.Echo "-=-"
Next
```

## Header Information

The Header information section is going to look very similar in each of the Exchange 2003 WMI scripts, so this is the only place you will look at it. You turn on *Option Explicit* and *On Error Resume Next*, and then name several variables, which are described in Table 20-2.

**Table 20-2   Variables Used in ExchangeSMTPQueue.vbs**

| Variable | Use |
| --- | --- |
| *strComputer* | Holds the name of the target computer |
| *wmiNS* | Holds the target namespace |
| *wmiQuery* | Holds the WMI query text |
| *objWMIService* | Holds the connection into WMI |
| *colItems* | Holds the returned data |
| *objItem* | Used to iterate through the data |

## Reference Information

The Reference information section of the script is used to assign values to variables that were declared in the Header information section. *StrComputer* is set to a period, which means that the query will run against the local computer. *WmiNS* is set to the "*\root\MicrosoftExchangeV2*" namespace to enable you to work with Exchange 2003. In most of our scripts, the *strComputer*, *wmiNS*, and *wmiQuery* references will remain exactly the same. The only item needing modification in the Reference information section of the script is the class from which *Select *￼* is going to run. You set *objWMIService* to be equal to the hook that comes back from using *GetObject* and the WMI moniker. This connection into WMI is targeted at *strComputer* and the namespace represented by *wmiNS*. The advantage of using variables to create the connection string is that the line of code will never need to be modified! Once you have the hook into WMI, you use that hook to cast your query. The query is contained in the *wmiQuery* variable, and as a result, you don't have to touch that line of code either.

```
strComputer = "."
wmiNS = "\root\MicrosoftExchangeV2"
wmiQuery = "Select * from Exchange_QueueSMTPVirtualServer"
Set objWMIService = GetObject("winmgmts:\\" & strComputer & wmiNS)
Set colItems = objWMIService.ExecQuery(wmiQuery)
```

## Worker Information

The Worker information section of the script is a *For Each...Next* construction. You use the *objItem* variable to iterate through the data held in the *colItems* collection. This code does not need to be modified. This construction looks like the following:

```
For Each objItem In colItems

Next
```

## Output Information

The Output information section of the script consists of a series of *WScript.Echo* statements. These statements are contained inside the *For Each...Next* construction in the Worker information section of the script. The Output information section will need to be customized for every WMI script you create using the *MicrosoftExchangeV2* namespace. For ExchangeSMTPQueue.vbs, the Output information section looks like the following:

```
WScript.Echo "Caption: " & objItem.Caption
WScript.Echo "Description: " & objItem.Description
WScript.Echo "GlobalActionsSupported: " _
    & objItem.GlobalActionsSupported
WScript.Echo "GlobalStop: " & objItem.GlobalStop
WScript.Echo "InstallDate: " & objItem.InstallDate
WScript.Echo "Name: " & objItem.Name
WScript.Echo "ProtocolName: " & objItem.ProtocolName
WScript.Echo "Status: " & objItem.Status
WScript.Echo "VirtualMachine: " _
    & objItem.VirtualMachine
WScript.Echo "VirtualServerName: " _
    & objItem.VirtualServerName
```

# Exchange Public Folders

Working with public folders in Exchange 2003 is a lot better than working with them in previous versions of Exchange. And with the addition of new and expanded WMI classes, working with public folders is especially easy. The script ExchangePublicFolders.vbs points this out. As you can see from the code listing, much of the process of connecting to and accessing useful information about Exchange 2003 public folders via the *Exchange_PublicFolder* class is similar to this process in other WMI scripts. Indeed, the only changes are using the *Exchange_PublicFolder* class to the select statement you will use for the query and, of course, the Output information section of the script.

```
Option Explicit
On Error Resume Next
Dim strComputer
Dim wmiNS
```

```
Dim wmiQuery
Dim objWMIService
Dim colItems
Dim objItem

strComputer = "."
wmiNS = "\root\MicrosoftExchangeV2"
wmiQuery = "Select * from Exchange_PublicFolder"
Set objWMIService = GetObject("winmgmts:\\" & strComputer & wmiNS)
Set colItems = objWMIService.ExecQuery(wmiQuery)

For Each objItem In colItems
    WScript.Echo "AddressBookName: " & objItem.AddressBookName
    WScript.Echo "AdministrativeNote: " & objItem.AdministrativeNote
    WScript.Echo "AdminSecurityDescriptor: " _
        & objItem.AdminSecurityDescriptor
    WScript.Echo "ADProxyPath: " & objItem.ADProxyPath
    WScript.Echo "AssociatedMessageCount: " _
        & objItem.AssociatedMessageCount
    WScript.Echo "AttachmentCount: " & objItem.AttachmentCount
    WScript.Echo "Caption: " & objItem.Caption
    WScript.Echo "CategorizationCount: " & _
        objItem.CategorizationCount
    WScript.Echo "Comment: " & objItem.Comment
    WScript.Echo "ContactCount: " & objItem.ContactCount
    WScript.Echo "ContainsRules: " & objItem.ContainsRules
    WScript.Echo "CreationTime: " & objItem.CreationTime
    WScript.Echo "DeletedItemLifetime: " _
        & objItem.DeletedItemLifetime
    WScript.Echo "Description: " & objItem.Description
    WScript.Echo "FolderTree: " & objItem.FolderTree
    WScript.Echo "FriendlyUrl: " & objItem.FriendlyUrl
    WScript.Echo "HasChildren: " & objItem.HasChildren
    WScript.Echo "HasLocalReplica: " & objItem.HasLocalReplica
    WScript.Echo "InstallDate: " & objItem.InstallDate
    WScript.Echo "IsMailEnabled: " & objItem.IsMailEnabled
    WScript.Echo "IsNormalFolder: " & objItem.IsNormalFolder
    WScript.Echo "IsPerUserReadDisabled: " _
        & objItem.IsPerUserReadDisabled
    WScript.Echo "IsSearchFolder: " & objItem.IsSearchFolder
    WScript.Echo "IsSecureInSite: " & objItem.IsSecureInSite
    WScript.Echo "LastAccessTime: " & objItem.LastAccessTime
    WScript.Echo "LastModificationTime: " _
        & objItem.LastModificationTime
    WScript.Echo "MaximumItemSize: " & objItem.MaximumItemSize
    WScript.Echo "MessageCount: " & objItem.MessageCount
    WScript.Echo "MessageWithAttachmentsCount: " _
        & objItem.MessageWithAttachmentsCount
    WScript.Echo "Name: " & objItem.Name
    WScript.Echo "NormalMessageSize: " & objItem.NormalMessageSize
    WScript.Echo "OwnerCount: " & objItem.OwnerCount
    WScript.Echo "ParentFriendlyUrl: " & objItem.ParentFriendlyUrl
    WScript.Echo "Path: " & objItem.Path
    WScript.Echo "ProhibitPostLimit: " & objItem.ProhibitPostLimit
    WScript.Echo "PublishInAddressBook: " _
```

```
                  & objItem.PublishInAddressBook
      WScript.Echo "RecipientCountOnAssociatedMessages: " _
          & objItem.RecipientCountOnAssociatedMessages
      WScript.Echo "RecipientCountOnNormalMessages: " _
          & objItem.RecipientCountOnNormalMessages
      WScript.Echo "ReplicaAgeLimit: " & objItem.ReplicaAgeLimit
      WScript.Echo "ReplicaList: " & objItem.ReplicaList
      WScript.Echo "ReplicationMessagePriority: " _
          & objItem.ReplicationMessagePriority
      WScript.Echo "ReplicationSchedule: " _
          & objItem.ReplicationSchedule
      WScript.Echo "ReplicationStyle: " & objItem.ReplicationStyle
      WScript.Echo "RestrictionCount: " & objItem.RestrictionCount
      WScript.Echo "SecurityDescriptor: " & objItem.SecurityDescriptor
      WScript.Echo "Status: " & objItem.Status
      WScript.Echo "StorageLimitStyle: " & objItem.StorageLimitStyle
      WScript.Echo "TargetAddress: " & objItem.TargetAddress
      WScript.Echo "TotalMessageSize: " & objItem.TotalMessageSize
      WScript.Echo "Url: " & objItem.Url
      WScript.Echo "UsePublicStoreAgeLimits: " _
          & objItem.UsePublicStoreAgeLimits
      WScript.Echo "UsePublicStoreDeletedItemLifetime: " _
          & objItem.UsePublicStoreDeletedItemLifetime
      WScript.Echo "WarningLimit: " & objItem.WarningLimit
WScript.Echo "-=-"
Next
```

## Exchange_FolderTree

To look at the folder structure defined on an Exchange 2003 server, you can use the *Exchange_FolderTree* class. The only changes you must make to your script are the same changes you made to the other scripts—changing the class portion of the *wmiQuery* to point to the *Exchange_FolderTree* class. Then you must modify the Output information section to echo out the properties you are interested in. The completed ExchangeFolder-Tree.vbs script is listed here:

```
Option Explicit
On Error Resume Next
Dim strComputer
Dim wmiNS
Dim wmiQuery
Dim objWMIService
Dim colItems
Dim objItem

strComputer = "."
wmiNS = "\root\MicrosoftExchangeV2"
wmiQuery = "Select * from Exchange_FolderTree"
Set objWMIService = GetObject("winmgmts:\\" & strComputer & wmiNS)
Set colItems = objWMIService.ExecQuery(wmiQuery)

For Each objItem In colItems
```

```
WScript.Echo "AdministrativeGroup: " _
    & objItem.AdministrativeGroup
WScript.Echo "AdministrativeNote: " _
    & objItem.AdministrativeNote
WScript.Echo "AssociatedPublicStores: " _
    & objItem.AssociatedPublicStores
WScript.Echo "Caption: " & objItem.Caption
WScript.Echo "CreationTime: " & objItem.CreationTime
WScript.Echo "Description: " & objItem.Description
WScript.Echo "GUID: " & objItem.GUID
WScript.Echo "HasLocalPublicStore: " _
    & objItem.HasLocalPublicStore
WScript.Echo "InstallDate: " & objItem.InstallDate
WScript.Echo "LastModificationTime: " _
    & objItem.LastModificationTime
WScript.Echo "MapiFolderTree: " & objItem.MapiFolderTree
WScript.Echo "Name: " & objItem.Name
WScript.Echo "RootFolderURL: " & objItem.RootFolderURL
WScript.Echo "Status: " & objItem.Status
WScript.Echo "-=-"

Next
```

# Summary

In this chapter, you examined querying WMI data by using the *MicrosoftExchangeV2* namespace. The *MicrosoftExchangeV2* namespace is located under the root WMI namespace and contains numerous classes that can be used to monitor nearly every aspect of daily exchange administrator activities. Because of a high level of consistency in the design of the *MicrosoftExchangeV2* namespace, many of the WMI scripts are reusable, requiring only a small degree of modification.

# Quiz Yourself

**Q. What is the WMI namespace for managing and monitoring Exchange 2003?**

**A.** The *MicrosoftExchangeV2* namespace is designed for managing and monitoring Exchange 2003.

**Q. How do you connect to the *MicrosoftExchangeV2* namespace?**

**A.** You connect to the *MicrosoftExchangeV2* namespace by using *GetObject*, the WMI moniker, and by specifying the target computer and the *root\MicrosoftExchangeV2* namespace.

**Q. To obtain information about Exchange 2003 public folders, what class should you query?**

**A.** To obtain information about Exchange 2003 public folders, you should query the *Exchange_PublicFolder* class in the *root\MicrosoftExchangeV2* namespace.

# On Your Own

# Lab 40 Using the *Exchange_Logon* Class

In this lab, you practice using the *Exchange_Logon* class from the *MicrosoftExchangeV2* namespace.

## Lab Instructions

1. Open Notepad.exe.

2. On the first line of a new file, type **Option Explicit**.

3. Save your file as **Lab40Solution.vbs**.

4. You need to declare six variables: *strComputer*, *wmiNS*, *wmiQuery*, *objWMIService*, *colItems*, and *objItem*. The completed Header information section of your script will look like the following:

```
Option Explicit
'On Error Resume Next
Dim strComputer
Dim wmiNS
Dim wmiQuery
Dim objWMIService
Dim colItems
Dim objItem
```

5. Assign the variable *strComputer* to be equal to ".". This line of code will look like the following:

```
strComputer = "."
```

6. Assign the variable *wmiNS* to be equal to "\*root*\*MicrosoftExchangeV2*". This line of code looks like the following:

```
wmiNS = "\root\MicrosoftExchangeV2"
```

7. Assign the *wmiQuery* variable to be equal to *"Select * from Exchange_Logon"*. This line of code looks like the following:

```
wmiQuery = "Select * from Exchange_Logon"
```

8. Set the variable *objWMIService* to be equal to the hook that comes back from using the *GetObject* command into WMI. Use the *winmgmts* moniker, specify the *strComputer* as the target computer, and specify *wmiNS* as the target namespace. This line of code looks like the following:

```
Set objWMIService = GetObject("winmgmts:\\" & strComputer & wmiNS)
```

9. Set the *colItems* variable to hold the data that comes back from running the query contained in the variable *wmiQuery* when you use the *ExecQuery* method. This line of code looks like the following:

```
Set colItems = objWMIService.ExecQuery(wmiQuery)
```

10. Create an empty *For Each...Next* construction. Use *objItem* as your placeholder, and use *colItems* as the collection to be iterated through. This will look like the following:

```
For Each objItem In colItems

Next
```

11. Open the Lab40Starter.vbs file. This file contains the series of *WScript.Echo* commands that go inside the empty *For Each...Next* construction that was created in step 10.

12. Copy all the *WScript.Echo* commands contained in StarterLab40.txt and paste them into the *For Each...Next* construction. When completed, the script will look like the following:

```
For Each objItem In colItems
    WScript.Echo "AdapterSpeed: " & objItem.AdapterSpeed
    WScript.Echo "Caption: " & objItem.Caption
    WScript.Echo "ClientIP: " & objItem.ClientIP
    WScript.Echo "ClientMode: " & objItem.ClientMode
    WScript.Echo "ClientName: " & objItem.ClientName
    WScript.Echo "ClientVersion: " & objItem.ClientVersion
    WScript.Echo "CodePageID: " & objItem.CodePageID
    WScript.Echo "Description: " & objItem.Description
    WScript.Echo "FolderOperationRate: " _
        & objItem.FolderOperationRate
    WScript.Echo "HostAddress: " & objItem.HostAddress
    WScript.Echo "InstallDate: " & objItem.InstallDate
    WScript.Echo "LastOperationTime: " & objItem.LastOperationTime
    WScript.Echo "Latency: " & objItem.Latency
    WScript.Echo "LocaleID: " & objItem.LocaleID
    WScript.Echo "LoggedOnUserAccount: " _
        & objItem.LoggedOnUserAccount
    WScript.Echo "LoggedOnUsersMailboxLegacyDN: "
    & objItem.LoggedOnUsersMailboxLegacyDN
    WScript.Echo "LogonTime: " & objItem.LogonTime
    WScript.Echo "MacAddress: " & objItem.MacAddress
    WScript.Echo "MailboxDisplayName: " & objItem.MailboxDisplayName
    WScript.Echo "MailboxLegacyDN: " & objItem.MailboxLegacyDN
    WScript.Echo "MessagingOperationRate: " _
        & objItem.MessagingOperationRate
    WScript.Echo "Name: " & objItem.Name
    WScript.Echo "OpenAttachmentCount: " _
        & objItem.OpenAttachmentCount
    WScript.Echo "OpenFolderCount: " & objItem.OpenFolderCount
    WScript.Echo "OpenMessageCount: " & objItem.OpenMessageCount
    WScript.Echo "OtherOperationRate: " & objItem.OtherOperationRate
```

```
        WScript.Echo "ProgressOperationRate: " _
            & objItem.ProgressOperationRate
        WScript.Echo "RowID: " & objItem.RowID
        WScript.Echo "RPCSucceeded: " & objItem.RPCSucceeded
        WScript.Echo "ServerName: " & objItem.ServerName
        WScript.Echo "Status: " & objItem.Status
        WScript.Echo "StorageGroupName: " & objItem.StorageGroupName
        WScript.Echo "StoreName: " & objItem.StoreName
        WScript.Echo "StoreType: " & objItem.StoreType
        WScript.Echo "StreamOperationRate: " _
            & objItem.StreamOperationRate
        WScript.Echo "TableOperationRate: " & objItem.TableOperationRate
        WScript.Echo "TotalOperationRate: " & objItem.TotalOperationRate
        WScript.Echo "TransferOperationRate: " _
            & objItem.TransferOperationRate
    WScript.Echo "-=-"
    Next
```

**13.** Save and run the script.

# Lab 41 Using the *Exchange_Mailbox* Class

In this lab, you create a script that connects to the *MicrosoftExchangeV2* namespace and queries the *Exchange_Mailbox* class.

## Lab Instructions

**1.** Open Notepad.exe.

**2.** On the first line of a new file, type **Option Explicit**.

**3.** Save your file as **Lab41Solution.vbs**.

**4.** You need to declare six variables: *strComputer*, *wmiNS*, *wmiQuery*, *objWMIService*, *colItems*, and *objItem*. The completed Header information section of your script will look like the following:

```
Option Explicit
'On Error Resume Next
Dim strComputer
Dim wmiNS
Dim wmiQuery
Dim objWMIService
Dim colItems
Dim objItem
```

**5.** Assign the variable *strComputer* to be equal to ".". This line of code will look like the following:

```
strComputer = "."
```

**6.** Assign the variable *wmiNS* to be equal to "\root\MicrosoftExchangeV2". This line of code looks like the following:

```
wmiNS = "\root\MicrosoftExchangeV2"
```

**7.** Assign the *wmiQuery* variable to be equal to *"Select * from Exchange_Logon"*. This line of code looks like the following:

```
wmiQuery = "Select * from Exchange_Logon"
```

**8.** Set the variable *objWMIService* to be equal to the hook that comes back from using the *GetObject* command into WMI. Use the *winmgmts* moniker, specify the *strComputer* as the target computer, and specify *wmiNS* as the target namespace. This line of code looks like the following:

```
Set objWMIService = GetObject("winmgmts:\\" & strComputer & wmiNS)
```

**9.** Set the *colItems* variable to hold the data that comes back from running the query contained in the variable *wmiQuery* when you use the *ExecQuery* method. This line of code looks like the following:

```
Set colItems = objWMIService.ExecQuery(wmiQuery)
```

**10.** Create an empty *For Each…Next* construction. Use *objItem* as your placeholder, and use *colItems* as the collection to be iterated through. This will look like the following:

```
For Each objItem In colItems

Next
```

**11.** Open the Lab41Starter.txt file. This file contains the series of *WScript.Echo* commands that go inside the empty *For Each…Next* construction that was created in step 10.

**12.** Copy all the *WScript.Echo* commands contained in Lab40Starter.txt and paste them into the *For Each…Next* construction. When completed, the script will look like the following:

```
For Each objItem In colItems
    WScript.Echo "AssocContentCount: " & objItem.AssocContentCount
    WScript.Echo "Caption: " & objItem.Caption
    WScript.Echo "DateDiscoveredAbsentInDS: " _
        & objItem.DateDiscoveredAbsentInDS
    WScript.Echo "DeletedMessageSizeExtended: " _
        & objItem.DeletedMessageSizeExtended
    WScript.Echo "Description: " & objItem.Description
    WScript.Echo "InstallDate: " & objItem.InstallDate
    WScript.Echo "LastLoggedOnUserAccount: " _
        & objItem.LastLoggedOnUserAccount
    WScript.Echo "LastLogoffTime: " & objItem.LastLogoffTime
    WScript.Echo "LastLogonTime: " & objItem.LastLogonTime
    WScript.Echo "LegacyDN: " & objItem.LegacyDN
    WScript.Echo "MailboxDisplayName: " & objItem.MailboxDisplayName
    WScript.Echo "MailboxGUID: " & objItem.MailboxGUID
    WScript.Echo "Name: " & objItem.Name
    WScript.Echo "ServerName: " & objItem.ServerName
    WScript.Echo "Size: " & objItem.Size
```

```
     WScript.Echo "Status: " & objItem.Status
     WScript.Echo "StorageGroupName: " & objItem.StorageGroupName
     WScript.Echo "StorageLimitInfo: " & objItem.StorageLimitInfo
     WScript.Echo "StoreName: " & objItem.StoreName
     WScript.Echo "TotalItems: " & objItem.TotalItems
     WScript.Echo "-=-"
  Next
```

**13.** Save and run your **Lab41Solution.vbs** script.

# Part 5
# Appendices

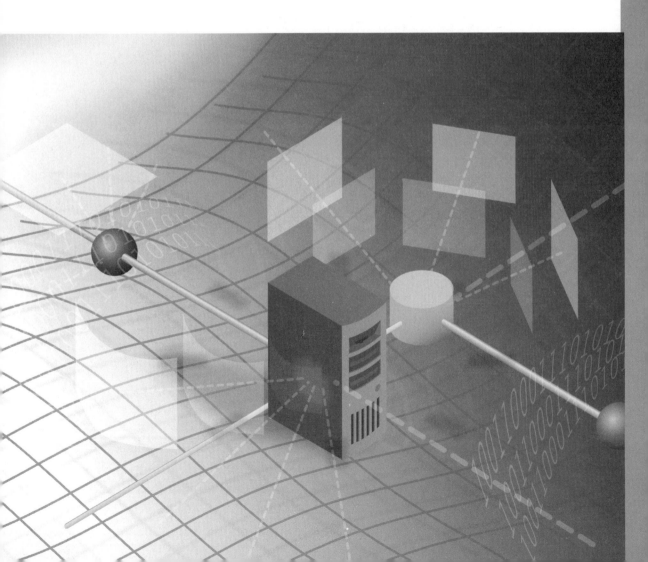

# Appendix A
# VBScript Documentation

## Constants

The constants in Tables A-1 through A-6 are built into VBScript and therefore do not need to be defined prior to use. You can use them anywhere in your code to represent the values shown.

**Table A-1  String Constants**

| Constant | Value | Description |
|---|---|---|
| *vbCr* | *Chr(13)* | Carriage return. |
| *VbCrLf* | *Chr(13)* and *Chr(10)* | Carriage return–linefeed combination. |
| *vbFormFeed* | *Chr(12)* | Form feed; not useful in Microsoft Windows. |
| *vbLf* | *Chr(10)* | Line feed. |
| *vbNewLine* | *Chr(13)* and *Chr(10)* or *Chr(10)* | Platform-specific newline character; whatever is appropriate for the platform. |
| *vbNullChar* | *Chr(0)* | Character having the value 0. |
| *vbNullString* | String having value *0* | Not the same as a zero-length string (""); used for calling external procedures. |
| *vbTab* | *Chr(9)* | Horizontal tab. |
| *vbVerticalTab* | *Chr(11)* | Vertical tab; not useful in Microsoft Windows. |

**Table A-2  Comparison Constants**

| Constant | Value | Description |
|---|---|---|
| *vbBinaryCompare* | 0 | Perform a binary comparison. |
| *vbTextCompare* | 1 | Perform a textual comparison. |

**Table A-3   Date and Time Constants**

| Constant | Value | Description |
|---|---|---|
| *vbSunday* | 1 | Sunday |
| *vbMonday* | 2 | Monday |
| *vbTuesday* | 3 | Tuesday |
| *vbWednesday* | 4 | Wednesday |
| *vbThursday* | 5 | Thursday |
| *vbFriday* | 6 | Friday |
| *vbSaturday* | 7 | Saturday |
| *vbUseSystemDayOfWeek* | 0 | Use the day of the week specified in your system settings for the first day of the week. |
| *vbFirstJan1* | 1 | Use the week in which January 1 occurs (default). |
| *vbFirstFourDays* | 2 | Use the first week that has at least four days in the new year. |
| *vbFirstFullWeek* | 3 | Use the first full week of the year. |

**Table A-4   Date Formatting Constants**

| Constant | Value | Description |
|---|---|---|
| *vbGeneralDate* | 0 | Display a date and/or time. For real numbers, display a date and time. If there is no fractional part, display only a date. If there is no integer part, display time only. Date and time display is determined by your system settings. |
| *vbLongDate* | 1 | Display a date using the long date format specified in your computer's regional settings. |
| *vbShortDate* | 2 | Display a date using the short date format specified in your computer's regional settings. |
| *vbLongTime* | 3 | Display a time using the long time format specified in your computer's regional settings. |
| *vbShortTime* | 4 | Display a time using the short time format specified in your computer's regional settings. |

**Table A-5   Tri-State Constants**

| Constant | Value | Description |
|---|---|---|
| *vbUseDefault* | -2 | Use default from your computer's regional settings. |
| *vbTrue* | -1 | True |
| *vbFalse* | 0 | False |

**Table A-6   Color Constants**

| Constant | Value | Description |
|----------|-------|-------------|
| *vbBlack* | *&h00* | Black |
| *vbRed* | *&hFF* | Red |
| *vbGreen* | *&hFF00* | Green |
| *vbYellow* | *&hFFFF* | Yellow |
| *vbBlue* | *&hFF0000* | Blue |
| *vbMagenta* | *&hFF00FF* | Magenta |
| *vbCyan* | *&hFFFF00* | Cyan |
| *vbWhite* | *&hFFFFFF* | White |

# VBScript Run-Time Errors

VBScript *run-time errors* result when your script attempts to perform an action that the system cannot execute. The errors are called run-time errors because they happen while your script is being executed. Run-time errors are listed in Table A-7.

**Table A-7   Run-Time Error Numbers and Descriptions**

| Error Number | Description |
|--------------|-------------|
| 429 | ActiveX component can't create object. |
| 507 | An exception occurred. |
| 449 | Argument not optional. |
| 17 | Can't perform requested operation. |
| 430 | Class doesn't support Automation. |
| 506 | Class not defined. |
| 11 | Division by zero. |
| 48 | Error in loading DLL. |
| 5020 | Expected ')' in regular expression. |
| 5019 | Expected ']' in regular expression. |
| 432 | Filename or class name not found during Automation operation. |
| 92 | *For* loop not initialized. |
| 5008 | Illegal assignment. |
| 51 | Internal error. |
| 505 | Invalid or unqualified reference. |
| 481 | Invalid picture. |
| 5 | Invalid procedure call or argument. |

**Table A-7   Run-Time Error Numbers and Descriptions**

| Error Number | Description |
| --- | --- |
| 5021 | Invalid range in character set. |
| 94 | Invalid use of Null. |
| 448 | Named argument not found. |
| 447 | Object doesn't support current locale setting. |
| 445 | Object doesn't support this action. |
| 438 | Object doesn't support this property or method. |
| 451 | Object not a collection. |
| 504 | Object not safe for creating. |
| 503 | Object not safe for initializing. |
| 502 | Object not safe for scripting. |
| 424 | Object required. |
| 91 | Object variable not set. |
| 7 | Out of memory. |
| 28 | Out of stack space. |
| 14 | Out of string space. |
| 6 | Overflow. |
| 35 | Sub or function not defined. |
| 9 | Subscript out of range. |

# VBScript Syntax Errors

VBScript *syntax errors* occur when the structure of one of your script statements violates one or more grammatical rules that govern the use of the scripting language. VBScript syntax errors occur during the program compilation stage, before the program has begun to be executed, and are therefore sometimes referred to as *compile time errors*. Syntax errors are listed in Table A-8.

**Table A-8   Syntax Error Numbers and Descriptions**

| Error Number | Description |
| --- | --- |
| 1052 | Cannot have multiple default properties/methods in a Class. |
| 1044 | Cannot use parentheses when calling a Sub. |
| 1053 | Class initialize or terminate do not have arguments. |
| 1058 | 'Default' specification can only be on property *Get*. |
| 1057 | 'Default' specification must also specify 'Public'. |
| 1005 | Expected '('. |

**Table A-8  Syntax Error Numbers and Descriptions**

| Error Number | Description |
|---|---|
| 1006 | Expected ')'. |
| 1011 | Expected '='. |
| 1021 | Expected 'Case'. |
| 1047 | Expected 'Class'. |
| 1025 | Expected end of statement. |
| 1014 | Expected 'End'. |
| 1023 | Expected expression. |
| 1015 | Expected 'Function'. |
| 1010 | Expected identifier. |
| 1012 | Expected 'If'. |
| 1046 | Expected 'In'. |
| 1026 | Expected integer constant. |
| 1049 | Expected *Let*, *Set*, or *Get* in property declaration. |
| 1045 | Expected literal constant. |
| 1019 | Expected 'Loop'. |
| 1020 | Expected 'Next'. |
| 1050 | Expected 'Property'. |
| 1022 | Expected 'Select'. |
| 1024 | Expected statement. |
| 1016 | Expected 'Sub'. |
| 1017 | Expected 'Then'. |
| 1013 | Expected 'To'. |
| 1018 | Expected 'Wend'. |
| 1027 | Expected 'While' or 'Until'. |
| 1028 | Expected 'While,' 'Until,' or end of statement. |
| 1029 | Expected 'With'. |
| 1030 | Identifier too long. |
| 1014 | Invalid character. |
| 1039 | Invalid 'exit' statement. |
| 1040 | Invalid 'for' loop control variable. |
| 1013 | Invalid number. |
| 1037 | Invalid use of 'Me' keyword. |
| 1038 | 'loop' without 'do'. |
| 1048 | Must be defined inside a class. |

**Table A-8   Syntax Error Numbers and Descriptions**

| Error Number | Description |
|---|---|
| 1042 | Must be first statement on the line. |
| 1041 | Name redefined. |
| 1051 | Number of arguments must be consistent across properties specification. |
| 1001 | Out of memory. |
| 1054 | Property *Set* or *Let* must have at least one argument. |
| 1002 | Syntax error. |
| 1055 | Unexpected 'Next'. |
| 1015 | Unterminated string constant. |

## Appendix B
# ADSI Documentation

For network administrators, one of the most frustrating aspects of using ADSI is trying to match what is found in Active Directory Users and Computers with what is expected in a Microsoft Visual Basic Script (VBScript) that uses ADSI to manipulate Active Directory. Although it is possible to use ADSI Edit to view the field names, reviewing Tables B-1 through B-20 will lessen some of your learning curve.

## Computer Object Mapping

Tables B-1 through B-4 show computer object names displayed in the Active Directory Users and Computers tool as they map to names available via ADSI scripting.

**Table B-1   Computer Object General Property Sheet**

| UI Label | Active Directory attribute | Comments |
|---|---|---|
| Computer Name (pre–Microsoft Windows 2000) | *sAMAccountName* | |
| DNS Name | *dNSHostName* | |
| Role | *userAccountControl* | Toggles a bit in the *userAccountControl* bitmask. |
| Description | *description* | |
| Trust Computer for delegation | *userAccountControl* | Toggles a bit in the *userAccountControl* bitmask. |

**Table B-2   Computer Object Location Property Sheet**

| UI label | Active Directory attribute |
|---|---|
| Location | *location* |

**Table B-3   Computer Object Member of Property Sheet**

| UI label | Active Directory attribute | Comments |
|---|---|---|
| Member of | *memberOf* | The member attribute of each of the groups in this list contains the distinguished name of this computer object. |
| Set Primary Group | *primaryGroupID* | |

**Table B-4  Computer Object Operating System Property Sheet**

| UI label | Active Directory attribute |
|---|---|
| Name | *operatingSystem* |
| Version | *operatingSystemVersion* |
| Service Pack | *operatingSystemServicePack* |

# Domain Object User Interface Mapping

Table B-5 shows user object names displayed in the Active Directory Users and Computers tool as they map to names available via ADSI scripting.

**Table B-5  Domain Object General Property Sheet**

| UI label | Active Directory attribute |
|---|---|
| Domain Name (pre–Windows 2000) | *DC* |
| Description | *description* |

# Group Object User Interface Mapping

Tables B-6 though B-8 show group object names displayed in the Active Directory Users and Computers tool as they map to names available via ADSI scripting.

**Table B-6  Group Object General Property Sheet**

| UI label | Active Directory attribute |
|---|---|
| Group Name (pre–Windows 2000) | *sAMAccountName* |
| Description | *description* |
| E-Mail | *mail* |
| Group Scope | *groupScope* |
| Group Type | *groupType* |
| Notes | *info* |

**Table B-7   Group Object Member of Property Sheet**

| UI label | Active Directory attribute | Comments |
|---|---|---|
| Member of | *memberOf* | Contains the distinguished names of the groups to which this group belongs. The member attribute of each of the groups in this list contains the distinguished name of this group object. |
| | | The user interface does not directly modify the *memberOf* attribute. It modifies the "*member*" attribute on the group object of which this object is made a member of. Active Directory maintains the *memberOf* attribute. |

**Table B-8   Group Object Member Members Property Sheet**

| UI label | Active Directory attribute | Comments |
|---|---|---|
| Members | *member* | Contains the distinguished names of the members of this group object. |

# Object Property Sheet

Table B-9 shows object property names displayed in the Active Directory Users and Computers tool as they map to names available via ADSI scripting.

**Table B-9   Object Property Sheet**

| UI label | Active Directory attribute | Comments |
|---|---|---|
| Fully qualified domain name of object | | This is the object's distinguished name in canonical form. |
| Object class | *objectClass* | |
| Created | *whenCreated* | |
| Modified | *whenChanged* | |
| Update Sequence Numbers: Current | *uSNChanged* | |
| Update Sequence Numbers: Original | *uSNCreated* | |

# Organizational Unit User Interface Mapping

Table B-10 and Table B-11 show organizational unit object names displayed in the Active Directory Users and Computers tool as they map to names available via ADSI scripting.

**Table B-10   OU General Property Sheet**

| UI label | Active Directory attribute | Comments |
|---|---|---|
| Description | *description* | |
| Street | *street* | |
| City | *l* | The *l* attribute name is a lowercase "L". |
| State/Province | *st* | |
| Zip/Postal Code | *postalCode* | |
| Country/Region | *c* | This is a lowercase "c". |

**Table B-11   OU Managed by Property Sheet**

| UI label | Active Directory attribute | Comments |
|---|---|---|
| Name | *managedBy* | |
| Manager can update membership list | *n/a* | Changes the ownership to the person named in the name (*managedBy*) attribute. |
| Office | *physicalDeliveryOfficeName* | |
| Street | *streetAddress* | |
| City | *l* | The *l* attribute name is a lowercase "L". |
| State/Province | *st* | |
| Country/Region | *c* | This is a lowercase "c". |
| Telephone Number | *telephoneNumber* | |
| Fax Number | *facsimileTelephoneNumber* | |

# Printer Object User Interface Mapping

Table B-12 shows printer object names displayed in the Active Directory Users and Computers tool as they map to names available via ADSI scripting.

**Table B-12    Printer Object General Property Sheet**

| UI label | Active Directory attribute |
|---|---|
| Location | *location* |
| Model | *driverName* |
| Description | *description* |
| Color | *printColor* |
| Staple | *printStaplingSupported* |
| Double-sided | *print DuplexSupported* |
| Printing Menu | *printRate* |
| Maximum Resolution | *printMaxResolutionSupported* |

# Shared Folder Object User Interface Mapping

Table B-13 shows shared folder object names displayed in the Active Directory Users and Computers tool as they map to names available via ADSI scripting.

**Table B-13    Shared Folder Object General Property Sheet**

| UI label | Active Directory attribute |
|---|---|
| Description | *description* |
| UNC Name | *uNCName* |
| Keywords | *keywords* |

# User Object User Interface Mapping

Tables B-14 through B-20 show user object names displayed in the Active Directory Users and Computers tool as they map to names available via ADSI scripting.

**Table B-14    User Object General Property Sheet**

| UI label | Active Directory attribute |
|---|---|
| First Name | *givenName* |
| Last Name | *sn* |
| Initials | *initials* |
| Description | *description* |
| Office | *physicalDeliveryOfficeName* |

**Table B-14 User Object General Property Sheet**

| UI label | Active Directory attribute |
|----------|---------------------------|
| Telephone Number | *telephoneNumber* |
| Telephone: Other | *otherTelephone* |
| E-Mail | *mail* |
| Web Page | *wwwHomePage* |
| Web Page: Other | *url* |

**Table B-15 User Object Account Property Sheet**

| UI label | Active Directory attribute | Comments |
|----------|---------------------------|----------|
| UserLogon Name | *userPrincipalName* | LDAP = loventPrincipalName, which prefixes the Logon Name drop-down list and adds the full text to the attribute. |
| User logon name (pre–Windows 2000) | *sAMAccountname* | |
| Logon Hours | *logonHours* | |
| Log On To | *logonWorkstation* | |
| Account is locked out | *userAccountControl* | Toggles a bit in the *userAccountControl* bitmask (flag: UF_ACCOUNTSDISABLE). |
| User must change password at next logon | *pwdLastSet* | |
| User cannot change password | N/A | This is the Change Password control in the ACL. |
| Other Account Options | *userAccountControl* | The remaining items in Account Options toggle bits in the *userAccountControl* bitmask (flags in a DWORD). |
| Account Expires | *accountExpires* | |

**Table B-16   User Object Address Property Sheet**

| UI label | Active Directory attribute | Comments |
|---|---|---|
| Street | *streetAddress* | |
| P.O. Box | *postOfficeBox* | |
| City | *l* | The *l* attribute name is a lowercase "L" as in Locale. |
| State/Province | *st* | |
| Zip/Postal Code | *postalCode* | |
| Country/Region | *c*, *co*, and *countryCode* | |

**Table B-17   User Object Member of Property Sheet**

| UI label | Active Directory attribute | Comments |
|---|---|---|
| Member of | *memberOf* | |
| Set Primary Group | *primaryGroupID* | LDAP: Tied to *primaryGroupToken* of the primary group. |

**Table B-18   User Object Organization Property Sheet**

| UI label | Active Directory attribute | Comments |
|---|---|---|
| Title | *title* | |
| Department | *department* | |
| Company | *company* | |
| Manager: Name | *manager* | |
| Direct Reports | *directReports* | Back linked by Active Directory to *directReports* |

**Table B-19  User Object Profile Property Sheet**

| UI label | Active Directory attribute | Comments |
|---|---|---|
| Profile Path | *profilePath* | |
| Logon Script | *scriptPath* | |
| Home Folder: Local Path | *homeDirectory* | If Local path is selected, the local path is stored in the *homeDirectory* attribute. |
| Home Folder: Connect | *homeDrive* | If Connect is selected, the mapped drive is stored in the *homeDrive* attribute. |
| Home Folder: To | *homeDirectory* | If Connect is selected, the path is stored in the *homeDirectory* attribute. |

**Table B-20  User Object Telephone Properties Sheet**

| UI label | Active Directory attribute | Comments |
|---|---|---|
| Home | *telephoneNumber* | LDAP: homePhone |
| Home: Other | *otherTelephone* | LDAP: otherHomePhone |
| Pager | *pager* | |
| Pager: Other | *pagerOther* | LDAP: otherPager |
| Mobile | *mobile* | |
| Mobile: Other | *otherMobile* | |
| Fax | *facsimileTelephoneNumber* | |
| Fax: Other | *otherFacsimileTelephoneNumber* | |
| IP phone | *ipPhone* | |
| IP phone: Other | *otherIpPhone* | |
| Notes | *info* | |

# Appendix C
# WMI Documentation

## Win32 Classes

Microsoft Windows classes give you the means to manipulate a variety of objects. Table C-1 identifies the categories of Windows classes.

**Table C-1   Win32 Classes**

| Category | Description |
| --- | --- |
| Computer system hardware | Classes that represent hardware-related objects. |
| Operating system | Classes that represent operating system-related objects. |
| Installed applications | Classes that represent software-related objects. |
| WMI service management | Classes used to manage WMI. |
| Performance counters | Classes that represent formatted and raw performance data. |

## WMI Providers

The providers in Table C-2 can request information from and send instructions to Windows Management Instrumentation (WMI) objects.

**Table C-2   WMI Providers**

| Provider | Description |
| --- | --- |
| Active Directory Provider | The Active Directory Provider maps Active Directory objects to WMI. By accessing the Lightweight Directory Access Protocol (LDAP) namespace in WMI, you can reference or make an object an alias in Active Directory. Supports the standard *IWbemInit* interface. |
| Cooked Counter Provider | Microsoft Windows XP: High-performance provider that is the preferred source of cooked (calculated) data. Cooked data is the same data displayed in the System Monitor. WMI supplies cooked classes such as *Win32_PerfFormattedData_PerfOS_Cache*, which allows applications to obtain cooked data for performance objects such as the cache. |
| DFS Provider | Microsoft Windows Server 2003 family: Supplies Distributed File System (DFS) functions that logically group shares on multiple servers and link them transparently to a tree-like structure in a single namespace. |

**Table C-2   WMI Providers**

| Provider | Description |
|---|---|
| Disk Quota Provider | Windows XP: Allows administrators to control the amount of data that each user stores on a Microsoft Windows NT File System (NTFS) volume. |
| Event Log Provider | Windows NT/2000: Provides access to data from the event log service to notifications of events. |
| IP Route Provider | Windows Server 2003: Supplies network routing information. |
| Job Object Provider | Windows XP: Provides access to data on named kernel job objects. |
| Performance Counter Provider | Microsoft Windows 2000 and later: High-performance provider that is the preferred source of raw performance data. WMI supplies raw classes such as *Win32_PerfRawData_PerfOS_Cache*, which allow applications to obtain raw performance data for performance objects such as the cache. |
| Performance Monitoring Provider | Windows NT/2000 and earlier: Provider for cooked data. In Windows XP, the Cooked Counter provider supplies the C++ and scripting APIs that access cooked data. |
| Ping Provider | Windows XP: Supplies WMI access to the status information provided by the standard ping command. |
| Policy Provider | Windows XP: Provides extensions to group policy and permits refinements in the application of policy. |
| Power Management Event Provider | Windows 2000 and later: Supplies information to the *Win32_PowerManagementEvent* class to describe power management events that result from power state changes by modeling the Windows 2000 power management protocols. |
| Security Provider | Retrieves or changes security settings that control ownership, auditing, and access rights to Windows NT/Windows 2000 file system (NTFS) files, directories, and shares. |
| Session Provider | Windows NT/2000 and later: Manages network sessions and connections. |
| SNMP Provider | Maps Simple Network Management Protocol (SNMP) objects defined in Management Information Base (MIB) schema objects to WMI CIM classes. This provider is not preinstalled but is available for Windows NT/Windows 2000 and later. |
| System Registry Provider | Enables management applications to retrieve and modify data in the system registry and receive notifications when changes occur. This provider is not preinstalled but is available for all operating systems. |
| Terminal Services Provider | WMI classes that you can use for consistent server administration in a Terminal Services environment. |

**Table C-2 WMI Providers**

| Provider | Description |
|---|---|
| Trustmon Provider | Windows Server 2003: Provides access information about domain trusts. |
| View Provider | Creates new instances and methods based on instances of other classes. |
| WDM Provider | Windows NT/2000 and later: Provides access to the classes, instances, methods, and events of hardware drivers that conform to the Windows Driver Model (WDM). |
| Win32 Provider | Provides access and updates data from Windows systems such as the current settings of environment variables and the attributes of a logical disk. |
| Windows Installer Provider | Provides access information collected from Windows Installer–compliant applications, and makes Windows Installer procedures available remotely. |
| | Windows Server 2003: The Windows Installer provider is included on the companion CD as an optional Windows component that you can install by using Control Panel. Optional installation of the Windows Installer provider ensures backward compatibility with the Windows XP and Windows 2000 feature sets. |
| Windows Product Activation Provider | Windows XP: Supports Windows Product Activation (WPA) administration by using WMI interfaces, and provides consistent server administration in Windows XP. |

# WMI Scripting API Objects

Table C-3 describes WMI scripting objects and how they are used.

**Table C-3 WMI Scripting API Objects**

| Object | Description |
|---|---|
| *SWbemDateTime* | Constructs and parses CIM date/time values. This is a helper object that is available in Windows XP. |
| *SWbemEventSource* | Retrieves events in conjunction with *SWbemServices.ExecNotificationQuery*. |
| *SWbemLastError* | Provides extended error information when an error occurs. |
| *SWbemLocator* | Obtains an *SWbemServices* object that can get access to WMI on a particular host computer. |
| *SWbemMethod* | Contains a single WMI method definition. |
| *SWbemMethodSet* | Gets a collection of *SWbemMethod* objects. |

**Table C-3   WMI Scripting API Objects**

| Object | Description |
| --- | --- |
| *SWbemNamedValue* | Contains a single named value. |
| *SWbemNamedValueSet* | Gets access to a collection of *SWbemNamedValue* objects. |
| *SWbemObject* | Contains and manipulates a single WMI object class or instance. |
| *SWbemObjectEx* | Extends the functionality of *SWbemObject* in Windows XP operating systems. This object adds the Refresh method for *SWbemRefresher* objects. |
| *SWbemObjectPath* | Generates and validates an object path. |
| *SWbemObjectSet* | Gets access to a collection of *SWbemObject* objects. |
| *SWbemPrivilege* | Sets or clears a privilege. |
| *SWbemPrivilegeSet* | Gets access to a collection of *SWbemPrivilege* objects. |
| *SWbemProperty* | Contains a single WMI property. |
| *SWbemPropertySet* | Gets access to a collection of *SWbemProperty* objects. |
| *SWbemQualifier* | Contains a single property qualifier. |
| *SWbemQualifierSet* | Gets access to a collection of *SWbemQualifier* objects. |
| *SWbemRefresher* | Collects and updates object property values in one operation. This object is available in Windows XP. |
| *SWbemRefreshableItem* | Represents a single refreshable element in an *SWbemRefresher* object, such as a property. This object is available in Windows XP. |
| *SWbemSecurity* | Manages security settings such as Component Object Model (COM) Privileges, *AuthenticationLevel*, and *ImpersonationLevel*. |
| *SWbemServices* | Creates, updates, and retrieves instances or classes. |
| *SWbemServicesEx* | Extends the functionality of *SWbemServices* in Windows XP operating systems. This object adds the *Put* and *PutAsync* methods to allow a class or instance to be saved to multiple namespaces. |
| *SWbemSink* | Receives the results of asynchronous operations and event notifications, which are used by client applications. |

# WMI Log Files

Table C-4 lists the log files created by WMI and the WMI providers.

**Table C-4   WMI Log Files**

| File | Description |
| --- | --- |
| Dsprovider.log | Traces information and error messages for the Directory Services Provider. |
| Framework.log | Traces information and error messages for the provider framework and the Win32 Provider. |
| Mofcomp.log | Compiles details from the MOF compiler. |
| Ntevt.log | Traces messages from the Event Log Provider. |
| | This provider requires that you set any bit value for the mask level in the system registry. |
| Setup.log | Reports MOF files that failed to load during the setup process. However, the error that caused the failure is not reported. You must review the Mofcomp.log file to determine the reason for the failure. After the error has been corrected, you can recompile the MOF file (using mofcomp) with the autorecover switch. |
| Viewprovider.log | Traces information from the View Provider based on the mask level you set in the registry. |
| Wbemcore.log | Reports wide spectrum of trace messages. |
| Wbemess.log | Logs entries related to events. |
| Wbemprox.log | Traces information for the WMI proxy server. |
| Wbemsnmp.log | Traces information from the Simple Network Management Protocol (SNMP) Provider. |
| Winmgmt.log | Traces information that is typically not used for diagnostics. |
| Wmiadap.log | Reports error messages related to the AutoDiscoveryAutoPurge (ADAP) process. |
| Wmiprov.log | Manages data and events from WMI-enabled Windows Driver Model (WDM) drivers. |

# Appendix D
# Documentation Standards

As network administrators begin to write lots of scripts, a need for standards becomes rapidly apparent. Large companies commonly maintain a collection of *enterprise scripts* that have been tested and approved for use as network tools. To ensure these scripts can be readily maintained, modified, and debugged, proper documentation must be included with them. This appendix offers suggestions for what kind of information to include with these scripts.

## Header Information Section

The following items should be considered for inclusion in the Header information section of a script:

- Script name
- Script writer
- Date the script was written
- Version information
- Description of the purpose of the script
- Special requirements for use of the script (for example, command-line arguments and access to Active Directory)

## Reference Information Section

The following items should be documented in the Reference information section of the script:

- Use of all variables
- Use of all constants

## Worker Information Section

The following items should be documented in the Worker information section of the script:

- Explanation of constructions used to gather information
- Explanation of constructions used to configure settings
- Explanation of any other constructions used in the script

# Sample of Documentation Use

The following script illustrates how you might include the elements described in the previous sections of this appendix to fully "document" a script. Although documenting a script does add considerably to its length, it also makes the script easier to understand when you need to modify it at a later date.

```
' +++++++++++++++++++++++++++++++++++++++++++++++++++++++++++
' Written by Ed Wilson, 7/13/2003
' version 1.0 basic script
' version 1.1 -- added additional documention, 1/14/2003
' Key concepts are listed below:

' This script displays various Computer Names by reading
' the registry
' +++++++++++++++++++++++++++++++++++++++++++++++++++++++++++
Option Explicit
On Error Resume Next

Dim objShell ' holds connection to wscript.shell
Dim regActiveComputerName ' holds registry string for
                          'active computer name
Dim regComputerName ' holds registry string for computer name
Dim regHostname ' holds registry string for hostname
Dim ActiveComputerName ' holds value found in registry
Dim ComputerName ' holds value found in registry
Dim Hostname 'holds value found in registry


regActiveComputerName = "HKLM\SYSTEM\CurrentControlSet" & _
    "\Control\ComputerName\ActiveComputerName\ComputerName"
regComputerName = "HKLM\SYSTEM\CurrentControlSet\Control" & _
    "\ComputerName\ComputerName\ComputerName"
regHostname = "HKLM\SYSTEM\CurrentControlSet\Services" & _
    "\Tcpip\Parameters\Hostname"


Set objShell = CreateObject("WScript.Shell")
Set objFileSystem = CreateObject("Scripting.FileSystemObject")

ActiveComputerName = objShell.RegRead(regActiveComputerName)
ComputerName = objShell.RegRead(regComputerName)
Hostname = objShell.RegRead(regHostname)


WScript.Echo activecomputername & " is active computer name"
WScript.Echo ComputerName & " is computer name"
WScript.Echo Hostname & " is host name"
```

# Index

## Symbols

## A

## X-Z

# About the Author

Ed Wilson is an Enterprise Consultant who works with Microsoft. Prior to joining Microsoft, Ed was a Senior Consultant with a solutions provider partner in Cincinnati. He is also a Microsoft Certified Trainer and has taught numerous networking and administration classes. His Microsoft Visual Basic Script (VBScript) workshop has been taught to hundreds of premier customers, as well as to Microsoft employees. Ed has written or contributed to seven books and holds nearly two dozen industry certifications including the MCSE and the CISSP.

# Microsoft Press

## Inside *security information* you can trust

**Microsoft® Windows® Security Resource Kit**
ISBN 0-7356-1868-2   Suggested Retail Price: $49.99 U.S., $72.99 Canada

**Comprehensive security information and tools, straight from the Microsoft product groups.** This official RESOURCE KIT delivers comprehensive operations and deployment information that information security professionals can put to work right away. The authors—members of Microsoft's security teams—describe how to plan and implement a comprehensive security strategy, assess security threats and vulnerabilities, configure system security, and more. The kit also provides must-have security tools, checklists, templates, and other on-the-job resources on CD-ROM and on the Web.

**Microsoft Encyclopedia of Security**
ISBN 0-7356-1877-1   Suggested Retail Price:  $39.99 U.S., $57.99 Canada

**The essential security reference for computer professionals at all levels.** Get the single resource that defines—and illustrates—the rapidly evolving world of computer and network security. The MICROSOFT ENCYCLOPEDIA OF SECURITY delivers more than 1000 cross-referenced entries detailing the latest security-related technologies, standards, products, services, and issues—including sources and types of attacks, countermeasures, policies, and more. You get clear, concise explanations and case scenarios that deftly take you from concept to real-world application—ready answers to help maximize security for your mission-critical systems and data.

**Microsoft Windows Server™ 2003 Security Administrator's Companion**
ISBN 0-7356-1574-8   Suggested Retail Price:  $49.99 U.S., $72.99 Canada

**The in-depth, practical guide to deploying and maintaining Windows Server 2003 in a secure environment.**  Learn how to use all the powerful security features in the latest network operating system with this in-depth, authoritative technical reference—written by a security expert on the Microsoft Windows Server 2003 security team. Explore physical security issues, internal security policies, and public and shared key cryptography, and then drill down into the specifics of the key security features of Windows Server 2003.

**Microsoft Internet Information Services Security Technical Reference**
ISBN 0-7356-1572-1   Suggested Retail Price:  $49.99 U.S., $72.99 Canada

**The definitive guide for developers and administrators who need to understand how to securely manage networked systems based on IIS.** This book presents obvious, avoidable mistakes and known security vulnerabilities in Internet Information Services (IIS)—priceless, intimate facts about the underlying causes of past security issues—while showing the best ways to fix them. The expert author, who has used IIS since the first version, also discusses real-world best practices for developing software and managing systems and networks with IIS.

### To learn more about Microsoft Press® products for IT professionals, please visit:

# microsoft.com/mspress/IT

# For Windows Server 2003 administrators

### Microsoft® Windows® Server 2003 Administrator's Companion
ISBN 0-7356-1367-2

The comprehensive, daily operations guide to planning, deployment, and maintenance. Here's the ideal one-volume guide for anyone who administers Windows Server 2003. It offers up-to-date information on core system-administration topics for Windows, including Active Directory® services, security, disaster planning and recovery, interoperability with NetWare and UNIX, plus all-new sections about Microsoft Internet Security and Acceleration (ISA) Server and scripting. Featuring easy-to-use procedures and handy workarounds, it provides ready answers for on-the-job results.

### Microsoft Windows Server 2003 Security Administrator's Companion
ISBN 0-7356-1574-8

The in-depth, practical guide to deployment and maintenance in a secure environment. With this authoritative ADMINISTRATOR'S COMPANION—written by an expert on the Windows Server 2003 security team—you'll learn how to use the powerful security features in the network server operating system. The guide describes best practices and technical details for enhancing security with Windows Server 2003, using a holistic approach to security enhancement.

### Microsoft Windows Server 2003 Administrator's Pocket Consultant
ISBN 0-7356-1354-0

The practical, portable guide to Windows Server 2003. Here's the practical, pocket-sized reference for IT professionals who support Windows Server 2003. Designed for quick referencing, it covers all the essentials for performing everyday system-administration tasks. Topics covered include managing workstations and servers, using Active Directory services, creating and administering user and group accounts, managing files and directories, data security and auditing, data back-up and recovery, administration with TCP/IP, WINS, and DNS, and more.

### Microsoft IIS 6.0 Administrator's Pocket Consultant
ISBN 0-7356-1560-8

The practical, portable guide to IIS 6.0. Here's the eminently practical, pocket-sized reference for IT and Web professionals who work with Internet Information Services (IIS) 6.0. Designed for quick referencing and compulsively readable, this portable guide covers all the basics needed for everyday tasks. Topics include Web administration fundamentals, Web server administration, essential services administration, and performance, optimization, and maintenance. It's the fast-answers guide that helps users consistently save time and energy as they administer IIS 6.0.

To learn more about the full line of Microsoft Press® products for IT professionals, please visit:

# microsoft.com/mspress/IT

# In-depth technical information and tools for
## Microsoft Windows Server 2003

### Microsoft® Windows Server™ 2003 Deployment Kit: A Microsoft Resource Kit
ISBN 0-7356-1486-5

Plan and deploy a Windows Server 2003 operating system environment with expertise from the team that develops and supports the technology—the Microsoft Windows® team. This multivolume kit delivers in-depth technical information and best practices to automate and customize your installation, configure servers and desktops, design and deploy network services, design and deploy directory and security services, implement Group Policy, create pilot and test plans, and more. You also get more than 125 timesaving tools, deployment job aids, Windows Server 2003 evaluation software, and the entire Windows Server 2003 Help on the CD-ROMs. It's everything you need to help ensure a smooth deployment—while minimizing maintenance and support costs.

### Internet Information Services (IIS) 6.0 Resource Kit
ISBN 0-7356-1420-2

Deploy and support IIS 6.0, which is included with Windows Server 2003, with expertise direct from the Microsoft IIS product team. This official RESOURCE KIT packs 1200+ pages of in-depth deployment, operations, and technical information, including step-by-step instructions for common administrative tasks. Get critical details and guidance on security enhancements, the new IIS 6.0 architecture, migration strategies, performance tuning, logging, and troubleshooting—along with timesaving tools, IIS 6.0 product documentation, and a searchable eBook on CD. You get all the resources you need to help maximize the security, reliability, manageability, and performance of your Web server—while reducing system administration costs.

To learn more about the full line of Microsoft Press® products for IT professionals, please visit:

# microsoft.com/mspress/IT